FORENSIC ANTHROPOLOGY TRAINING MANUAL

Karen Ramey Burns

University of North Carolina at Charlotte

Illustrations by Joanna Wallington

Prentice Hall, Upper Saddle River, New Jersey 07458

Library of Congress Cataloging-in-Publication Data

BURNS, KAREN RAMEY.
Forensic anthropology training manual/Karen Ramey Burns.
p. cm.
Includes bibliographical references and index.
ISBN 0-13-010576-7
1. Forensic anthropology—Handbooks, manuals, etc. I. Title.
GN69.8.B87 1998
599.9—dc21 98-50154
CIP

Editorial director: Charlyce Jones Owen
Acquisitions editor: Nancy Roberts
Editorial assistant: Maureen Diana
Marketing manager: Christopher DeJohn
Editorial/production supervision: Kari Callaghan Mazzola
Electronic page makeup: Kari Callaghan Mazzola
Illustrator: Joanna Wallington
Electronic art scanning/labeling: John P. Mazzola
Interior design: Kari Callaghan Mazzola
Cover director: Jayne Conte
Cover design: Bruce Kenselaar
Buyer: Lynn Pearlman

This book was set in 10/12 New Century Schoolbook by Big Sky Composition
and was printed and bound by Banta Company.
The cover was printed by Banta Company.

Upper Saddle River, New Jersey 07458

Printed in the United States of America
10 9 8

ISBN 0-13-010576-7

PRENTICE-HALL INTERNATIONAL (UK) LIMITED, *London*
PRENTICE-HALL OF AUSTRALIA PTY. LIMITED, *Sydney*
PRENTICE-HALL CANADA INC., *Toronto*
PRENTICE-HALL HISPANOAMERICANA, S.A., *Mexico*
PRENTICE-HALL OF INDIA PRIVATE LIMITED, *New Delhi*
PRENTICE-HALL OF JAPAN, INC., *Tokyo*

EDITORA PRENTICE-HALL DO BRASIL, LTDA., *Rio de Janeiro*

Forensic Anthropology Training Manual

This manual is dedicated to my children, Tasha, Lara, and Alec, as well as to the many students I have known who take the time to ask questions, search for understanding, and decide to make a difference through knowledge.

CONTENTS

PREFACE

The *Forensic Anthropology Training Manual* is designed to serve as a general introduction to the discipline of forensic anthropology, a training guide, and a practical reference tool. The general introduction informs judges, attorneys, law enforcement personnel, and human rights workers of the range of information and services available from a professional forensic anthropologist. The training guide assists in the study of human osteology and provides an introduction to the discipline of forensic anthropology. The tables, formulae, and forms are provided as practical tools for general use and reference when working in the field or laboratory.

The chapters of this manual are presented in a sequence designed for effective teaching. Basic human osteology precedes laboratory analysis, and information on the skeleton is completed before the chapters on field work and human rights applications are presented. In life, the topics unfold in reverse—human rights violations are followed by field investigation and laboratory analysis. The reason for the opposite learning sequence is simple: People must *learn* to see. We fail to notice many of the things that are not already part of our life experience. Beginning students, for example, fail to recognize 80 percent of the human skeleton and confuse bones of other animals with human bones. The most effective workers go into the field equipped with knowledge from the laboratory along with their equipment and supplies.

This is *not* a self-instruction manual. This manual contains the basic knowledge necessary to successfully collect and process skeletonized human remains, but effective education requires professional guidance and plenty of hands-on experience. Anyone seeking proficiency should use this manual as one of many steps to knowledge. Be persistent in the pursuit of information, supplement class work with additional reading, and use every opportunity available for practical self-testing.

The *Forensic Anthropology Training Manual* is ideal for use as a practical text for a laboratory course. The overview of general information will introduce students to the knowledge and work of a forensic anthropologist.

Of course, a single book cannot substitute for a library of reference materials. But this manual distills much of the essential information and provides it in a format that helps to move the student along in a rapid but orderly fashion. Basic tables, formulae, illustrations, diagrams, and forms are included. Wherever necessary, information is repeated in the interest of complete coverage of topics within chapters.

This manual can serve as a supplement for four related courses:

1. Human Osteology: a complete course in human skeletal anatomy, including recognition of fragments, the range of normal variation, sexual and racial differences, and the basics of age determination.
2. Forensic Anthropology: an advanced course in the methods for human identification from skeletal remains, proper handling of physical evidence for legal purposes, and forensic report writing.
3. Forensic Archaeology: location and investigation of burial sites, excavation and disinterment of human remains and associated physical evidence.
4. Forensic Anthropology and Human Rights Applications: application of the methods of forensic anthropology to international human rights missions, planning and following through with international missions, and final report writing.

Each of the four courses listed above can be taught as intensive short courses or as term-length college courses. Both formats have about the same amount of student-teacher contact time. The intensive course, however, has less time out of class for reading and reflecting on the material. The standard college course tends to have less usable time in class because of the considerable time lost to starting and stopping.

The human osteology course and the forensic archaeology course require a large amount of laboratory and field time. Therefore, they work well in an intensive short-course format. The forensic anthropology course and the human rights applications course require more time for reading, lecture, and discussion. They are better taught in a regular-length college term (ten to fifteen weeks).

Acknowledgments

The genesis of this work can be traced to Dr. Audrey Chapman, Director of the Science and Human Rights Program of the American Association for the Advancement of Science (AAAS). Dr. Chapman encouraged me to put information into a format that can be translated for use in areas of the world trying to recover from war and the ultimate in human rights violations. The AAAS supplied the initial funding.

Questions and comments from my students in Guatemala, at the University of Georgia, and at the University of North Carolina at Charlotte generated many additions and revisions, and the following reviewers made helpful comments and suggestions: Jeffrey H. Schwartz, University of Pittsburgh; William R. Adams, University of Indiana; and Paul W. Sciulli, Ohio State University. Also, I thank Scott Saunders at the UGA Instructional Resource Center for his expertise and patience in digitizing illustrations.

My professor and mentor, the late Dr. William R. Maples, contributed through his no-nonsense attitude and profound knowledge of the discipline. Dr. Clyde C. Snow shared his unique perspective on the world and the work of an anthropologist.

As always, I'm grateful to my family for their love, support, and good humor. They have done a good job of reconciling their lives with a nontraditional wife and mother. Finally, a very special thank you to Larry.

About the Author

Karen Ramey Burns, Ph.D., received her graduate education in forensic anthropology under the direction of the late Dr. William R. Maples at the University of Florida. Dr. Burns is presently teaching at the University of North Carolina at Charlotte, while maintaining an active consulting practice. She gained experience in major crime laboratory procedures while working for the Georgia Bureau of Investigation, Division of Forensic Sciences (1988–1991). She continues to serve the State of Georgia as Consultant in Forensic Anthropology and as an appointed member of the Georgia Council on American Indian Concerns.

Dr. Burns has devoted much of her professional career to human rights work by providing educational and technical assistance in the excavation and identification of human remains. She has worked on numerous missions to Latin America, as well as Haiti, the Middle East, and Africa. She is the author of the "Protocol for Disinterment and Analysis of Skeletal Remains," in the *Manual on the Effective Prevention and Investigation of Extra-Legal, Arbitrary, and Summary Executions* (1991), a United Nations publication.

Dr. Burns works for the National Disaster Medical System in times of national emergency. She contributed to the identification of the 405 bodies unearthed from cemeteries during the Flint River flood of 1994. She has also analyzed ancient skeletal remains from archaeological excavations of ancient Romans and Phoenicians in northern Africa, as well as historic cemeteries in the United States. Her research interests include microstructure of mineralized tissues, effects of burning and cremation, and remote sensing.

About the Illustrator

Joanna Wallington, B.F.A., is a freelance professional illustrator and photographer. She graduated from the University of Georgia, College of Fine Arts. Ms. Wallington is proficient in a wide range of artistic media, from pen and pencil to computer graphics and photography. Her major educational emphasis was scientific illustration with a minor in anthropology. She completed a senior thesis in comparative primate anatomy.

Ms. Wallington, a native of Great Britain, has lived in the United States since 1977. She served in the United States Marine Corps as a firefighter emergency medical technician.

INTRODUCTION TO FORENSIC ANTHROPOLOGY

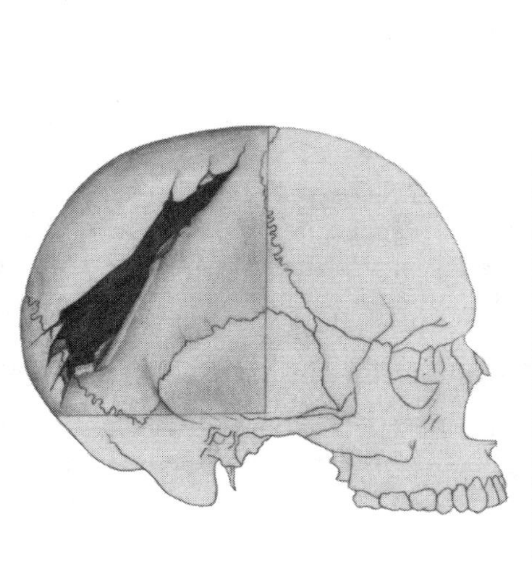

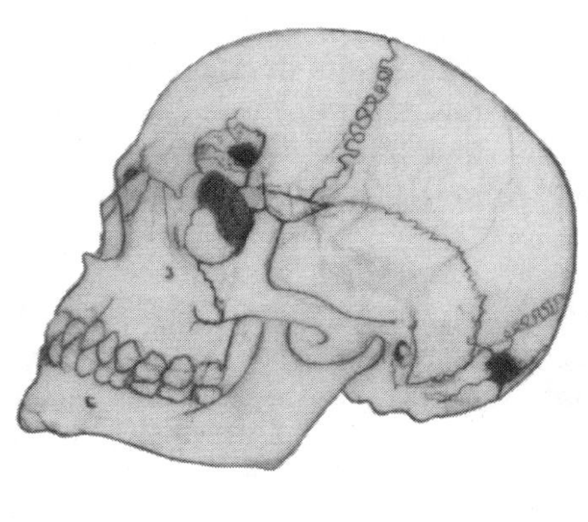

CHAPTER OUTLINE

The Basic Problem

Who Are the "Missing, Unidentified, and Disappeared"?

Why Is Identification so Difficult?

The Discipline of Forensic Anthropology

What Are the Objectives of an Anthropological Investigation?

What Are the Educational Requirements of a Forensic Anthropologist?

How Is the Work of an Anthropologist Different from the Work of a Pathologist or Medical Examiner?

What Are the Stages of Investigation in Forensic Anthropology?

The body of knowledge known as forensic anthropology offers a unique humanitarian service in a world troubled by violence. Forensic anthropology is a relatively new specialization. It is a subfield of physical anthropology, but it is also an amalgam of contributions from several other scientific disciplines. It is practiced on a full-time basis by relatively few qualified experts.

The major service of forensic anthropology is the description and identification of human remains that are unrecognizable and therefore unidentifiable by standard methods. Analysis of human remains and associated materials can reveal considerable information such as cause of death, manner of death, events occurring around the time of death, and treatment of the remains after death. Successful analysis is dependent on careful retrieval of the remains, often under difficult conditions.

THE BASIC PROBLEM

Clandestine deaths cast a shadow on everyone. Missing persons and unidentified dead—the "disappeared" of this world—are prime evidence of the worst criminal and political behavior of man. Peace and humanity begin with the effort to identify the dead and understand their fate.

WHO ARE THE "MISSING, UNIDENTIFIED, AND DISAPPEARED"?

Some unidentified bodies are those of derelicts who simply wandered off and died. Some are suicides who didn't want to be found. But many are evidence of the worst types of crime plaguing our society. They are teenagers executed by their companions, women raped by men in uniform, and children abused by their caretakers. The unidentified are the evidence of serial killers who walk the streets with us and eat at the next table. In many countries, the missing and unidentified are known as "the disappeared." They are evidence of genocide and extreme misuse of authority.

The odd thing about an unidentified body is its *silence*. It may seem that all dead bodies are silent, but an unidentified body is even more silent. No one calls and complains when it is forgotten. No one exerts pressure or wields political or financial power on behalf of an unidentified person. If shipped off to a morgue or buried as a "John Doe," it doesn't even take up space at a responsible agency.

It appears that no one cares, but this is a patent falsehood. Those who care suffer in silence with nowhere to turn for relief. They suffer the agony of not knowing the fate of their loved ones. They put their lives on hold. They become victims who are afraid to move to a new location, to remarry, or to rebuild their lives. They feel that they might show a lack of love by giving up hope and assuming the person to be dead. After all, what if the person does return and finds his or her home gone?

Parents of soldiers missing in action say that not knowing is far worse than being able to grieve. Instead of feeling buoyed by hope, they are paralyzed by the fear that their child is suffering somewhere.

Families of missing persons say that they experience a sense of relief when the bodies of loved ones are finally identified. They find a sense of closure and even empowerment through the process of funeral rituals.

WHY IS IDENTIFICATION SO DIFFICULT?

The general attitude of law enforcement personnel toward unidentified bodies is defeatist. Standard comments are, "If it is not identified within two weeks, it won't be identified," or "If it is not a local person with a well-publicized missing person record, forget it." These are self-fulfilling prophecies. While the law of diminishing returns is no doubt applicable, the door *can* be left open for success. But leaving the door open is not easy. It requires a thorough analysis of the remains and a recording of *correct* information.

Unfortunately, correct information is as useless as incorrect information if it is not communicated. This may be the Information Age, but the world is still struggling with the responsible use of information. The technology is available, but efficient use of technology is a challenge. Within the United States, the National Crime Information Center is the ideal place to deposit information. In developing countries, it is necessary to transfer and build technology. This is being accomplished with slow determination by nongovernmental organizations such as the American Association for the Advancement of Science in Washington, D.C., Physicians for Human Rights in Boston, and the Carter Center of Emory University in Atlanta.

When the doors are left open for identification, and a "hit" is finally made, the remains must be relocated. Storing human remains (especially decomposing remains) is not as easy as storing most other types of evidence, but it can be done. However, the ethics of the situation are confused. Is it more important to identify a deceased person, inform a tormented relative, and possibly apprehend a murderer, or is it more important to "honor" the dead with an anonymous burial?

The Discipline of Forensic Anthropology

Forensic anthropology is the scientific discipline that applies the methods of physical anthropology and archaeology to the collection and analysis of legal evidence. Description and identification of skeletonized human remains are standard work for forensic anthropologists, but the expertise of the forensic anthropologist is also applicable to a wide variety of other problems. The common denominator is hard tissues: bones, teeth, and sometimes cartilage.

What Are the Objectives of an Anthropological Investigation?

The objectives of anthropological investigation are the same as those of a medical-legal investigation of a recently deceased person: identification, determination of cause and manner of death, estimation of time of death, and collection of any physical evidence supporting the conclusions or leading to further information.

The work of anthropologists overlaps the work of both the crime scene investigator and the medical examiner (or forensic pathologist). The difference is in the methods used by each specialist. The choice of methods is dictated by the location and the nature of the material to be examined.

- The anthropologist with osteological training (usually a physical anthropologist) maximizes information obtained from *skeletonized* human remains.
- The anthropologist with archaeological training optimizes recovery of evidence from a crime scene that is *underground* and requires careful excavation.
- The physical anthropologist or archaeologist with training in *forensic science* works with law enforcement when crime scenes involve skeletonized or buried evidence.

What Are the Educational Requirements of a Forensic Anthropologist?

Forensic anthropologists specialize first in physical anthropology, then obtain graduate or postgraduate training in forensic anthropology. Most are competent in human biology, anatomy, and osteology. Many have additional training in other medical fields such as emergency medicine, nursing, anatomy, pathology, and dentistry.

Most forensic anthropologists learn the basics of medical-legal death investigation through on-the-job training. The education itself is a never-ending process. It is actively renewed by reading scientific periodicals, participating in short courses, and attending professional meetings.

The degree of Ph.D. is highly desirable because the degree implies competence in research methods, writing, and teaching. All of these skills are useful to the professional forensic anthropologist.

How Is the Work of an Anthropologist Different from the Work of a Pathologist or Medical Examiner?

Typically, a medical doctor is called upon to examine a fleshed body, whereas an anthropologist is called to examine a skeleton. The medical doctor focuses on information from soft tissues, and the anthropologist focuses on information from hard tissues. However, since decomposition is a continuous process, the work of these specialists tends to overlap. An anthropologist is useful when decomposition is advanced or when bone trauma is a major element in the death.

A medical doctor may be useful when mummified tissues are present on the skeleton. Simple visual identification is usually impossible in an anthropological investigation. Therefore, more time and attention are devoted to the *basics* of personal identification.

Questions Basic to Personal Identification

- Are the remains human? (Frequently they are not.)
- Do the remains represent a single individual or several individuals?
- What did the person look like? The description should include sex, age, race, height, physique, and handedness.
- Who is it? Are there unique skeletal traits or anomalies that could serve to provide a tentative or positive identification?

Forensic anthropologists also collect physical evidence that aids in solving questions about the circumstances of death. This is another area in which broad-spectrum anthropological training is very useful, particularly in cross-cultural circumstances.

Questions Regarding the Circumstances of Death

- When did death occur?
- Did the person die at the place of burial, or was he or she transported after death?
- Was the grave disturbed or was the person buried more than once?
- What was the cause of death (e.g., gunshot wound, stabbing, asphyxiation)?
- What was the manner of death (i.e., homicide, suicide, accident, or natural)?
- What is the identity of the perpetrator(s)?

WHAT ARE THE STAGES OF INVESTIGATION IN FORENSIC ANTHROPOLOGY?

There are three major stages of investigation in a typical case: collection of verbal evidence, collection of physical evidence, and analysis of the evidence. Within the United States, the collection of verbal evidence is usually carried out by the police investigator using information provided by the forensic scientists working with the physical evidence. There are other countries, however, in which the anthropologist is expected to take the initiative in obtaining verbal evidence. Under such circumstances, forensic anthropologists become involved in the entire process of interviewing and record searching with little more than official approval.

The flowchart below reveals the orderly stages of investigation leading to a synthesis and interpretation of information. Each box within the flowchart is a subject unto itself. Subsequent chapters will endeavor to introduce all parts of the chart, but aspects related to physical evidence will be explored in greater detail.

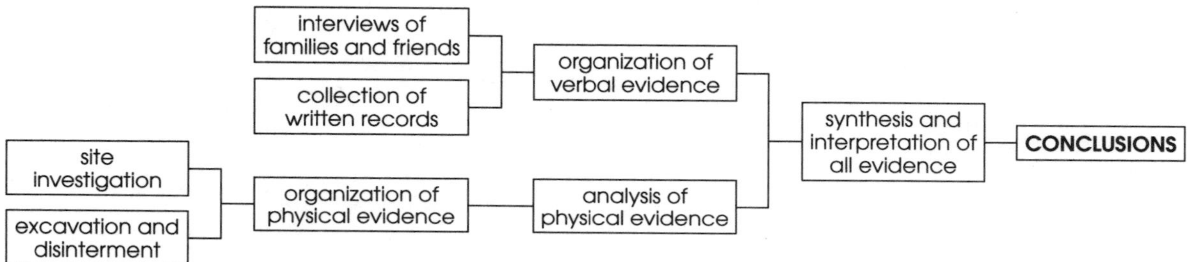

PART I

SKELETAL ANATOMY

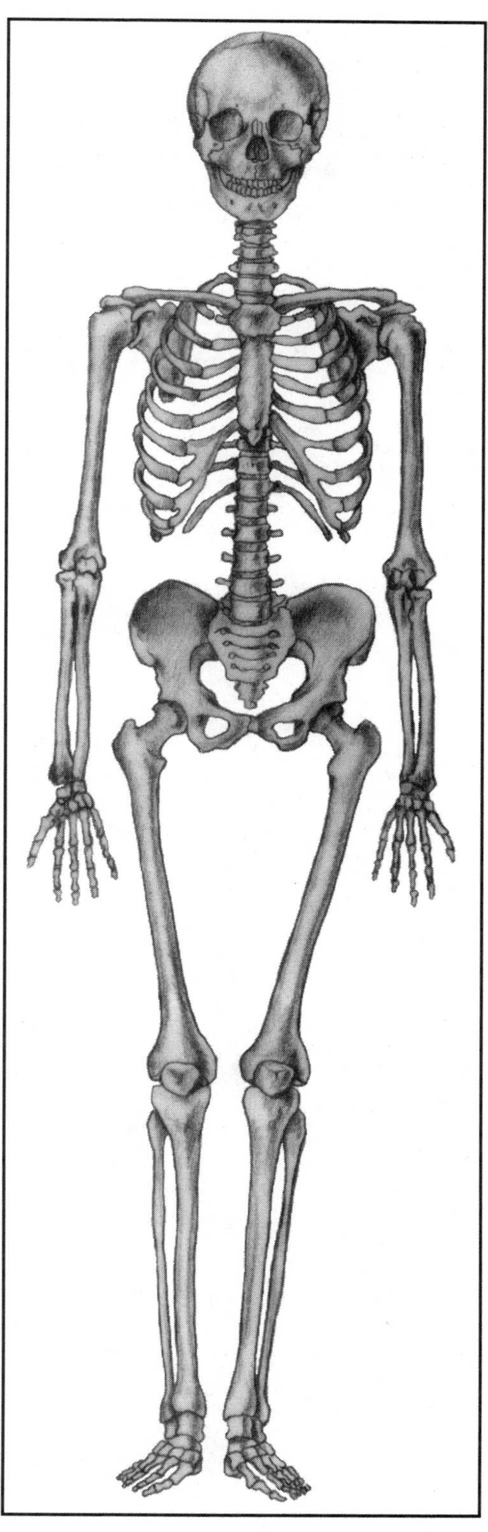

PART OUTLINE

CHAPTER 1

INTRODUCTION TO HUMAN OSTEOLOGY

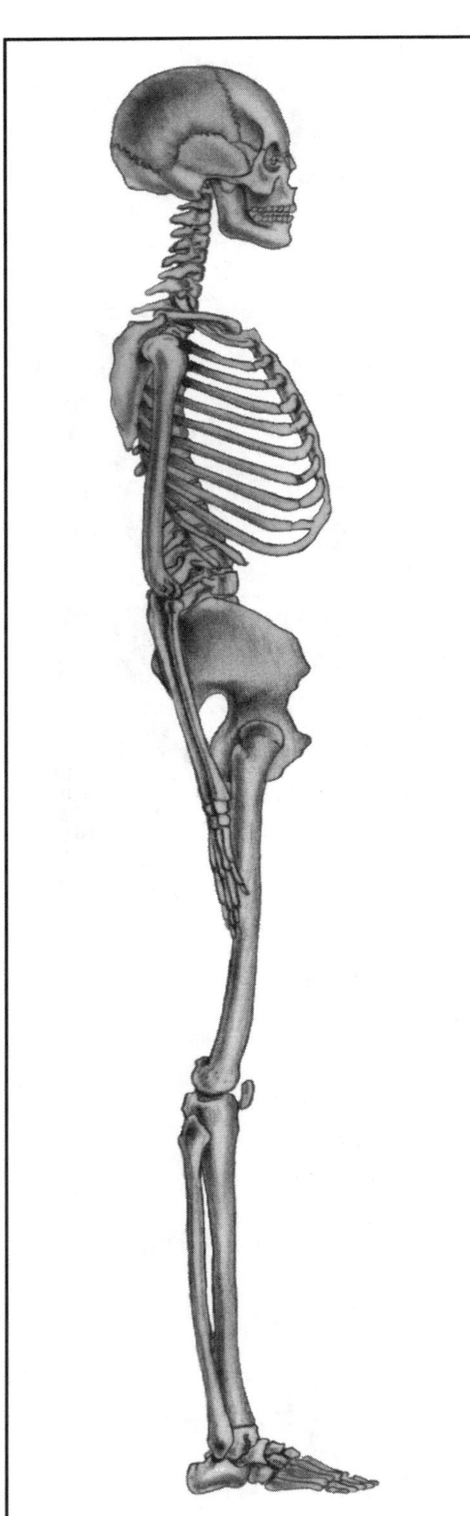

CHAPTER OUTLINE

Why Learn Human Osteology?

Key Term
osteology The study of bones, their development, structure, function, and degeneration.

Osteology is the study of bones. It is the science that explores the development, structure, function, and variation of bones. The knowledge of *human osteology* is prerequisite to reading the record of man. The skeleton is more durable than the rest of the human body. It is often the only surviving record of a life on this earth.

Imagine receiving a book written in an obscure language. If you have no knowledge of the language, you could describe the color and texture of the pages, but you would not be able to read the information that the writer intended to communicate.

It is the same with bones. You may describe them, but you will not understand their meaning until you learn the language. And just as you find that a dictionary is still useful in your own language, you will find it necessary to continue learning the language of bones as long as you work with them.

Practical Applications for Human Osteology

Depending on the condition of the remains and the availability of antemortem information, a competent osteologist can provide much of the following information from skeletal remains:

- A description of the living person
- An evaluation of the health of the deceased
- Recognition of habitual activities
- Identification of the deceased person
- Recognition of the cause and manner of death
- Determination of the approximate time since death
- Information about postmortem events

What to Expect from a Human Osteology Course

The Basics

This course is designed to train you to recognize and understand the entire human skeleton. Begin by learning to recognize every curve and facet of each bone that is presented, then compare one set of bones with another and note the variation. Work at understanding the concept of normal or average. Then work at recognizing the many deviations from normal. Competent work in forensic anthropology is based on this knowledge.

Course Description

During this course, the human skeleton is studied in detail, including recognition of whole and fragmentary bones and teeth.

- Vocabulary of calcified tissues is stressed. It is essential to be able to communicate with other osteologists as well as physicians and dentists.
- The dynamics of bone growth, healing, and aging are studied at both macroscopic and microscopic levels.
- The basics of skeletal description are introduced. The student learns to determine age, sex, genetic heritage, and stature.
- Interpretation of pathology and trauma are introduced.

Course Time Allotment

The course consists of a minimum of two weeks of lecture and laboratory. Each day begins with a practical quiz covering the previous day's work. The quizzes are designed as self-help tools. Success in the course is measured by the final practical exam and the final report.

Use of Human Skeletons

The human skeletal remains utilized in the laboratory sessions are from recently excavated graves or from the professor's teaching collection. They are human. Obscure origin or lack of identification do not in any way lessen the humanity of these people. *They will be treated with respect and dignity.*

If the skeletal remains are of forensic significance, appropriate security will be maintained, and chain of custody will be documented.

Schedule of Study

The following course outline covers the basics of skeletal analysis and related forensic topics in a generalized format. One must, however, be flexible with the schedule in order to allow for the specific nature of the available study materials.

A course that utilizes newly recovered remains as study material is, by its very nature, full of contingencies. It is not possible to plan examples for every major point of study. Occasionally, an atypical skeleton requires extra attention.

Information versus Experience

The course is intense and the successful student will absorb a large amount of information. However, the time is short for developing experience. We never cease to be students. Self-testing is advised whenever opportunities present themselves. Lecturers should supplement class materials with case studies in order to share experience in the time available.

Also, the most successful students work with their classmates. They help each other, quiz each other, and share discoveries. Begin on the first day of class to become acquainted with your classmates. Find common free time and organize study groups. Ask questions and explain what you have learned to each other!

Tissues

A **tissue** is a group of closely associated cells that perform related functions and are similar in structure. The cells are bound together in matrices of nonliving extracellular material that varies greatly from one tissue to another. The body's organs are built from tissues, and most organs contain all four tissue types. Study Table 1.1 for a comparison of tissue types, functions, and examples of each.

Key Terms

tissue A community of cells with a common purpose.

connective tissue The most durable tissue of the body.

Connective Tissue

Connective tissues are primary tissues derived from the mesenchyme, and this derives in turn from the mesoderm of the embryo. There are many forms of connective tissue, but all connective tissues consist of more or less numerous cells surrounded by an extracellular matrix of fibrous and ground substance.

Table 1.1 Basic Tissue Types

Basic Tissue Types	Tissue Functions	Examples
epithelial tissue	covering	skin, hair, nails
connective tissue	support, protection	bone, cartilage, fat, blood
muscle tissue	movement	muscle
nervous tissue	control	nerves

FUNCTIONS COMMON TO CONNECTIVE TISSUES

- Support in areas that require durable flexibility
- Protection for bones and joints during activity
- Hydration and maintenance of body fluids

CLASSES AND SUBCLASSES OF CONNECTIVE TISSUE

Connective tissue proper forms the supporting framework of many large organs of the body. Connective tissues are classified as either loose connective tissue or dense connective tissue. *Loose connective tissues* are areolar, adipose (fat), and reticular tissues. *Dense connective tissues* contain more collagen than loose connective tissues. The thick collagen fibers can resist extremely strong pulling forces. Dense connective tissues can be irregular (fibrous capsules that surround certain organs of the body), regular (ligaments, tendons, aponeuroses, and fascia), or elastic (vocal cords and some ligaments connecting adjacent vertebrae).

Cartilage and bone are discussed in a separate section. Blood is also a connective tissue as it consists of cells surrounded by a nonliving matrix. In blood, the ground substance is a liquid.

BASIC CONNECTIVE TISSUE CELL

Mesenchymal cells are primitive cells that have the capability to differentiate into other types of cells, including the cells that produce the connective tissues. The differentiated cells produce and maintain the tissues. The mature cells are discussed in their appropriate sections.

Dense Connective Tissue and Fibrous Tissue

Dense regular connective tissue and dense elastic connective tissue are the fibrous tissues directly associated with bone and cartilage. Both types of dense connective tissue are capable of providing enormous tensile strength. The dense elastic connective tissue combines greater elasticity with strength. Bundles of white fibers are sandwiched between rows of connective tissue cells. The fibers all run in the same direction, parallel to the direction of pull.

Additional functions of dense connective tissues are attachment and encasement. In attachment, connective tissues form many necessary points of attachment and connection within the body. In encasement, connective tissues wrap organs, helping each organ to maintain its integrity despite the many bumps and bruises of life. Connective tissues also bind various structures of the body together.

TYPES OF DENSE CONNECTIVE TISSUE

- Ligaments attach (or connect) *bone* to bone, cartilage, and other structures. They are bands or sheets of fibrous tissue.
- Tendons attach (or connect) *muscle* to bone. They tend to be narrower and more cord-like than ligaments.

- Periosteum encases (covers) the *outer* surfaces of compact bone. It is a fibrous sheath that is cellular and vascularized.
- Endosteum covers the *inner* surfaces of compact bone. It is a thinner fibrous sheath than the periosteum.
- Fascia encases muscles, groups of muscles, and large vessels and nerves. It is the "plastic sandwich wrap" of the body, binding structures together wherever necessary.

CONNECTIVE TISSUE CELLS

Fibroblasts are the cells that produce collagen fibers, the basic organic fibers of connective tissues. Inactive fibroblasts are sometimes called fibrocytes.

CARTILAGE

Key Term

cartilage A strong but flexible connective tissue.

Cartilage consists primarily of water (60–80 percent by weight). Because of its high water content, cartilage is very *resilient*. It is capable of springing back when compressed. It contains no blood vessels. Nutrients are passed from the surrounding perichondrium by diffusion, an adequate method because of the high water content.

Cartilage is also resistant to *tension* because of a strong network of collagen fibrils. It is not, however, resistant to shear forces (twisting and bending). This weakness is the reason for the large number of torn cartilages in sports injuries.

Unlike bone, cartilage has very little capacity for regeneration in adults. Chondrocytes can no longer divide, so the little healing that does take place is due to the ability of the surviving chondrocytes to secrete more extracellular matrix.

FUNCTIONS OF CARTILAGE

Cartilage acts as a model for growing bones. It is capable of fast growth because there is no need for vascular formation; a slow process. Cartilage also provides a framework for nose and ears. Structures that must protrude from the body would be broken far more frequently if it were not for flexible cartilaginous support.

Cartilage is a cushion and shock absorber for movable joints, intervertebral disks, and the interpubic joint. It also provides a flexible attachment between the ribs and the sternum. In all of these areas of the body, cartilage protects bone by withstanding compression far more effectively than bone.

TYPES OF CARTILAGE

- Hyaline, or articular cartilage, caps the ends of bones, shapes the nose, completes the rib cage, and forms the fetal skeleton.
- Elastic cartilage is hyaline cartilage with elastic fibers added. It forms the epiglottis and the external ear.
- Fibrocartilage is embedded in dense collagenous tissue. It forms the vertebral discs, the interpubic joint, joint capsules, tendon insertions, and related ligaments.

CARTILAGE CELLS

Chondroblasts and chondroclasts live in the extracellular matrix and maintain the cartilage. Chondroblasts build the cartilage. They are capable of rapid multiplication when necessary. Chondroclasts break down and absorb cartilage when replacement and repair is necessary.

EXTRACELLULAR MATRIX

The extracellular matrix is a jelly-like ground substance, with collagen fibers and watery tissue fluid. It is important for transport of cells and maintenance of homeostasis.

Bone

Function

Key Terms

bone The strongest, least flexible connective tissue.

macrostructure Gross anatomy; a structure large enough to be viewed with the naked eye.

microstructure Microscopic anatomy; a structure that cannot be seen without magnification.

Support is the primary function of **bone**. Without bone, the body would be like a string without a bow or a sail without a mast. Protection is provided, particularly by the armor-like bones of the skull and the pelvis. The rib cage is also effective protection. Movement is made possible by the lever action of one bone on another by opposing muscle groups.

Blood cell formation takes place within the marrow cavities of bone. Mineral storage takes place in bone when there is an abundance in the diet. The bone then gives up the needed minerals when there is a shortage in the diet.

Macrostructure (Gross Anatomy)

- Epiphysis—the end of a bone; a secondary center of ossification
- Diaphysis—the shaft or primary center of ossification
- Metaphysis—the area of epiphysis-diaphysis union or fusion
- Medullary cavity—the marrow cavity within the shaft of a long bone
- Nutrient canals—holes in bone for passage of blood vessels

Microstructure (Microscopic Anatomy)

Compact bone is also called dense bone. It forms the bone cortex. The structural component is the osteon or Haversian system, a cylinder-shaped structure oriented parallel to the long axis of the bone and the main compression stresses. Each osteon is made of concentric lamella.

Cancellous bone is also called spongy bone or trabecular bone. It contains red marrow.

Lamellar bone is bone with tubular lamellae. Each lamella is characterized by having parallel collagen fibers. The fibers of adjacent lamella run in opposite directions. The alternating pattern is optimal for withstanding torsion.

Woven bone is fibrous, nonlamellar, primitive, embryonic, or healing bone. The matrix is irregular.

Compare the characteristics of bone and cartilage in Table 1.2 and consider the reasons for each functional difference.

Table 1.2 Characteristics of Bone and Cartilage

	Bone	Cartilage
Characteristics	solid	solid
	inflexible	flexible
	vascular	avascular
Functions	weight bearing	weight bearing
	anchor for muscles	model for growing bone
	stores calcium	supports flexible parts of the body
	houses marrow	decreases friction at joints
Cellular Component	osteocytes	chondrocytes
	osteoblasts	chondroblasts
	osteoclasts	chondroclasts
Organic Matrix	collagenic fibrils embedded in an amorphous intercellular substance	gelatinous
Inorganic Component	crystalline lattice of hydroxyapatite (3Ca3(PO4)2 ß Ca(OH)2)	no inorganic component

The Layers of a Long Bone Shaft

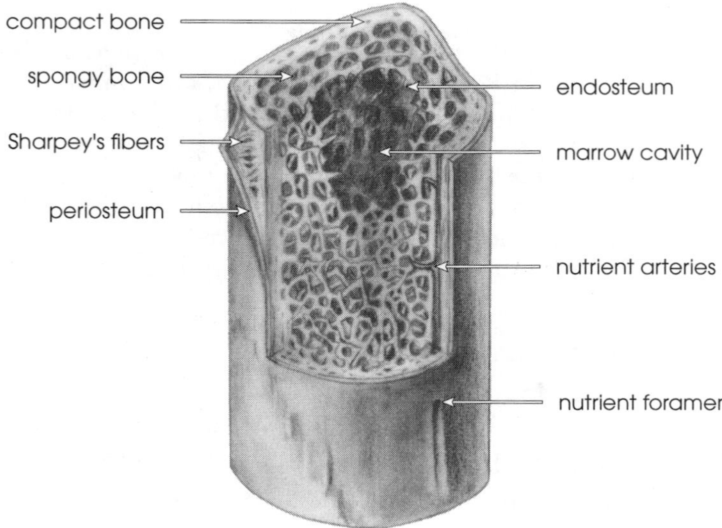

The periosteum is the fibrous membrane that surrounds bone. Sharpey's fibers hold the periosteum tightly in place. Nutrient foramina pierce the periosteum and the bone, providing access for blood vessels. The vessels carry blood between the exterior and the interior of the bone.

The periosteum, Sharpey's fibers, and nutrient vessels usually decompose after death. Therefore, they are not visible on clean, dry bone, but evidence of their presence remains.

The Building Blocks for Bone

Chemical Composition

Key Term
hydroxyapatite The natural mineral structure that the crystal lattice of bones and teeth most closely resembles.

The organic component is 35 percent of the bone mass. It is composed of cells, collagen fibers, and ground substance. Ground substance is amorphous material in which structural elements occur. It is composed of protein polysaccharides, tissue fluids, and metabolites.

The inorganic component is 65 percent of the bone mass. It is composed of hydroxyapatites. **Hydroxyapatites**—3Ca3(PO4)2 ß Ca(OH)2—are mineral salts, primarily calcium phosphate, that form tiny crystals and pack tightly into the extracellular matrix of collagen fibers.

Bone Cells

- Osteoblasts are bone-forming cells. They are found at the sites of bone growth, repair, and remodeling.
- Osteoclasts are large multinucleated cells that are capable of breaking down bone. They are found at sites of repair and remodeling.
- Osteocytes are long-term maintenance cells. They are found in the lacunae of lamellar bone with cellular processes extending into the canaliculi of the bone.

Osteogenesis

There are two basic ways for bone to form and develop—in between two membranes or within a cartilaginous model. *Intramembranous ossification* is bone formation between membranes. It is also called subperiosteal bone apposition. The flat bones of the skull, pelvis, and scapula form by intramembranous ossification.

Endochondral ossification is bone formation within a cartilaginous model. First, mesenchymal cells differentiate into chondroblasts that form hyaline cartilage. Then some of the mesenchymal cells differentiate into osteoblasts and hematopoietic cells. The result is the development of a primary center of ossification. Long and short bones form by endochondral ossification.

BONE STRENGTH

The forces of compression and tension have profound effects on bone growth, development, and strength. Healthy bone is half as strong as steel in resisting compression and fully as strong as steel in resisting tension. Bone grows and thrives under tension. It fails and reabsorbs under long-term compression. Bone is normally under tension because of the balance of muscle groups—flexors and extensors, adductors and abductors.

BONE ARCHITECTURE

Stress is the key to form. The shape of each bone is a result of the stresses most commonly placed on it. Bones are subjected to compression as weight bears down on them or as muscles pull on them. The loading is rarely uniform, however, and tends to bend the bone. Bending compresses one side and stretches the other. Compression and tension are greatest at the outer parts of the bones and least at the inner parts. Therefore, strong, compact bone tissue is necessary at the periphery of bones and spongy bone is sufficient in the internal regions.

The internal regions of bones appear weak because of the porous, spongy nature. In fact, the trabeculae of spongy bone align along stress lines and provide light-weight struts that buttress and further strengthen the bone. At the same time, they provide well-protected space for essential bone marrow.

WOLFF'S LAW ("FORM FOLLOWS FUNCTION")

According to PDR Medical Dictionary (first edition): "Every change in the form and the function of a bone, or in its function alone, is followed by certain definite changes in its internal architecture and secondary alterations in its external conformation."

Wolff's Law explains the observed phenomenon that damage to muscles or the nerves that enervate them results in bone remodeling or resorption. Change in use patterns of muscles also results in bone remodeling or resorption.

CLASSIFICATION AND DESCRIPTION OF BONES

The skeletal system can be described and classified by several different systems, depending on the aspect of the skeleton that is the focus of attention. Bones are categorized by location, by size and shape, by origin, and by structure.

BY LOCATION

The *axial skeleton* is the foundation or base to which the appendicular skeleton is attached. Some parts of the axial skeleton are singular, other parts are paired. The axial skeleton is composed of the following:

- The skull—the multiple bones of the cranium together with the jaw or mandible
- The hyoid—the small U-shaped bone beneath the mandible
- The backbone—the vertebral column
- The sternum—the manubrium, the body of the sternum, and the xiphoid process
- The ribs—twelve pair

The *appendicular skeleton* is attached to the axial skeleton. All of the appendicular skeleton is paired (i.e., a right a left version). The appendicular skeleton is composed of the following:

- The pectoral girdle—the clavicle and scapula
- The arm—the humerus, radius, and ulna
- The hand—the carpals, metacarpals, phalanges
- The pelvic girdle—the innominate bones
- The leg—the femur, patella, tibia, and fibula
- The foot—the tarsals, metatarsals, and phalanges

BY SIZE AND SHAPE

Long bones are much longer than wide. The arm, leg, fingers, and toes are long bones. *Short bones* are small rounded bones. The carpal bones of the wrist and the tarsal bones of the ankle are short bones. Bones of the fingers and toes may seem short, but they are longer than wide and are therefore long bones.

Flat bones are, as you might expect, flat. The skull, pelvis, and shoulder blade are flat bones. Irregular bones are the bones of the spine. Many other bones may seem irregular, but only the vertebrae are *called* irregular.

BY ORIGIN

See *osteogenesis* in the previous section for explanations of intramembranous and endochondral ossification.

BY STRUCTURE

Compact bone is dense. The outer layer of most bones is compact *circumferential lamellae*. The inner layers of bone are osteonal in structure. The *osteons* are also built of lamellae. Circumferential lamellae encase the entire bone, and osteonal lamellae are wound tightly into columnar structures (also called Haversian systems). Each lamella of bone is a layer of bone matrix in which all of the collagen fibers run in a single direction. Fibers of adjacent lamellae run in opposite directions. The result is much like well-made plywood. Many layers of lamellae resist torsion. Compact bone is nourished by self-contained blood vessels that travel within the central canals of the osteon and interconnect by Volkmann's canals.

Cancellous (spongy) bone is much less complex in organization than compact bone. Spongy bone is made up of trabeculae, each of which has a few layers of lamellae, but lacks osteons and self-contained blood vessels. Cancellous bone is nourished by diffusion from capillaries in the surrounding endosteum.

Test your vocabulary by classifying and describing the bone below.

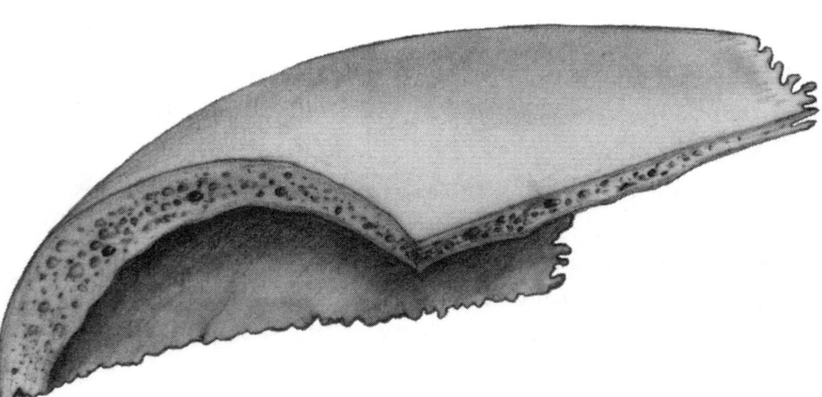

Example of Bone Classification

Classify and describe the bone shown here (e.g., location, size and shape, origin, structure).

Answer: This is a parietal bone, one of the *paired bones* of the skull. It is part of the *axial skeleton*. It is also a *flat bone, intramembranous* in origin. The outer and inner tables of the parietal are *compact bone*. The internal layer is *spongy bone*.

Directional and Sectional Terms for the Human Body

The sets of terms in Tables 1.3 and 1.4 all must be known in order to find your way around the human body and communicate with others who are trying to do the same. Correct terminology is required to avoid misunderstanding in written reports. Begin by talking with your laboratory partners. Use the terms and names, rather than simply pointing at structures. Practice new vocabulary as each new chapter is presented.

Table 1.3 Sections of the Body

Term	Usage	Opposite
coronal	a frontal section cut through the head or skull	sagittal
frontal	a midline section cut from side to side of the body	sagittal
sagittal	a midline section cut from front to back	frontal or coronal
transverse	a section cut parallel to the floor	vertical
vertical	a section cut at 90% to the floor	transverse

Table 1.4 Directional Terms for the Human Body

Term	Definition	Opposite
anterior	toward the front of the body	posterior
axillary	in the armpit area	
caudal	in the area of the tail (the coccyx in man)	cranial
cranial	in the area of the head or toward the head	caudal
distal	away from the body (used with limbs)	proximal
dorsal	toward the back of the body, the back of the hand, or the top of the foot	ventral, palmar, or volar
external	outside the body	internal
frontal	toward the front	dorsal, occipital
inferior	below	superior
internal	inside the body	external
lateral	toward the side	medial
medial	toward the midline	lateral
posterior	toward the back	anterior
palmar or volar	toward the palm of the hand	dorsal
plantar or volar	toward the sole of the foot	dorsal
profundus	deep inside the body	superficial
proximal	toward the body (used with limbs)	distal
radial	toward the radius; the lateral side of the arm	ulnar
superficial	toward the surface of the body	profundus
superior	above	inferior
ulnar	toward the ulna; the medial side of the arm	radial
ventral	toward the abdomen	dorsal
volar	palm of the hand, sole of the foot	dorsal

Examples of Directions and Sections

Read the following sentences and picture the spatial relationships described by the terms. Then practice using correct terms consistently when describing any part of the body.

- The forehead is *superior* to the nose.
- The sternum is *anterior* to the spine.
- The sole of the foot is *plantar*.
- The palm of the hand is *palmar*.
- The brain is *internal* to the skull.
- The skin is *superficial* to the skeleton.
- The arm is *lateral* to the body.
- The wrist is *distal* to the elbow.
- The ribs are *external* to the lungs.
- The incisors are *medial* to the molars.
- The thumb is *radial*; the little finger is *ulnar*.
- The clavicle is *intermediate* to the sternum and scapula.
- The armpit is *axillary*.
- The nose is divided into halves by a *sagittal* section.
- The ears are cut by a *coronal* section.
- Both arms are cut by the same *frontal* section.
- A waistband makes a *transverse* mark on the body.

Osteological Terms

The terms in Table 1.5 are terms for general communication about bone. The terms in Table 1.6 are terms to describe form and function. The terms in Table 1.7 are terms for structures.

Table 1.5 Terms for General Communication about Bone

Function	Name	Definition
articulation with other bones	articular surface	any joint surface normally covered by articular cartilage
	articular facet	a small, smooth area; a small joint surface normally covered by articular cartilage
attachments	attachment area	any area of tendon or ligament attachment
	attachment site	a circumscribed area of attachment
attachment or protection	fossa	any depression
passage	aperture	any hole

Directional Terms and Sections

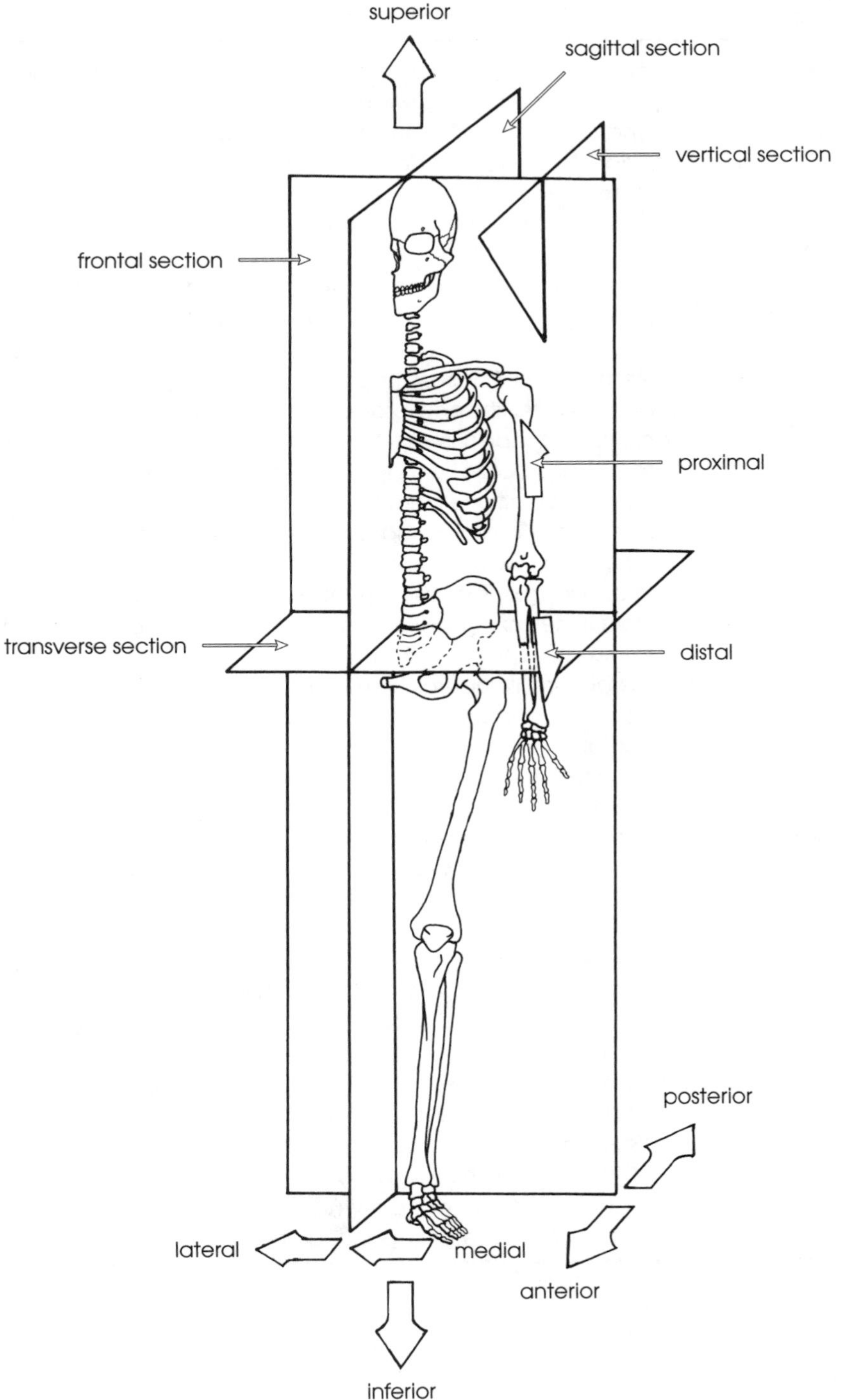

Table 1.6 Terms to Describe Form and Function

Form	Function	Name, Definition, and Example
projection	articulation with other bones	*capitulum*: a small, ball-shaped surface (e.g., c. of humerus for articulation with the head of the radius)
		condyle: a rounded, hinge-like projection (e.g., mandibular c., occipital c.)
		head: a rounded, smooth eminence on long bone (e.g., humeral h., femoral h., radial h., ulnar h.)
		process: any kind of projection, including articular (e.g., superior articular p. of vertebrae)
		trochlea: a pulley-like structure (e.g., t. of the distal humerus)
	attachment or support	*ala*: wing-like structure (e.g., a. of sacrum)
		apophysis: a process formed from a separate center of ossification (e.g., temporal a. (mastoid) basilar a. of occipital)
		conoid: cone-shaped process (e.g., c. tubercle of clavicle)
		coronoid: shaped like a crow's beak (e.g., c. process of ulna)
		crest: sharp border or ridge (e.g., interosseous c.)
		epicondyle: above a condyle (e.g., medial e.)
		promontory: a projecting part (e.g., sacral p.)
		ridge: a narrow elongated, elevation (e.g., supraorbital r.)
		spine: a long, sharp prominence (e.g., scapular s., iliac s.)
		styloid: resembling a stylus; a long, thin, pointed projection (e.g., s. processes of radius, ulna, and fibula)
		tubercle: small tuberosity (e.g., rib t.)
		tuberosity: rounded eminence—larger than a tubercle (e.g., deltoid t., radial t., ischial t.)
		trochanter: large prominence for rotator m. attachment (e.g., greater and lesser t. of the femur)
depression or hole	articulation with another bone	*cavity*: hollow space or sinus (e.g., glenoid c.)
		fossa: an indentation in a structure (e.g., mandibular f.)
		notch: an indentation at the edge of a structure (e.g., clavicular, radial, and ulnar notch)
		pit: a small hole or pocket (e.g., costal pit on vertebral body)
	passage or protection of vessels, nerves, and tendons; also enclosures	*foramen*: a hole (e.g., occipital, vertebral, nutrient, and sternal f.)
		fovea: a pit or cup-like depression (e.g., fovea capitis in the head of the femur)
		groove: a narrow depression extending for some distance (e.g., intertubercular groove of the humerus)
		incisure: a notch or indentation at the edge of a structure (e.g., i. acetabuli of the femur, i. mastoidea of the temporal)
		sinus: hollow space or cavity (e.g., nasal or frontal sinus)
		sulcus: a groove (e.g., preauricular sulcus)

Table 1.7 Terms for Structures

Term	Definition and Examples
ala	a wing-like structure, e.g. ala of sphenoid
apophysis	a prominence formed directly upon a bone, an outgrowth of bone with an independent center of ossification, e.g., basilar apophysis of occipital
articular surface	a joint; the place at which one bone comes into contact with another bone; normally smooth, dense, and covered with articular cartilage
bone	1. a hard tissue consisting of cells in a matrix of ground substance and collagen fibers. The fibers are impregnated with mineral substance, chiefly calcium phosphate and carbonate. Adult bone is about 35 percent organic matter by weight. 2. a portion of osseous tissue of definite shape and size, forming a part of the skeleton. A bone consists of an outer layer of dense compact tissue covered by the periosteum and an inner loose, spongy tissue, filled with marrow.
calvaria	the uppermost portion of the skull; the dome-like covering of the brain
canal	a narrow passage or channel, e.g., auditory canal of the temporal bone
capitulum	a small, rounded articular end of a bone, e.g., c. of the distal humerus
cavity	a hollow space, e.g., cranial cavity or glenoid cavity
condyle	a rounded articular projection, e.g., mandibular or occipital condyle
conoid	cone shaped, e.g., conoid tubercle of the lateral clavicle
coronoid	shaped like a crow's beak, e.g., coronoid process of the ulna or mandible
cranium	the bones of the head collectively or, more specifically, the bones of the head excluding the face
crest	a sharp border or ridge; usually prominent, e.g., interosseous c. of radius
dens	tooth-shaped process (odontoid process), e.g., dens epistropheus
diaphysis	shaft of a long bone, a primary center of ossification, e.g., femoral d.
diploë	lattice-like bone, e.g., cranial diploë
epicondyle	a raised area on or above a condyle, e.g., lateral epicondyle of humerus
epiphysis (pl. epiphyses)	1. a secondary center of ossification that fuses to the primary center when growth is complete, e.g., medial epiphysis of the clavicle 2. also the extremity of a bone expanded for articulation
facet	a small, smooth, somewhat flat articular surface, e.g., superior and inferior articular facets of vertebra
fissure	a narrow, slit-like opening, e.g., superior orbital fissure
foramen	a round or oval hole passing through a bone or a membranous structure, e.g., supraorbital foramen
fossa	a shallow depression; sometimes for articulation, e.g., mandibular fossa
fovea	a pit or cup-like depression, e.g., fovea capitis in the femoral head for attachment of the ligamentum teres
glenoid	having the appearance of a socket, e.g., glenoid fossa of scapula
groove	a furrow or sulcus, e.g., lacrimal groove
head	a rounded, smooth articular eminence on a neck of bone, e.g., femoral h.
line	a narrow ridge of bone; less prominent than a crest, e.g., temporal line
meatus	a canal-like passageway, e.g., auditory meatus
malleolus	a rounded bony prominence, e.g., medial malleolus
notch	an indentation at the edge of a structure, e.g., clavicular or costal notch
odontoid	tooth-like; a small, strong process, e.g., odontoid process of axis
pit	a tiny hole or pocket, e.g., costal pit on thoracic vertebrae
process	any kind of bony projection, e.g., alveolar, mastoid, or coronoid process
promontory	a projecting part, e.g., sacral promontory
ramus	an arm-like bar of bone, e.g., mandibular ramus
ridge	a rough, narrow elevation extending some distance, e.g., alveolar ridge
shaft	the major portion of a long bone, e.g., femoral shaft

Table 1.7, continued

Term	Definition and Examples
sinus	a cavity within bone filled with air and lined with mucous membrane, e.g., nasal sinus
spine	a sharp, slender projection, e.g., nasal spine
spinous process	a long pointed projection, e.g., spinous process of a vertebra
styloid process	a small pointed projection, e.g., styloid process of ulna or radius
trochanter	a very large prominence for muscle attachment and bone articulation, e.g., greater and lesser trochanter of the femur
tubercle	a small, rounded projection or process, e.g., dorsal tubercle of the radius
tuberosity	large rounded projection or eminence (It may have a roughened surface), e.g., ischial tuberosity

CHAPTER 2

THE SKULL: CRANIUM, MANDIBLE, AND HYOID

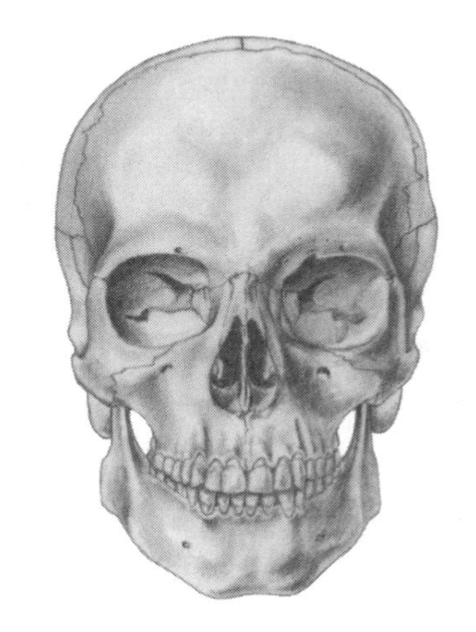

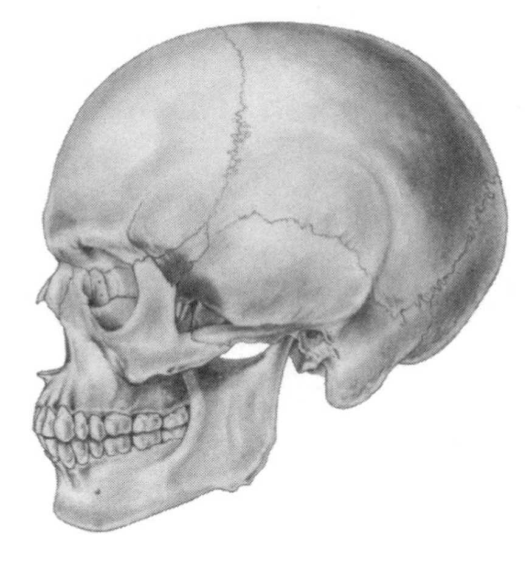

CHAPTER OUTLINE

The skull is a singular term, but it is actually made up of at least twenty separate bones. Seven are paired bones and six are unpaired. The skull may be further subdivided into regions, many of the regions overlapping with one another. There are cranial vault bones, ear bones, facial bones, orbital bones, nasal bones, and jaw bones. As you examine each bone of the skull, think about its contribution to the overall architecture of the skull. Mentally place each bone in its proper location and consider its function.

Individual variation sometimes results in a few extra bones. Many of the extra bones are small bones isolated within skull sutures. They are called *wormian bones*. An extra suture across the occipital can result in a triangular bone at the back of the skull called an *Inca bone*. Lack of union of the frontal bone results in a retained midline suture, a *metopic* suture, and paired frontal bones.

In the following pages, the skull is presented from several standard perspectives. Compare the skulls in the illustrations with as many sample skulls as possible—male and female, young and old, and genetically diverse. Look for patterns of similarity and details of difference.

Table 2.1 Osteological Terms for the Skull

Term	Definitions and Examples
ala	a wing-like structure (e.g., ala of sphenoid)
apophysis	a prominence formed directly upon a bone, an outgrowth of bone with an independent center of ossification (e.g., basilar apophysis of the occipital bone)
arch	any vaulted or arch-like structure (e.g., palatal a.; dental a.)
arch, zygomatic	the arch composed of processes from the zygomatic and temporal bones (e.g., zygomatic arch)
bone	**1.** a hard tissue consisting of cells in a matrix of ground substance and collagen fibers. The fibers are impregnated with mineral substance, chiefly calcium phosphate and carbonate. Adult bone is about 35 percent organic matter by weight; **2.** a portion of osseous tissue of definite shape and size, forming a part of the skeleton. A bone consists of an outer layer of dense compact tissue covered by the periosteum and an inner loose, spongy tissue, filled with marrow. (e.g., frontal; parietal; occipital; temporal; sphenoid; maxilla; nasal; zygomatic or malar; ethmoid; lacrimal; palatine; vomer; inferior nasal concha; malleus, incus, stapes; mandible)
boss	a rounded eminence (e.g., frontal boss)
calvaria, calvarium	skullcap, the upper dome-like portion of the skull (e.g., the calvaria is superior to the brain)
cranium	**1.** skull, bones of the head collectively; **2.** in a more limited sense, the bony brain case without the face or jaw (e.g., the cranium surrounds the brain)
foramen	any aperture or perforation through bone or membranous structure (e.g., occipital foramen)
line	a thin mark distinguished by texture or elevation—often the outer edge of a muscle or ligament attachment (e.g., temporal line on the frontal and parietal bones)
skull	the bones of the head as a unit
suture	the interface of two bones of the skull (e.g., coronal suture)

Frontal View

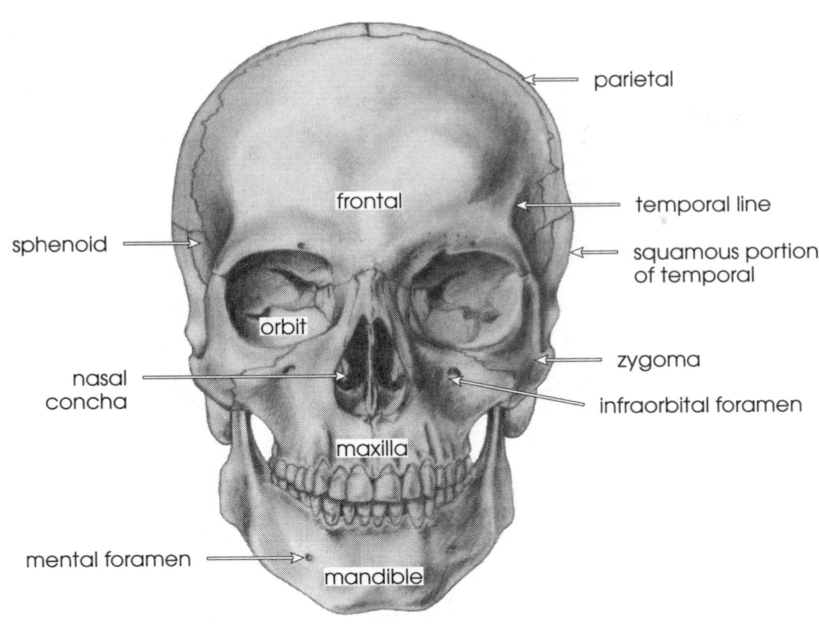

Lateral View

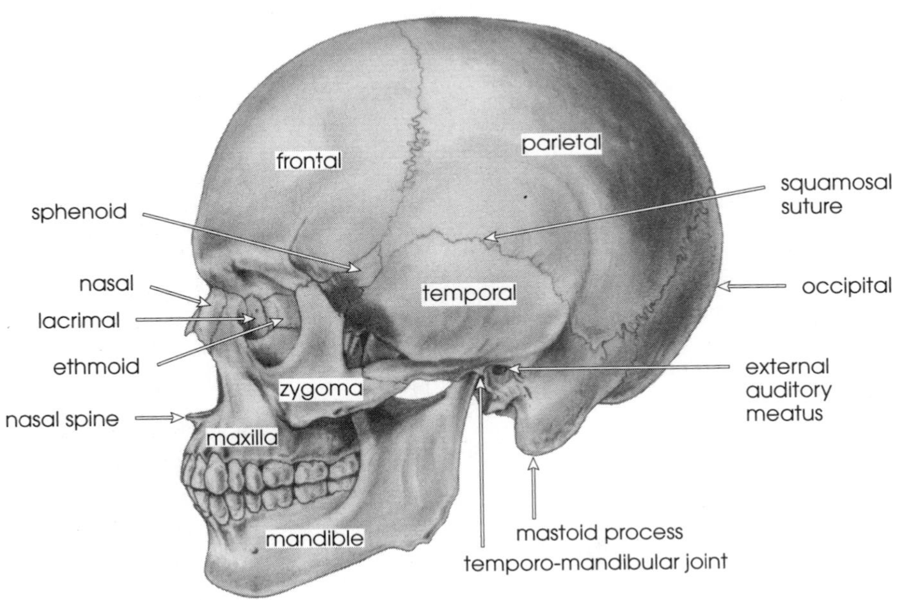

Basilar View

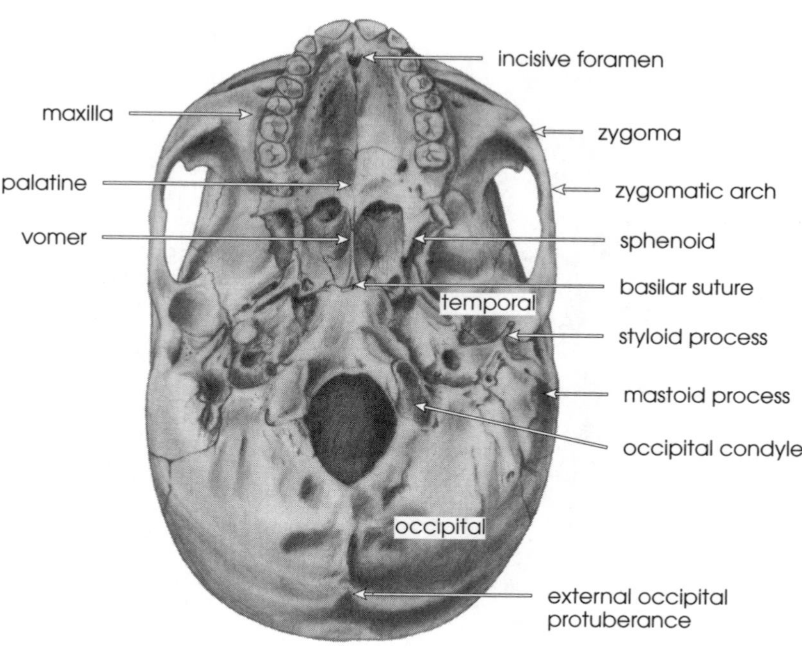

Coronal View

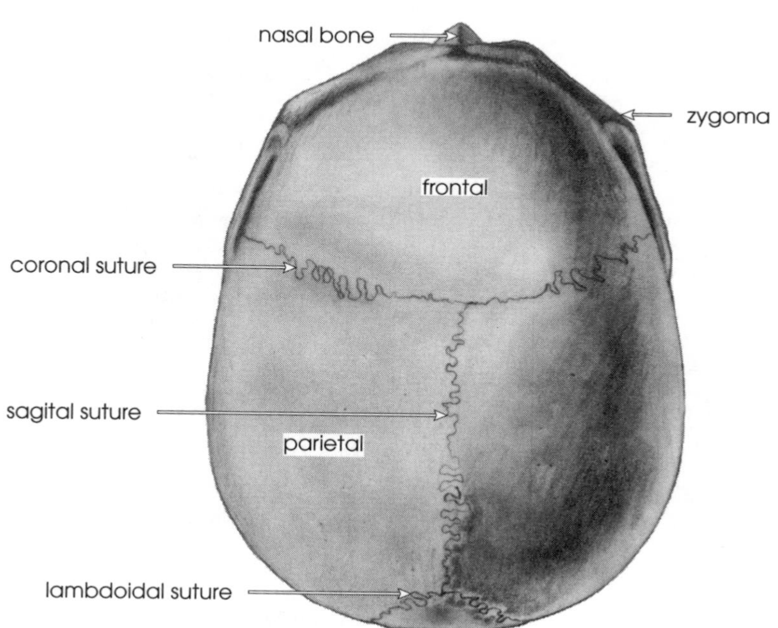

Posterior View

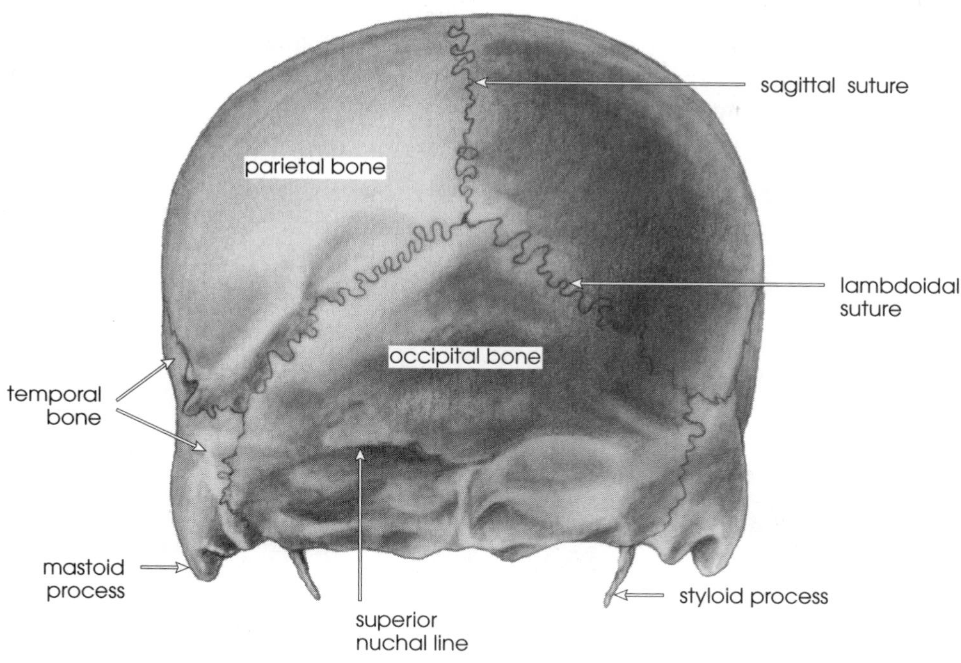

Table 2.2 Bones of the Skull

Bone	Parts to Identify
ethmoid	superior and middle nasal concha, cribriform plate, crista galli, orbital plate
frontal	supraorbital ridge or margin, supraorbital notch, superciliary arch, frontal boss, temporal line, zygomatic process, foramen cecum, frontal crest
hyoid	body and two horns (The hyoid is not a skull bone, but it is included here because of its proximity to the skull. It is the U-shaped bone lying between the mandible and the larynx and articulating with no other bone.)
lacrimal	lacrimal groove or duct
mandible	mental eminence, mental foramen, angle, coronoid process, mandibular condyles, lingula, mandibular foramen, mylohyoid groove, symphysis
maxilla	orbital margin, palate, alveolar ridges, maxillary sinus, frontal process, lacrimal groove, infraorbital foramen, nasal spine, zygomatic process
nasal	superior, inferior, lateral, and medial borders
occipital	basioccipital, foramen magnum, occipital condyles
palatine	horizontal plate
parietal	parietal foramen, parietal eminence, superior and inferior temporal lines, meningeal vascular grooves, frontal, parietal, occipital, and occipital borders
sphenoid	greater and lesser wings, lateral and medial pterygoid plates, sella turcica, occipital articulation, frontal border, temporal border
temporal	petrous portion, squamous portion, mastoid process
vomer	posterior border, nasopalatine groove
zygoma	orbital margin, maxillary process, temporal process, frontosphenoidal process

Bone Recognition

For each bone, there are numerous areas or structures to identify in addition to the bone itself and the side. Try to follow a logical order for the identification of any part of any bone. Here is a step-by-step sequence that seems to work for most students:

- First, identify the bone itself.
- Then identify the side. If it is a paired bone, is it from the right or left side? If it is not a paired bone, is it complete or is it the right or left part of a medial bone?
- Finally, identify specific parts of the bone. Table 2.2 (on page 27) includes the parts of each bone that can be easily recognized.

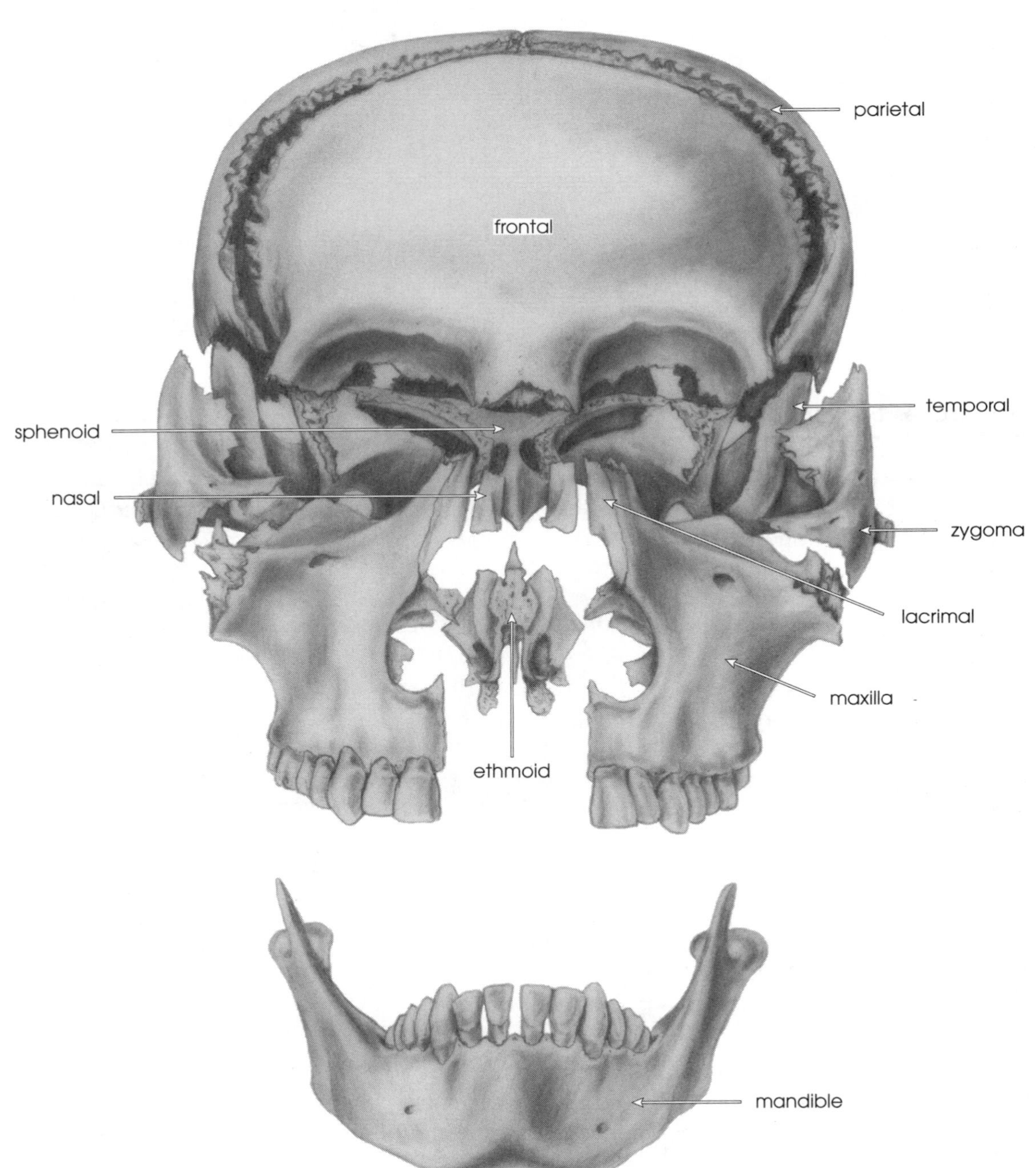

Frontal, External Surface

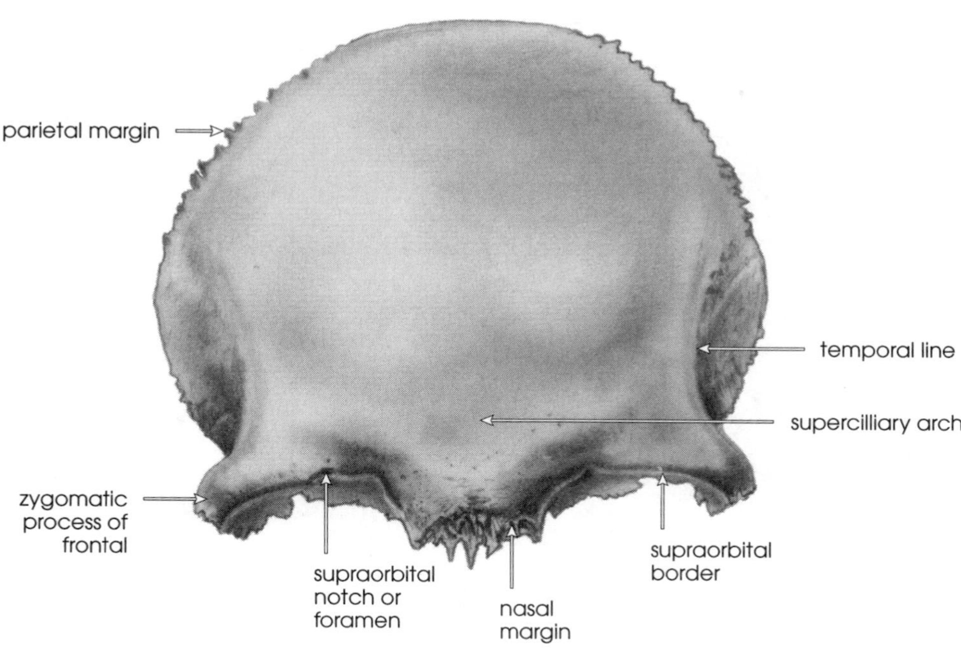

Frontal, Cerebral Surface

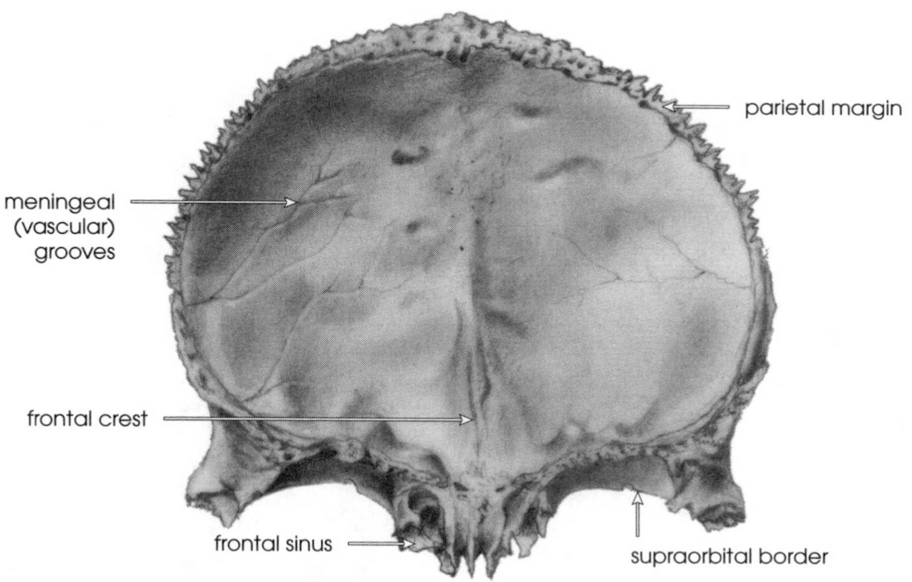

Left Parietal, External Surface

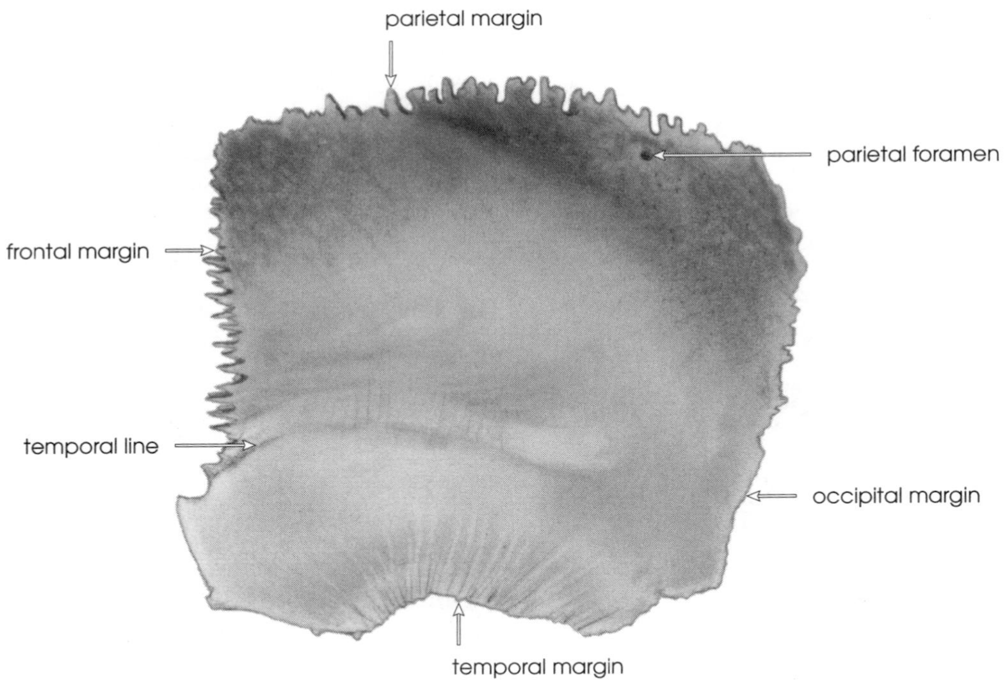

Left Parietal, Cerebral Surface

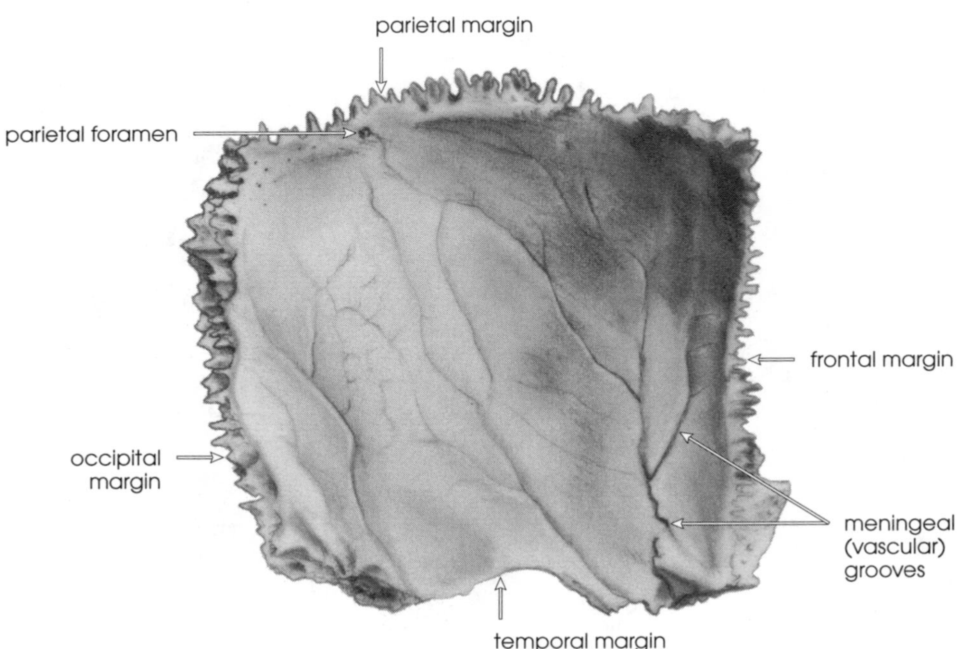

Occipital, External Surface

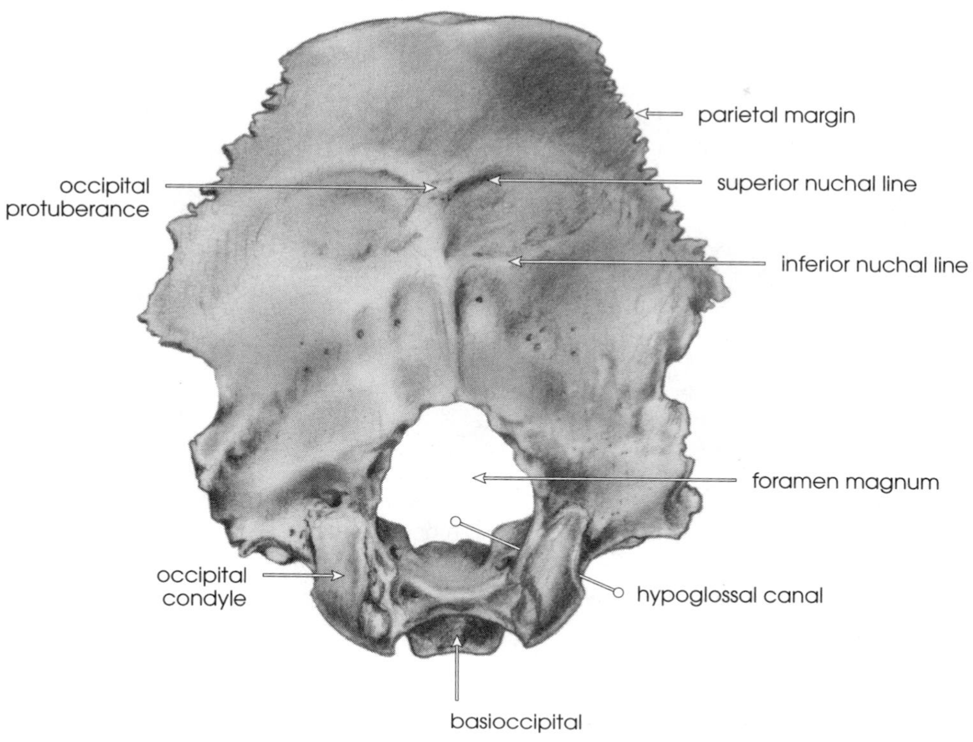

Occipital, Cerebral Surface

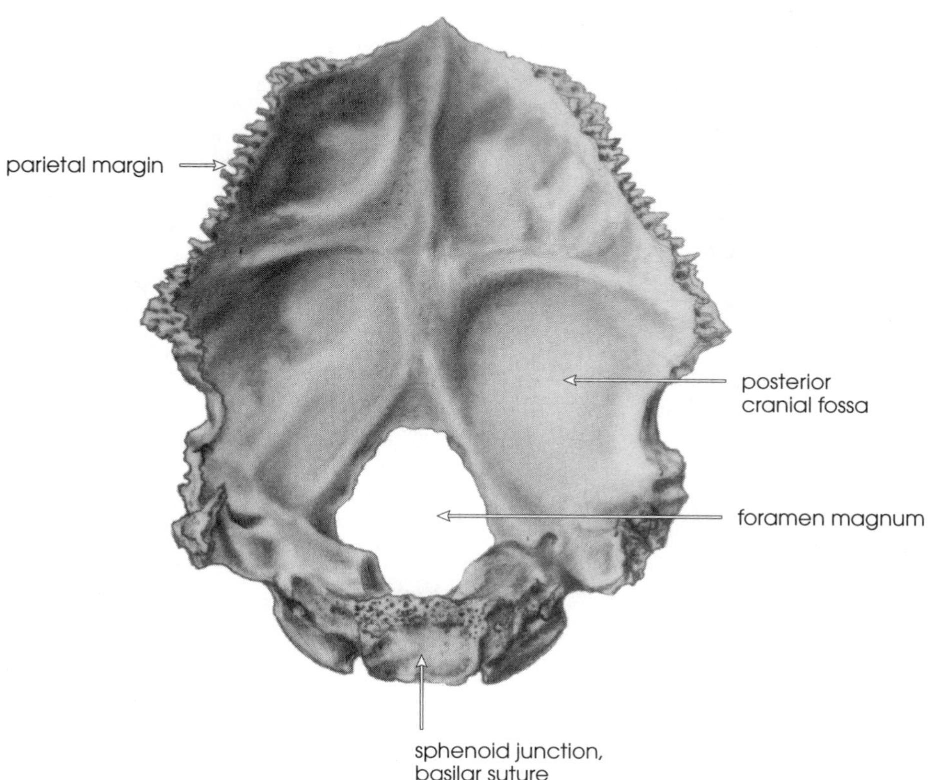

Left Temporal, External Surface

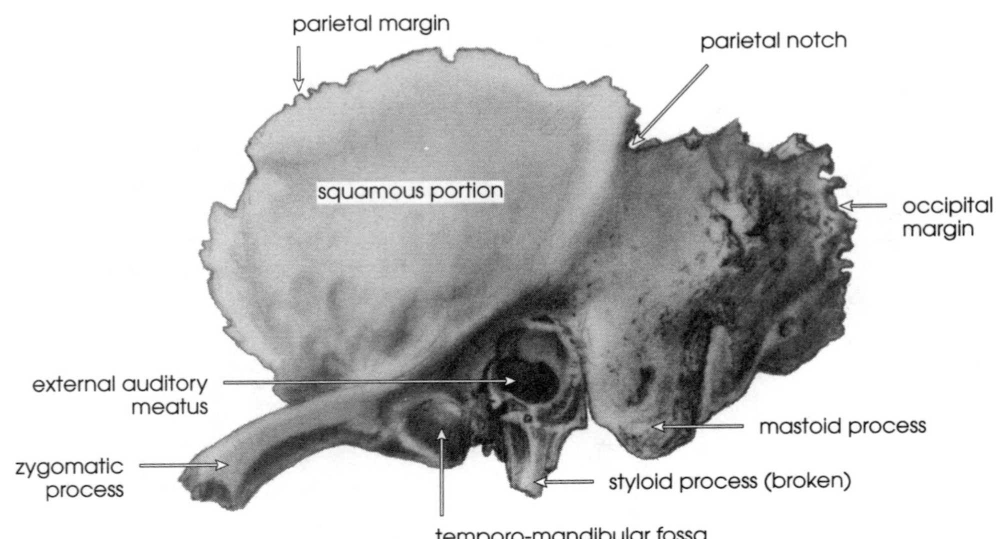

Left Temporal, Cerebral Surface

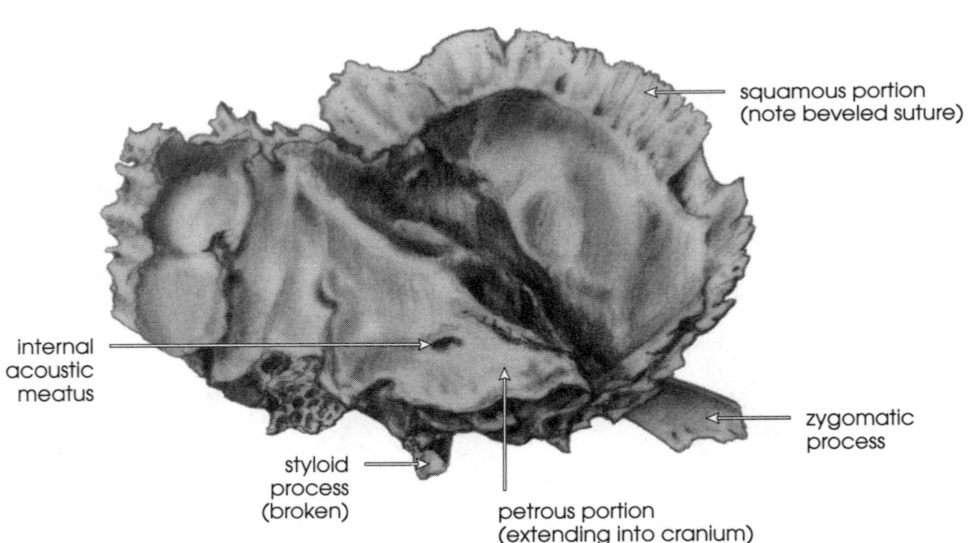

Sphenoid, Superior View

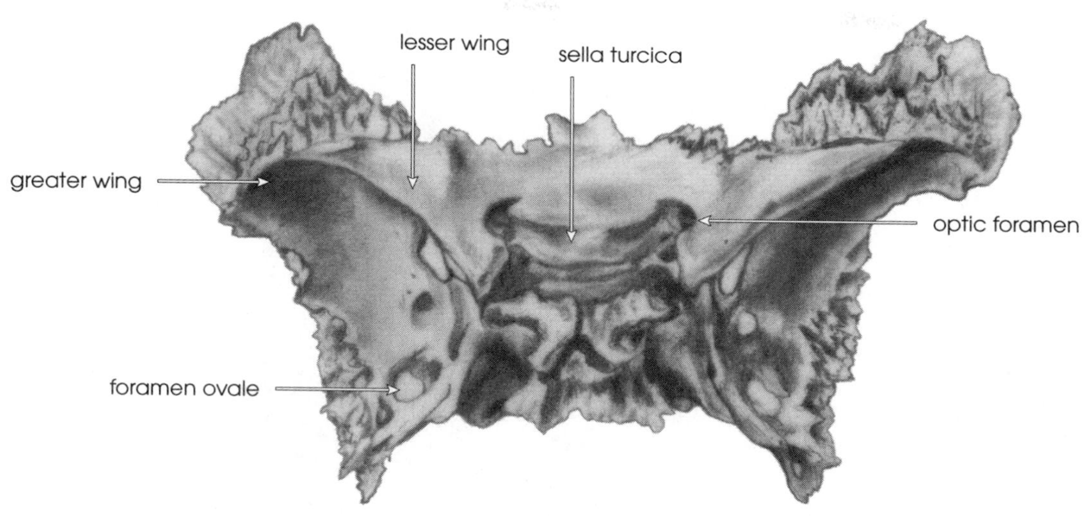

Sphenoid, Posterior View

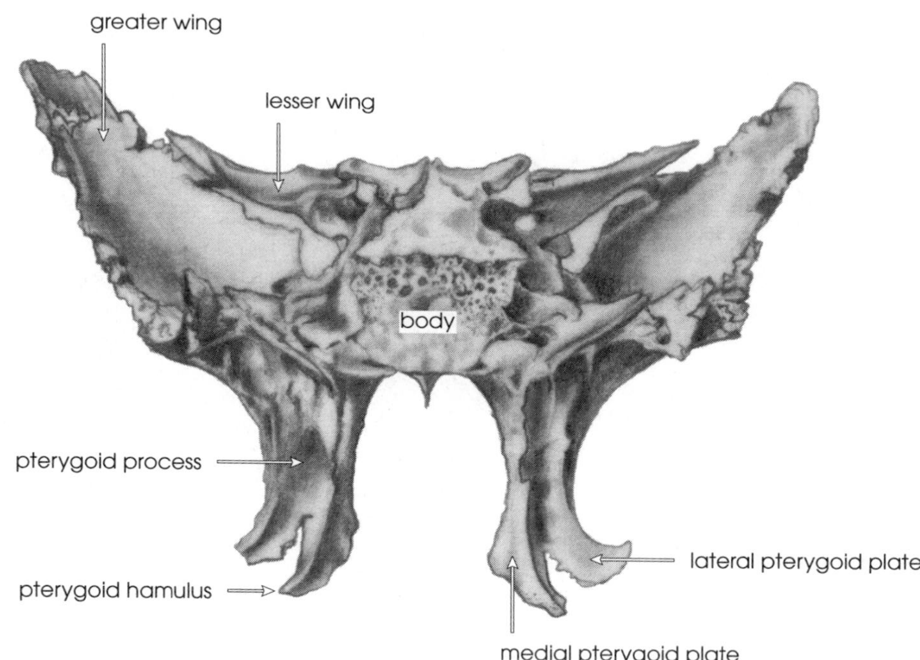

Left Maxilla and Mandible, Internal Surface

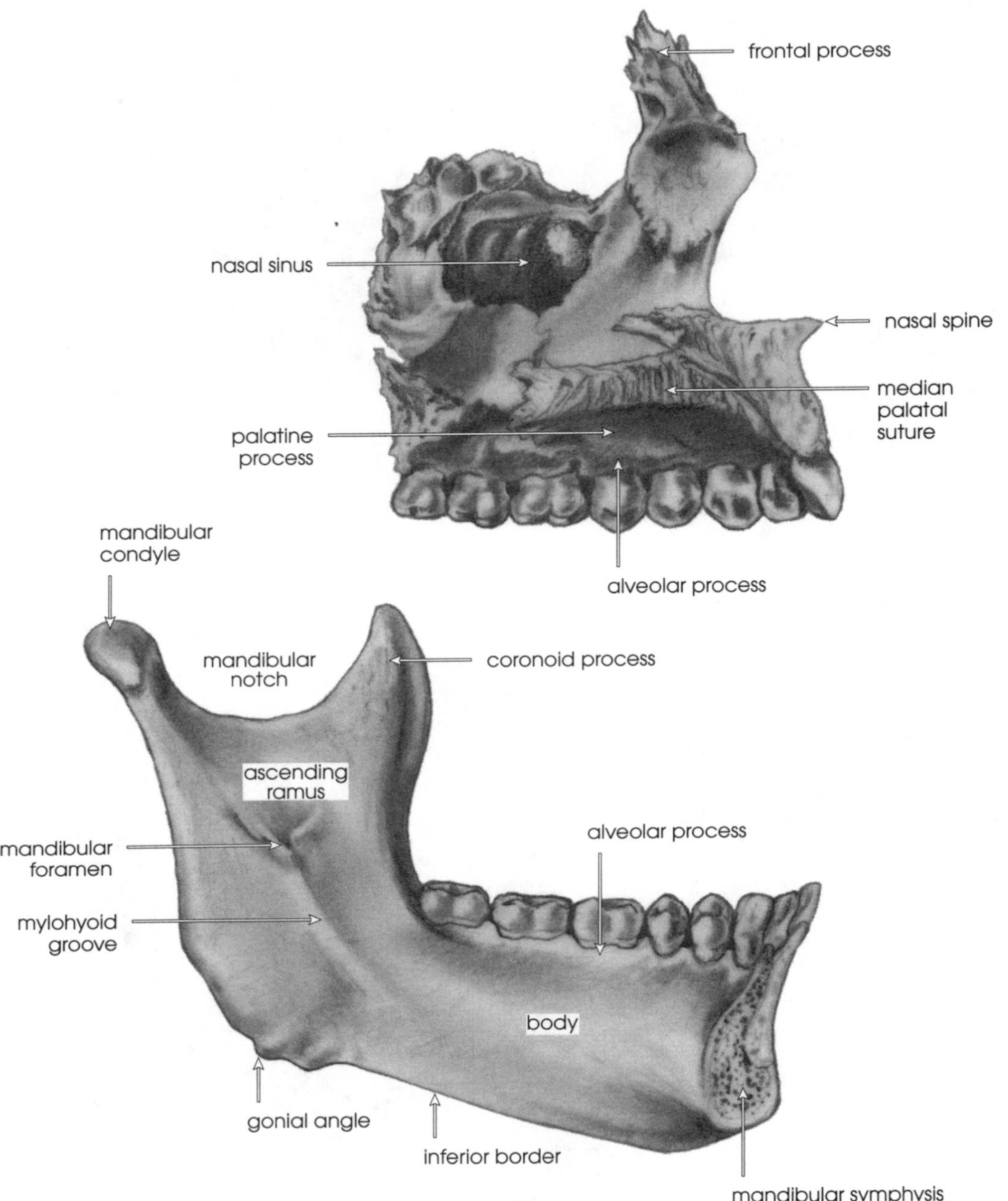

Left Maxilla and Mandible, External Surface

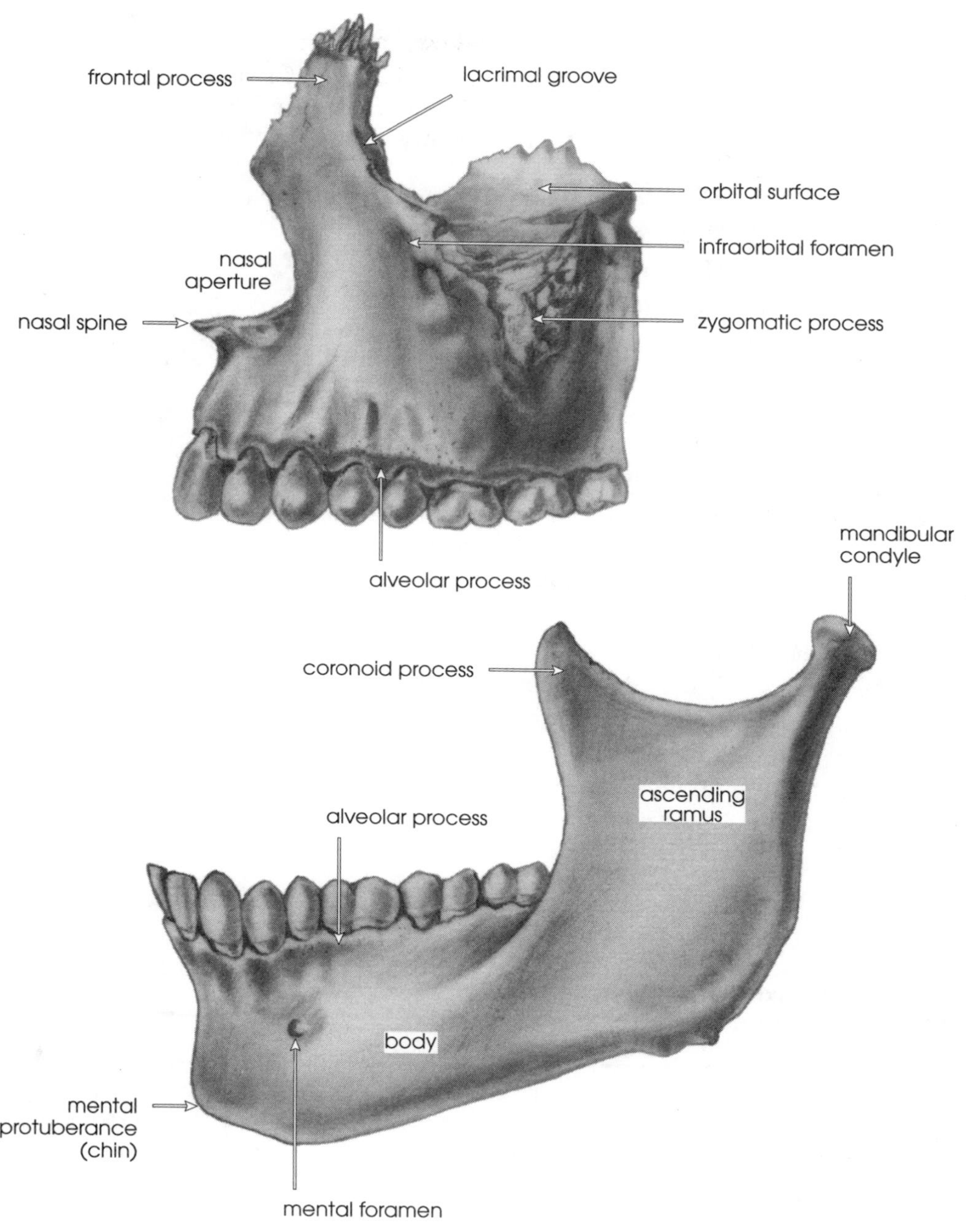

Sex Differentiation

Examining Male and Female Skulls for Sexual Differences

When examining male and female skulls for sexual differences, use as large a sample as possible. You will find yourself misled by your own observations if you try to learn with a small number of individuals.

1. First note the differences in overall size, shape, and rugosity.
2. Then compare foreheads:
   How large is the supraorbital ridge?
   How sharp is the orbital rim?
   Are there bumps on the frontal? How many?
3. Next, compare the jaws:
   Is the chin squared or oval?
   Can the flare of the mandible be seen?
4. Now, turn the skull and compare the facial profiles:
   What is the shape and contour of the forehead?
   How large is the brow ridge?
5. Look at the area of the skull where the ear once was:
   How sharp is the angle of the mandible? Is it flared?
   How large is the mastoid process?
   Where does the zygomatic arch end?
6. Finally, compare the cranial bases:
   Are the nuchal ridges rough or smooth?
   Is there a bony projection in the middle of the occipital?

Table 2.3 Non-Metric Sexual Cranial Traits

Bone	Elements of Difference	Male	Female
frontal	supraorbital ridge	prominent	absent
	frontal bossing	double boss	single central boss
temporal	mastoid process	large	small
	zygomatic process length	extends to the external auditory meatus and beyond	ends before the external auditory meatus
occipital	nuchal ridges	strong muscle attachment	slight muscle attachment
mandible	ramus	wide and sharply angled	narrow and less angled
	chin shape	square	rounded or pointed

Comparison of Male and Female Skulls, Frontal View

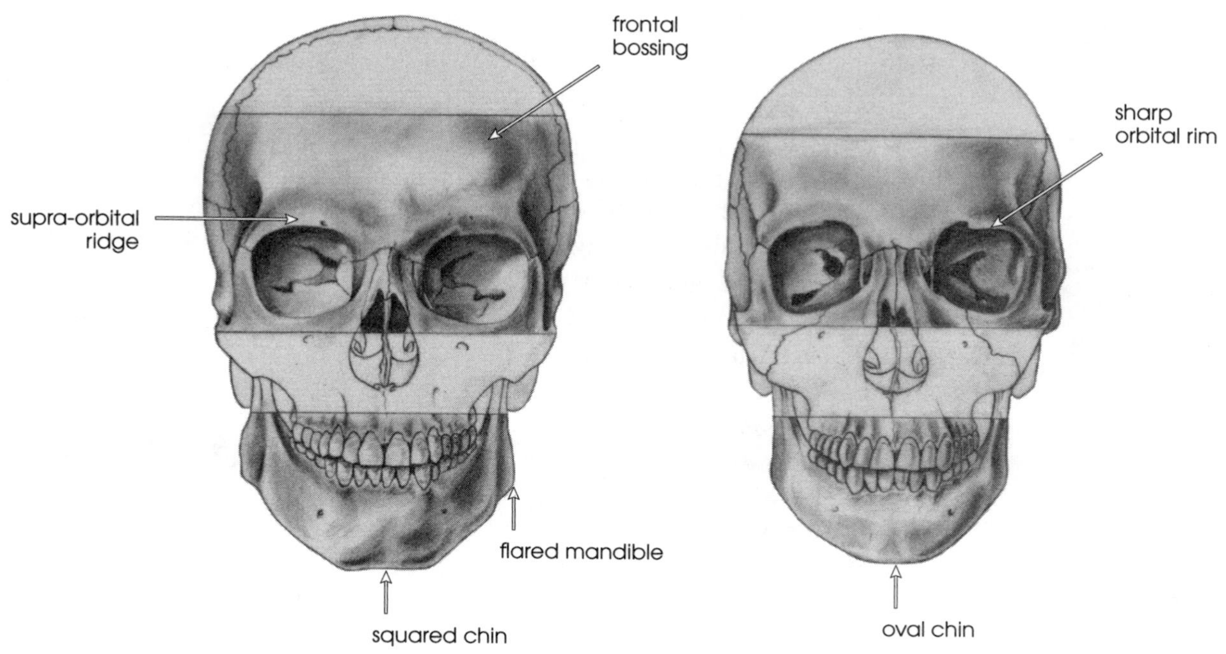

Comparison of Male and Female Skulls, Lateral View

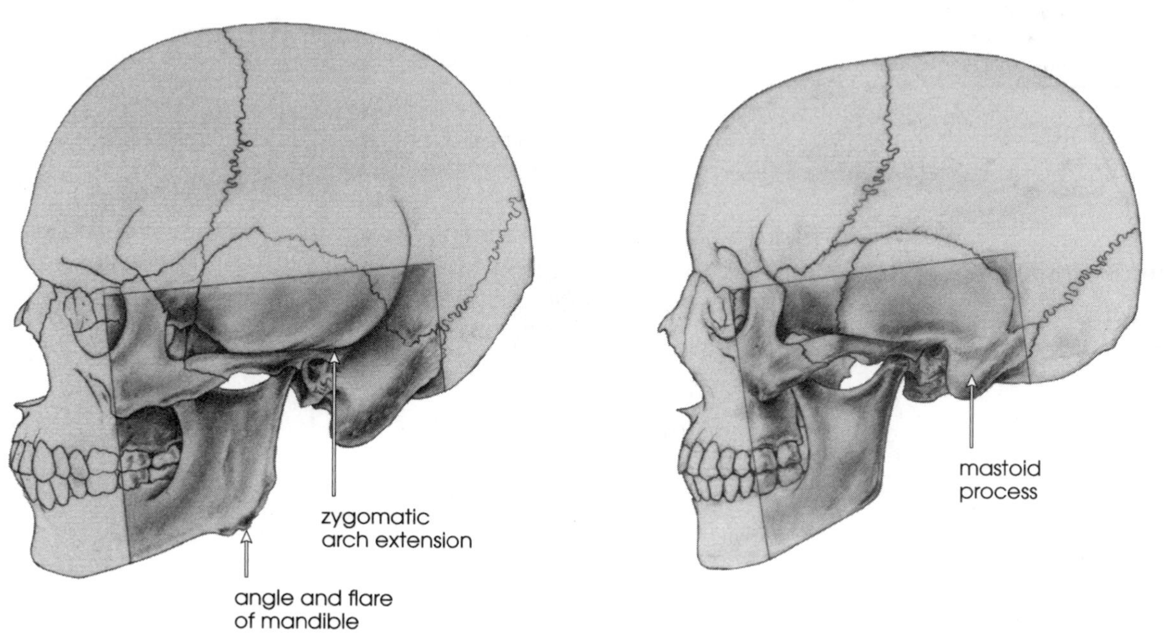

Racial Analysis

Examining Skulls from Persons of Different Races

Using as large a sample as possible, look at each skull and determine what characteristic impresses you the most.

1. Compare the center of the face in each racial type. Examine each trait separately. Is one racial trait more reliable than the others? Should all traits be considered in combination with the others?
   Shape and size of the zygoma
   Line of the zygomaxillary suture
   Shape of the nasal bones
   Width of the nasal aperture
   Form of the nasal sill
   Orbital shape
2. Compare the profile of each racial type. Examine each trait separately.
   Degree of prognathism
   Shape of the zygoma
   Projection of the nasal spine
   Shape of the chin
   Width of the mandibular ramus
   Cranial shape

Table 2.4 Nonmetric Cranial Traits

Elements of Difference	American Indians	European Origin	African Origin
incisors	shovel-shaped incisors	blade-form incisors	blade-form incisors
dentition	not crowded, often well-sclerosed	crowded, frequently impacted 3rd molars	not crowded
malars (zygoma)	robust and flaring, with malar tubercle	small, retreating malars	small, retreating malars
zygomaxillary suture	angled	jagged or S-shaped	curved or S-shaped
profile	moderate alveolar prognathism	little prognathism, orthognathic	strong alveolar prognathism
palatal shape	elliptic	parabolic	hyperbolic
palatal suture	straight	z-shape	arched
cranial sutures	complex, with Wormian bones	simple	simple
nasal bones	low "tented" nasals	high and arched, with nasion depression	low flat "quonset hut"
nasal aperture	medium	narrow	wide
nasal spine	medium, tilted	large, long	little or none
nasal sill	sharp	very sharp	"guttered"
chin	blunt median chin	square bilateral, projecting	retreating
ramus	wide ascending ramus		narrow ascending ramus
cranium	low, sloping	high	low, with post-bregmatic depression
hair form	straight round cross section	wavy oval cross section	curly or kinky flat cross section

Source: Adapted from Gill, 1995.

3. Determine which characteristic is most consistently different. Is it possible that there is no consistent difference?
   Prognathism/orthognathism?
   The nasal spine?
   The mandible?
   Something else?

Racial Differences in the Mid-Face, Frontal View

Asian

African

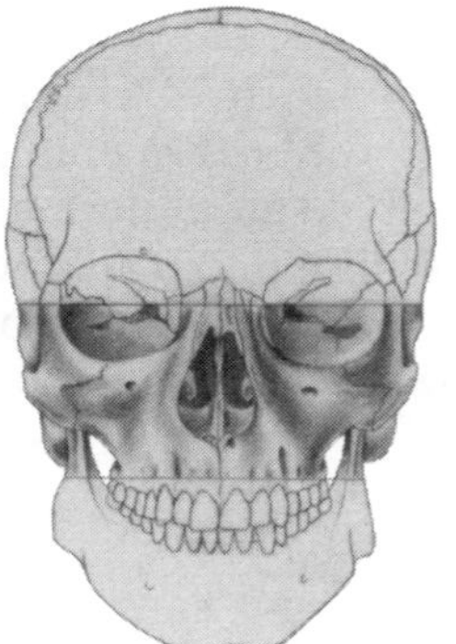

European

Racial Differences in the Face, Lateral View

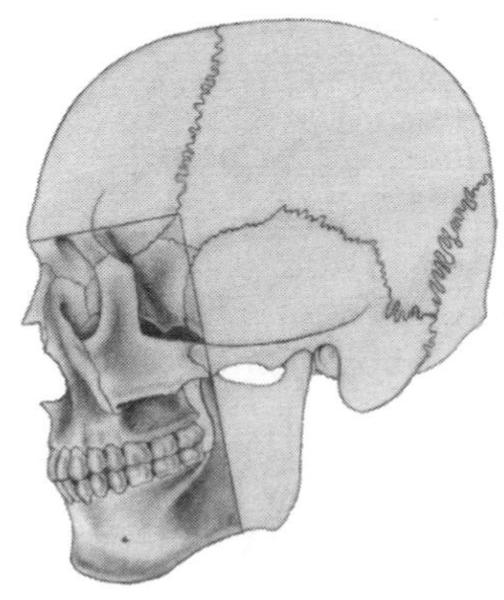

Asian

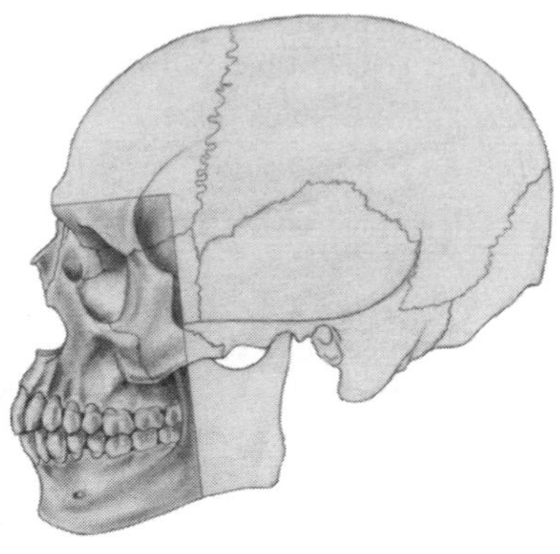

African

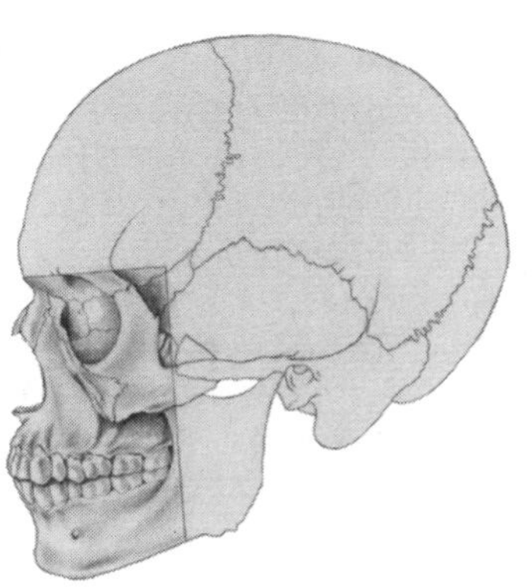

European

RACIAL ANALYSIS BY CRANIOMETRIC MEASUREMENTS AND COMPUTERIZED ANALYSIS

A complete set of measurements from an unidentified person can be compared with a large database of known persons for race and sex assessment. A computer program, FORDISC 2.0, designed by Douglas Ousley and Richard Jantz,1996, is highly recommended for this purpose. It is quite user friendly. All of the measurements are described and pictured within the help files.

ANTHROPOMETRY

Do you know why people of an unfamiliar race "all look alike?" Have you noticed that houses on an unfamiliar street are hard to tell apart, but the houses on your home street are easy? The answer is details, details, details. No matter what we look at, we see the grand picture before we see the details. When the grand picture is familiar, we unconsciously begin sorting through minutia. Details of the faces that we see every day are so well known to us that the briefest glance is sufficient for recognition.

But the process of absorbing details takes time. Instrumentation can speed up the process and help one to focus on significant differences. Exact measurements can also serve to support or refute hunches, suspicions, or intuitions about differences; this is where **anthropometry**—the measurement of the size and proportions of the human body—comes in. Spend some time learning the what, how, and why of measurements so that they will serve you well.

Key Term

anthropometry The measurement of the size and proportions of the human body.

Numerous sets of measurement techniques exist. When the body is alive or still fleshed, the techniques are somatometry for the body and cephalometry for the skull and face. Measurement techniques regularly used for the skeleton are osteometry. If only the skull is considered, the term is craniometry.

POSITION

When a bare skull is placed on a flat surface, it appears to be looking upward. It was in a different position in the living person. Most people carry their heads with the chin below the base of the skull. A line drawn through the ear openings is about the same distance from the floor as a line drawn between the shadows under each eye. If you connect the ear line with the under-eye line, a plane is formed that is parallel to the floor.

FRANKFORT PLANE (A.K.A. FRANKFORT HORIZONTAL)

The anatomically correct position for the skull is defined by three cranial points: left and right porion and left orbitale. Thus the external ear openings and the lower edge of the eye orbit provide a standardized plane for a "normal" skull position. This plane is called the Frankfort Plane or Frankfort Horizontal. It is a worldwide standard in physical anthropology, accepted by the International Congress of Anthropologists in Frankfort, Germany, 1877.

CRANIOMETRIC POINTS

Craniometric points are carefully defined points used for cranial measurements. Some are single points on the midsagittal plane of the skull, others are bilaterally paired points. Names of craniometric points are used not only to locate points for precise measurements, but also to describe specific areas of the skull when a precise word is needed. Each point is listed on pages 41–43 in alphabetical order.

- *Alare*—the paired point at the widest place on the margin of the nasal aperture. Instrumentally determined, it is used to measure *nasal width*.
- *Alveolare*—the lowest single point on the bony septum between the upper central incisors. This can be confused with infradentale, which is the comparable point between the *lower* central incisors. It is used to measure *upper facial height*.
- *Alveolon*—the single point at the intersection of sagittal suture of the hard palate and a line drawn from the posterior point of the right alveolar process to the posterior point of the left alveolar process. This point can be determined with sliding calipers or with a rubber band stretched around the entire alveolar process. It is used to measure *maxilloalveolar length*.
- *Apex*—the highest single point on the frontal section defined by left and right porion with the skull oriented to the Frankfort Plane. The apex is posterior to bregma.
- *Basion*—the single point at the anterior margin of the foramen magnum. It is the point most distant from bregma and is used to measure *maximum cranial height*.
- *Bregma*—the single point at the intersection of the sagittal and coronal sutures. It is used to measure *maximum cranial height*.
- *Condylion laterale*—a paired point at the most lateral edge of the mandibular condyle. It is used to measure *bicondylar width*.
- *Dacryon*—a paired point on the medial wall of the orbit where the lacrimomaxillary suture meets the frontal bone. It is between maxillofrontale and lacrimale and is used to measure *orbital width* and *interorbital width*.
- *Ectoconchion*—a paired point at the outer edge of the eye orbit. Instrumentally determined, this is the point at which the orbital length line meets the outer orbital rim. It is used to measure *maximum orbital width*.
- *Ectomolare*—a paired point on the lateral (buccal) surface of the alveolar process. Instrumentally determined, it is usually located at the upper second molar. It is used to measure *maximum alveolar width*.
- *Endobasion*—the single point at the posterior margin of the anterior border of the foramen magnum. It is usually internal to basion. It is used for facial measurements, not cranial height.
- *Endomolare*—a paired point on the lingual surface of the alveolar process at the location of the second molar. It is used to measure *palatal width*.
- *Euryon*—a paired point used to measure *maximum cranial width*. Instrumentally determined, it is located on the parietal or temporal. Note: Left and right euryon must be directly opposite each other on the skull.
- *Frontotemporale*—a paired point on the curve of the temporal line. Instrumentally determined, it is the point on the frontal bone that gives the smallest measurement from left to right temporal line and is used to measure *minimum frontal width*.
- *Glabella*—the most anterior single point in the midsagittal section of the frontal bone at the level of the supraorbital ridges. It is above nasion and is used to measure *maximum cranial length*.
- *Gnathion*—the lowest point on the midsagittal plane of the mandible; the bottom of the chin. It is used to measure *total facial height* and *mandibular symphysis height*.

- *Gonion*—a paired point at the outer corner of the angle of the mandible. It is the junction of the body and ramus of the mandible and is used to measure *bigonial width* and *ascending ramus height*.
- *Incision*—the single point at the incisal level of the upper central incisors; the lower edge of the upper central incisors.
- *Infradentale*—the highest single point on the bony septum between the lower central incisors. This can be confused with alveolar, which is the comparable point between the *upper* central incisors. It is used to measure *mandibular symphysis height*.
- *Inion*—a single point at the intersection of the left and right superior nuchal lines. It is at the base of the external occipital protuberance, and there may be a slight projection of bone at this point.
- *Lacrimale*—a paired point on the medial wall of the orbit at the intersection of the posterior lacrimal crest and the frontolacrimal suture. It is posterior to dacryon and maxillofrontale.
- *Lambda*—the single point at the intersection of the sagittal suture and the lambdoidal suture.
- *Mastoidale*—a paired point at the inferior tip of the mastoid process. It is used to measure *mastoid length*.
- *Maxillofrontale*—a paired point at the intersection of the anterior lacrimal crest (on the frontal process of the maxilla) and the frontomaxillary suture. It is on the medial margin of the orbit and can be used to measure *orbital width*.
- *Nasion*—the single point at the intersection of the nasofrontal suture and the internasal suture. It is used to measure *total facial height* and *upper facial height*.
- *Nasospinale*—the single point on the intermaxillary suture at the base of the nasal aperture. It is used to measure *nasal height*.
- *Opisthion*—the single point at the posterior margin of the foramen magnum.
- *Opisthocranion*—the single most posterior point on the skull, but not on the occipital protuberance. Instrumentally determined, it is used to measure *maximum cranial length*.
- *Orale*—the single most anterior point on the hard palate where a line drawn lingual to the central incisors intersects the palatal suture. It is used to measure *palatal length*.
- *Orbitale*—a paired point at the lowest part of the orbital margin. It is used to define the Frankfort Plane and to measure *orbital height*.
- *Pogonion*—the most anterior single point on the midsagittal plane of the mandible; the front of the chin.
- *Porion*—a paired point at the most lateral part of the superior margin of the external auditory meatus. It is used to define the Frankfort Plane and to measure *mastoid length*.
- *Prosthion*—the most anterior single point on the upper alveolar process. It is superior to alveolare and is used to measure *maxilloalveolar length*.
- *Pterion*—a paired point on the upper end of the greater wing of the sphenoid. This is more often a region than a point.
- *Staphylion*—the single point on the posterior hard palate where the palatal suture is crossed by a line drawn tangent to the curves of the posterior margin of the palatal bones. It is used to measure *palatal length*.

- *Vertex*—the highest single point on the midsagittal section of the skull when positioned in the Frankfort Plane.
- *Zygion*—a paired point at the most lateral edge of the zygoma. It is used to measure *bizygomatic width* (mid-facial width).

Directions for Accurate Measurements

Some measurements, such as maximum cranial height and width are simple and obvious. Others are rather awkward and require practice. The goal is consistent results that can be duplicated by yourself and others. Start by working through all of the measurements on your own. Then test yourself by measuring a study skull and comparing your results with the results recorded by an experienced person. Wherever discrepancies occur, review the method and ask for help.

Measuring the Orbit

- Orbital height—orbitale to the superior orbital border while perpendicular to the natural horizontal axis of the orbit. Some orbits are naturally oriented on a horizontal plane, but many are oriented with the lateral border inferior to the medial border.
- Orbital width—maxillofrontale to ectoconchion
- Biorbital width—ectoconchion to ectoconchion
- Interorbital width—dacryon to dacryon

Craniometric Points, Medial Orbital Wall

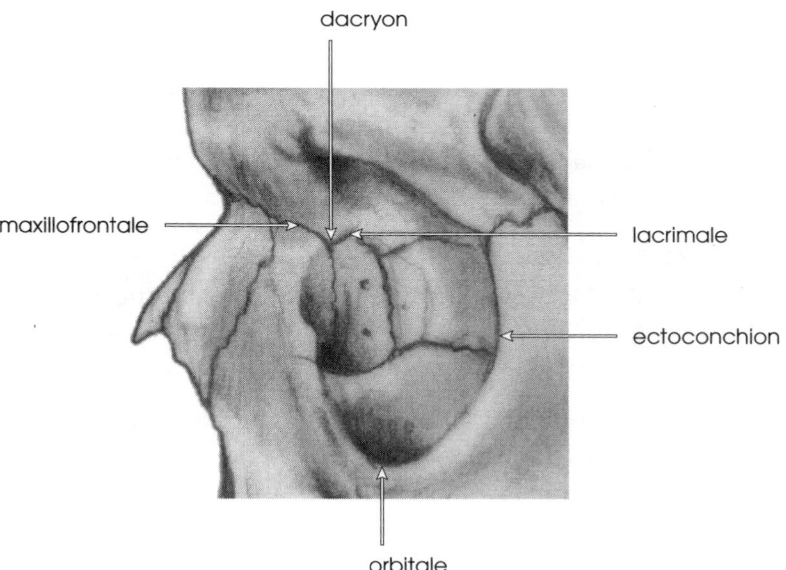

MEASURING THE PALATE

- Maxilloalveolar length—prosthion to alveolon
- Maxilloalveolar width—ectomolare to ectomolare
- Palatal length—orale to staphylion
- Palatal width—endomolare to endomolare

Craniometric Points, Palatal View, No 3rd Molars

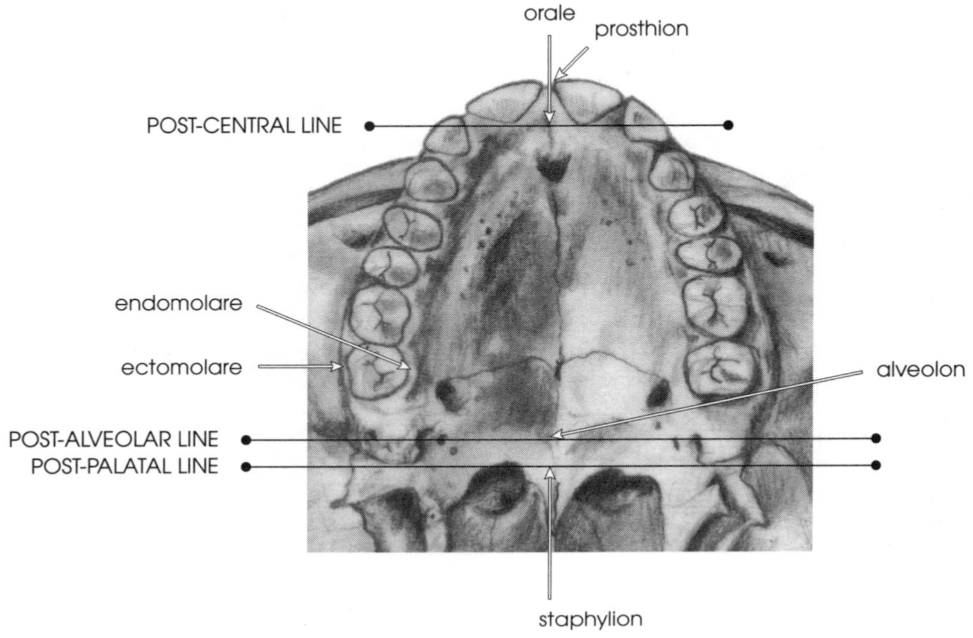

MEASURING THE MANDIBLE

- Bicondylar width—condylion to condylion
- Bigonial width—gonion to gonion
- Ascending ramus height—gonion to superior mandibular condyle
- Mandibular symphysis height—gnathion to infradentale

CHORD MEASUREMENTS

The chord is a standardized method for obtaining a straight line measurement from a curved surface. The curvature is not important, only the direct distance from beginning point to end point.

- Frontal chord (frontal bone)—nasion to bregma
- Parietal chord (parietal bone)—bregma to lambda
- Occipital chord (occipital bone)—lambda to opisthion

HEAD SHAPE AND CRANIAL INDICES

The cranial (or cephalic) indices are simple ratios of cranial measurements. They are used to describe the general shape of a skull and the general appearance of the face in life. A person with a long narrow head looks quite different from a person with a wide round head. For those who understand the terms, indices help translate a skull shape to a face shape.

Computer analysis has made the calculation of multiple cranial indices rather obsolete. Most people would prefer to analyze everything at once rather than piece by piece. Nonetheless, it is good to understand the roots of the computer programs for skeletal analysis.

Cranial Index (CI) = (maximum cranial width x 100) ÷ maximum cranial length

long, narrow head (dolichocranic)
(CI) = 74.99 or less

average head (mesocranic)
(CI) = 75.00 to 79.99

broad, round head (brachycranic)
(CI) = 80.00 to 84.00

very broad, round head (hyperbrachycranic)
(CI) = 85.00 or more

If computer analysis is not available, it is also possible to work out the analysis by direct computation. The Fordisc database is, however, changing with the addition of new cases. It is, therefore, a dynamic resource, more appropriate for modern cases than formulae derived from static collections.

In case the measurements must be taken without computer assistance, Table 2.5 and the illustrations on pages 46–47 can be used for quick reference.

Table 2.5 Major Cranial Measurements

Name	Measurement Name	From This point	To This point
GOL	maximum cranial length	glabella (g)	opisthocranion (op)
XCB	maximum cranial width	euryon (eu)	euryon (eu)
ZYB	bizygomatic width	zygion (zy)	zygion (zy)
BAB	maximum cranial height (basion-bregma height)	basion (ba)	bregma (b)
BAN	cranial base length	basion (ba)	nasion (n)
BAPR	basion-prosthion length	basion (ba)	prosthion (pr)
MAB	maxillo-alveolar width	ectomolare (ecm)	ectomolare (ecm)
MAL	maxillo-alveolar length	prosthion (pr)	alveolon (al)
AUB	biauricular width	zygomatic process root	zygomatic process root
TFHT	total facial height	nasion (n)	gnathion (gn)
UFHT	upper facial height	nasion (n)	prosthion (pr)
MFB	minimum frontal width	frontotemporale (ft)	frontotemporale (ft)
NLH	nasal height	nasion (n)	nasospinale (ns)
NLB	nasal width	alare (al)	alare (al)
ORBR	orbital width	dacryon (d)	ectoconchion (ec)
OBH	orbital height	superior margin	inferior margin
BIOB	biorbital width	ectoconchion (ec)	ectoconchion (ec)
INTB	interorbital width	dacryon (d)	dacryon (d)
FRC	frontal chord	nasion (n)	bregma (b)
PAC	parietal chord	bregma (b)	lambda (l)
OCC	occipital chord	lambda (l)	opisthion (o)
FOL	foramen magnum length	opisthion (o)	basion (ba)
	mastoid length	porion	mastoidale

Note: The word "width" is used instead of "breadth" for names of measurements. The two words have the same meaning, but "width" is more commonly used in the English language. It is, therefore, easier for nonnative English speakers to translate.

Craniometric Points, Frontal View

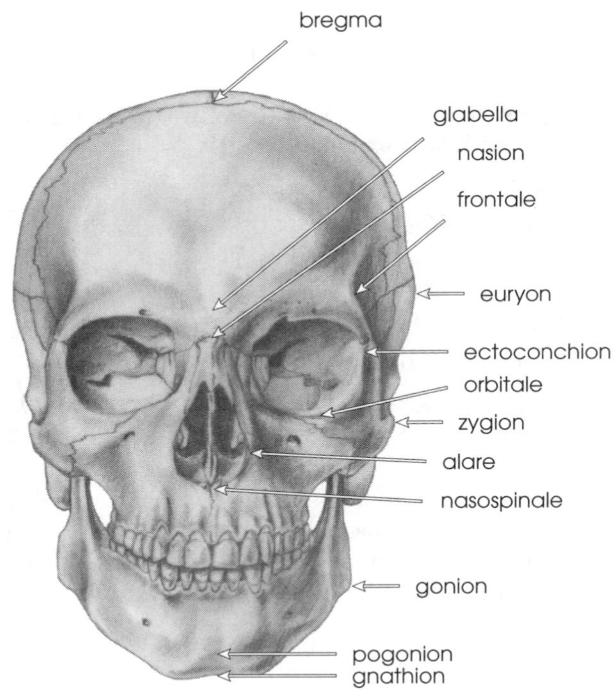

Craniometric Points, Lateral View

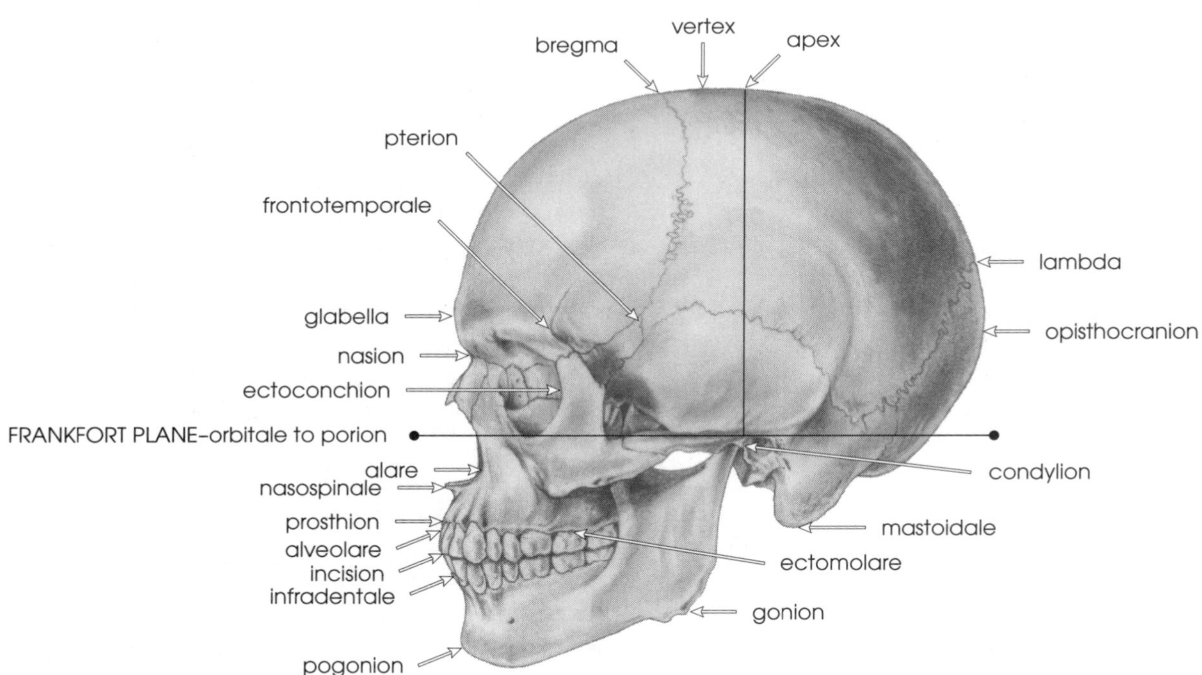

Craniometric Points, Basilar View

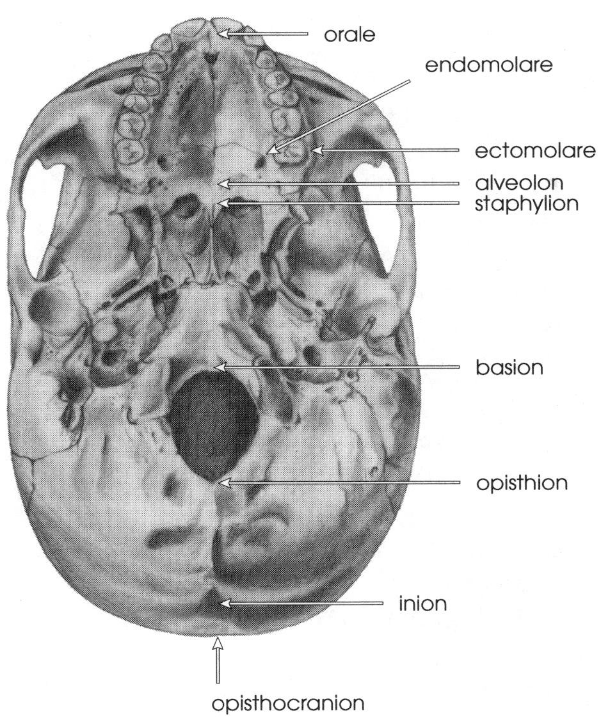

Craniometric Points, Coronal View

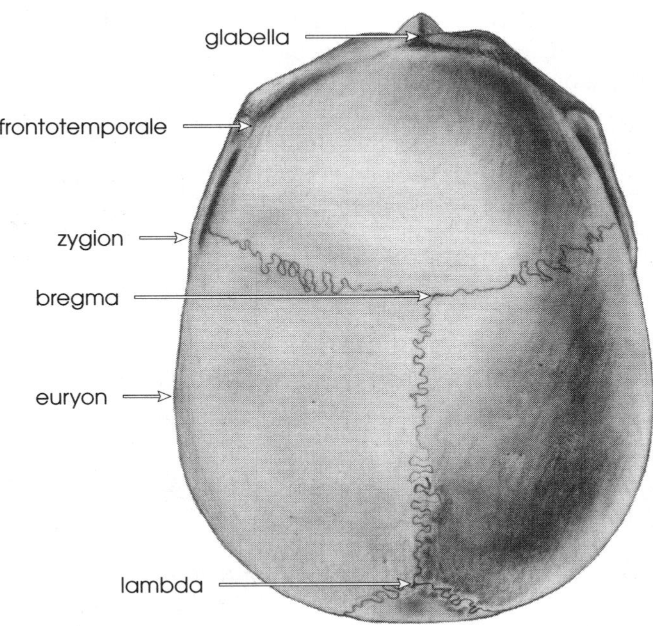

Review of Skull Measurement Terms

Find each point on a skull and describe it in a way that helps you to remember:

1. Alare (al)
2. Alveolon (alv)
3. Basion (ba)
4. Bregma (b)
5. Dacryon (d)
6. Ectoconchion (ec)
7. Ectomolare (ecm)
8. Euryon (eu)
9. Frontotemporale (ft)
10. Glabella (g)
11. Gonion (go)
12. Lambda (l)
13. Nasion (n)
14. Nasospinale (ns)
15. Opisthion (o)
16. Opisthocranion (op)
17. Prosthion (pr)
18. Pterion (pt)
19. Zygion (zy)

The Hyoid

Key Term

hyoid The *os hyoideus* or hyoid apparatus; a small, three-part, U-shaped bone within the anterior upper neck.

The **hyoid** is a small U-shaped bone in the upper part of the neck. It is tucked between the mandible and the larynx, suspended from the styloid processes of the temporal bone by delicate stylohyoid ligaments.

The complete hyoid is composed of three parts—a central body and two lateral horns. The body is slightly cup-shaped and the horns taper from the articulation with the body to the lateral ligament attachments. It is not unusual for the horns to fuse to the body of the hyoid, sometimes on only one side.

Hyoid, Three-Quarter View

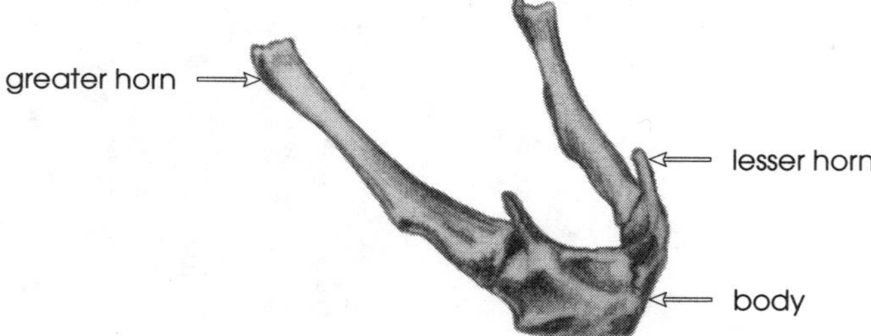

Chapter 3

The Shoulder and Ches
Clavicle, Scapula,

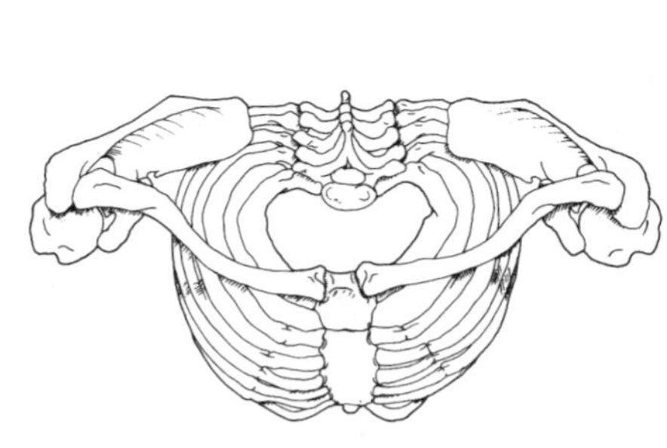

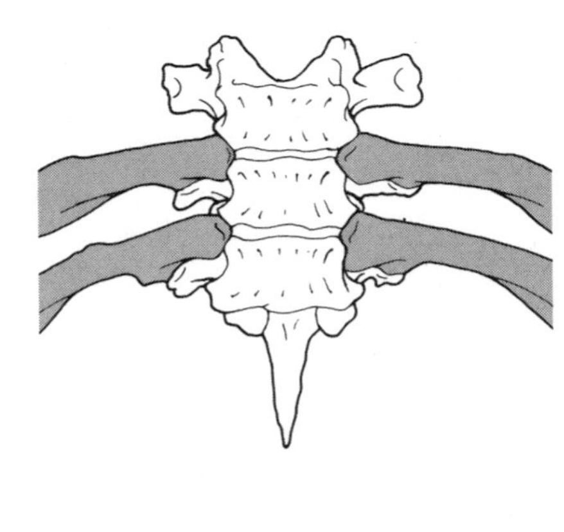

CHAPTER OUTLINE

The Shoulder Girdle

The Clavicle

- Epiphyseal Fusion

The Scapula

The Ribs

- Costo-Vertebral Articulations
- Age Determination

The Sternum

...ER GIRDLE

The shoulders provide a suspension system for the arms. The bones of the shoulders function like a carpenter's belt. The belt wraps around the hips and tools hang from it. The scapula and the clavicle wrap around the upper part of the barrel of the chest and the arms hang from this "girdle." The system provides both stability and an enormous range of flexibility.

The **shoulder girdle** is incomplete across the back. The bony articulations occur only at two points on each side. The medial articulation is between the clavicles and the manubrium of the sternum. The lateral articulation is between the clavicles and the acromion processes of the scapulae.

The main articulation of the humerus is at the glenoid fossa of the scapula. When compared with the acetabulum of the hip joint, the glenoid fossa provides a very small bony socket. Less weight bearing is expected of the arm, but the arm is allowed a far greater range of movement.

Key Term

shoulder girdle The bones that articulate to form a supporting framework for the shoulders and arms; the clavicles and scapulae.

Superior View of the Articulated Shoulder Girdle

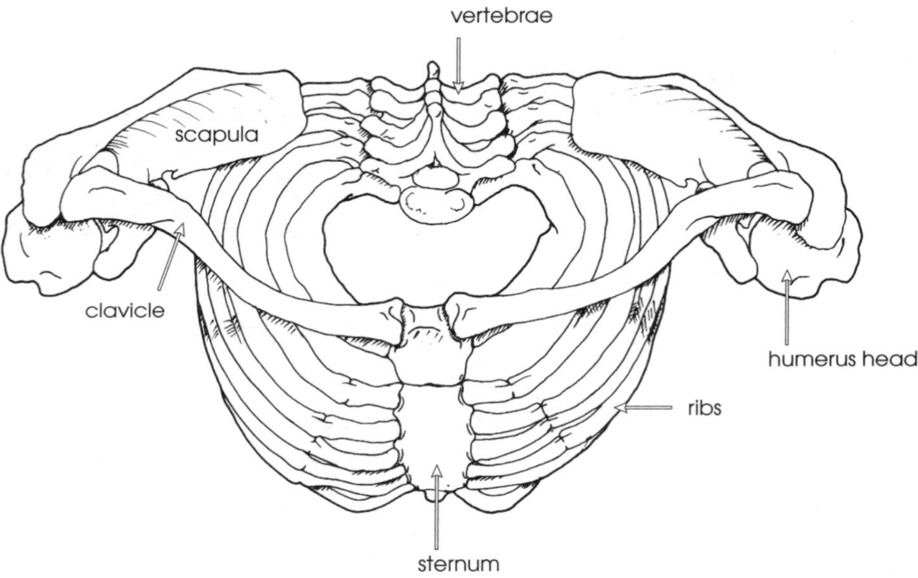

THE CLAVICLE

The **clavicle** is commonly known as a "collar bone." Clavicles are S-shaped long bones. The medial end is circular in cross section and abuts against the manubrium of the sternum. The lateral end is compressed and spatulate in shape. It touches the acromion process of the scapula, forming a small point of articulation. Beginning at the medial end, the clavicle curves anteriorly before it curves posteriorly. The roughened surface is internal and the smoother surface is external.

Key Term

clavicle The S-shaped paired bone that forms the anterior of the shoulder girdle; the "collar bone."

Anterior-Superior View of the Left Clavicle

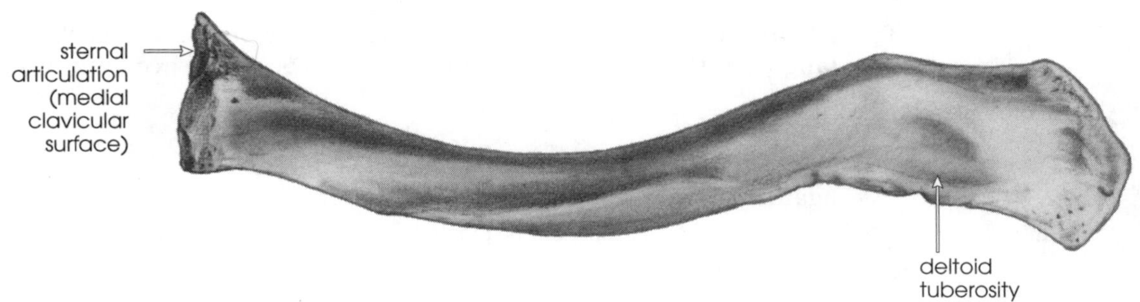

Posterior-Inferior View of the Left Clavicle

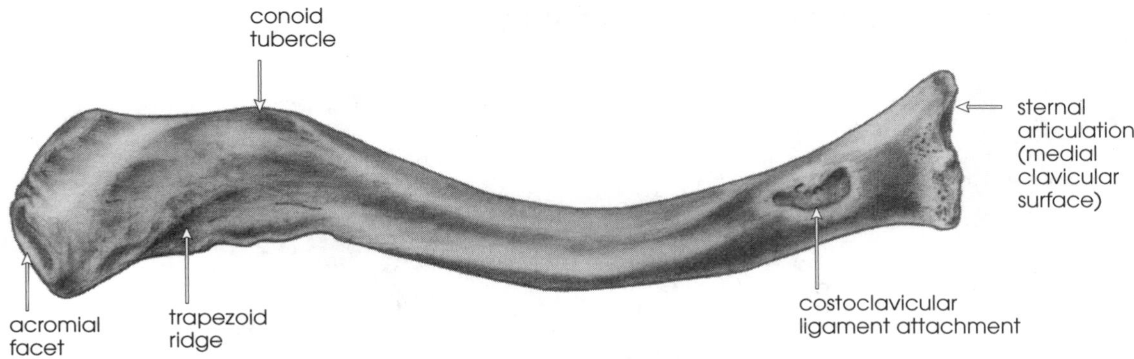

Epiphyseal Fusion

In the human body, the medial clavicular epiphysis is the last epiphysis to fuse. Fusion usually takes place in the mid-twenties; however, the widest age range reported is fifteen to thirty-two.

The illustration below shows a medial view of the epiphyseal surface of the clavicle before, during, and after fusion.

The Medial Clavicular Surface in Three States of Development

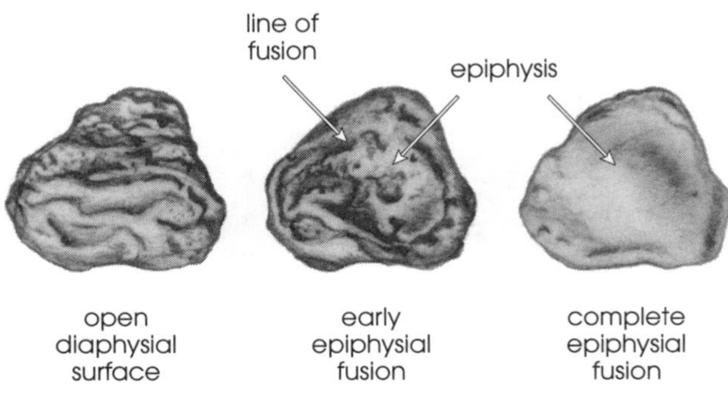

THE SCAPULA

Key Term

scapula (pl. scapulae) The flat, triangular paired bone overlying the posterior portion of the upper ribs; the "shoulder blade."

The **scapulae** are flat bones that cover the upper part of the back. In common language, they are called shoulder blades. Scapulae are built of several parts.

- The body is the large triangular part. The flat side of the body is against the ribs and the spine is posterior.
- The coracoid process curls close to the anterosuperior part of the upper arm.
- The acromion process swings higher and wider than the coracoid. The acromion is known as the "shoulder bone."
- The glenoid fossa is the articular surface for the humerus.

Costal View of the Left Scapula

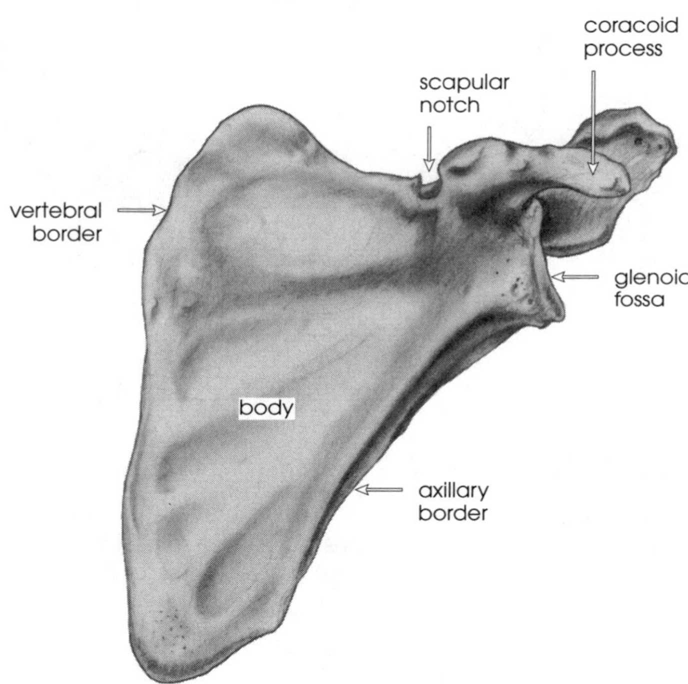

Lateral and Dorsal Views of the Left Scapula

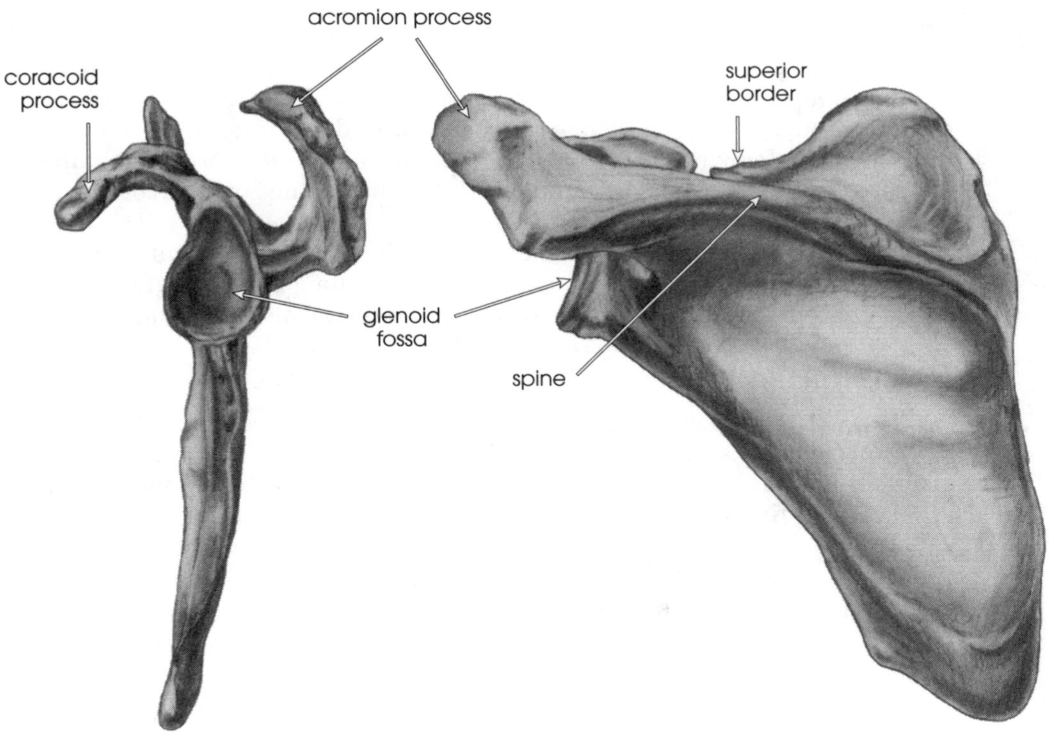

Table 3.1 Osteological Terms for the Shoulder

Bone	Term	Definition and Attachments
clavicle	conoid tubercle	the bump on the posterior superior surface of the lateral end of the clavicle—attachment for the trapezius muscle
	medial epiphysis	the epiphysis on the sternal end of the clavicle (the clavicle has no lateral epiphysis)—articulates with the clavicular notch on the manubrium; attachment on the inner surface for the sternohyoid
scapula	acromion process	the larger, more posterior and superior of the two scapular processes—articulates with the lateral end of the clavicle; attachment for the trapezium and the deltoid
	body of scapula	the main part of the shoulder blade; a large, thin triangular plate of bone
	coracoid process	the smaller, more anterior of the two scapular processes—attachment for the coracobrachialis and the pectoralis minor
	border, axillary	the lateral border of the scapula—attachment for the teres major
	border, superior	the uppermost border of the scapula
	border, vertebral	the medial border of the scapula—attachment for the levator scapulae and the rhomboids
	costal surface	the anterior (rib) surface—covered by the subscapularis
	dorsal surface	the posterior (back) surface—covered by the supraspinatus, the infraspinatus, and the teres minor
	glenoid cavity	the large ovoid articular surface on the superior-lateral corner of the scapula—articulates with the head of the humerus
	supra-glenoid tubercle	the bump at the superior edge of the glenoid fossa—attachment for the biceps brachii
	scapular notch	the notch on the superior border of the scapula
	spine	the long thin elevation on the dorsal surface of the scapula that ends laterally as the acromion process—attachment for the trapezius (superior edge) and the deltoid (inferior edge)

The Ribs

Key Term
rib One of the twelve paired bones of the rib cage—the bones surrounding the organs of the chest.

The rib cage houses several of the organs essential to life. Careful examination of the **ribs** may provide evidence for the determination of cause or manner of death. Gunshot wounds, knife wounds, and fractures that occurred on living bone can be used to draw inferences about the condition of underlying organs at the time of death. Of course, the value of the evidence is greatly diminished if the ribs are not on the correct side or in the correct order.

Begin the study of ribs by learning to sort all twenty-four ribs and place them in correct numerical order. With the guidelines given here and plenty of practice, it is possible to sort all of the ribs correctly and determine which may be missing or damaged.

1. Begin with the first rib. The first ribs are short, tightly curved, and almost flat. They also have relatively long necks. (The neck is the extension of bone between the two vertebral facets.) Place the first ribs on a flat surface. If the head is angled downward and touching the surface of the table, the dorsal (superior) surface is facing upward.
2. Find the floating ribs (#11 and #12) and separate them out. They have fan-shaped heads, no neck, and tapered sternal ends. The sternal end is not cup-shaped.
3. Sort the other nine pairs of ribs into groups of right ribs and left ribs. The sharper edge and the costal groove are inferior. The head is posterior.
4. With rib #1 as a starting point, sort one side from top to bottom, then the other. The shape of the heads changes gradually from long and narrow to fan-shaped. The length of the necks gradually shortens. The curvature of the ribs changes as the ribs conform to the outer surface of the barrel-shaped chest. The inner surface of the upper ribs faces toward the table surface; the inner surface of the lower ribs faces away from the table surface.
5. Finally, check the arrangement of ribs from first to last. The head of rib #7 or #8 is usually highest from the surface. Each rib conforms to the curvature of the adjacent ribs. Each rib is also easily compared to the rib from the opposite side for consistency in overall shape and length.

Rib heads articulate with the vertebrae and the sternal ends attach to the sternum by means of costal cartilage. Costal cartilage tends to ossify with advancing age. It provides one method of relative age determination.

Ribs #1, #7, and #12, Inferior (Internal) View

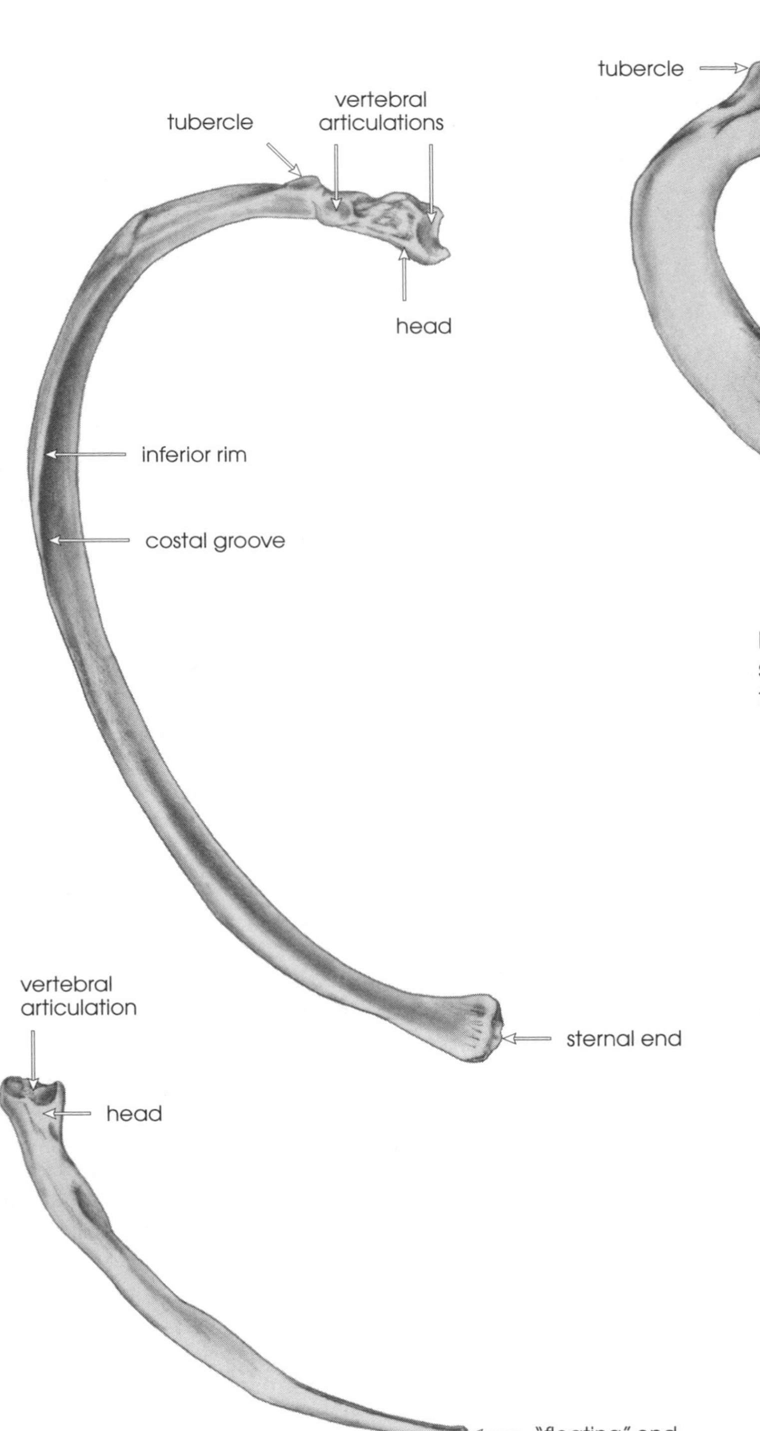

Note the major differences from the most superior rib to the most inferior rib in each of the following characteristics:

1. The cross-sectional shape of the body
2. The shape of the head
3. The presence or absence of a neck
4. The curvature of the body of the rib
5. The shape of the sternal end

Use a sequence of steps for sorting ribs:

1. Separate left from right.
2. Separate long thin necks and narrow heads from no necks and wide or fanning heads.
3. Match curvatures and vertical angles.
4. Check the left with the right for bilateral consistency.

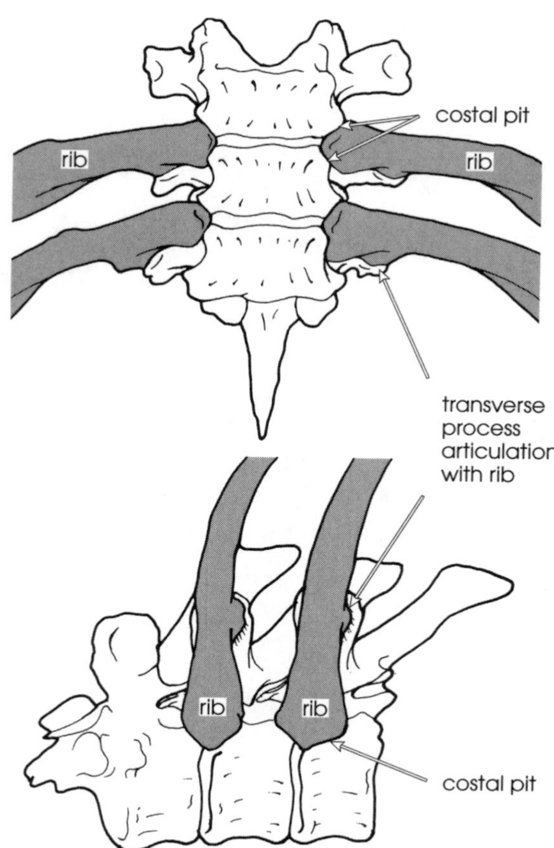

Rib Articulations, Anterior and Lateral Views

Ribs #2 through #10 usually abut against adjacent vertebral bodies as well as the intervertebral disk.

Costo-Vertebral Articulations

Considerable individual variation exists in costo-vertebral articulations. Ribs appear to have moved slightly cerebrally (toward the head) in some individuals and caudally (toward the lower back) in others. The configuration described here is fairly common, but do not be surprised by variations.

The body of the first thoracic vertebra has a complete costal pit for rib #1. The body of T12 has a complete costal pit for rib #12. T2 through T10 have half-pits on both the superior and inferior edges of the bodies. T1 may have a half-pit on the inferior edge. T11 is probably the most variable, exhibiting one complete pit, two half-pits, or a superior half-pit and an inferior complete pit.

The first ten thoracic vertebrae also have articular facets on the anterior surface of the transverse processes. T11 and T12 do not have facets on the transverse process. (The transverse processes on the lowest of the thoracic vertebrae are reduced in size from those of the upper thoracic vertebrae.)

Age Determination

Ribs, like the rest of the skeleton, change with advancing age. The sternal end of the rib is connected to the sternum by cartilage. As the bone-cartilage interface is subjected to the normal stresses of life, the bone responds by steadily remodeling and further ossifying the cartilage. The pattern of change is predictable. It tends to differ, however, between the sexes. Males are more likely to ossify along the margins of the rib cartilage, and females are more likely to ossify outward from the rib end and through the center of the rib cartilage. The elderly male is more likely to exhibit rib ends with a "crab-claw" appearance (McCormick and Stewart, 1983 and 1984).

Isçan et al. (1985) published
They describe rib age changes by
series of ribs illustrated here is si
vides an overview of the basic char
read the original publication and pı
available through France Casting.

CHILD (YOUNGER THAN MID-TEENS)

The rib end begins as a fairly flat sur
and the surface is only slightly undula

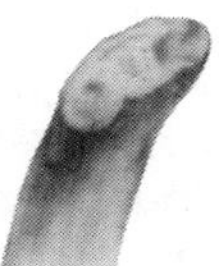
stage 0

TEENAGER+ (MID-TEENS TO EARLY TWENTIES)

The edges are sharper and have a scallope
is beginning to look V-shaped (Stage 1–2).

stage 1

stage 2

YOUNG ADULT (MID-TWENTIES TO EARLY THIRTIES)

The edges are less regular and the centers projec
and inferior edges. The V is deepening (Stage 3–4

stage 3

stage 4

OLDER ADULT (AGE MID-THIRTIES TO MID-FIFTIES)

The superior and inferior edges have grown to the lengt
V has expanded into a cup-shaped center (Stage 5–6).

stage 5

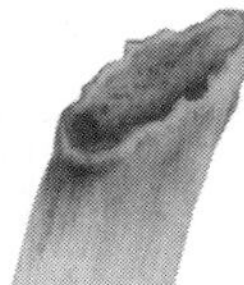
stage 6

ELDERLY ADULT (OLDER THAN MID-FIFTIES)

The edges are elongated, ragged, and sometimes have a crab
ance. The center is porous and irregular (Stage 7–8).

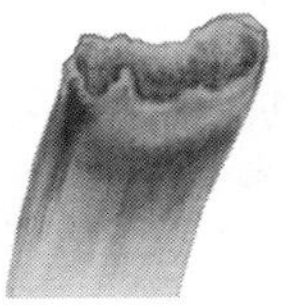
stage 7

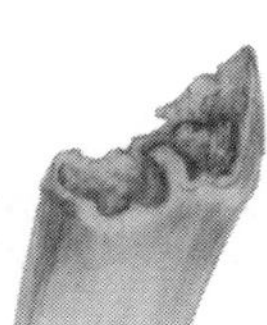
stage 8

THE STERNUM

Key Terr

sternum The
part of the ant
chest; the med
articulation fo
clavicles and
ment for rib c

n

e bony
erior
ial
r the
ttach-
artilage.

The adult **sternum** is comprised of three elements: the manubrium, the body, and the xiphoid process. The body is comprised of four primary centers of ossification. The xiphoid process usually fuses with the body of the sternum. Occasionally the body also fuses with the manubrium.

The clavicles articulate with the manubrium and the first ten ribs attach to the sternum by cartilaginous extensions known as "costal cartilage." The costal cartilage of the first rib attaches to the manubrium. Costal cartilage of the second rib attaches at the junction of the manubrium and the body of the sternum. Costal cartilage of ribs three through six connects at the junctions of each of the sternal elements. Ribs seven through ten attach to the inferior border of the sternal body through a single cartilaginous connection.

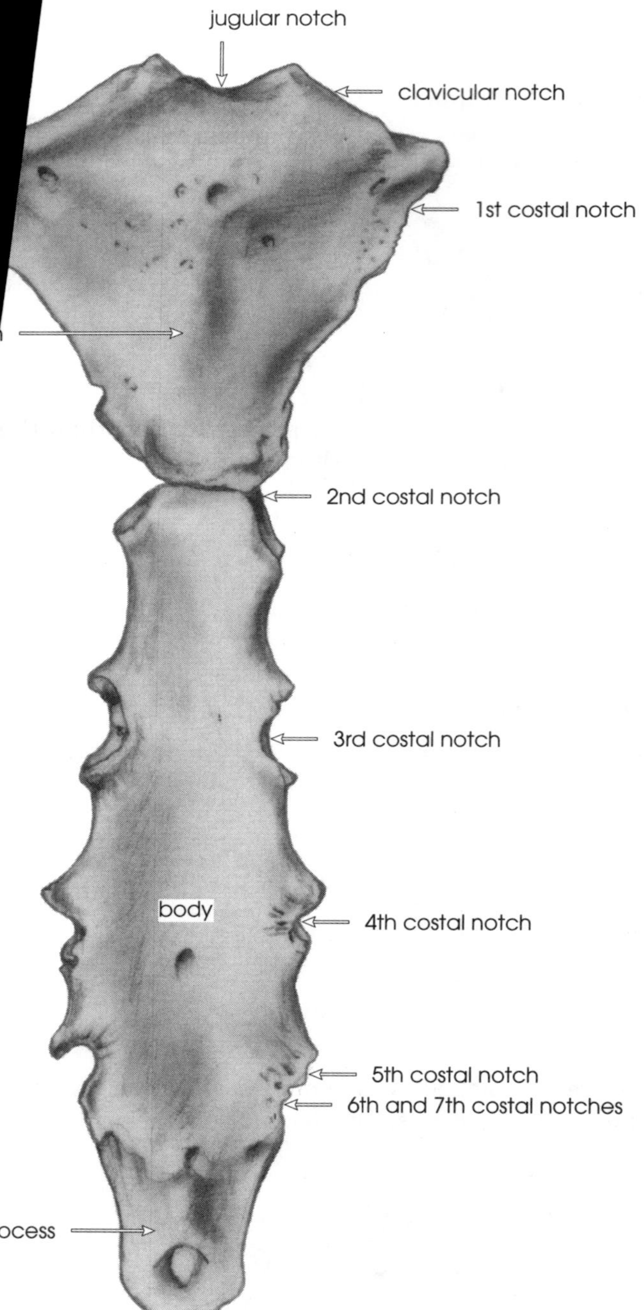

Sternum: Manubrium, Body, and Xiphoid Process

The sternum appears to be a very simple bone; therefore, it is often neglected. The following questions help to focus thought on the structure of the sternum and the anterior chest wall:

- How many ribs attach to the manubrium of the sternum?
- How many ribs attach to the body of the sternum?
- Are the rib attachment sites evenly distributed?
- If the rib attachment sites are not evenly distributed, which attachment sites are closest to one another?
- Where is the widest part of the body of the sternum?
- Where is the narrowest part of the body of the sternum?
- Are there any articular surfaces on the sternum? How many and where?

Table 3.2 Osteological Terms for the Chest

Bone	Term	Definition and Examples
rib	groove, costal	the groove on the inferior edge of the inner surface of the rib
	body of rib	the main part of the rib
	rib head	the vertebral end of the rib
	rib neck	the constricted part below the rib head on upper ribs (not obvious on lower ribs)
	rib tubercle	the center of ossification below the neck; *part* of the tubercle articulates with the vertebral transverse process
	rib, sternal end	the open end of the rib that connects to the sternal cartilage; useful for aging purposes
	true rib	1–7 attach directly to the sternum via cartilage
	false rib	8–10 join the sternum via the 7th rib cartilage
	floating rib	11–12 do not attach to the sternum
	sternal-end ossification	osteophytic growth from the rib end into the sternal cartilage; cartilaginous calcification; it increases with age and varies with sex.
sternum	body of sternum	the main part of the sternum, the corpus sterni, fused from the four central centers of ossification
	clavicular notch	the articular facets for the clavicles, located on either side of the jugular notch of the manubrium
	costal notch	the 7 pairs of notches for joining of the costal cartilage with the sternum
	jugular notch	the medial, superior notch on the manubrium
	manubrium	the superior-most section of the sternum
	sternal foramen	an anomalous foramen in the sternal body
	xiphoid process	the inferior projection or tip of the sternum

The Vertebral Column

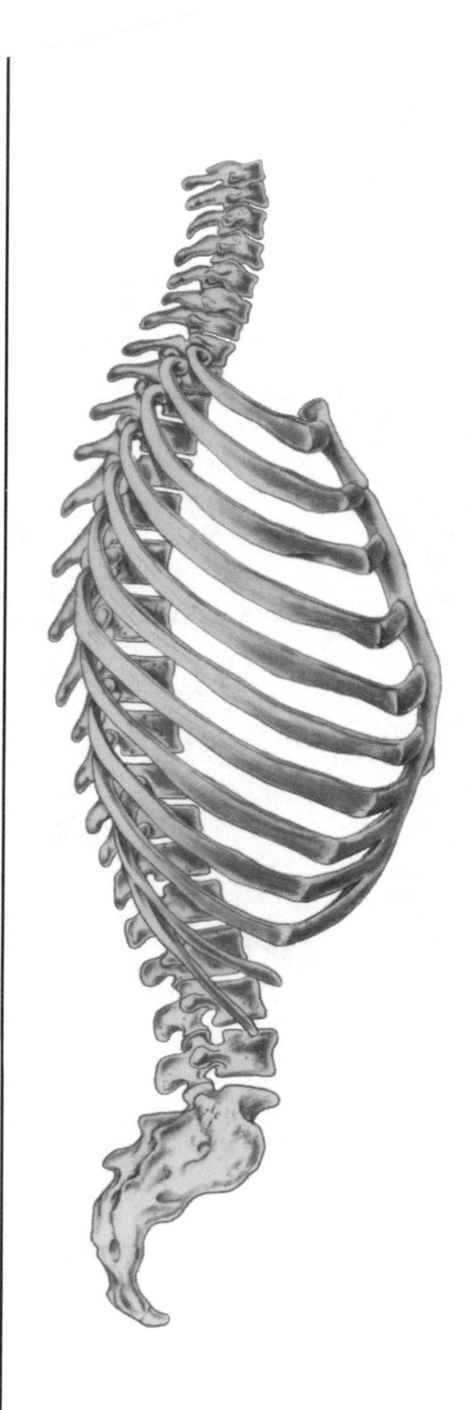

CHAPTER OUTLINE

Overview of Vertebral Sections

The vertebral column or "backbone" has five sections—cervical, thoracic, lumbar, sacral, and coccygeal. There are seven cervical vertebrae, twelve thoracic, five lumbar, and four or five coccygeal vertebrae. The first two cervical verte-

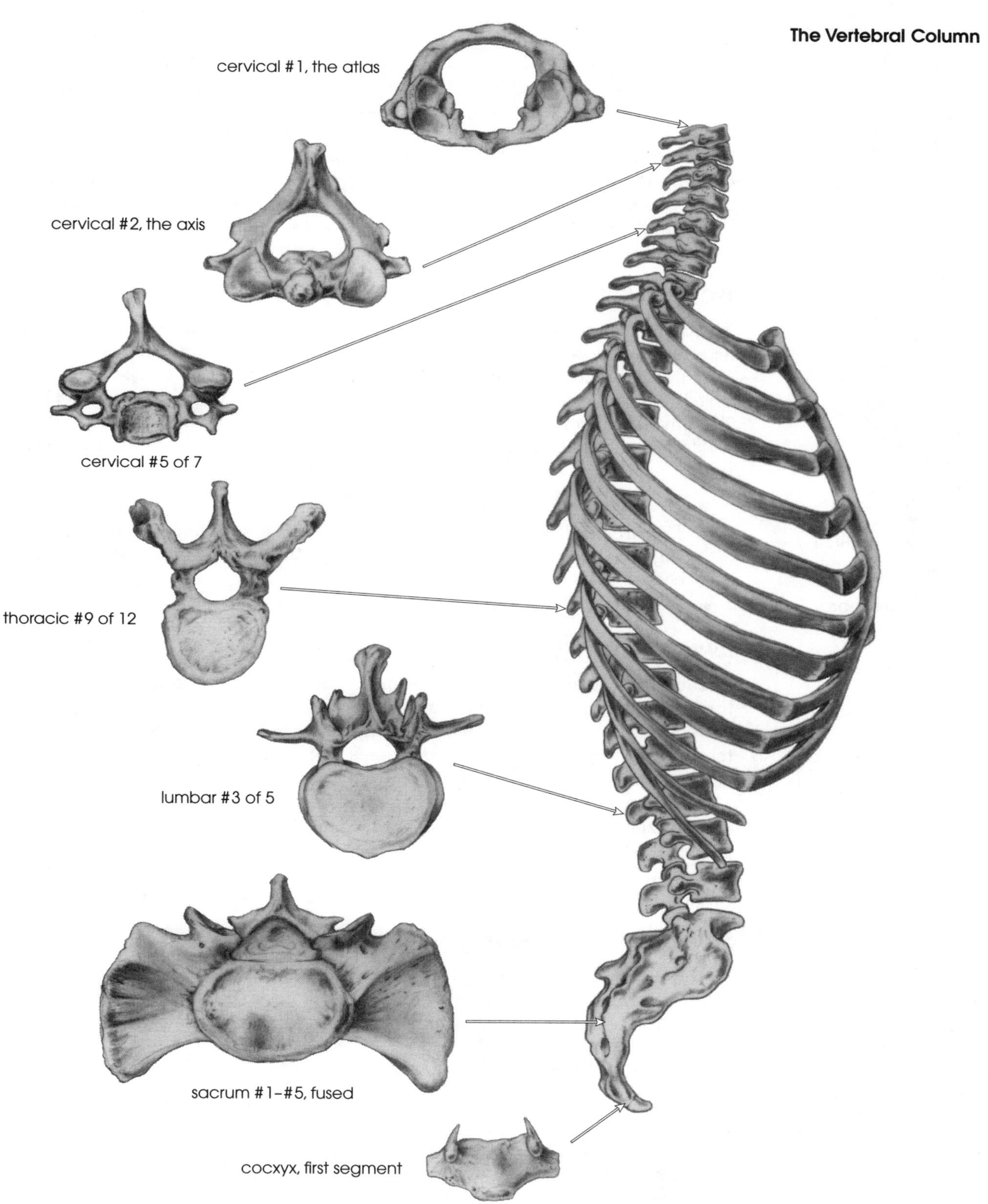

brae have their own names—the atlas and the axis. Every vertebra of the backbone is characterized by a vertebral body or "disk," a vertebral arch, and numerous processes for attachment and articulation.

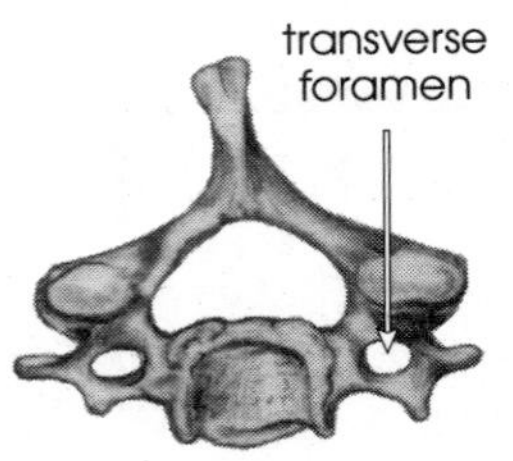

Cervical Vertebra

Cervical Vertebrae (Atlas, Axis, and C3–C7)

The cervical vertebrae make up the neck. Each cervical vertebra is characterized by *transverse foramina*, one on each side of the centrum, within the transverse processes. No other vertebrae have transverse foramina.

The occipital condyles of the cranium articulate with the atlas. The atlas is a ring-like bone with no apparent centrum. The atlas rotates on the *dens* of the axis (also called an *odontoid process* because of its tooth-like appearance). The dens is, in fact, the "misplaced" centrum of the atlas. During fetal development, the center of ossification that appears in the position of the first centrum proceeds to fuse with the second centrum, becoming part of the axis instead of the atlas. The atlas and the axis, by their curious arrangement of parts, aid in providing both stability and mobility for the head.

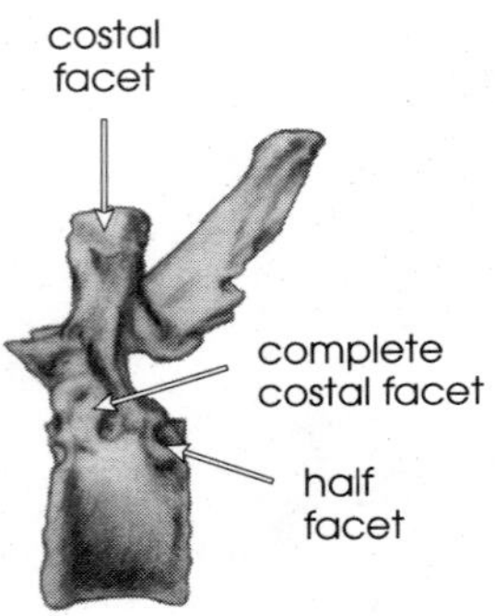

Thoracic Vertebra

Thoracic Vertebrae (T1–T12)

The thoracic vertebrae connect with the rib cage. Each thoracic vertebra is characterized by the presence of *rib facets*, also known as *costal pits*. Rib facets are the articular facets for rib heads. T1 through T10 have rib facets on each side of the vertebral bodies and on the anterior surface of the transverse processes. T11 and T12 have facets only on the vertebral bodies, not on the transverse processes.

There is variation in the way ribs articulate with vertebrae, but there is a typical pattern as viewed from one side:

- T1 has one complete facet and a half facet.
- T2 through T9 have two half facets—at the superior and inferior edges of the centrum. The ribs through this area connect with the bodies of two adjacent vertebrae.
- T9 through T12 have complete facets.

Lumbar Vertebrae (L1–L5)

The lumbar vertebrae are the bones of the lower back. The key characteristic of lumbar vertebrae is not what you see, but rather what you don't see. Lumbar vertebrae have neither transverse foramina nor costal pits. They are large vertebrae with short, wide spinous processes and slender transverse processes. L1 is easily confused with T12, but T12 has a clear costal pit whereas L1 has none.

Note also that the shape of the vertebral articular facets changes from flat and horizontal in the cervical area to flat and angled in the thoracic area to U-shaped in the lumbar area. The lumbar area is the region of the back most likely to sustain damage from strenuous activity. The U-shaped articular facets help counter this tendency by limiting the range of movement and providing stability.

Sacral Vertebrae (S1–S5)

In the adult, all five sacral vertebrae fuse into one bone, the **sacrum**. The sacrum connects with the pelvic bones and provides the posterior section of the pelvic girdle. (See the illustration on page 63.)

Key Terms

sacrum The fused vertebra that form the posterior wall of the pelvis.

coccyx The small bones that form the lower extremity of the spinal column.

Coccygeal Vertebrae (Coccyx)

The coccygeal vertebrae make up the **coccyx**, or "tail bone." The first section is distinctive, but the others are very small and highly variable. It is not unusual for all of the coccygeal bones to fuse with each other or for the coccyx to fuse with the sacrum. If not fused, these tiny bones are frequently lost or go completely unnoticed. (See the illustration on page 63.)

Sacrum and Coccyx, Dorsal (Posterior) View and Lateral View

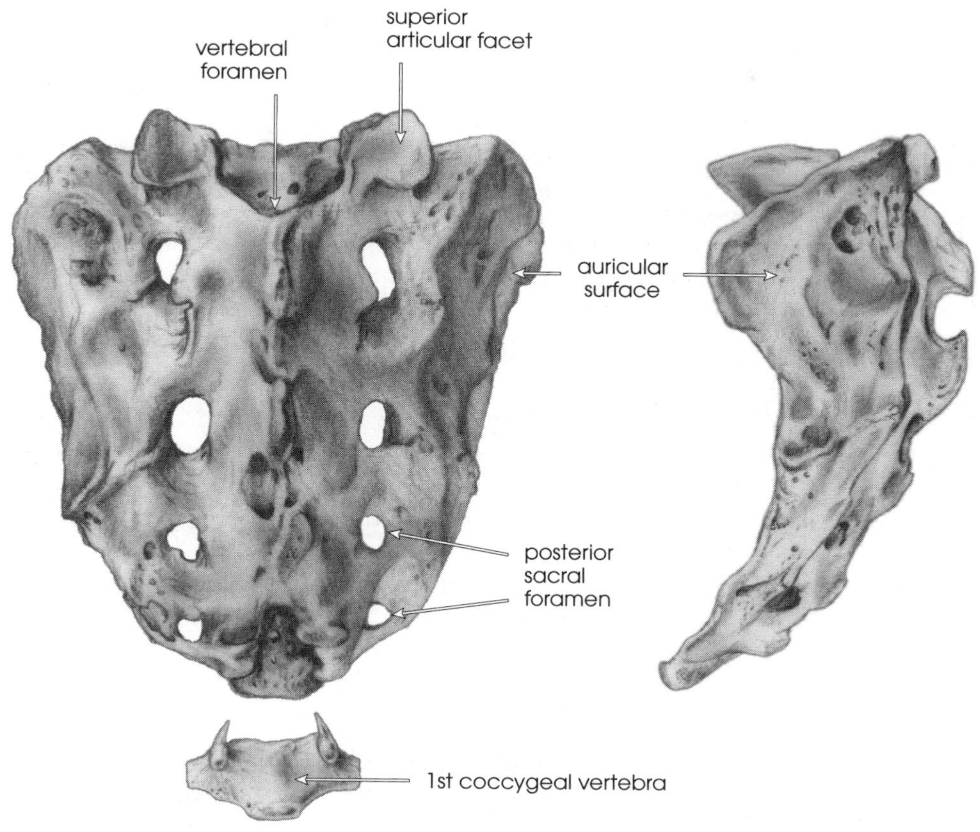

Sacrum and Coccyx, Ventral (Anterior) View

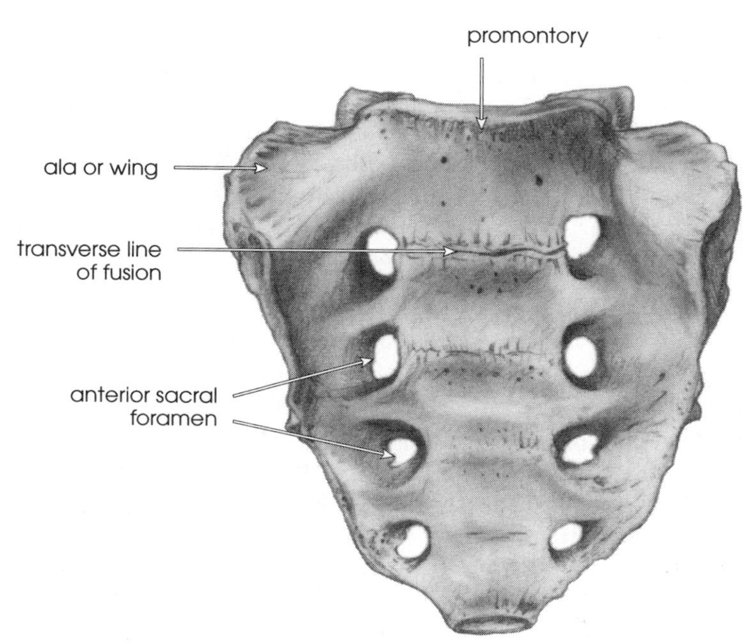

Reassembling the Vertebral Column

The process of reassembling a vertebral column in correct order need not be difficult. Approach it methodically and the bones will usually go together quickly and easily. *Sort first.* Then begin at the top and work downward using the steps described here.

The assembled column is easier to examine and photograph if it is placed on a towel or paper that is rolled from two sides to make a long central groove. Rubber bands work well to secure the ends and keep the apparatus from unrolling. The vertebrae can be placed on the groove in any direction—with the dorsal spine down, a transverse process down, or the vertebral bodies down.

Sorting

- Sort the vertebra by section in three rows—cervical, thoracic, and lumbar.
- Place each vertebra on the table with the dorsal spine pointed away.
- Turn each one so that the superior surface is up and the inferior surface is on the table.

Beginning at the Top

- Fit the atlas and axis together.
- Look at the inferior surface of the axis—then look for the cervical with a superior surface that closely resembles the inferior surface of the axis.
- When you find C3 and fit it to the axis, look at the inferior surface of C3 and search the remaining cervicals for a matching superior surface.
- Continue matching the surfaces of adjacent vertebral bodies one by one from top to bottom.

Viewing the Results

Look at the completed assemblage from all sides. Compare each element of each vertebra—vertebral bodies, spinous processes, transverse processes, articular surfaces. There should be consistency in the flow from one vertebra to another with no sudden changes in size or shape. All of the articular surfaces should approximate neatly.

The Aging Vertebral Body

The vertebral body changes with advancing age, just as the rest of the skeleton does. Albert and Maples (1995) showed that two decades of life can be distinguished by assessing the advancement of epiphyseal ring fusion. Further analysis can be accomplished by assessing the development of osteoarthritic lipping at the edges of vertebral disks.

Age Changes in Vertebral Bodies, Dorsal and Lateral Views

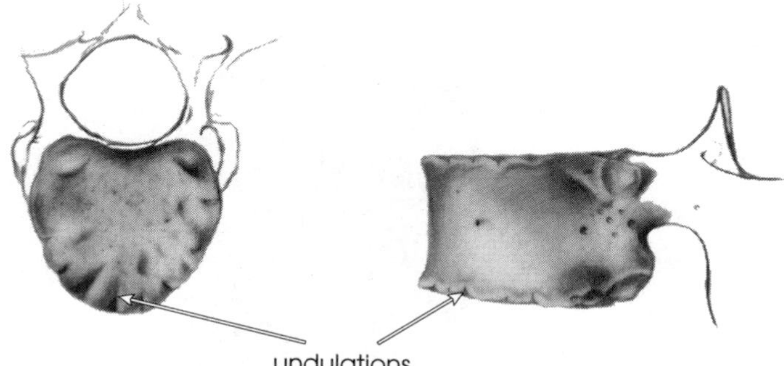

Child (under 16 Years)

The epiphyseal ring is completely absent. Note the regular undulations on the edges of the vertebral body.

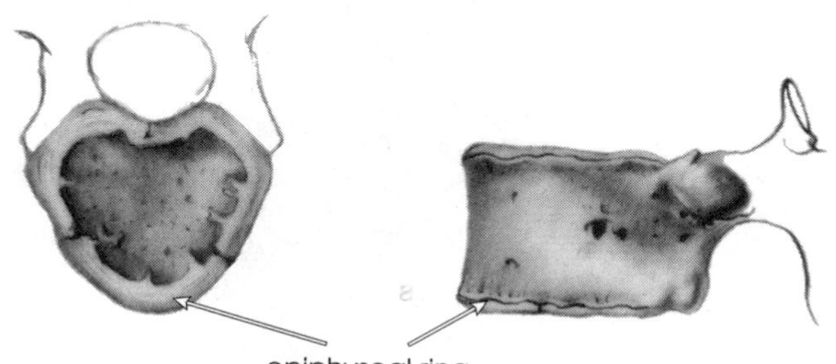

Late Teenager (16–20 Years)

The epiphyseal ring is in the process of fusing. Note the line of fusion on the lateral view and the slight chipping of the ring on the superior view.

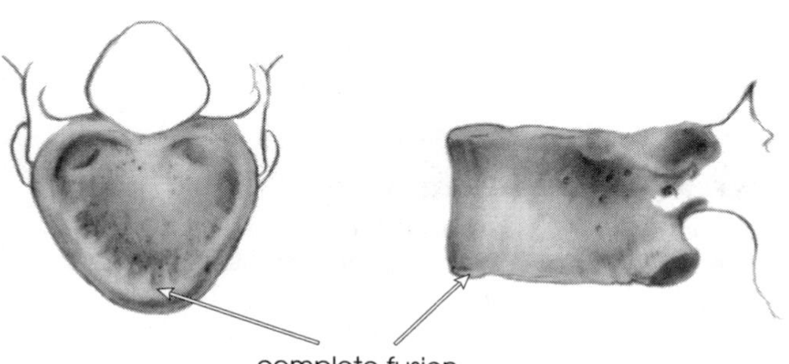

Young Adult (20–29 Years)

The epiphyseal ring is fused, but no osteoarthritis is visible. The bone is smooth and solid.

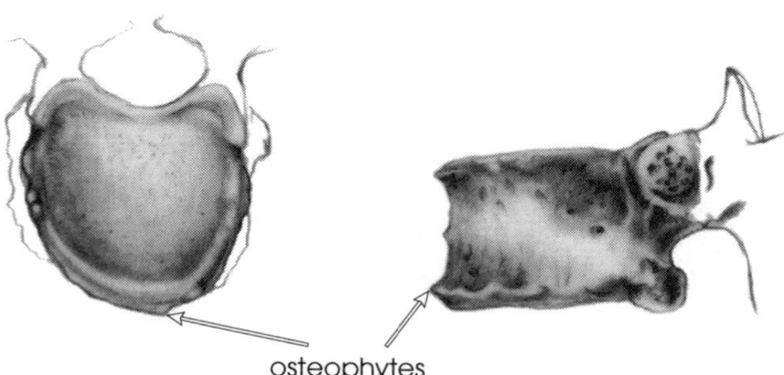

Older Adult (over 30 Years)

Osteoarthritis is obvious and the vertebral body is beginning to degenerate. Note the osteophytes at the vertebral edges and the porous nature of the bone.

Osteoarthritis in the Lower Back

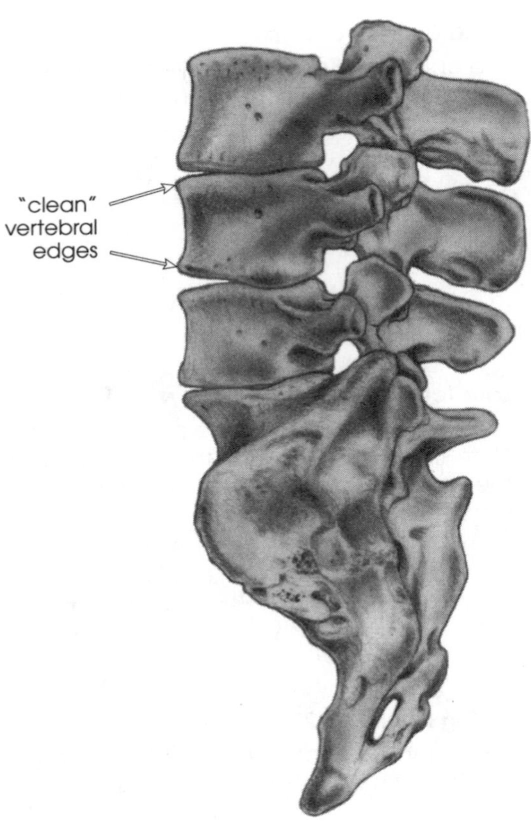

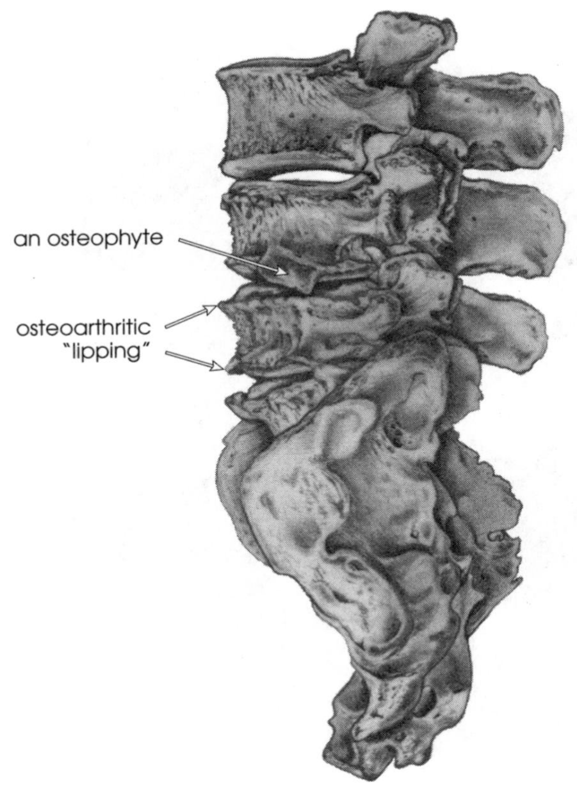

A "Young-Looking" Back

The lumbar vertebrae on the left are typical of a young person who has experienced no unusual back trauma. The edges of the vertebral bodies are smooth and regular in shape. The auricular surface of the sacrum is billowed or smooth, but not lipped.

An Elderly or "Hard Working" Back

The lumbar vertebrae on the right are typical of an elderly person or a history of heavy labor. The edges of the vertebral bodies are sharp and irregular. Sometimes bony "bridges" will develop between adjacent vertebra. These are called *osteophytes.* The auricular surface of the sacrum is rough and porous with sharply defined edges.

Table 4.1 Osteological Terms for the Backbone

Term	Definition
arch, vertebral	the neural arch—formed from two halves that fuse between the ages of 1 and 3 years
articular facet	any bony surface that articulates with another bony surface. (superior articular facet of the vertebra)
auricular surface	the lateral ear-shaped surface of the sacrum that articulates with the innominate; sacroiliac articulation
centrum	the body of the vertebra, especially the body without epiphyseal rings
costal pit	articular surface for rib on the vertebral body and on the transverse processes; rib facet
dens	a tooth-like projection; odontoid process (*dens epistropheus*)
epiphyseal ring	the secondary centers of ossification that fuse to the superior and inferior surfaces of the vertebral centrum
epiphysis (pl. epiphyses)	a secondary center of ossification that fuses to the primary center when growth is complete
foramen (pl. foramina)	a round or oval aperture in bone or a membranous structure for the passage or anchorage of other tissue
foramen, transverse	the aperture in the transverse process of the cervical vertebrae
foramen, vertebral	the aperture between the vertebral arch and the vertebral body for the passage of the spinal cord
process	any bony projection
process, transverse	lateral vertebral processes, some of which articulate with ribs
process, superior articular	vertebral processes that articulate with the inferior articular processes of the next higher vertebra
process, inferior articular	vertebral processes that articulate with the superior articular processes of the next lower vertebra
process, spinous	the process that projects toward the dorsal surface of the back
process, articular	any projection that serves to articulate
promontory; promontorium	a raised place; the most ventral prominent median point of the lumbosacral symphysis; the most anterosuperior point on the sacrum
vertebra (pl. vertebrae)	a single segment of the spinal column. There are 7 cervical vertebrae, 12 thoracic vertebra, 5 lumbar, 5 sacral (fused to form the sacrum) and 4 coccygeal (often fused to form the coccyx and sometimes fused to the sacrum)
vertebral body	the centrum and its epiphyseal rings; the arch and the body fuse between the ages of 3 and 7 years

CHAPTER 5

THE ARM: HUMERUS, RADIUS, AND ULNA

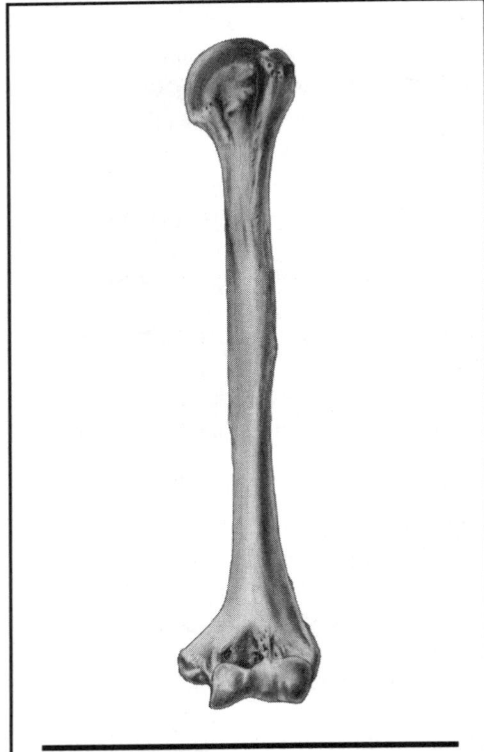

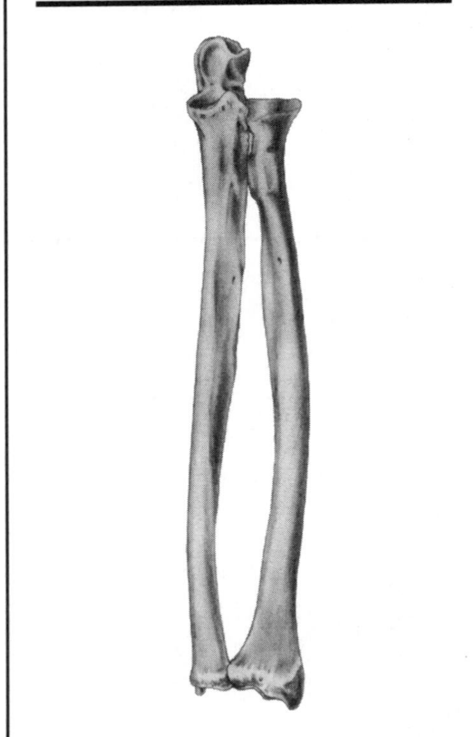

CHAPTER OUTLINE

There are three bones between the shoulder and the wrist—one in the upper arm, two in the forearm. The upper arm bone is the humerus; the forearm bones are the radius and the ulna.

THE HUMERUS

Key Term

humerus The upper (proximal) arm bone; the bone between the shoulder and the elbow.

The **humerus** articulates at the shoulder with the glenoid fossa of the scapula. The humerus articulates with the radius and ulna at the elbow. Note that the nutrient foramen enters the humeral shaft toward the elbow.

The humerus is particularly useful in human identification because the deltoid tuberosity provides one of the more obvious indicators of the degree of muscular development. The *deltoideus*, one of the major abductor muscles of the arm, attaches at the deltoid tuberosity. As muscle size increases, the attachment area enlarges. This is accomplished more by changing the shape of the tuberosity than by increasing the diameter of the attachment area. Gain experience by lining up a series of adult humeri and comparing the size, shape, and rugosity of the deltoid tuberosities.

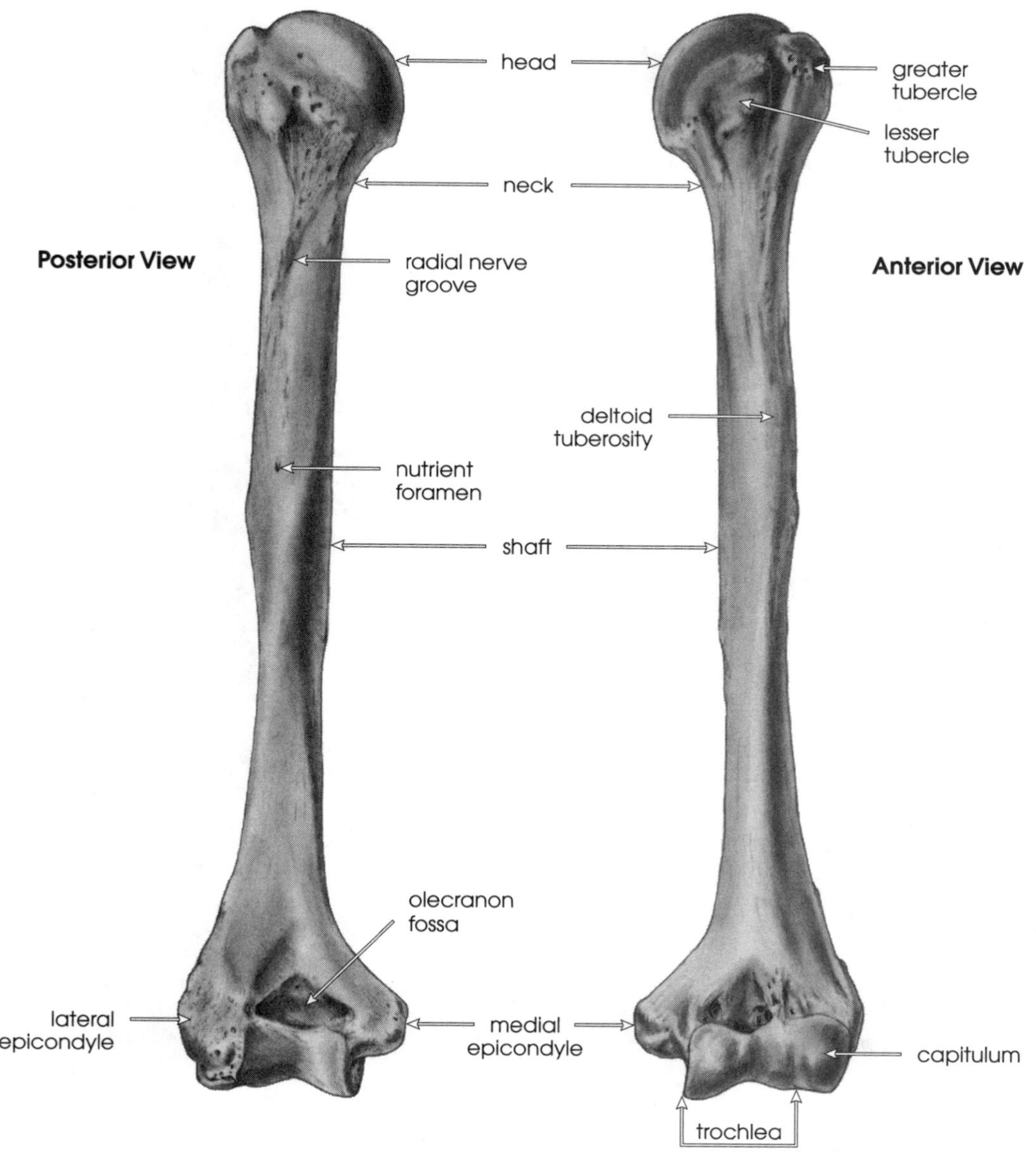

The Forearm

Key Term
forearm The lower (distal) part of the arm; the radius and ulna are the bones of the forearm.

Two bones, the radius and the ulna, make up the **forearm**. They lie parallel to each other between the elbow and the wrist. The clever construction of the elbow joint makes pronation of the hand possible without a change in upper arm position.

Think of each articular surface in terms of function. In the forearm, the radius takes care of rotation, and the ulna takes care of flexion. The cylinder of the radial head rotates on the ulna and the capitulum of the humerus, and the semilunar notch of the olecranon process moves bidirectionally on the trochlea of the humerus. The result is both a wide range of motion and stability.

Left Radius and Ulna Articulated, Anterior View

Note that the head of the radius is *proximal* and the head of the ulna is *distal.* Also examine the nutrient foramena of the radius and ulna. Both foramena enter the shafts *toward the elbow,* just as the foramen of the humerus.

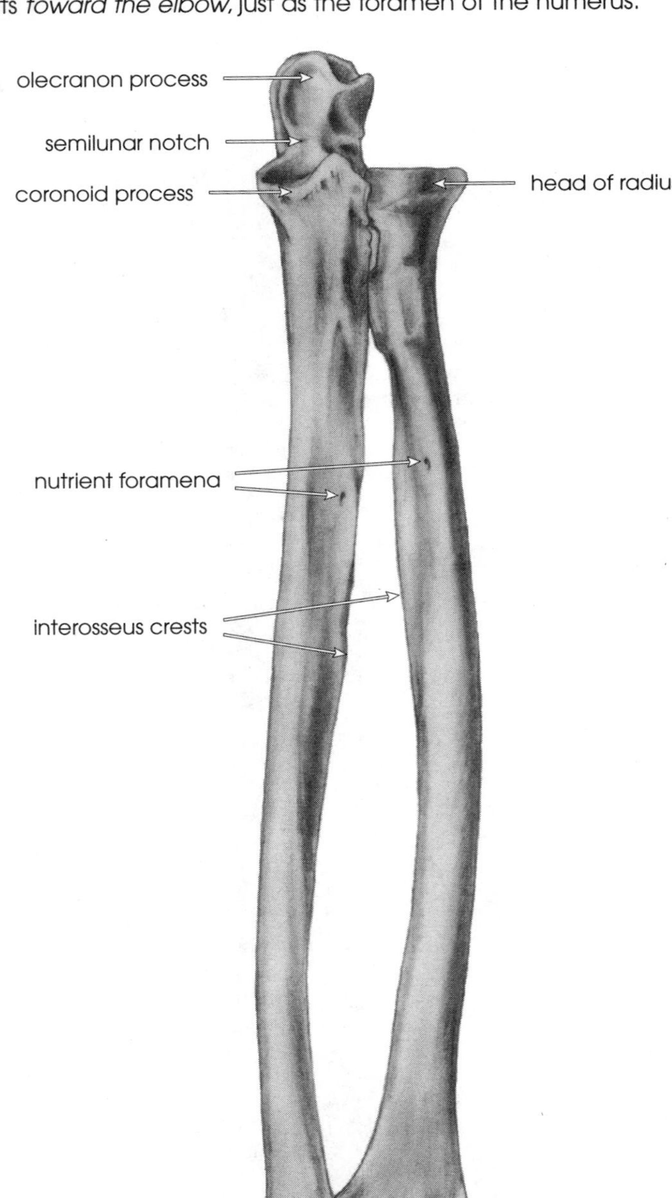

Elbow Joint

Note that the ulna moves in only two directions; the radius rotates.

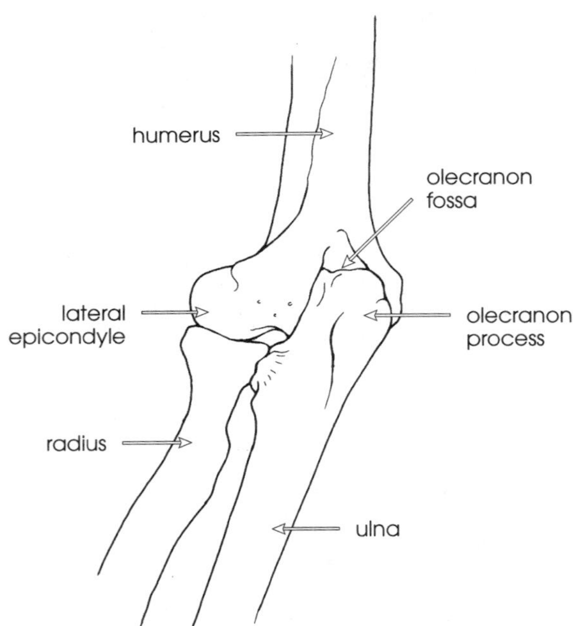

THE RADIUS

Key Term
radius The lateral of the two bones in the forearm; the radius "rotates" around the ulna.

The **radius** is lateral to the ulna. It is on the same side of the forearm as the thumb. The head of the radius is proximal, articulating with the capitulum of the humerus. The expanded part of the radius is distal, articulating with the scaphoid carpal bone. The styloid process of the radius indicates the direction of the thumb.

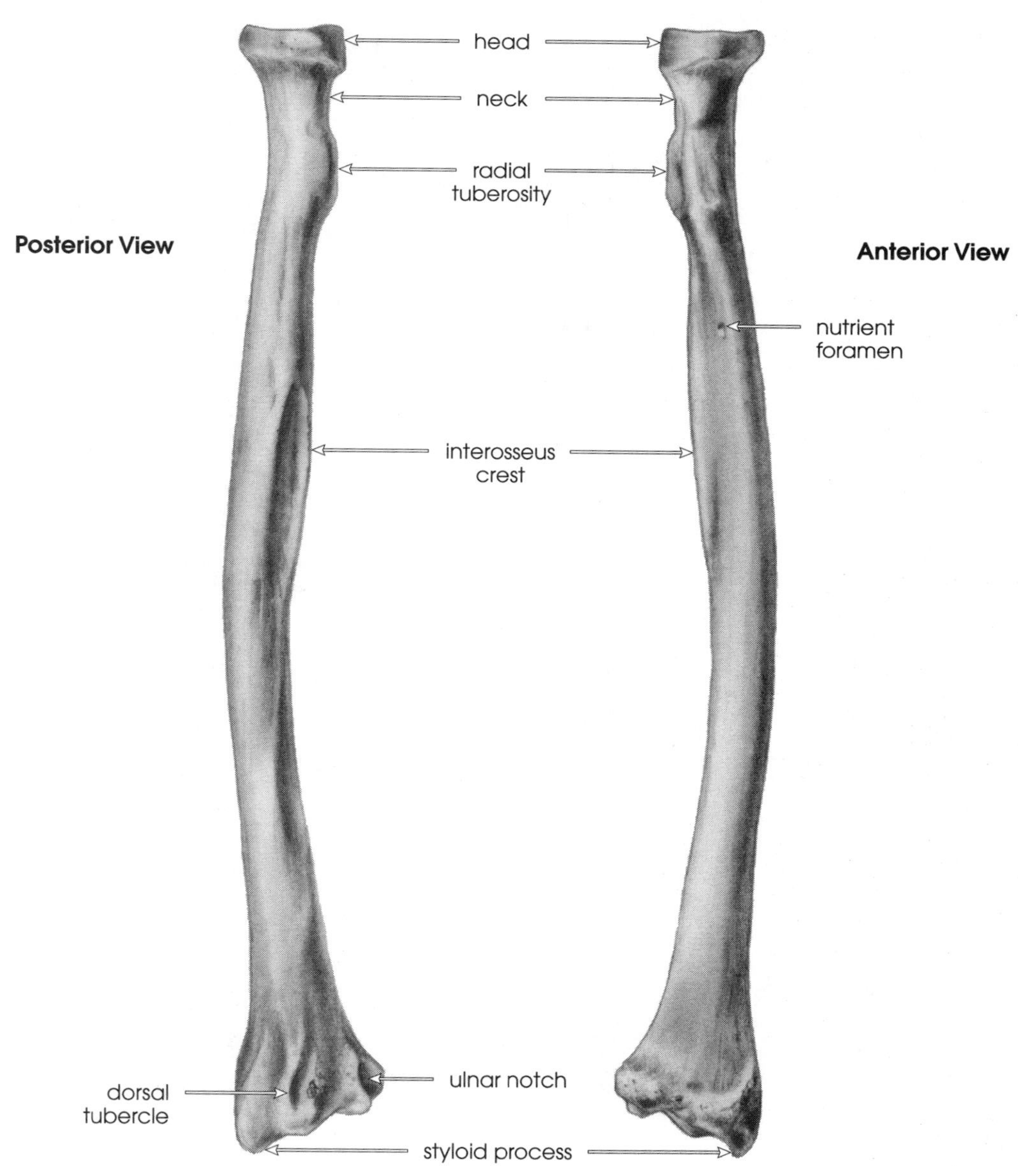

The Ulna

Key Term

ulna The medial of the two bones in the forearm; the proximal end of the ulna is the bone of the elbow.

The **ulna** is medial to the radius. The proximal end of the ulna is the olecranon process, otherwise known as the "elbow bone." The head of the ulna is distal (opposite of the radius), articulating with the lunate carpal bone. The styloid process of the ulna indicates the direction of the fifth finger.

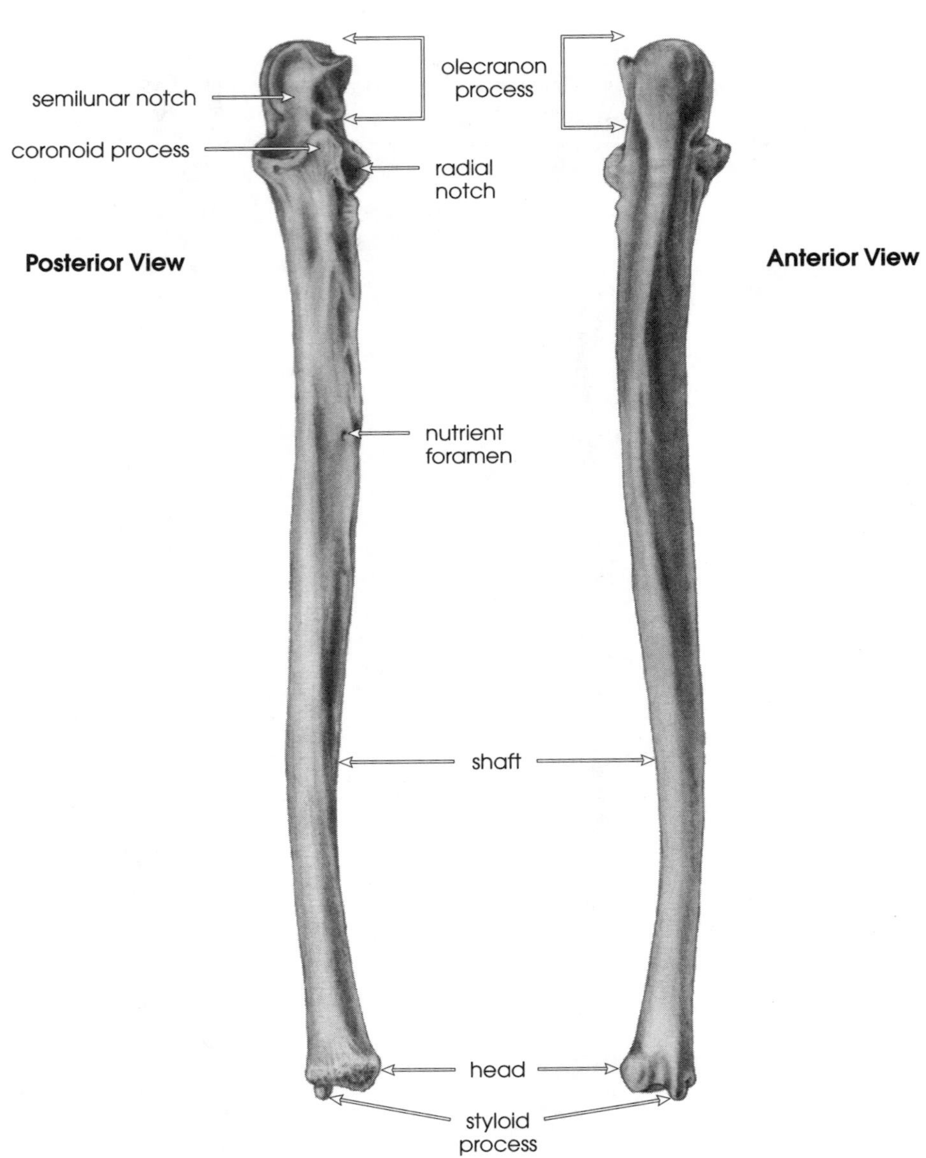

Table 5.1 Osteological Terms for the Arm

Bone	Term	Definition
humerus	capitulum	the articular surface for the head of the radius on the distal end of the humerus
	deltoid tuberosity	the attachment area for the deltoid on the lateral part of the anterior surface of the humeral shaft
	greater tubercle	the larger of the two tubercles on the proximal end of the humerus—more lateral than the lesser tubercle
	head	the proximal articular surface of the humerus—hemispherical in shape
	intertubercular groove	the groove between the greater and lesser tubercles of the humerus
	lateral epicondyle	the bulbous area on the lateral side above the distal condyle; the origin of the extensor muscles of the hand
	lesser tubercle	the smaller of the two tubercles on the proximal end of the humerus
	medial epicondyle	the bulbous area on the medial side above the distal condyle; the origin of the flexor muscles of the hand
	neck	the area immediately distal to the head of the humerus; a common fracture site; this is also a surgical neck
	nutrient foramen	the major vascular opening on the shaft of the humerus; enters the shaft pointing toward the *distal* end
	olecranon fossa	the large depression on the posterior surface of the distal humerus for the olecranon process of the ulna
	radial nerve groove	the slight diagonal groove on the posterior surface of the shaft the humerus
	septal aperture	the olecranon foramen—infrequent appearance, more common in females
	shaft	the diaphysis of the humerus
	trochlea	the articular surface for the ulna on the distal end of the humerus
radius	distal articular surface	the end that articulates with the scaphoid carpal bone
	dorsal tubercles	the bumps on the dorsal surface of the distal end
	head	the *proximal* end of the radius; the head articulates with the capitulum of the humerus and the radial notch of the ulna
	interosseous crest	the somewhat sharp edge on the shaft directed toward the ulna for attachment of the interosseous ligament
	neck	the area of the shaft immediately distal to the head of the radius
	nutrient foramen	the major vascular opening on the shaft of the radius; enters the shaft pointing toward the *proximal* end
	radial tuberosity	the bump distal to the neck of the radius, one insertion of the biceps muscle
	shaft	the diaphysis of the radius
	styloid process	the point on the lateral edge of the distal end of the radius; the brachio-radialis m. inserts on the styloid
	ulnar notch	the facet for the ulna on the medial side of the distal end of the radius
ulna	coronoid process	the smaller of the two processes at the proximal end of the ulna (anterior)
	head	the *distal* end of the ulna; the head articulates with the ulnar notch of the radius and the lunate carpal bone

Table 5.1, continued

Bone	Term	Definition
	interosseous crest	the somewhat sharp edge on the shaft directed toward the radius for attachment of the interosseous ligament
	nutrient foramen	the major vascular opening on the shaft of the ulna; enters the shaft pointing toward the *proximal* end
	olecranon process	the larger process at the proximal end of the ulna (posterior); the elbow
	radial notch	the concavity for articulation of the radius on the lateral side of the proximal end of the ulna.
	semilunar notch	the articular surface for the trochlea of the humerus; bounded by the olecranon and coronoid processes
	shaft	the diaphysis of the ulna
	styloid process	the small process extending from the head of the ulna toward the fifth finger

CHAPTER 6

THE HAND: CARPALS, METACARPALS, AND PHALANGES

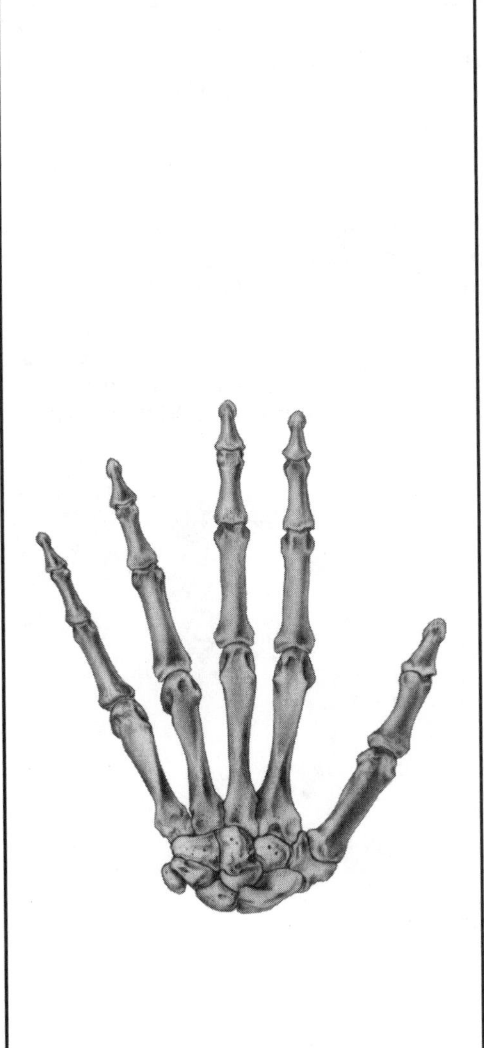

CHAPTER OUTLINE

Key Term

carpal bone Relating to the wrist or carpus; a carpal bone is one of the eight small bones of the wrist.

Half of the bones in the adult human body are found in the hands and feet—a total of 106 bones! Anyone who thinks the hands and feet can be disregarded is greatly mistaken. Each hand is built of 27 bones. There are 8 **carpal bones** (wrist bones), 5 metacarpal bones (the bones of the palm), and 14 phalanges (finger bones). The words *carpal* and *metacarpal* are adjectives, not nouns; nevertheless, *carpal bones* and *metacarpal bones* are often just called *carpals* and *metacarpals* by osteologists.

Each of the carpals and metacarpals is unique and can be recognized by side and name. The phalanges are more difficult. Right and left can be confused and second and fourth finger can be interchanged because of their size similarity.

The first challenge is basic orientation. Standard anatomical position is used with the hand as with any other part of the body. *Remember "thumbs out."* The thumbs always point away from the body. The back of the hand is dorsal; the palm of the hand is palmar (or anterior). The thumb is lateral; the little finger is medial.

Carpal Bones

It takes time and practice to be able to recognize each carpal bone and tell right from left. The illustration on page 77 gives carpal nicknames provided by other students to help you get started. Use your own imagination to carry you further.

Dorsal View of Bones of the Left Hand and Wrist: Carpals, Metacarpals, and Phalanges

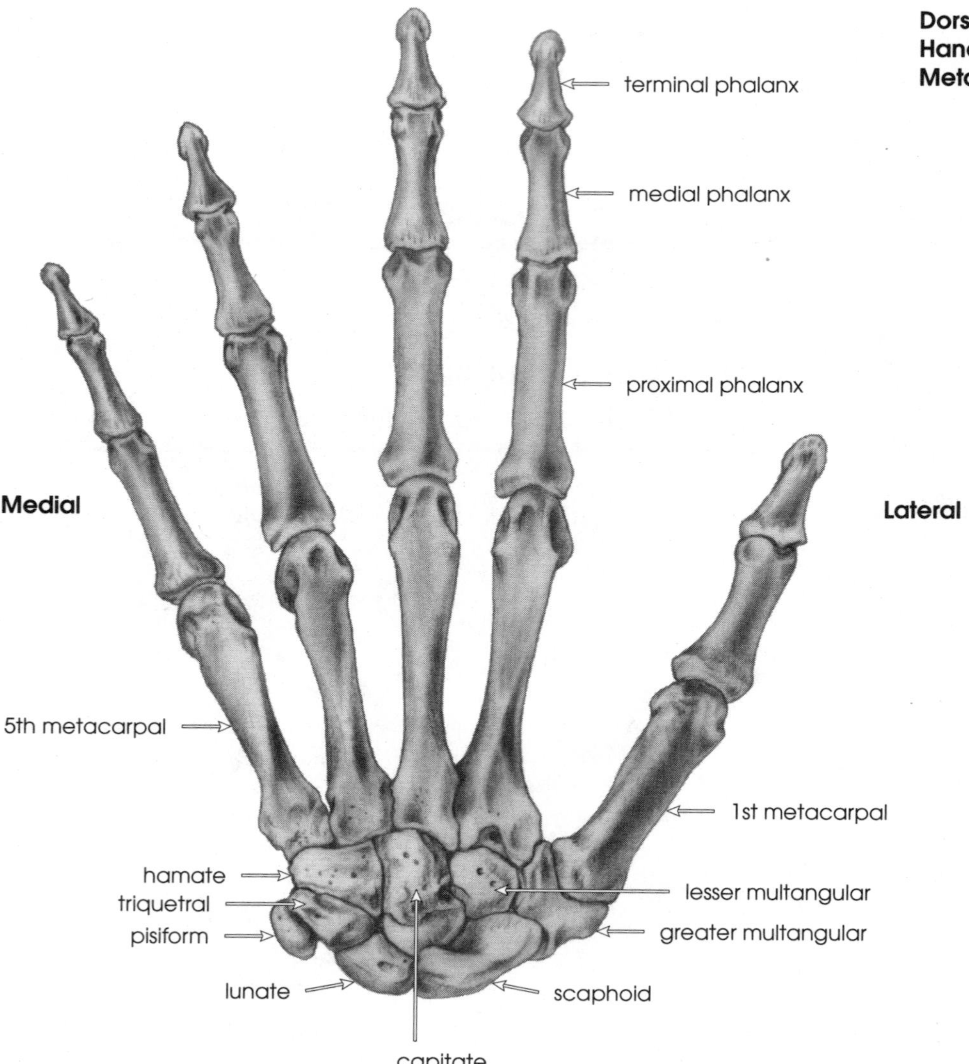

Left Carpal Bones

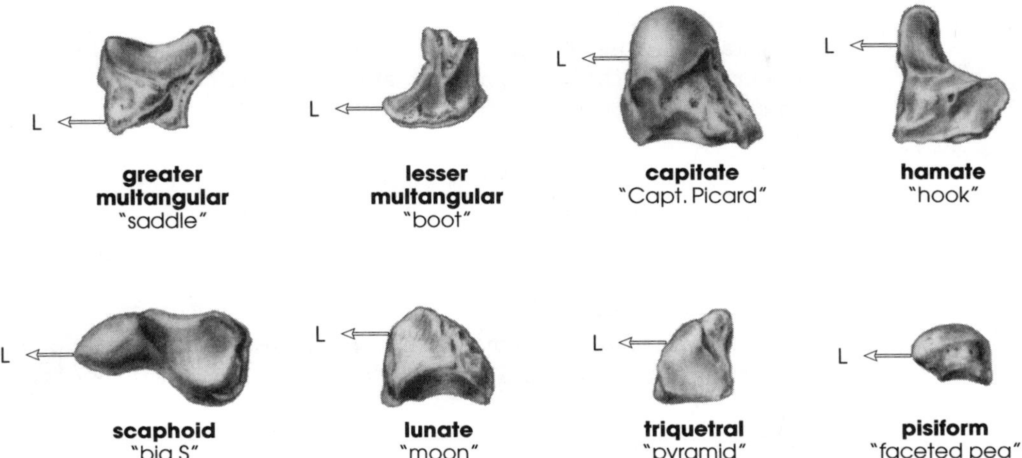

As with all other bones, examine the same bone from as many individuals as possible. Learn through experience to recognize key characteristics for each bone and separate out individual variation. Key characteristics are important for *bone* identification; individual variation is important in *human* identification.

Table 6.1 Carpal Articulations

Carpals	Alternate Terms	Articulations
scaphoid	navicular	radius, lunate, capitate, lesser multangular, greater multangular
lunate	semilunar	ulna, scaphoid, capitate, triquetral
triquetral	triquetrium	lunate, hamate, pisiform
pisiform		triquetral
greater multangular	trapezium	metacarpal 1, scaphoid, lesser multangular
lesser multangular	trapezoid	metacarpal 2, greater multangular, capitate, scaphoid
capitate		metacarpal 3, lesser multangular, scaphoid, lunate, triquetral
hamate		metacarpals 4 and 5, triquetral, capitate

Metacarpal Bones

> **Key Term**
>
> **metacarpal bone** Relating to the area of the hand between the carpus and the phalanges; a metacarpal bone is one of the five bones that supports the palm of the hand.

The **metacarpal bones** support the palm of the hand. There are five metacarpals in each hand. They articulate proximally with the carpal bones and distally with the phalanges. Students often confuse metacarpals with finger bones. This confusion may be the result of studying articulated skeletal hands without using a fleshed hand for comparison. The solution is your own hand. Identify the location of the knuckles on both the fleshed hand and the skeletal hand. Remember that the metacarpal *heads* are the large rounded knuckles at the *base* of the fingers.

The base (proximal end) of each metacarpal is the key to both the side (right or left) and the metacarpal number. In the illustrations on page 78, each metacarpal is pictured twice. The lateral view is on the left; the medial view is on the right. The palmar surfaces face each other.

Look at the head of each metacarpal and look at the shape of your own knuckles when you make a fist. The knuckles are rounded. In contrast, the joints of the fingers are flat or indented.

Examine the length, width, and curvature of the shaft of each metacarpal, and then compare the shape of each base. Look for the facets on each side of the base. Note the following characteristics:

- Metacarpal #1 is different from the other four. It is short and *wide*. From the dorsal side, the base *points toward* #2.
- Metacarpal #2 is one of the *two* larger metacarpals. It is the only metacarpal with *two* major processes at the base. From the dorsal side, the longer of the two processes *points toward* #3.
- Metacarpal #3 is the other large metacarpal. It has only one major process at the base. From the dorsal side, the process *points back toward* #2.
- Metacarpal #4 is one of the two smaller metacarpals. It has no processes on the base, and it has facets on *both sides* of the base. The simpler of the facets is on the side of #5.
- Metacarpal #5 is the other small metacarpal. It has no processes on the base, and it has *only one* facet. The facet, of course, faces #4.

Metacarpals #1 through #5, Lateral View on Left, Medial View on Right

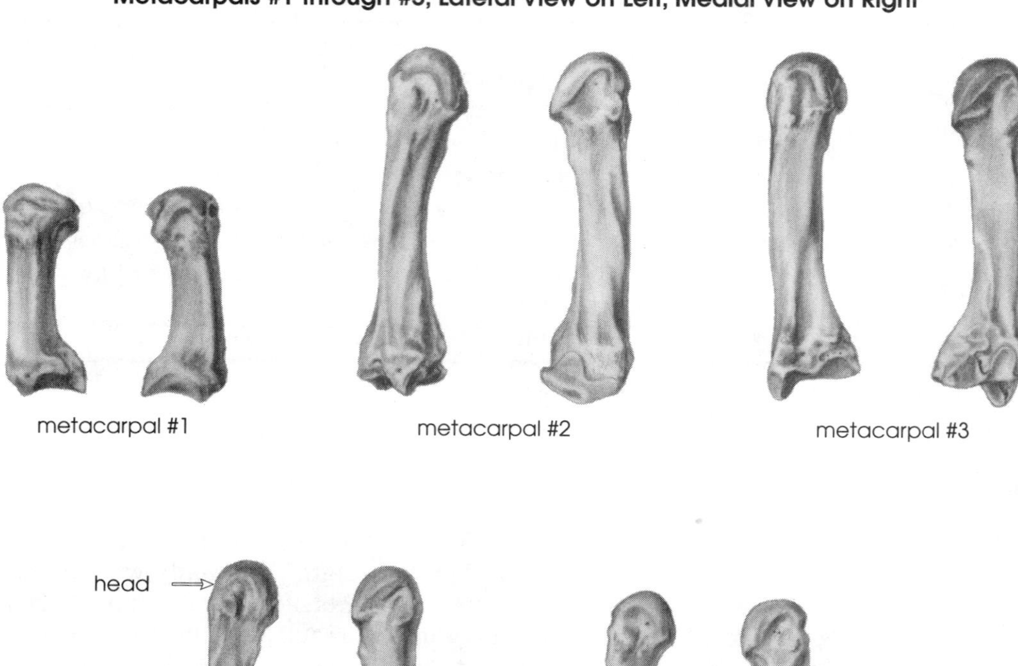

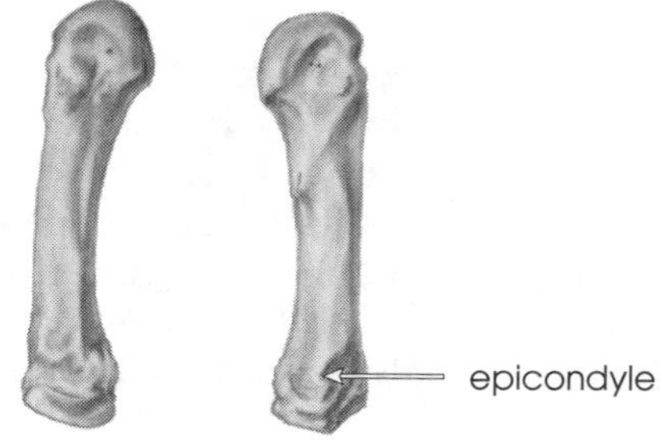

Table 6.2 Metacarpal and Phalanx Articulations

Bone	Articular Facet	Adjacent Bone
metacarpal #1	base	greater multangular
	medial surface	no bone—*not even #2*
	lateral surface	no bone
	head	proximal phalanx
metacarpal #2	base	lesser multangular
	medial surface	metacarpal #3
	lateral surface	greater multangular
	head	proximal phalanx
metacarpal #3	base	capitate
	medial surface	metacarpal #4
	lateral surface	metacarpal #2
	head	proximal phalanx
metacarpal #4	base	hamate
	medial surface	metacarpal #5
	lateral surface	metacarpal #3
	head	proximal phalanx
metacarpal #5	base	hamate
	medial surface	no bone—only an epicondyle
	lateral surface	metacarpal #4
	head	proximal phalanx
proximal phalanx	base	metacarpal head
	head	medial phalanx
medial phalanx	base	proximal phalanx
	head	distal phalanx
distal (terminal) phalanx	base	medial phalanx
	head	no bone—only fingernail

KEY CHARACTERS OR INDIVIDUAL VARIATION?

Key characters are attributes that can be readily recognized, formally analyzed, and used as a basis for generalization. Key characters are used to recognize *groups*; therefore, they are essential for *bone* identification.

Individual variation is deviation from the general type in form or structure. Individual variation is used to recognize the *individual* within the group; therefore, it is important in *human* identification.

Don't expect to learn to distinguish key characters from individual variation from pictures. You *must* examine and compare bones from as many individuals as possible.

PHALANGES OF THE HAND

Key Term
phalanx (pl. phalanges) A bone of a finger or toe.

A **phalanx** is one of the fourteen bones in the fingers of a hand or toes of a foot. The thumb has two phalanges. Each of the other four digits has three phalanges. They are distinguishable as proximal, medial, or terminal.

The left and right side *cannot* be determined with phalanges. During recovery, hands should be bagged separately. But even with separate bags, the second and fourth digits of the same hand cannot be reliably separated. However, the proximal, medial, and terminal phalanges *can* be separated from one another.

A METHOD FOR SORTING PHALANGES

1. First, identify all of the terminal phalanges.
   a. The terminal (or distal) phalanx can be recognized by the shape of the distal end. It is flat and roughened on the palmar side.
   b. The distal end has no facet for articulating with another bone. Instead, it is shaped to hold a fingernail, attach tendons, and provide support for a fingertip.
2. Next, examine the *proximal* ends of the other phalanges.
   a. The medial phalanx has a double-faceted proximal end with a scalloped appearance. The double-facet fits the indented surface of the distal end of the proximal phalanx.
   b. The proximal phalanx has a single, cup-shaped proximal end that fits against the rounded head of the metacarpal.

Phalanges: Terminal, Medial, and Proximal

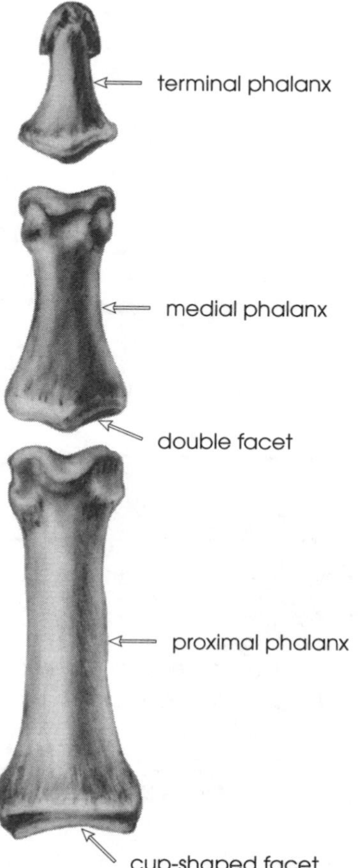

CHAPTER 7

THE PELVIS (HIP): THE INNOMI… COMPOSED OF THE ILIUM, ISCHIUM, AND PU…

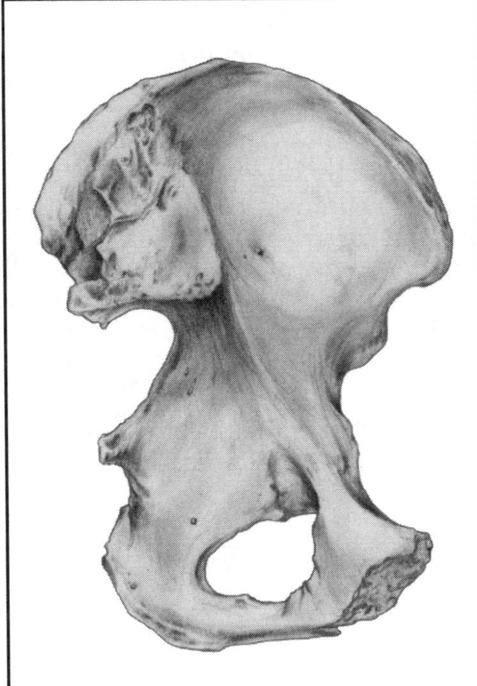

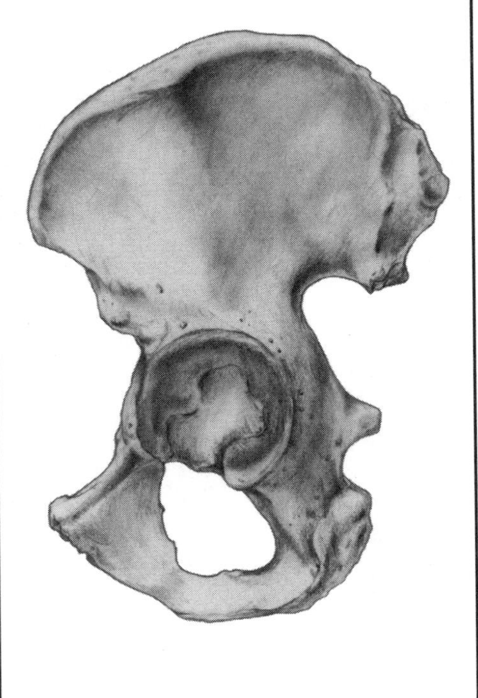

CHAPTER OUTLINE

THE STRUCTURE OF THE INNOMINATE

Key Terms

innominate A paired bone resulting from the fusion of the ilium, ischium, and pubis; one side of the pelvis; the "hip bone" or *os coxae*.

ilium (pl. ilia) The large, flaring portion of the innominate; the ilium forms the structure that is commonly recognized as "hip bones." The waist is immediately above the iliac crest.

ischium (pl. ischia) The most inferior bone of the innominate; the bone that carries the weight of the sitting person.

pubis (or pubes) The anteroinferior bone of the innominate; the pubic bones meet at the *symphysis pubis*, a cartilaginous union in the lower midline of the trunk.

The two **innominate** bones join with the sacrum to form the pelvis. Together, the innominates and sacrum create a bowl-shaped support for the organs of the lower trunk—the intestines, bladder, uterus, and so forth.

Each innominate is an adult bone resulting from the fusion of three separate bones—the ilium, ischium, and pubis. (See the illustration on page 83.)

The **ilium** is the large, flaring portion of the innominate. The ilium forms the structure that is commonly recognized as "hip bones." The waist is immediately above the iliac crest.

The **ischium** is the most inferior bone of the innominate. It is the bone that carries the weight of the sitting person.

The **pubis** is the most anterior bone of the innominate. Left and right pubic bones meet at the lower midline of the trunk.

Fusion of the ilium, ischium, and pubis takes place near the time of puberty, between the ages of 12 and 17. When the bones of the innominate fuse, the acetabulum (hip socket) and the obturator foramen are complete. (See the illustration on page 83.) The complete adult bone is called the innominate, but the specific name (ilium, ischium, or pubis) is used for a part of the innominate. This is no different from using specific names for parts of the skull.

Innominate, Left Side, Lateral View

Fusion of the ilium, ischium, and pubis takes place near the time of puberty, between the ages of 12 and 17. When the bones of the innominate fuse, the acetabulum (hip socket) and the obturator foramen are complete.

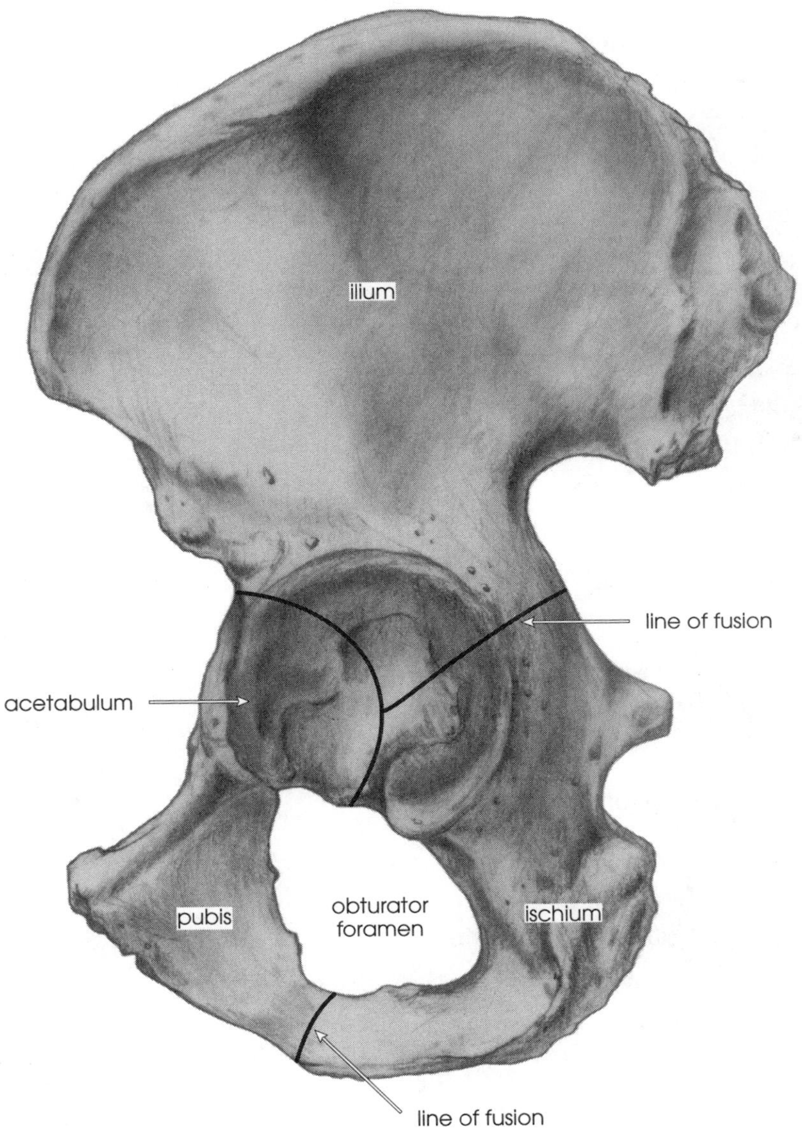

Side Differences and Specific Structures of the Pelvis

The illustrations below show medial and lateral views of the left innominate. The illustrations on page 85 show sexual differences in the pubis, and the illustrations on page 86 show sexual differences in the ilium.

Medial View (Inner Surface) of the Left Innominate

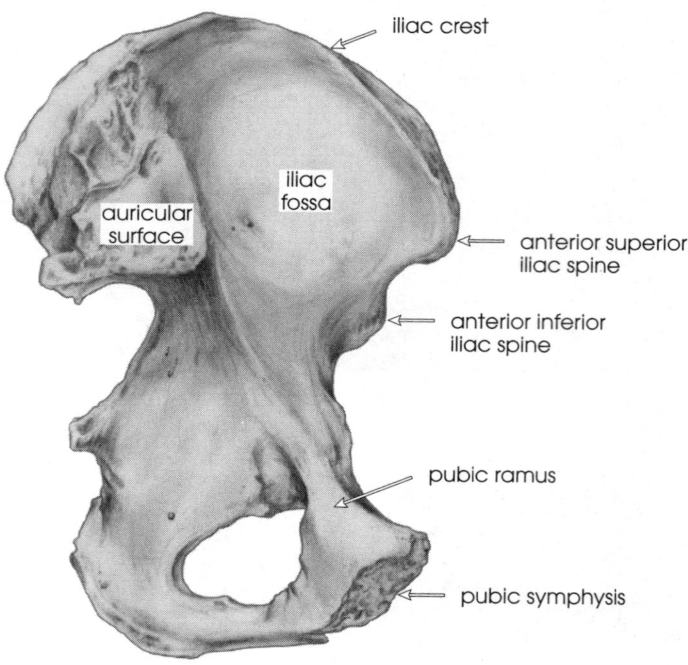

Note each of the following points as you examine the innominate:

- The sacrum articulates on the *inner* surface of the ilium at the auricular surface.
- The femur articulates on the *lateral* surface of the innominate at the acetabulum.
- The pubis curves in the opposite way from the expected—outward like the *lip* of a bowl, not inward like the greater part of a bowl.
- The thickest part of the innominate is the ischial tuberosity, the bone in closest association with the chair.
- The auricular surface, the pubic symphysis, and the rim of the acetabulum change considerably with advancing age.

Lateral View (Outer Surface) of the Left Innominate

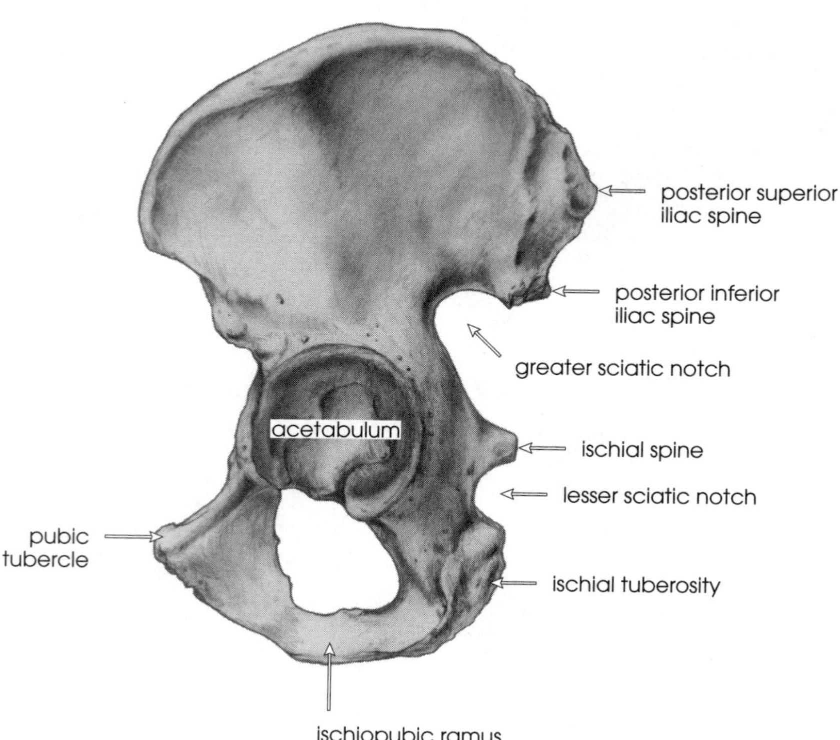

Sexual Differences in the Pubis

The pelvis is the most reliable bone for sex determination in the adult. Key sexual characters can be seen in the pubis and the ilium. The male pubis is *narrower* than the female pubis, and the male *subpubic angle* is more acute.

When compared to the male pubis, the female pubis appears to have been stretched toward the midline. The female *subpubic angle* is broad and the pubic part of the ischiopubic ramus develops a slight *ventral arc*. The pelvic differences result in wider female hips and a larger pelvic inlet.

Male

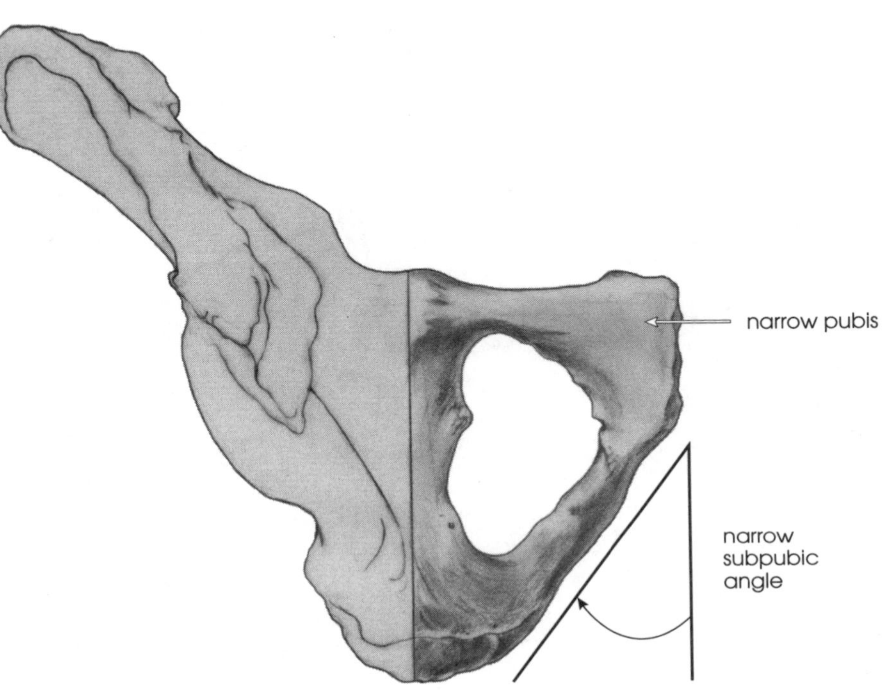

Female

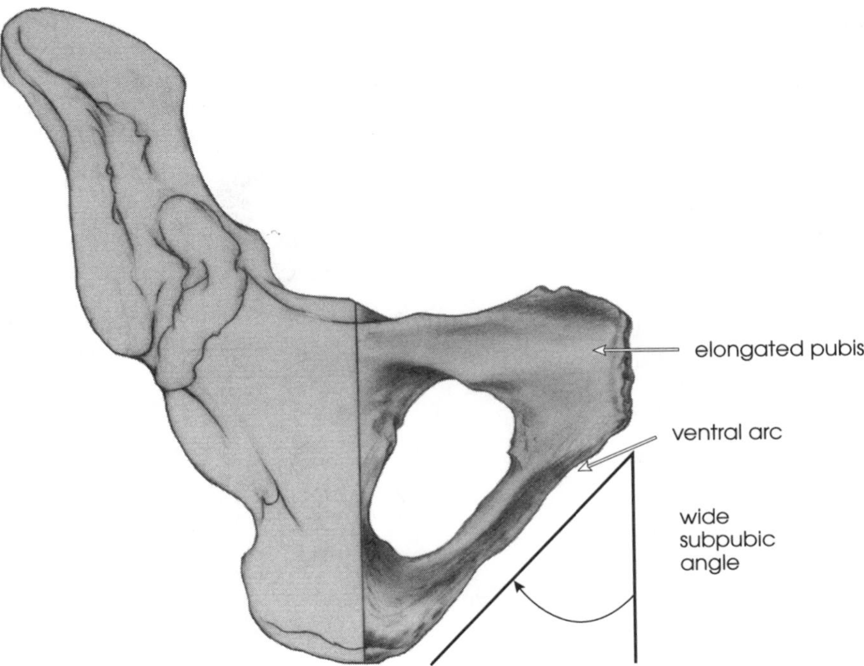

Sexual Differences in the Ilium

At the time of puberty, the female *sciatic notch* widens as the hips tend to flare outward. The male ilium retains a narrow sciatic notch.

An adult female may also develop a groove, or sulcus, anterior and inferior to the auricular surface. The presence of a *preauricular sulcus* is usually associated with the trauma of childbirth.

Male

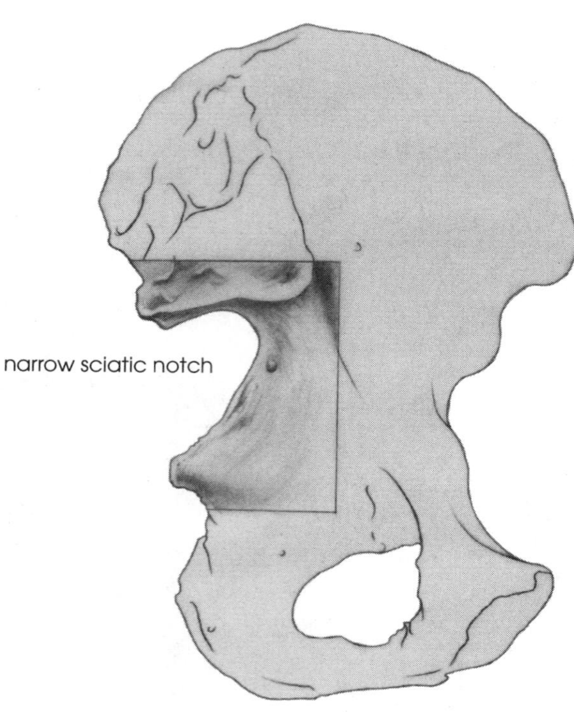

Female

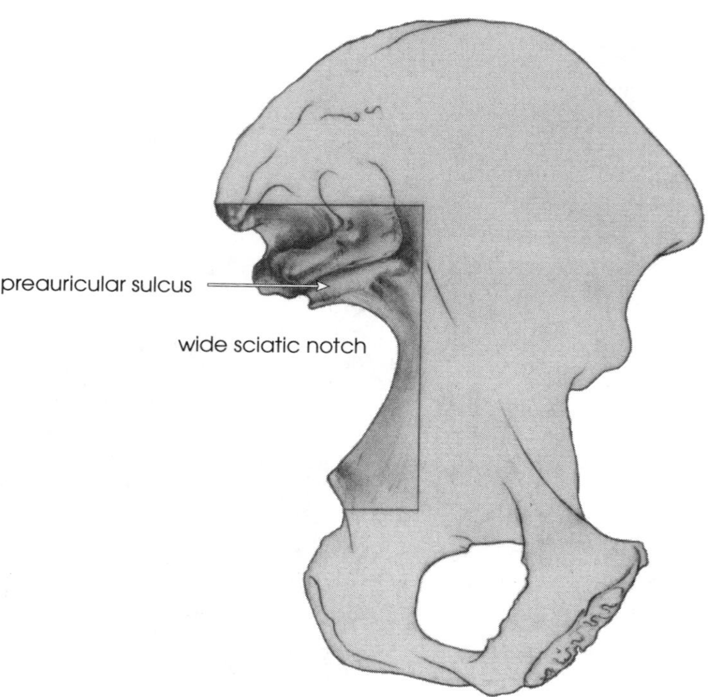

AGE DIFFERENCES IN THE MALE PUBIC SYMPHYSIS

Component analysis of pubic symphyses was first suggested by T. W. Todd in 1920. He published a readable description of ten phases of the pubic symphysis with illustrations of each phase. Todd's sample is not an adequate representation of the wide variation encountered throughout the world, but Todd's work is quite helpful as an aid to understanding the sequence of aging events. It is included here for general use.

I. *First post-adolescent phase (age 18–19).* Symphysial surface rugged, traversed by horizontal ridges separated by well-marked grooves; no ossific (epiphyseal) nodules fusing with the surface; no definite delimiting margin; no definition of extremities (Todd 1920, p. 301).

II. *Second post-adolescent phase (age 20–21).* Symphysial surface still rugged, traversed by horizontal ridges, the grooves between which are, however, becoming filled near the dorsal limit with a new formation of finely textured bone. This formation begins to obscure the hinder extremities of the horizontal ridges. Ossific (epiphyseal) nodules fusing with the upper symphysial face may occur; dorsal limiting margin begins to develop; no delimitation of extremities; foreshadowing of ventral bevel (Todd 1920, pp. 302–303).

III. *Third post-adolescent phase (age 22–24).* Symphysial face shows progressive obliteration of ridge and furrow system; commencing formation of the dorsal plateau; presence of fusing ossific (epiphyseal) nodules; dorsal margin gradually becoming more defined; beveling as a result of ventral rarefaction becoming rapidly more pronounced; no delimitation of extremities (Todd 1920, p. 304).

IV. *Fourth phase (age 25–26).* Great increase of ventral beveled area; corresponding diminution of ridge and furrow formation; complete definition of dorsal margin through the formation of the dorsal plateau; commencing delimitation of lower extremity (Todd 1920, p. 305).

V. *Fifth phase (age 27–30).* Little or no change in symphysial face and dorsal plateau except that sporadic and premature attempts at the formation of a ventral rampart occur; lower extremity, like the dorsal margin, is increasing in clearness of definition; commencing formation of upper extremity with or without the intervention of a bony (epiphyseal) nodule (Todd 1920, p. 306).

VI. *Sixth phase (age 30–35).* Increasing definition of extremities; development and practical completion of ventral rampart; retention of granular appearance of symphysial face and ventral aspect of pubis; absence of lipping of symphysial margin (Todd 1920, p. 308).

VII. *Seventh phase (age 35–39).* Changes in symphysial face and ventral aspect of pubis consequent upon diminishing activity; commencing bony outgrowth into attachments of tendons and ligaments, especially the gracilis tendon and sacro-tuberous ligament (Todd 1920, p. 310).

VIII. *Eighth phase (age 39–44).* Symphysial face generally smooth and inactive; ventral surface of pubis also inactive; oval outline complete or approximately complete; extremities clearly defined; no distinct "rim" to symphysial face; no marked lipping of either dorsal or ventral margin (Todd 1920, p. 311).

IX. *Ninth phase (age 45–50)*. Symphysial face presents a more or less marked rim; dorsal margin uniformly lipped; ventral margin irregularly lipped (Todd 1920, p. 312).

X. *Tenth phase (age 50 and upward)*. Symphysial face eroded and showing erratic ossification; ventral border more or less broken down; disfigurement increases with age (Todd 1920, p. 313).

Todd's work was tested and modified by Brooks (1955), McKern and Stewart (1957), Hanihara and Suzuki (1978), Gilbert (1973), Snow (1983), Katz and Suchey (1986), Suchey, Wiseley, and Katz in Reichs, ed. (1986), and others. Each investigator set out to find out if the method really worked and, if so, how to improve or simplify it.

Each investigator became extremely proficient in analyzing the hills and valleys of the pubic symphysis, but none actually made the method any easier for anyone else to use. There are no simple cookbook methods. The investigators have proven, however, that intense study of large quantities of information leads to better and better observation of detail.

The pubic symphysis, like the rest of the body, changes with age. But, as with all things biological, there are many variables and many responses. The result has the appearance of trends rather than clearly delineated steps. Study the trends, use the methods, compare your samples to casts from people of known ages, but do not rely wholly on the pubic symphysis or any other single method alone for age determination. In a mass grave of people from the same population group, it is at least possible to derive a fairly good age sequence.

Note that the terms used repeatedly in pubic symphysis aging are "dorsal plateau, ventral rampart, and symphysial rim." These terms are in Table 7.2 on pages 90–91 and in the glossary at the end of the book. They are also pointed out in the illustrations on page 89.

Examples from the Male Pubic Symphysis

The illustrations on page 89 are adapted for the male pubic bone casts by France casting. I recommend regular use of casts rather than illustrations whenever possible. The casts were developed specifically for use with the six-phase system of pubic aging published by Katz and Suchey, 1986.

Note that the number of years within the age range increases by over 15 percent between phase 1 and phase 6. In other words, the higher the phase number, the less it tells you.

Table 7.1 Correlation and Comparison of the Katz and Suchey Six-Phase System and the Todd Ten-Phase System

Todd	Katz and Suchey	Age Range	Years
I, II, III	1	15–23	8
IV, V	2	19–35	16
VI	3	22–43	21
VII, VIII	4	23–59	36
IX	5	28–78	50
X	6	36–87	51

EXAMPLES OF THE SIX PHASES OF PUBIC SYMPHYSIS AGING

Pubic aging is described in an abbreviated form adapted from descriptions in Katz and Suchey (1986). Only the more obvious features are emphasized.

Pubic Aging in 6 Phases

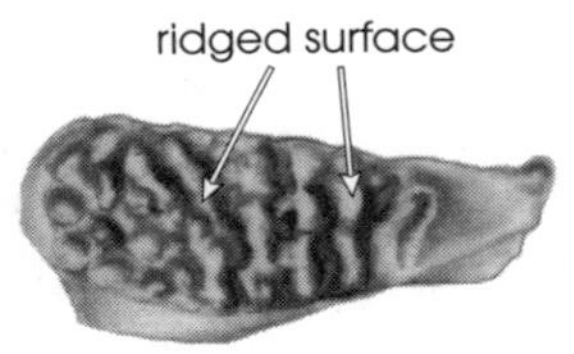

PHASE 1: 15 TO 23 YEARS—COMPLETELY RIDGED SURFACE

- Early: *completely ridged surface*, no nodules, no beveling, no symphysial rim, no lipping
- Late: ossified nodules begin to form as ridges slowly disappear

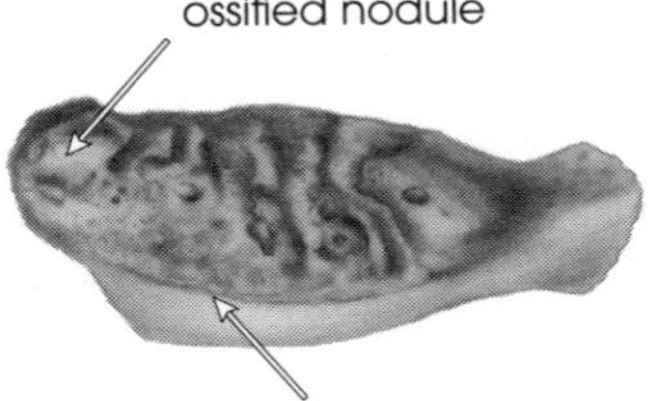

PHASE 2: 19 TO 35 YEARS—OSSIFIED NODULES

- *Ossified nodules* obvious
- Dorsal plateau formed
- Ventral beveling begins

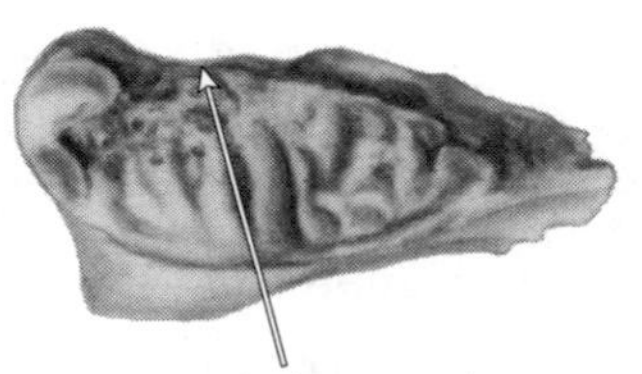

PHASE 3: 22 TO 43 YEARS—VENTRAL RAMPART

- Definition of extremities (superior and inferior parts of symphysis)
- *Ventral rampart* completed
- No symphysial rim, no lipping

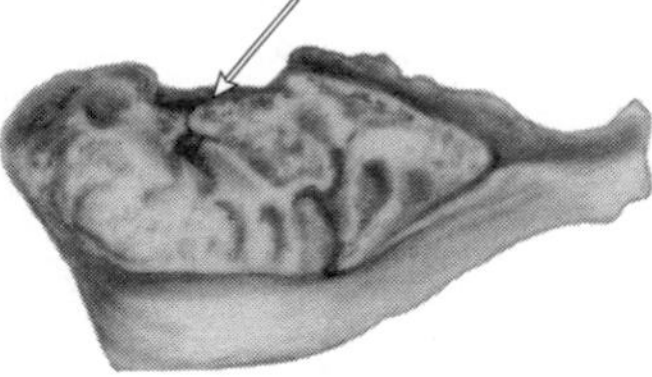

PHASE 4: 23 TO 59 YEARS—OVAL OUTLINE

- Smoother symphysial face
- *Oval outline* almost complete
- No symphysial rim, no lipping

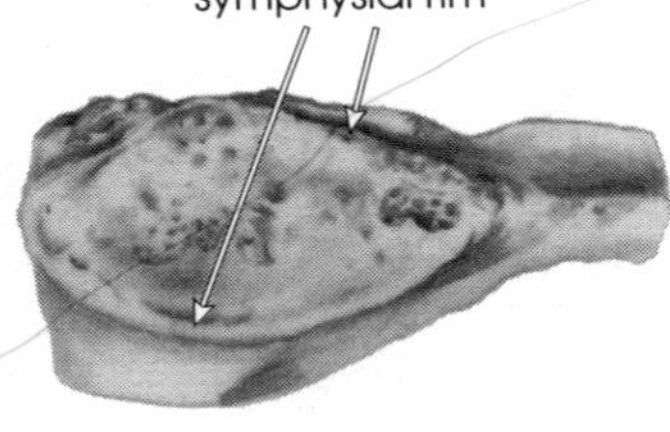

PHASE 5: 28 TO 78 YEARS—SYMPHYSIAL RIM

- Marked *symphysial rim*
- Dorsal margin lipped
- Ventral margin irregularly lipped

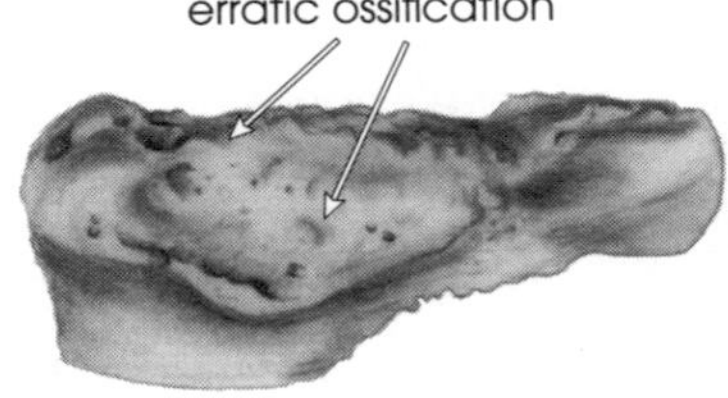

PHASE 6: 36 TO 87 YEARS—ERRATIC OSSIFICATION

- Eroded *erratic ossification*
- Irregular lipping
- Broken down ventral border

Table 7.2 Osteological Terms for the Hip (Pelvis)

Bone	Term	Definition
innominate	acetabulum	the articular surface for the rotation of the head of the femur
	acetabular fossa	the nonarticular central surface deep within the acetabulum
	obturator foramen	large opening bordered by the pubis, the ischium, and ischio-pubic ramus
ilium	auricular surface	ear-shaped surface for the articulation of the sacrum
	preauricular sulcus	groove adjacent to the auricular surface related to the trauma of bearing children
	iliac crest	superior edge of the ilium
	iliac fossa	smooth, depressed inner surface of the ilium
	iliac tuberosity	the posterior, inner thickening of the ilium, superior to the auricular surface
	anterior superior iliac spine	the upper of the two projections on the ventral edge of the ilium
	anterior inferior iliac spine	the lower of the two projections on the ventral edge of the ilium
	posterior superior iliac spine	the upper of the two projections on the dorsal edge of the ilium
	posterior inferior iliac spine	the lower of the two projections on the dorsal edge of the ilium; the projection that forms the superior boundary of the greater sciatic notch
	greater sciatic notch	the large notch on the posterior edge of the ilium and extending down onto the ischium; an area of distinct sexual dimorphism (male narrow, female wide)
ischium	ischial tuberosity	the largest, thickest portion of the ischium; man sits on the two ischial tuberosities
	ischial spine	the projection of bone that forms the inferior boundary of the greater sciatic notch
	lesser sciatic notch	the smaller notch inferior to the greater sciatic notch
pubis	dorsal plateau	the elevated ridge that appears on the dorsal surface (the convex innermost surface of the pubis) in the early phases of pubic symphysis aging.
	ischiopubic ramus	the bridge of bone formed from processes of both ischium and pubis
	pubic ramus	the superior bridge of the pubis extending toward the ilium
	pubic symphysis	the cartilaginous joint between the two pubic bones; the surface of the symphysial bone changes progressively with age
	pubic tubercle	the small bony bump on the superior anterior surface of the pubic bone
	subpubic angle	the angle formed beneath the pubic symphysis when the two pubic bones are anatomically aligned
	subpubic concavity	the lateral curvature inferior to the female pubic symphysis

Table 7.2, continued

Bone	Term	Definition
	symphysial rim	the lip that circumscribes the face of the pubic symphysis in later phases of pubic symphysis aging
	ventral rampart	the bevel that appears on the ventral surface (the concave, outer surface) in middle phases of pubic symphysis aging
	ventral arc	the slightly elevated ridge of bone on the ventral aspect of the female pubis
	parturition pits	indentations on the inner surface of the pubis adjacent to the pubic symphysis

CHAPTER 8

THE LEG: FEMUR, TIBIA, FIBULA, AND PATELLA

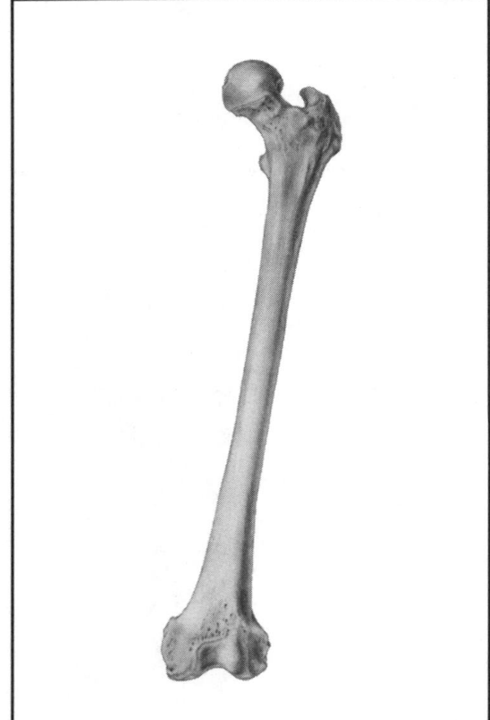

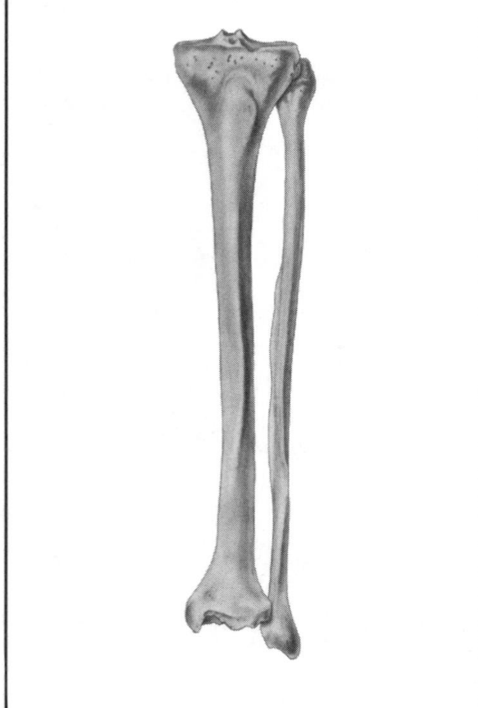

CHAPTER OUTLINE

The Femur
The Tibia
The Fibula
The Patella
Sexual Differences in the Bones of the Leg

The Femur

Key Term
femur (pl. femora) The upper leg bone; the largest of the leg bones; the "thigh bone."

The **femur** is commonly called the thigh bone. It is usually the heaviest and strongest long bone of the body. The femur has a slight anterior curvature. There is individual variation and racial variation in the extent of "anterior bowing," as well as variation in the angle created by the anatomical neck and the shaft.

The femur is *not* in direct line with the tibia. The illustration below shows the femur in normal anatomical position; the distal surface of the medial and lateral condyles is horizontal, but the shaft is not vertical. It angles medially (inward) from the acetabulum of the pelvis toward the knee. The orientation of the femur and the tibia in the human leg is essential to a smoothly balanced walk.

Left Femur

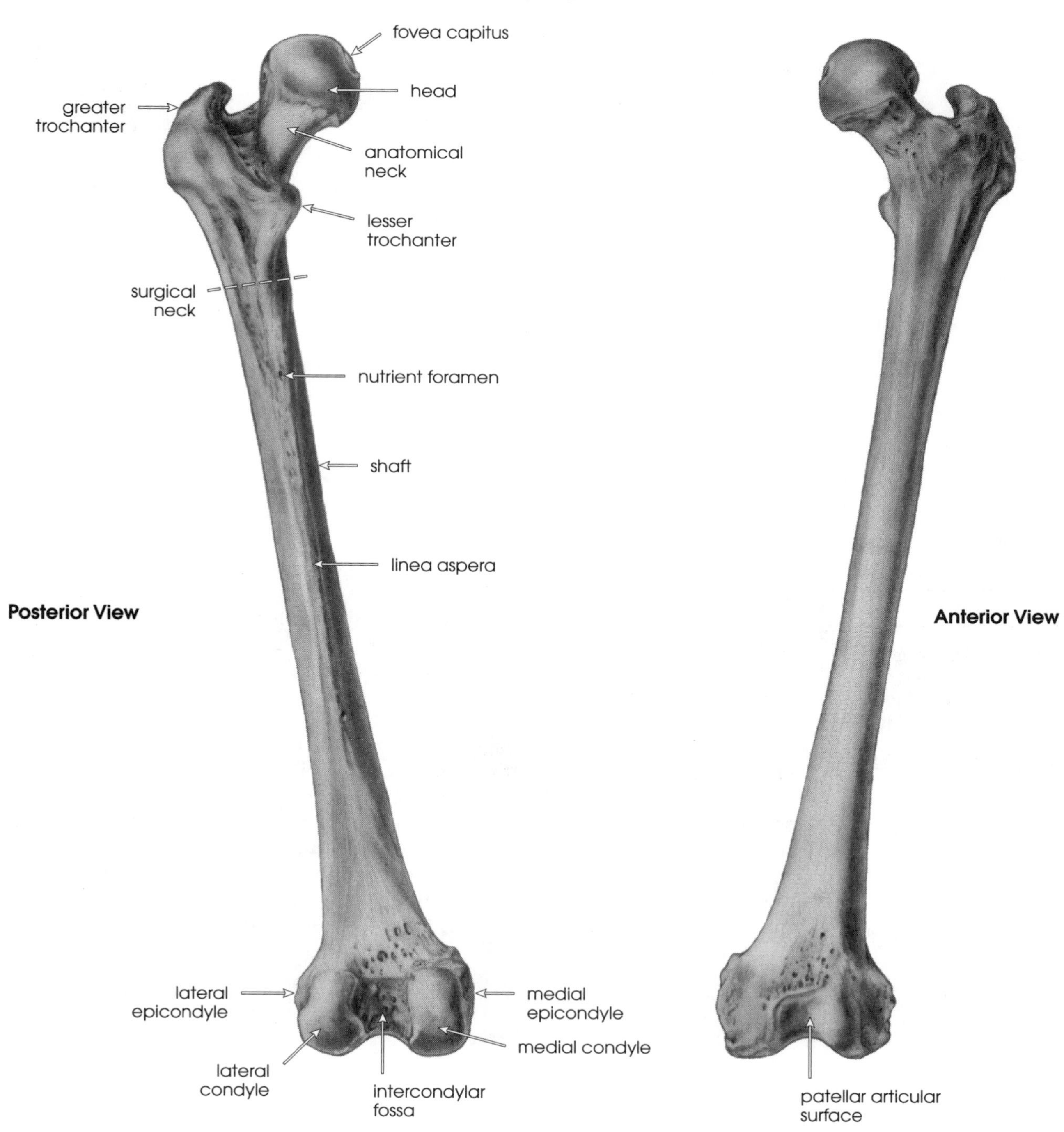

Comparison of the Head of the Femur with the Head of the Humerus

The head of the femur has a fovea capitus and an extended neck; the humerus has neither.

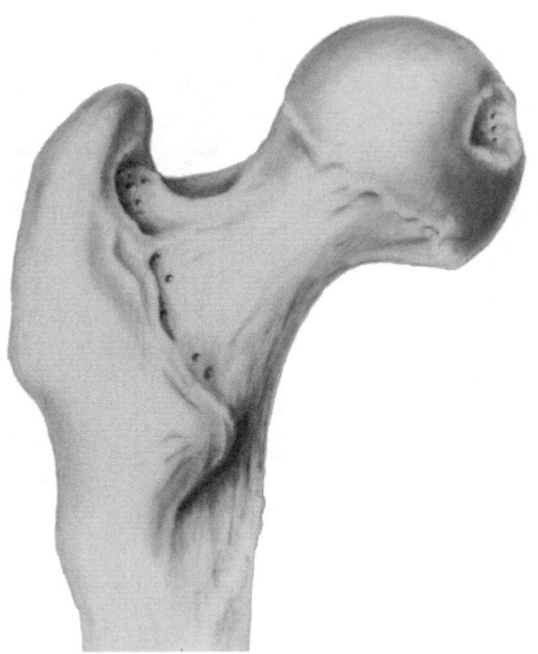

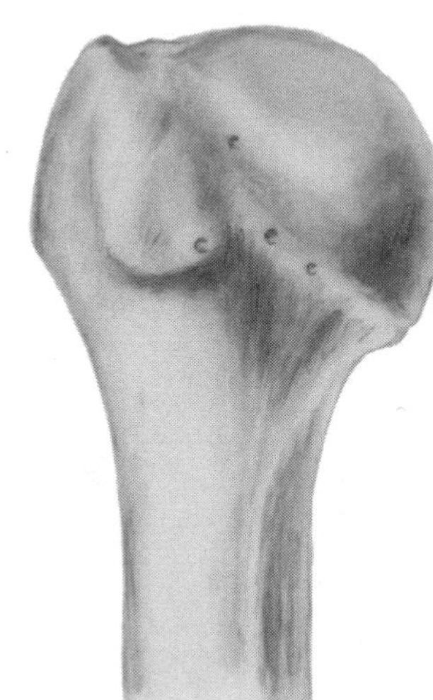

THE TIBIA

Key Term
tibia The large, medial bone of the lower leg; the "shin bone," also the medial "ankle bone."

The **tibia** is the second largest long bone and is commonly known as the shin bone. It is straighter than the femur and positioned vertically. Whereas the femur was rounded with a linea aspera projecting from the posterior, the tibia is more triangular with the sharpest angle anterior. It is the anterior crest of the tibia that frequently sustains bumps and bruises in the course of an active life.

In the illustration on page 95, observe the thin ridge on the lateral side of the tibia. This is the interosseous crest, which serves as an attachment area for the interosseous membrane between the tibia and fibula. This crest serves the same function as the interosseous crests on the radius and ulna, the other set of limb bones that are neatly bound together.

The distal end of the tibia is identified by the projection of the medial malleolus, commonly known as an ankle bone. The tibia contributes only the inner ankle bone. The fibula provides the outer ankle bone.

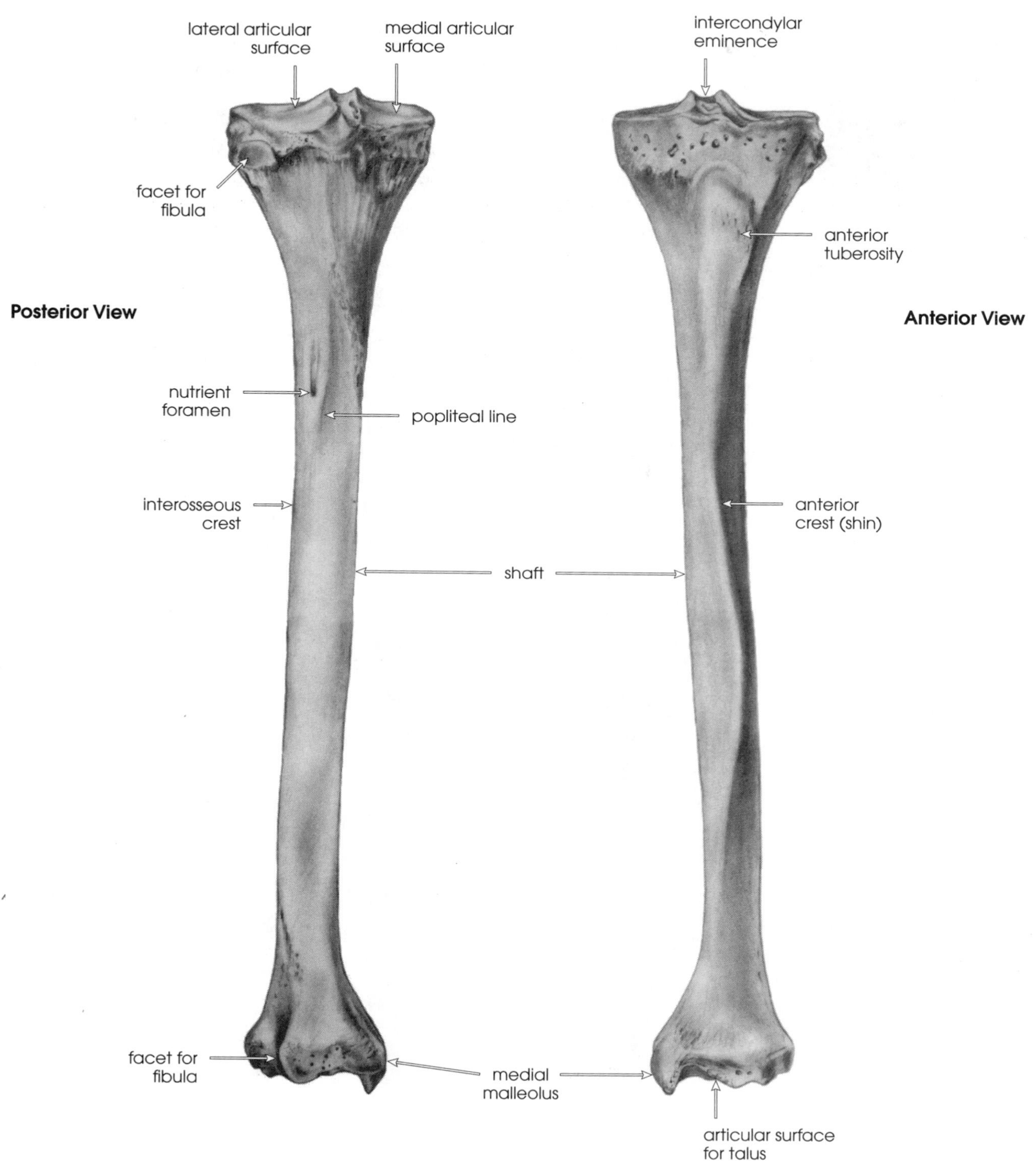
Left Tibia
lateral articular surface
medial articular surface
intercondylar eminence
facet for fibula
anterior tuberosity
Posterior View
Anterior View
nutrient foramen
popliteal line
interosseous crest
anterior crest (shin)
shaft
facet for fibula
medial malleolus
articular surface for talus

The Fibula

Key Term
fibula The slender, lateral bone of the lower leg; the lateral "ankle bone."

The illustration below shows the left **fibula**, lateral and medial views. The illustration on page 97 shows the tibia and fibula together, anterior view. Note the following features when comparing the tibia and fibula:

- The *medial* malleolus (of the tibia) points toward the *anterior*.
- The *lateral* malleolus (of the fibula) points toward the *posterior*.
- The interosseous crests of the tibia and fibula point toward each other.
- The *major* curvature of the fibula is in the direction of the side.

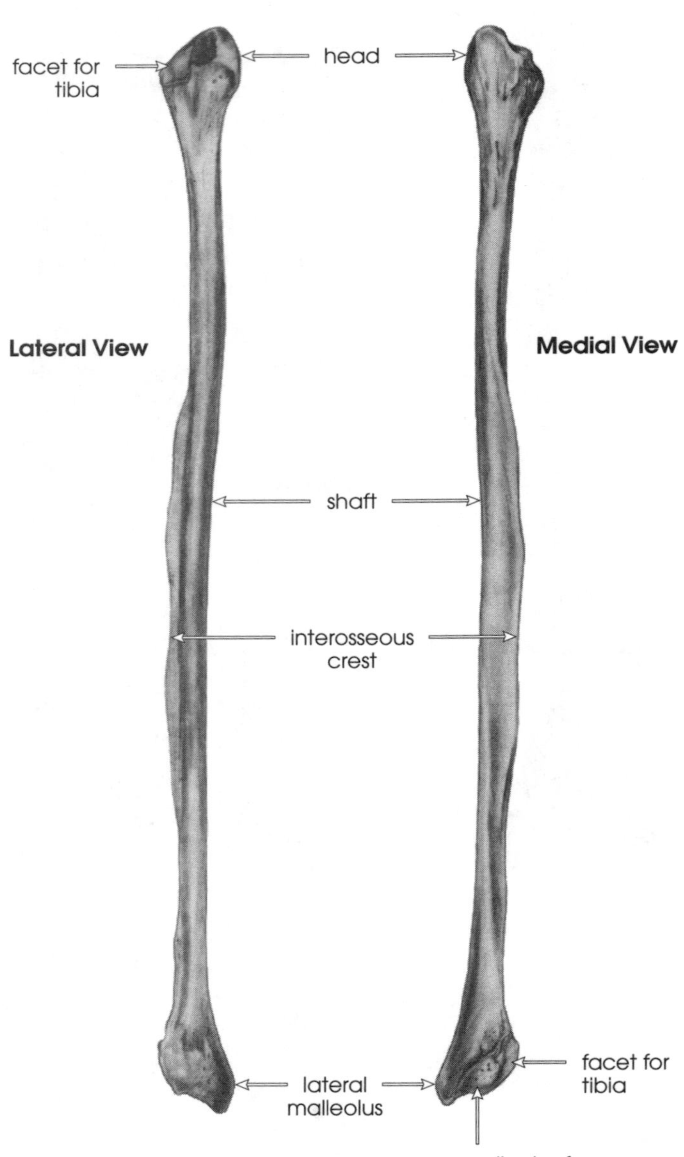

Note the manner in which the fibula fits against the outside of the tibia:

- The *head* of the fibula is lateral and inferior to the ledge of the proximal end of the tibia.
- The *malleolus* of the distal end of the fibula mirrors the malleolus of the distal end of the tibia.
- Each malleolus is commonly called an *ankle bone*.

Tibia and Fibula Together, Anterior View

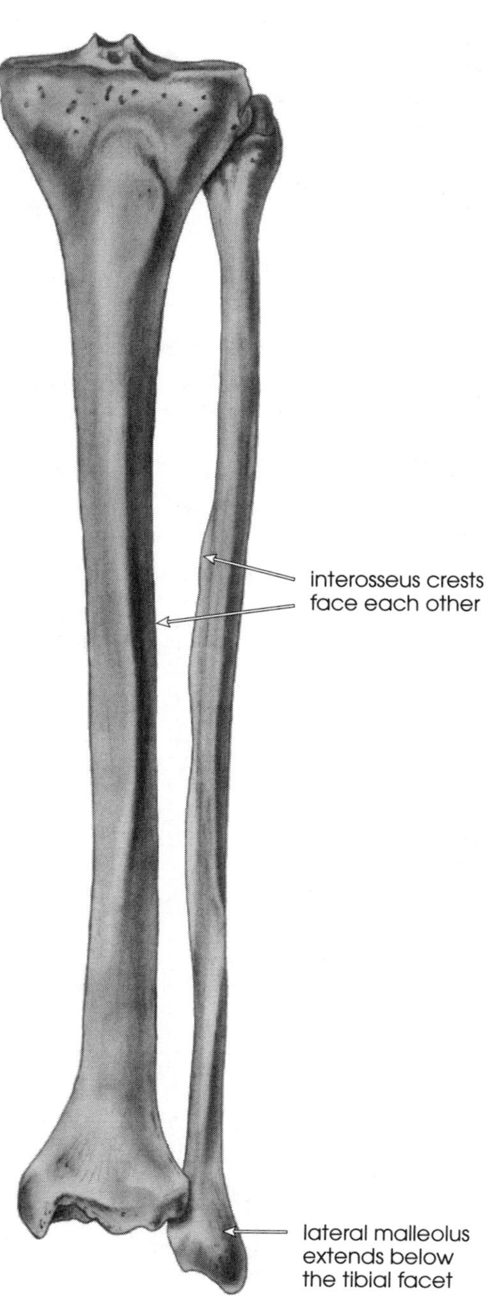

The Patella

Key Term

patella (pl. patellae)
The flat, rounded bone articulating with the anterior of the distal end of the femur; the "kneecap."

The **patella**, commonly known as the kneecap, is the flat, rounded bone articulating with the anterior of the distal end of the femur. The illustrations below show the anterior and posterior views of the left patella.

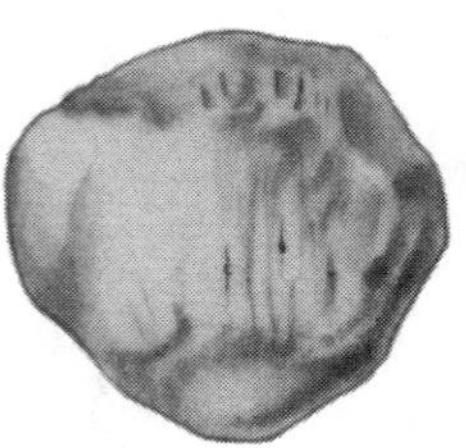

Left Patella, Anterior View

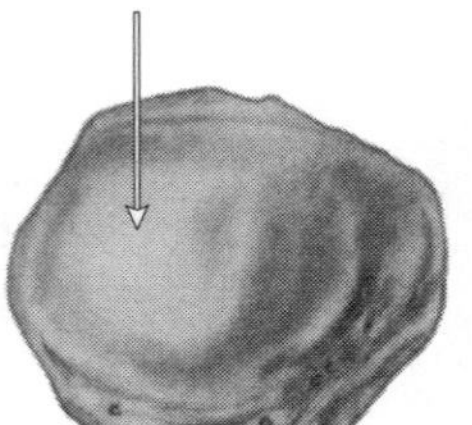

Left Patella, Posterior View
Note that the lateral portion of the articular surface is larger.

The illustration below shows the knee joint and vertical location of the patella. The patella actually rides higher on the femur than is shown in the illustration below. Note the location of the patellar articular surface on the femur.

- The patella is held above the tibia by the quadriceps muscle. The quadriceps tendon inserts on the superior beveled edge of the patella.
- The inferior aspect of the patella is held in place by the patellar ligament, which originates on the pointed inferior apex and inserts on the anterior tibia.
- The largest facet of the patella articulates with the wide lateral condyle of the femur. If the inferior apex is pointed away, and the patella is placed on a flat surface, it will fall toward the larger lateral facet. This is the side of origin (i.e., the right patella falls to the right and the left patella falls to the left).

Knee Joint and Vertical Location of Patella

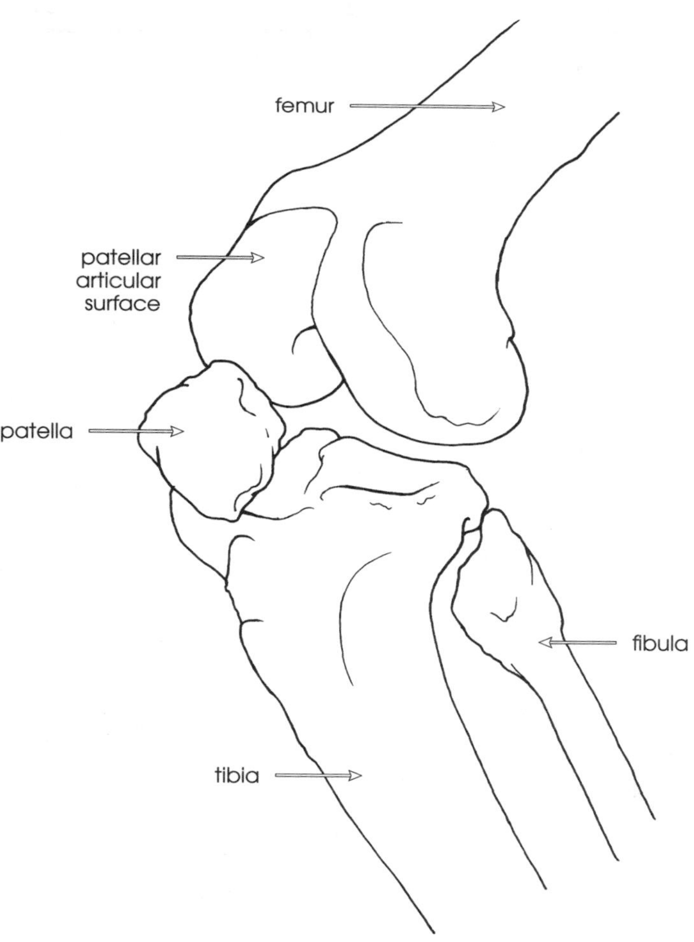

Sexual Differences in the Bones of the Leg

It is possible to estimate (not determine) sex with femoral head measurements. This is based on basic sexual dimorphism, anticipating that males are larger than females. The method is useful if there is no pelvis or skull and if the unidentified individual is from a well-documented population. An unknown corpse from an heterogeneous population such as is found in major U.S. cities may not be a good candidate for this type of analysis.

Stewart (1979, 120) offers the set of numbers in Table 8.1 based on his tests of the earlier work of Pearson (1917–1919) for use in sexing dry bones of American whites.

Measure the greatest diameter of the femur with standard sliding calipers and compare femoral head measurements with the measurements above. If possible, establish normative data for the population before using this method with confidence.

Table 8.1 Sexing Dry Bones of American Whites

Female	Female?	Indeterminate	Male?	Male
42.5 mm	42.5–43.5 mm	43.5–46.5 mm	46.5–47.5 mm	47.5 mm

Table 8.2 Osteological Terms for the Leg

Bone	Term	Definition
femur	head	the ball-shaped upper extremity of the femur; the femoral head articulates within the acetabulum of the innominate; the proximal epiphysis
	fovea capitis	the pit in the femoral head providing attachment for the ligamentum teres
	neck	the constricted portion just below the head of the femur; the anatomical neck is proximal to the two trochanters; the surgical neck is distal to the trochanters
	greater trochanter	the larger and more superior of the two protuberances between the neck and the shaft; a separate center of ossification
	lesser trochanter	the smaller and more inferior of the two protuberances between the neck and the shaft; a separate center of ossification
	shaft	the major portion of the femur; the diaphysis
	linea aspera	the muscle attachment line on the posterior surface of the femoral shaft
	nutrient foramen	the aperture through which vessels pass between the inner and outer surfaces of the femoral shaft; the vessels pass inward as they progress *away from* the knee
	patellar articular surface	the anterior-most articular surface on the distal end of the femur
	medial epicondyle	the protuberance proximal and medial to the medial condyle
	medial condyle	the medial articular surface for the tibia
	lateral epicondyle	the protuberance proximal and lateral to the lateral condyle
	lateral condyle	the lateral articular surface for the tibia
	intercondylar fossa	the depression between the two condyles on the posterior surface of the femur
patella	medial articular facet	the articular surface that articulates with the anterior of the medial condyle of the femur
	lateral articular facet	the articular surface that articulates with the anterior of the lateral condyle of the femur
tibia	medial condyle	the proximal articular surface that articulates with the medial condyle of the femur
	lateral condyle	the proximal articular surface that articulates with the lateral condyle of the femur
	malleolar fossa	the indentation on the lateral surface of the distal end of the tibia, the groove for the lateral malleolus of the fibula
	intercondylar eminence	the bony projection between the two condylar platforms of the tibia; also called intercondyloid eminence
	fibular articular surfaces	the surfaces on the lateral side of the tibia providing articulation for the ends of the fibula; the proximal surface is a flat oval facet under the shelf of the lateral articular surface; the distal articulation is the groove opposite the medial malleolus; the groove is also called the malleolar fossa
	shaft	the diaphysis of the tibia
	anterior crest	the sharp ridge on the anterior shaft of the tibia, the shin
	interosseous crest	the low sharp border the length of the lateral side, the attachment site for the interosseous membrane between tibia and fibula
	medial malleolus	the projection on the disto-medial end of the tibia; the inner "ankle bone"

Table 8.2, continued

Bone	Term	Definition
	popliteal line	on the superior and posterior surface of the tibia, a curved roughened attachment surface
	nutrient foramen	the aperture through which vessels pass between the inner and outer surfaces of the femoral shaft; the vessels pass inward as they progress *away from* the knee
fibula	styloid process	the slightly sharp projection of bone pointing upward from the proximal end (the head) of the fibula
	head	the proximal end
	shaft	the diaphysis of the fibula
	lateral malleolus	the distal end of the fibula, the lateral "ankle bone"
	interosseous crest	the sharp border on the length of the medial side, the attachment site for the interosseous membrane between tibia and fibula

Chapter 9

The Foot: Tarsals, Metatarsals, and Phalanges

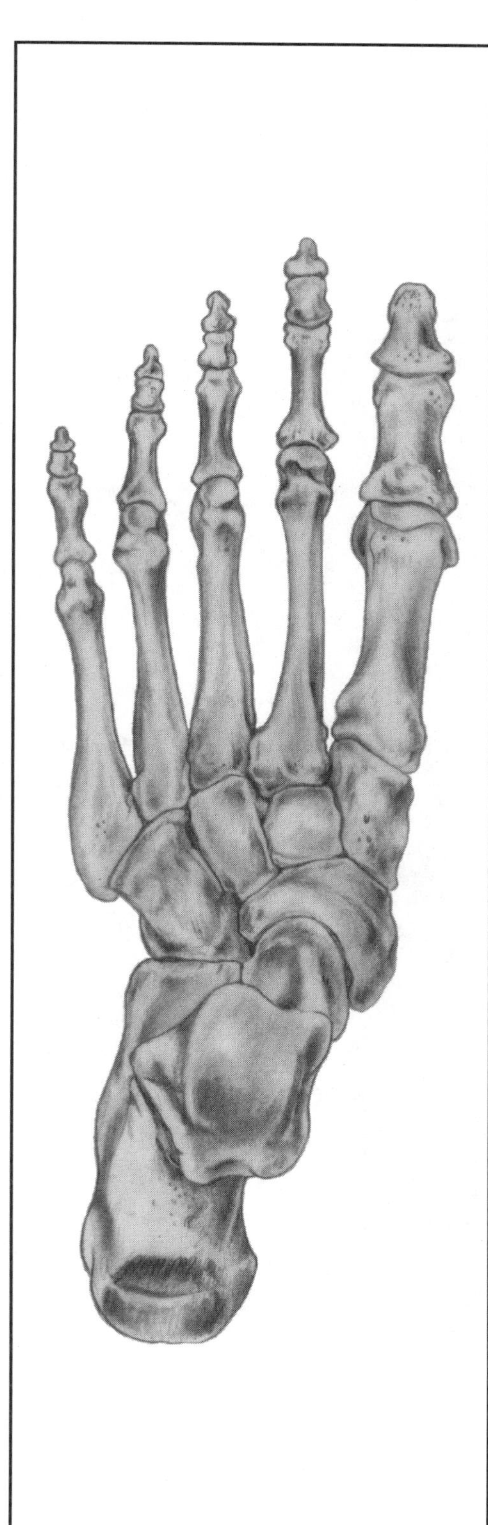

CHAPTER OUTLINE

The human foot is built of twenty-six bones: seven tarsal bones, five metatarsal bones, and fourteen phalanges. Just as with the carpal and metacarpal bones, *tarsal bones* and *metatarsal bones* are often just called *tarsals* and *metatarsals*.

The tarsals articulate with the leg and form the heel and arch of the foot. The metatarsals extend from the arch to the toes, and the phalanges form the toes.

Each tarsal and metatarsal can be recognized, and right can be distinguished from left. The phalanges are more difficult. Proximal, medial, and terminal phalanges can be distinguished, but right and left cannot be separated with certainty in any but the first toe. Thus, it is most important to bag the feet separately during disinterment. Any toe that may contribute to identification because of trauma or anomaly should be separated and labeled by number.

Left Foot and Ankle Bones, Superior View

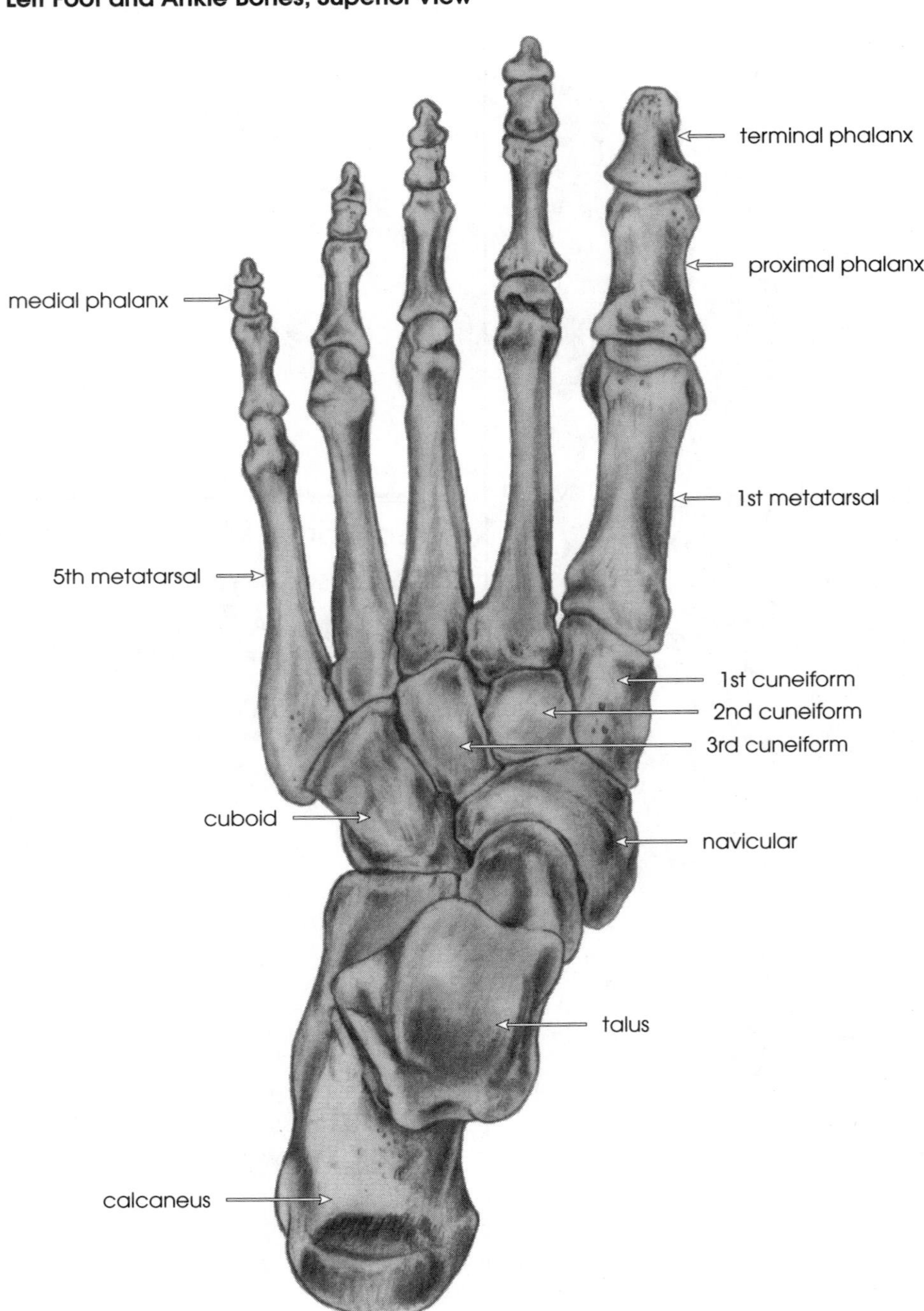

Tarsal Bones

Key Term

tarsal bone One of the seven bones within the proximal portion of the foot; the bones of the heel and arch.

Only one of the **tarsal bones**, the talus, is part of the ankle. The other six tarsals are foot bones. The illustration on page 106 shows all seven tarsals: the first cuneiform, the second cuneiform, the third cuneiform, the navicular, the cuboid, the talus, and the calcaneus. Table 9.1, below, lists tarsal articulations.

Table 9.1 Tarsal Articulations

Bone	Articular Facet	Adjacent Bone
talus	trochlea	tibia
	head	navicular
	planar facets	calcaneus
calcaneus	dorsal facet	talus
	sustentaculum tali facet	talus
	distal facet	cuboid
navicular	proximal surface	talus
	distal surfaces	all three cuneiforms
first cuneiform	proximal surface	navicular
	medial surface	no bone
	lateral surface	second cuneiform and metatarsal #2
	distal surface	metatarsal #1
second cuneiform	proximal surface	navicular
	medial surface	first cuneiform
	lateral surface	third cuneiform
	distal surface	metatarsal #2
third cuneiform	proximal surface	navicular
	medial surface	second cuneiform and metatarsal #2
	lateral surface	cuboid
	distal surface	metatarsal #3
cuboid	proximal surface	calcaneus
	medial surface	3rd cuneiform and navicular
	distal surface	metatarsals #4 and #5

Tarsal Bones (L = Left Side)

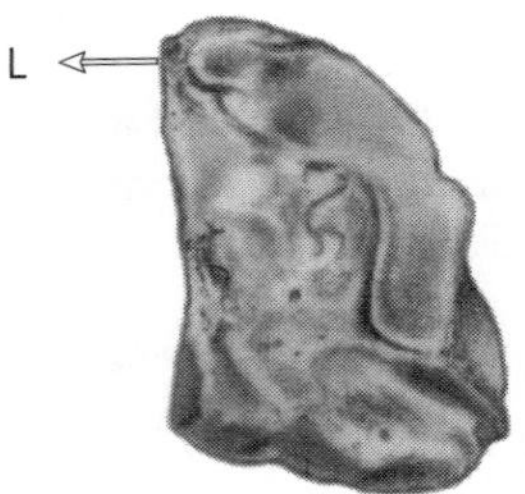

first cuneiform
lateral surface

When the lateral facet faces you and the point is up, the bone points toward the correct side.

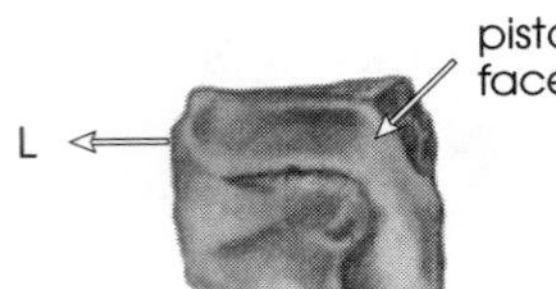

second cuneiform
medial surface

When the pistol-shaped facet faces you, the "barrel" points toward the correct side.

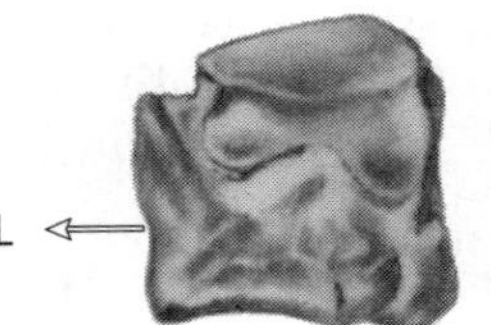

third cuneiform
medial surface

When the "butterfly" facet faces you, the narrow plantar surface points toward the correct side.

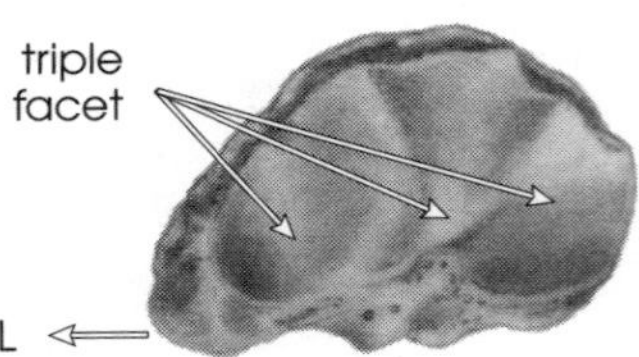

navicular
distal surface

When the triple facet faces you with the rounded dorsal surface up, the bone points toward the correct side.

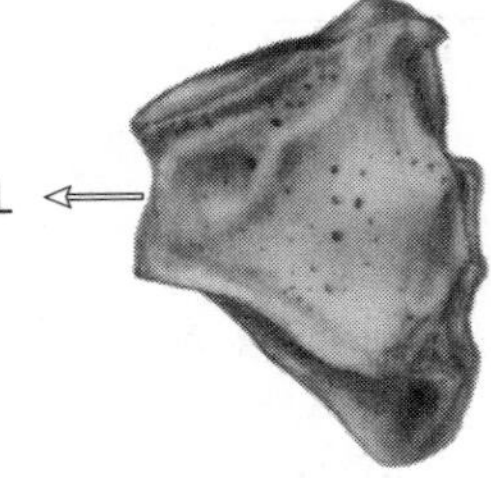

cuboid
superior-lateral surface

When the largest process points downward with the smooth dorsal side up, the narrow side points toward the correct side.

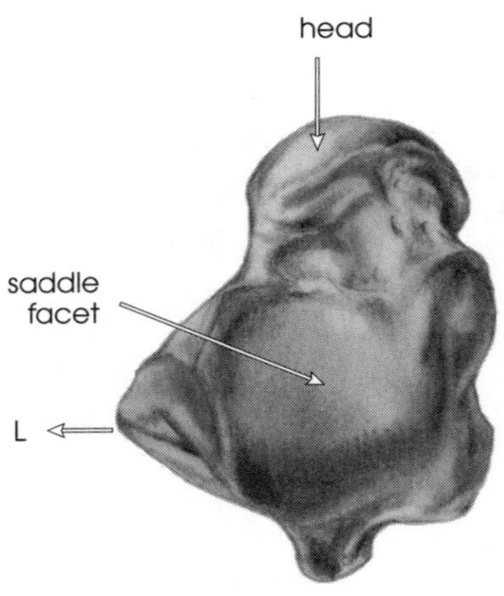

talus
superior surface

When the head points away from you with the saddle facet up, the lateral process points toward the correct side.

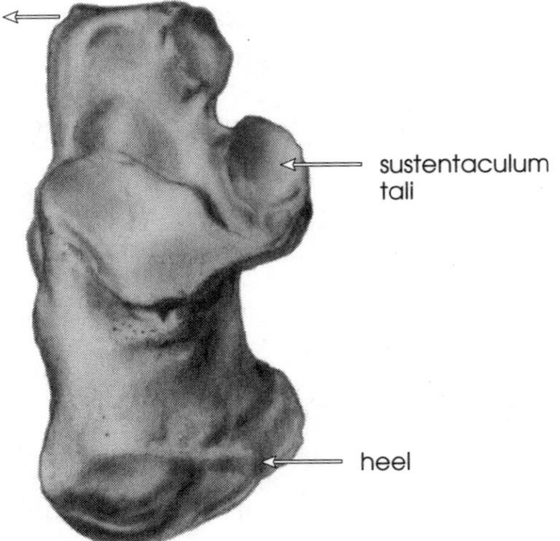

calcaneus
superior surface

When the heel points toward you with the talar facet up, the distal articulation is on the correct side.

Metatarsal Bones

Key Term
metatarsal bone One of the five bones extending from the arch to the toes of the foot.

The **metatarsal bones** are longer and thinner than metacarpals. The bases of the second through the fifth slant so that the lateral edge is an acute angle that points toward the correct side.

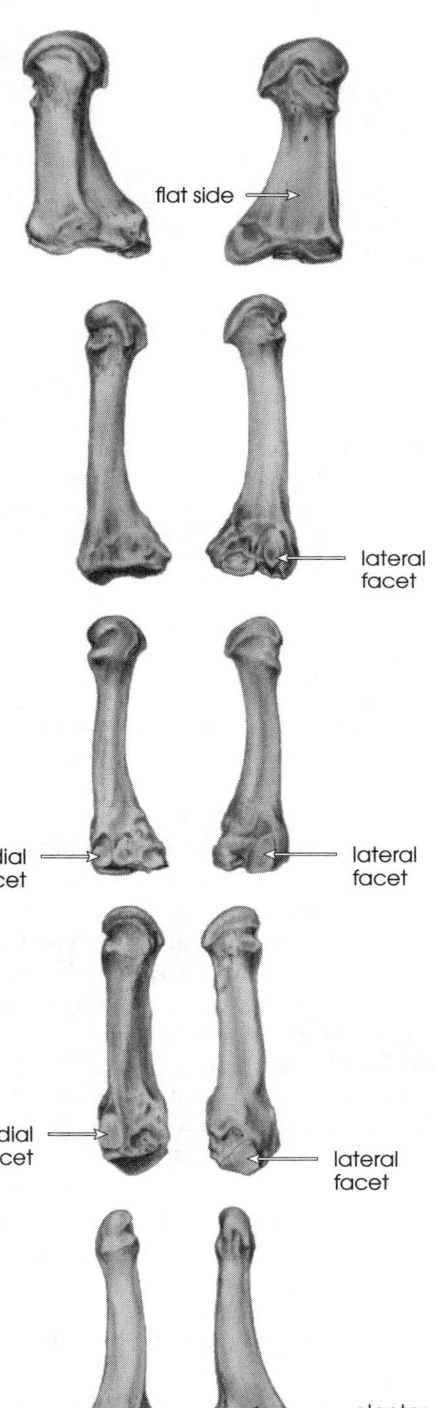

Metatarsal #1

The thickest metacarpal has a D-shaped base. The flat side of the "D" is lateral. The curved side of the "D" is the medial side of the foot.

Metatarsal #2

The base of #2 is inset between the distal ends of the first and third cuneiforms. The result is a *lateral* facet that sits well above the base. The proximal facet is triangular.

Metatarsal #3

The facets on the sides of the base of #3 are *both* adjacent to the base. The proximal facet is triangular.

Metatarsal #4

This metatarsal is also inset, but only on the medial side. Unlike #2, the *medial* facet sits above the base. The lateral facet is larger. The proximal facet is rectangular, *not* triangular.

Metatarsal #5

This is the only metatarsal with a long process that has the appearance of a tail. When viewed from the smoother dorsal side with the head pointed away, the tail points toward the correct side. The only facet is, of course, on the medial side.

Table 9.2 Metatarsal and Phalanx Articulations

Bone	Articular Facet	Adjacent Bone
metatarsal #1	base	first cuneiform
	medial surface	no bone
	lateral surface	no bone—not even metatarsal #2
	head	proximal phalanx
metatarsal #2	base	second cuneiform
	medial surface	sometimes first cuneiform
	lateral surface	third cuneiform and metatarsal #3
	head	proximal phalanx
metatarsal #3	base	third cuneiform
	medial surface	metatarsal #2
	lateral surface	metatarsal #4
	head	proximal phalanx
metatarsal #4	base	cuboid
	medial surface	metatarsal #3
	lateral surface	metatarsal #5
	head	proximal phalanx
metatarsal #5	base	cuboid
	medial surface	metatarsal #4
	lateral surface	no bone—only a process
	head	proximal phalanx
proximal phalanx	base	metatarsal head
	head	medial phalanx
medial phalanx	base	proximal phalanx
	head	distal phalanx
distal or terminal phalanx	base	medial phalanx
	head	no bone—only a toenail

Phalanges: A Finger-Toe Comparison

Key Term

phalanx (pl. phalanges) A bone of a finger or toe.

Now that you are familiar with the bones of the fingers and toes, take time to compare and differentiate the two types of **phalanges**.

The proximal phalanges of the finger and toe look a lot alike, but the finger phalanx is flatter and more oval in cross section than the toe phalanx, which is narrower in the middle. The central portion of the toe phalanx is waistlike.

The medial finger phalanx is much longer than the medial toe phalanx. The proximal and medial finger phalanges can be confused if the proximal articular surfaces are not closely examined. The proximal and medial toe phalanges are not likely to be confused because of the great difference in size. Frequently, the tiny distal toe phalanx fuses to the medial phalanx, particularly with the fourth and fifth toes. Fusion is unusual with medial and distal finger phalanges.

All of the finger phalanges are dorso-palmarly compressed. The cross section is a flattened oval shape. In contrast, the proximal toe phalanx is medio-laterally compressed at the center. The result is a circular cross section.

Cross Sections of Finger Phalanx and Toe Phalanx

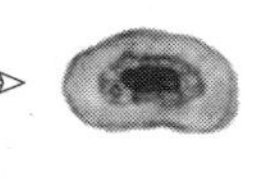

Finger phalanges are oval or flattened in cross section.

Toe phalanges are circular in cross section.

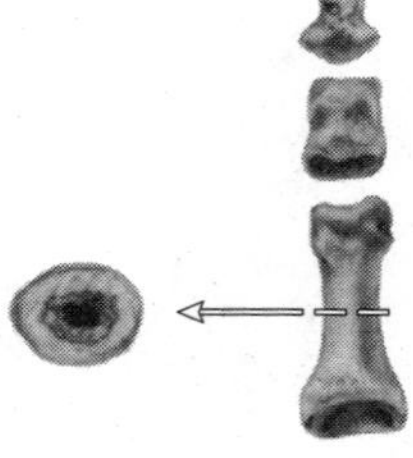

CHAPTER 10

HUMAN ODONTOLOGY (THE TEETH)

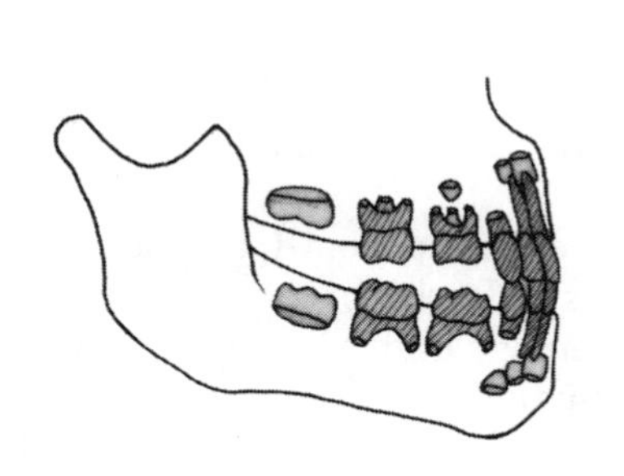

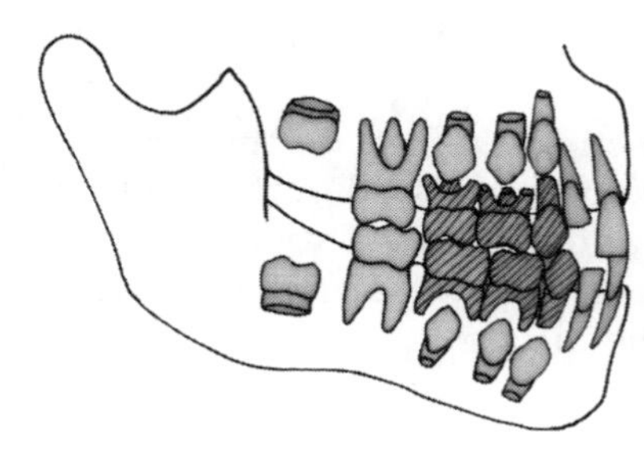

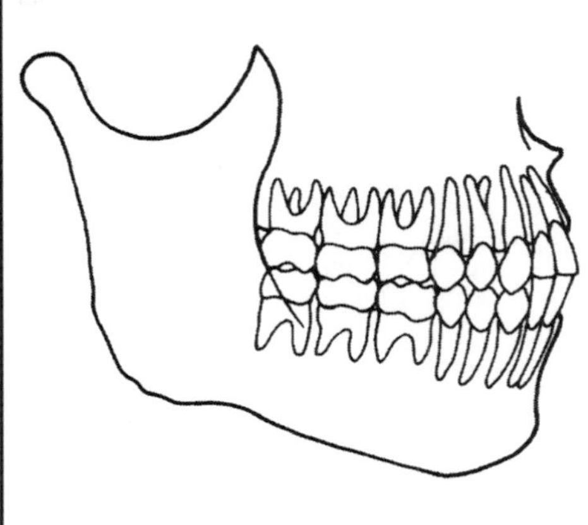

CHAPTER OUTLINE

Introduction to Odontology

Key Term
odontology The study of teeth, their development, structure, function, and degeneration; dentistry.

The teeth are just another part of the skull, but the amount of information in a single tooth makes it a subject unto itself. Use this introductory section to learn the correct terminology for the structures of the oral cavity—the basic vocabulary of dental anatomy and **odontology**. The objective is better communication between the forensic anthropologist and the professional odontologist or dentist.

As with any scientific discipline, the most reliable work is accomplished by the best-trained person. The odontologist—a dentist, orthodontist, periodontist, oral surgeon or oral pathologist—has years of study and experience with the structures of the oral cavity. A well-trained odontologist will see detail in teeth that the untrained eye does not. Thus an odontologist will be more likely to do the best dental analysis.

If the mouth contains restored (filled or crowned) teeth, a practicing dentist from the same region as the victim is usually the best person to provide the analysis. If dental prostheses are present, a dentist can often date the work and sometimes even identify the workmanship.

After extolling the virtues of dental professionals, I insist that the forensic anthropologist learn about teeth. Why not just call a dentist? There are at least three good reasons.

1. There may be no dentist to call. Under such conditions, the anthropologist who knows more about teeth is going to find more, see more, and understand more.
2. The anthropologist who can use clear dental and oral terminology can communicate with dental professionals and make accurate use of dental records.
3. Some dental information is of no practical interest to the dentist. The anthropologist is more likely to become involved in the study of genetic variation due to geographic and ethnic isolation, cultural differences in hygiene and nutrition, ritual dental practices, and diagenetic alterations due to burial conditions.

Table 10.1 Directional Terms for Teeth

Term	Definition	Opposite
apical	toward the root tip	incisal or occlusal
buccal	surface toward the cheek (posterior teeth only)	lingual
cervical	around the base of the crown, the neck of the tooth, or the C-E junction (cementoenamel junction)	none
distal	away from the midline of the mouth	medial
facial	toward the lips or cheek (i.e., both labial and buccal surfaces)	lingual
incisal	toward the cutting edge of the anterior teeth	apical
interproximal	between adjacent teeth	none
labial	surface toward the lips (anterior teeth only)	lingual
lingual	surface toward the tongue (all teeth)	labial or buccal
mesial	toward the midline of the mouth	distal
occlusal	toward the grinding surface of the posterior teeth	apical

An Example of Directional Terms Applied to a Single Tooth

This is tooth #10, the upper left lateral incisor. Each surface is named according to its position in the mouth.

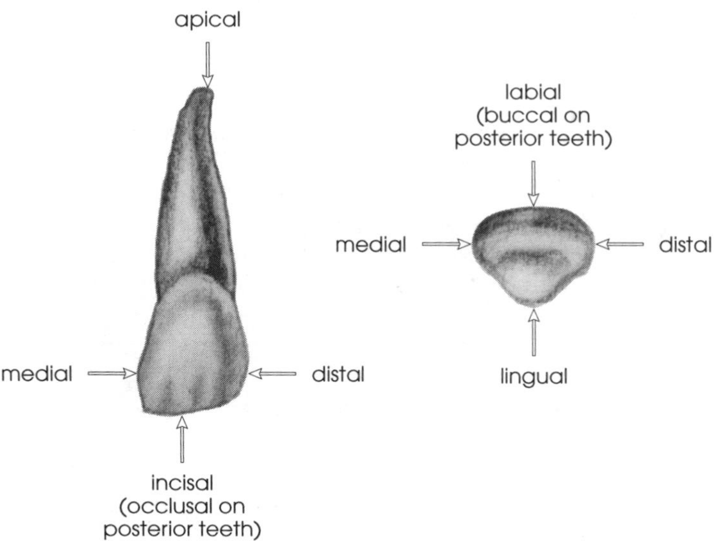

An Example of Anatomical Terms Applied to a Single Tooth

This is tooth #22, the lower left canine, labial surface. The canine has one cusp and one root. It is located between the incisors and the premolars.

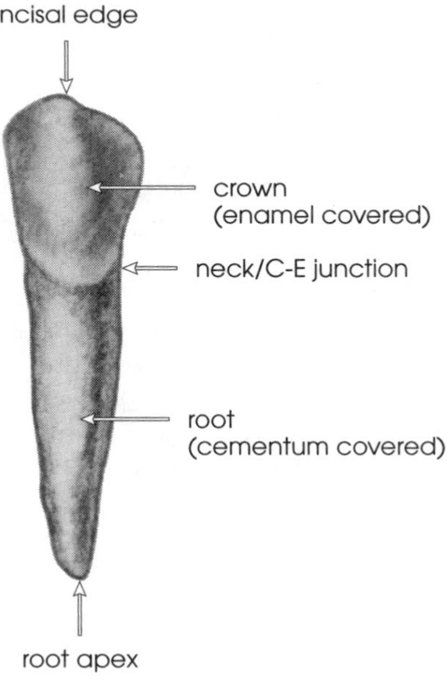

Table 10.2 Odontological Terms for Tooth and Socket

Term	Definition
alveolar process	the ridge of the maxilla or mandible that supports the teeth
alveolus dentalis	the tooth socket in which teeth are attached by a periodontal membrane
attrition	the wearing down of a tooth surface due to abrasion and age
bicuspid	synonym for a premolar
caries, dental	a localized, progressively destructive disease beginning at the external surface with dissolution of inorganic components by organic acids produced by microorganisms.
cementum	a porous layer of calcification covering the tooth root; the cementum provides a site for periodontal fibers to anchor
cervix (neck)	the slightly constricted part of the tooth between the crown and the root
cingulum	the lingual ridge or shelf at the base of upper incisors and canines; in normal occlusion, the lower anterior teeth oppose (touch) on the cingulum of the upper anterior teeth.
crown	the enamel-capped portion of the tooth that normally projects beyond the gum line
crown, clinical	the portion of the tooth visible in the oral cavity
crown, anatomic	the portion of a natural tooth that extends from the cementoenamel junction to the occlusal surface or incisal edge
cusp	a conical elevation arising on the surface of a tooth from an independent calcification center; cusps are named according to their position (e.g., mediolingual cusp, distobuccal cusp)
cusp, Carabelli's	an extra cuspid on the mediolingual surface of upper molars; more common in the Caucasian race
cuspid	synonym for a canine tooth; a small cusp
cusp pattern	the recognizable alignment of cusps on a particular tooth type
dentin, primary	the original dentin of the tooth; ceases to form when the root is completed
dentin	the main mass of the tooth; 20 percent is organic matrix, mostly collagen with some elastin and a small amount of mucopolysaccharide; 80 percent is inorganic, mainly hydroxyapatite with some carbonate, magnesium, and fluoride; structured of parallel tubules.
dentin, secondary	forms after the tooth has erupted, due to age or irritation from caries, abrasion, or injury
dentin, sclerotic	generalized calcification of dentinal tubules as a result of aging
dentin, reparative	calcification of dentinal tubules immediately beneath a carious lesion, abrasion, or injury
dentinal tubule	the tubules extending from the pulp to the dentinoenamel junction; odontoblastic processes extend into the tubules from the pulp surface
enamel	the dense mineralized outer covering of the tooth crown; 99.5 percent inorganic hydroxyapatite with small amounts of carbonate, magnesium, and fluoride, and 0.5 percent organic matrix of glycoprotein and keratin-like protein; structured of oriented rods consisting of rodlets encased in an organic prism sheath.
gingiva	the gum; the dense fibrous tissue covered by mucous membrane that envelops the alveolar processes of the upper and lower jaws and surrounds the necks of the teeth
junction, cementoenamel (C-E junction)	the line around the neck of the tooth at which the cementum and enamel meet
junction, cementodentinal	the surface at which the cementum and dentin meet
junction, dentinoenamel (D-E junction)	the surface at which the dentin and enamel meet
mamelons	small, regular bumps on the incisal edges of recently erupted incisors; indication of youth or (occasionally) lack of occlusion.
periapical	around the tip of the root

Table 10.2, continued

Term	Definition
periodontal disease	inflammation of the tissues surrounding the teeth resulting in resorption of supporting structures and tooth loss
periodontal ligament	the fibrous tissue anchoring the tooth by surrounding the root and attaching to the alveolus
periodontosis	lowering of the attachment level of the periodontal ligament
pits and fissures	the depressed points and lines between cusps
pulp	the soft tissue in the central chamber of the tooth, consisting of connective tissue containing nerves, blood vessels, lymphatics, and, at the periphery, odontoblasts capable of dentinal repair
pulp chamber	the central cavity of the tooth surrounded by dentin and extending from the crown to the root apex
root	the cementum-covered part of the tooth, usually below gum line
root, anatomical	the portion of the root extending from the cementoenamel junction to the apex or root tip
root, clinical	the imbedded portion of the root; the part not visible in the oral cavity
shovel-shaped incisors	central incisors formed with lateral margins bent lingually, resembling the form of a flat shovel or a snow shovel; common within the Mongoloid race (e.g., American Indians)

Tooth Structure

The tissues of the tooth and surrounding structure are pictured below. Note that both hard and soft tissues are essential to healthy teeth.

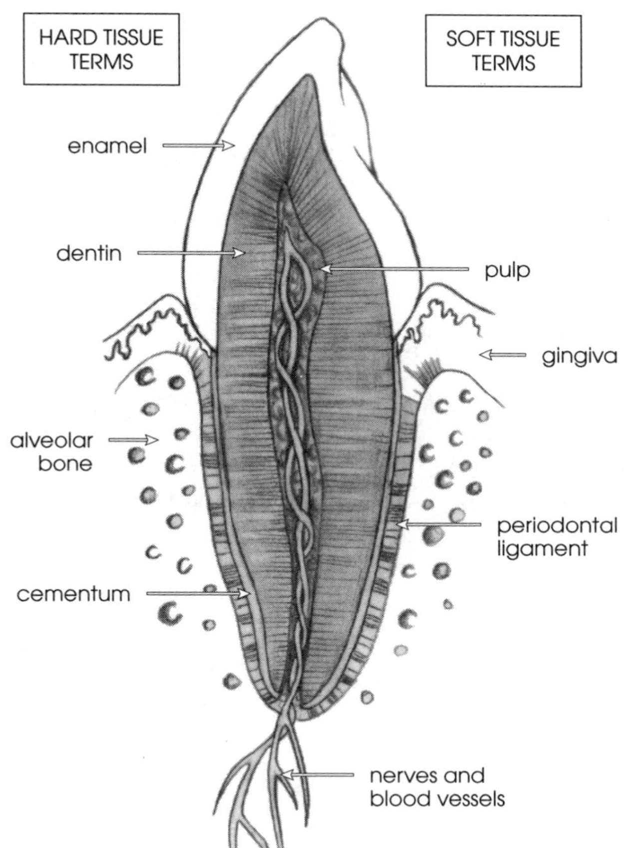

- Enamel is very dense hard tissue.
- Dentin is dense but tubular.
- Alveolar bone is mostly spongy (cancellous) bone.
- Cementum is hard but very porous.
- Pulp is soft connective tissue filled with vessels and nerves.
- Periodontal ligament is soft fibrous connective tissue.
- Gingiva is soft connective tissue covered with mucous membrane.

Tooth Recognition

Key Terms

incisor One of eight anterior single-rooted teeth with straight cutting edges; function: biting.

canine One of four anterior single-rooted teeth with single cusps; syn. cuspid; function: holding and ripping.

premolar One of eight posterior double and single-rooted teeth with two cusps; syn. bicuspid; function: chewing.

molar One of twelve posterior, multi-rooted teeth with more than three cusps; function: chewing.

There are four categories of teeth: **incisors**, **canines**, **premolars**, and **molars**. The child has twenty deciduous teeth (baby teeth), five in each quadrant (two incisors, one canine, and two molars). There are no premolars in the deciduous dentition.

The normal adult has thirty-two permanent teeth, eight in each quadrant (two incisors, one canine, two premolars, and three molars). The premolars form and erupt beneath the deciduous molars. The permanent molars erupt distal to the deciduous molars.

There are many variations on the ideal dental model. This is due to both genetic heritage and the dynamic nature of the oral cavity. It is best to begin by studying "normal." It will then be easier to recognize individual anomalies and population variation in more advanced studies.

In the following sections, each permanent tooth is described briefly. For a more complete description, I recommend *Concise Dental Anatomy and Morphology* (Fuller and Denehy 1977).

Incisors

Incisors are the biting teeth in the anterior part of the mouth. They have single, relatively straight incisal edges and single roots. When incisors first erupt into the oral cavity, the incisal edge tends to be scalloped. The scallops or "bumps" are called mamelons.

Dentists often refer to incisors as "centrals" and "laterals." Centrals are medial; laterals are distal. The central incisors are sometimes abbreviated, I_1 and the lateral incisors, I_2. The upper central has the greatest length and breadth of all the incisors; the four lower incisors are the most narrow of the incisors.

An Incisor Tooth

Canines

Canines are the pointed teeth on either side of the incisors. They are the longest four teeth in the mouth. Canines have one cusp and one root. The canine is sometimes abbreviated with the letter C. Dentists may refer to canines as "cuspids," but a common name in English is "eye tooth."

A Canine Tooth

Premolars

Premolars are the two teeth distal to the canine. They have two cusps and one or two roots. Premolars are abbreviated P_1 and P_2. Dentists may call premolars "bicuspids." Lower premolars are rounded in cross section whereas upper premolars tend to be mesiodistally compressed. The buccal cusp is larger on both upper and lower premolars, but the cusp size difference is greater on the lower premolars. The difference is so pronounced on the lower premolar that it is commonly mistaken by students for a canine. The main cusp of the lower premolar occludes between the two cusps of the upper premolar.

A Premolar Tooth

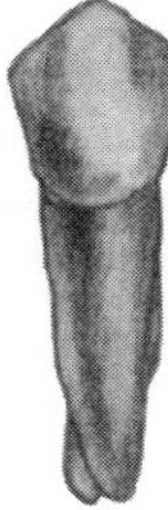

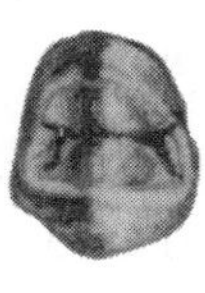

Molars

Molars are the three teeth distal to the premolars. They are the chewing or grinding teeth. Molars have multiple cusps and multiple roots. They vary more than any of the other teeth in size and shape. In biology, the molars are abbreviated as M_1, M_2, and M_3.

Dentists call molars the "first molar, second molar, and third molar." In common language, they are often referred to by the general time of eruption—the 6-year molar, 12-year molar, and 18-year molar. The third molar is more commonly called the "wisdom tooth" because it erupts after puberty.

Upper molars usually have three roots; lower molars usually have two roots. The cusp patterns are distinctive. The first molars usually have the largest occlusal area, whereas the third molars tend to be reduced in size, often with fewer roots or fused roots.

The third molars are more variable in form than the first and second molars, therefore they can be more difficult to recognize. Learn the first and second molars first.

A Molar Tooth

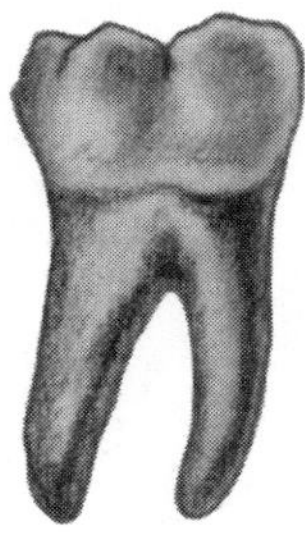

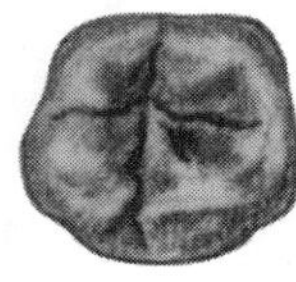

Tips for Recognizing Similar Teeth

Distinguishing Maxillary Incisors from Mandibular Incisors

Study the two incisors in the illustration below. The maxillary incisor is wider; the mandibular incisor is narrower. The root of the mandibular incisor is very narrow. The incisal edge of the maxillary incisor is more likely to be slanted from a longer mesial corner to a shorter distal corner. The incisal edge of the mandibular incisor is more likely to be horizontal. In other words, the incisal corners of the mandibular incisor will be nearer to 90 degree angles whereas the incisal corners of the maxillary incisor will be mesially acute and distally obtuse.

A cingulum is well-defined on the maxillary incisor, but not on the mandibular incisor. (This is also true of the canine. A cingulum is present on the maxillary canine, but not on the mandibular canine.)

Two Incisors, Labial and Incisal Surfaces

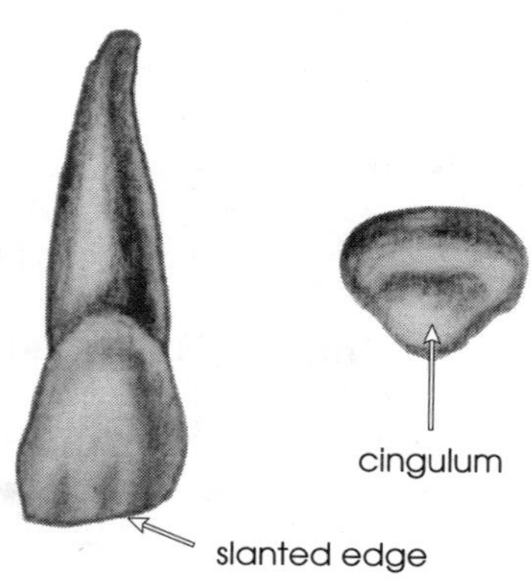

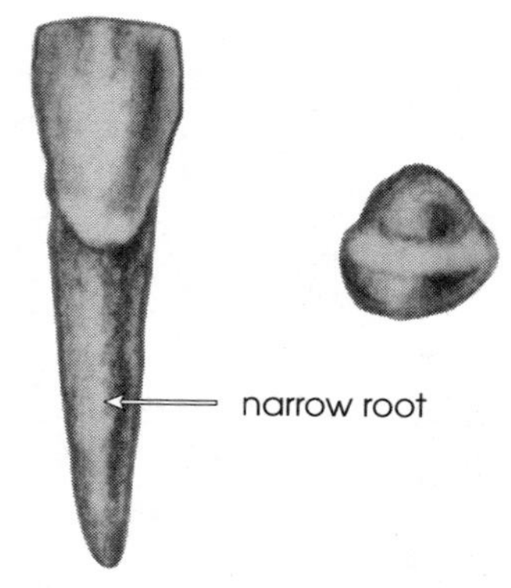

mandibular lateral
incisor #23

Distinguishing Maxillary Premolars from Mandibular Premolars

Examine the two premolars in the illustration below. On both premolars the buccal cusps are larger than the lingual cusps. The difference, however, is much greater between the size of the two cusps on the mandibular premolar than on the maxillary premolar.

The cross sectional shape is also different. The maxillary premolar is mesiodistally compressed, whereas the mandibular premolar is rounded.

The maxillary first premolar usually has two well-defined roots, whereas the maxillary second and the mandibular premolars usually have a single root.

The first maxillary premolar is the same size or slightly larger than the second maxillary premolar. The first mandibular premolar is almost always smaller than the second mandibular premolar.

A Premolar Comparison

right maxillary first premolar

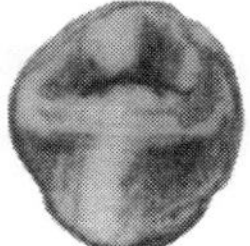

right mandibular first premolar

Distinguishing Maxillary Molars from Mandibular Molars

Take a good look at the two molars in the illustration below. Notice that the cusps and grooves form a completely different pattern. The cusps of the maxillary molar are not in a symmetrical relationship, whereas the cusps of the mandibular molar are symmetrical. The mesiolingual cusp predominates on the maxillary molar, whereas no single cusp predominates on the mandibular molar. The distolingual cusp of the maxillary molars is separated from the other three by the diagonal distolingual groove. The cusps of the mandibular molar are squared-off and the grooves tend to form a plus sign.

A Molar Comparison

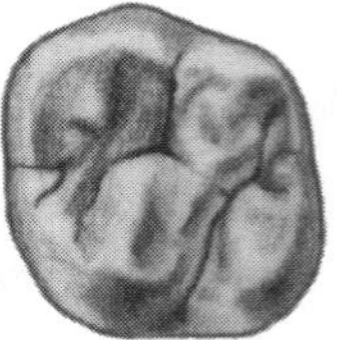

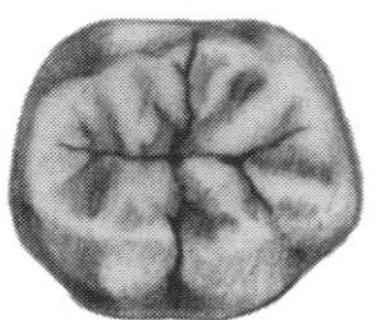

Recognizing Racial Traits

Two dental traits stand out as easily recognized characteristics of major racial groups. Maxillary incisors tend to be "shovel-shaped" among groups derived from Mongoloid ancestry. This includes Asians and American Indians. The lateral edges of the incisor fold lingually to form a rough version of a straight-edged shovel (see illustration below).

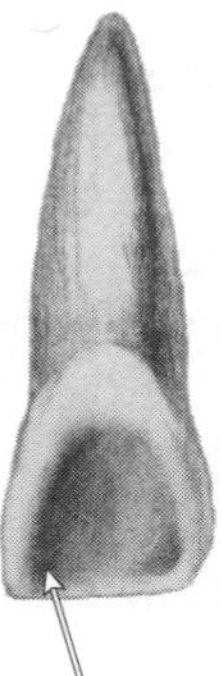

shovel-shaped central incisor (#8, lingual view)

An extra cusp occasionally appears on the mesiolingual surface of the maxillary first molar. This is called "Carabelli's cusp" (see illustration below). It can be found in a range of sizes from a small "leaflet" to a cusp as large as any of the other four cusps. Carabelli's cusp is found most frequently in European-derived populations (i.e., Caucasians or whites).

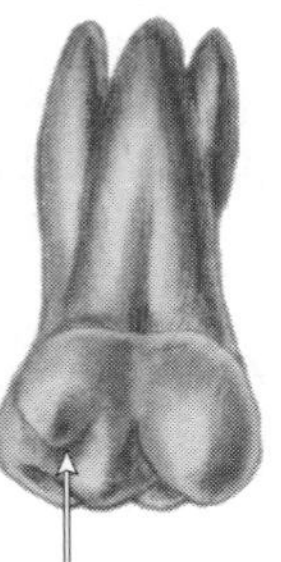

Carabelli's cusp on maxillary molar (#3, lingual view)

The Universal Numbering System

Many parts of the skeleton can be seen or felt by the observer within his own body. In other words, bones from the left side are easily pictured within the left side of the observer's body.

The mouth is different. Most people look at their own mouth in a mirror. Left and right are immediately confused. Therefore, in order to study the mouth and teeth, I highly recommend that the observer utilize the methods of a dental professional. Always visualize mouth and teeth of another person. This way, the observer's right is always left, and the observer's left is always right.

The Universal Numbering System is easy to understand, but it requires a little time and concentration before each tooth can be visualized by number. First look at the open mouth as if it were a clock. Begin the count at 9:00 and always move clockwise.

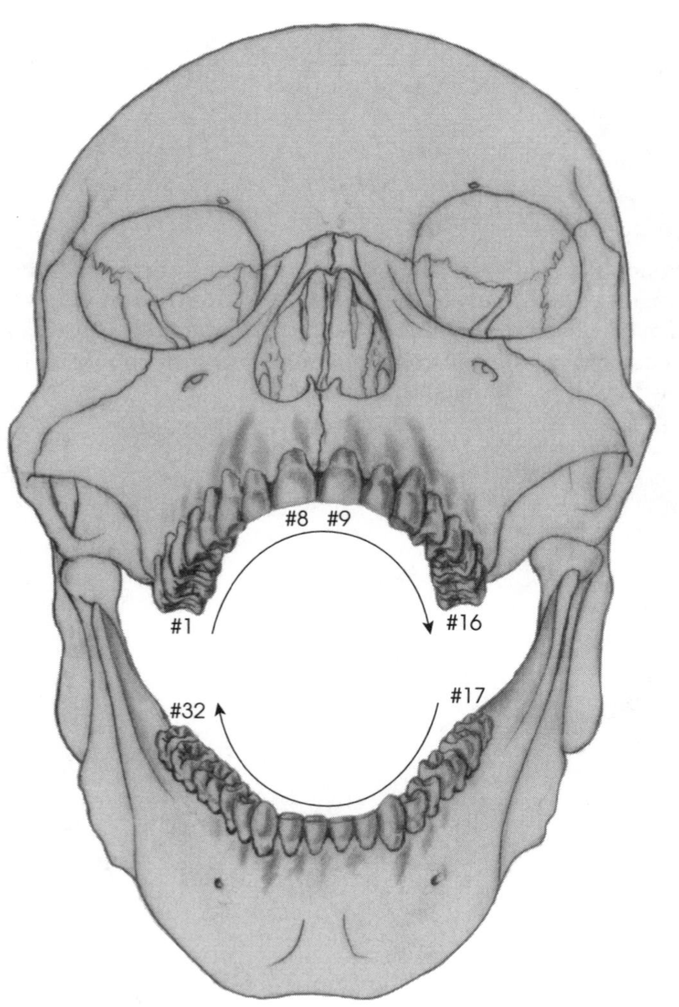

Open-Mouth View of the Universal Numbering System

9:00 The count begins with a mid-morning yawn to open the mouth wide enough to view the upper right 3rd molar. This is tooth #1.

12:00 Noon is between the two upper central incisors, tooth #8 and tooth #9.

3:00 The count shifts from the maxillary arch to the mandibular arch in the afternoon. The last tooth in the maxilla is #16, the upper left 3rd molar. The first in the mandible is the lower left 3rd molar, #17.

6:00 The midpoint of the mandibular arch is between the two lower central incisors, #24 and #25.

9:00 The lower right 3rd molar is #32. It occludes with #1.

Complete Permanent Dentition

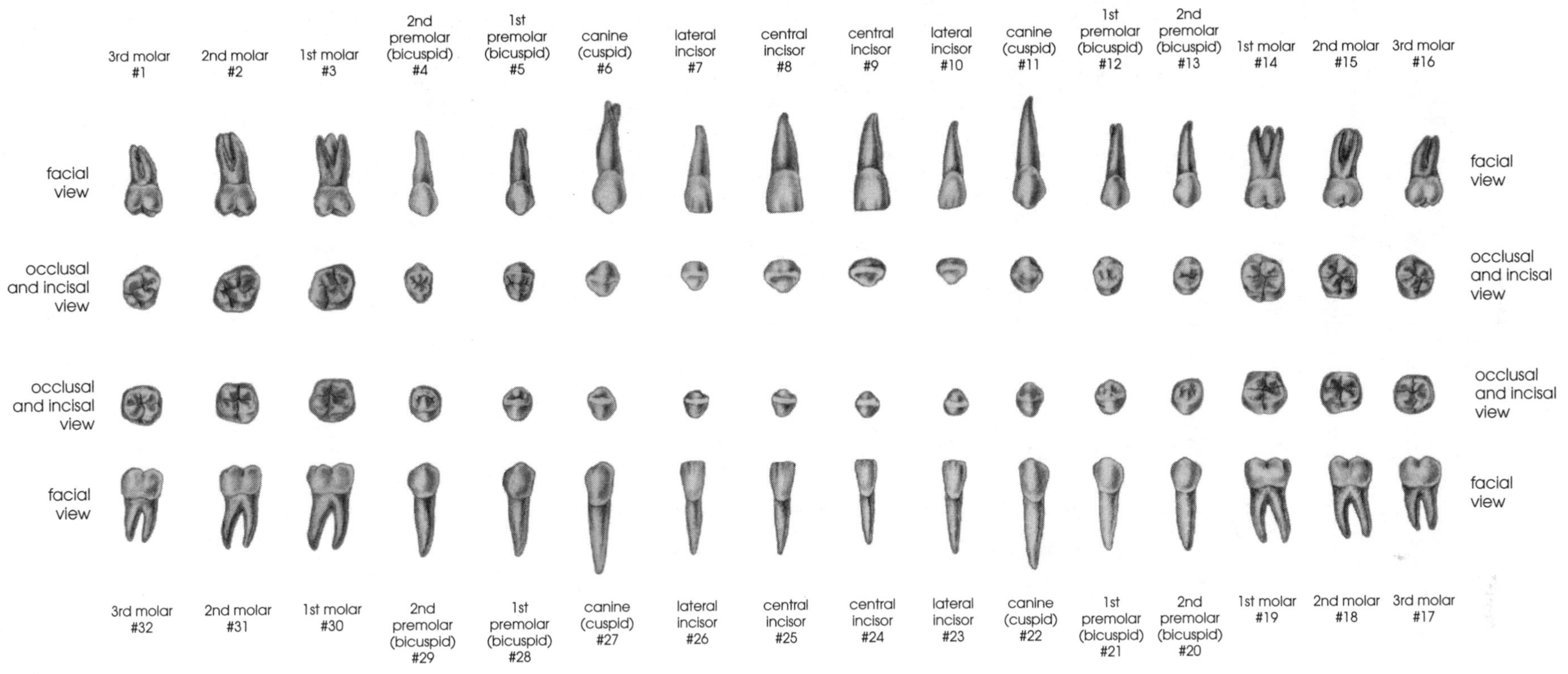

3rd molar #1
2nd molar #2
1st molar #3
2nd premolar (bicuspid) #4
1st premolar (bicuspid) #5
canine (cuspid) #6
lateral incisor #7
central incisor #8
central incisor #9
lateral incisor #10
canine (cuspid) #11
1st premolar (bicuspid) #12
2nd premolar (bicuspid) #13
1st molar #14
2nd molar #15
3rd molar #16
facial view
occlusal and incisal view
occlusal and incisal view
facial view
facial view
occlusal and incisal view
occlusal and incisal view
facial view
3rd molar #32
2nd molar #31
1st molar #30
2nd premolar (bicuspid) #29
1st premolar (bicuspid) #28
canine (cuspid) #27
lateral incisor #26
central incisor #25
central incisor #24
lateral incisor #23
canine (cuspid) #22
1st premolar (bicuspid) #21
2nd premolar (bicuspid) #20
1st molar #19
2nd molar #18
3rd molar #17

Dental Aging

Age estimation from teeth has been employed by numerous researchers seeking better and more convenient ways to determine age from human remains. Just as with bone, the formative years provide better age estimates than the degenerative years. The sequence of tooth formation and eruption is well documented. Formation is influenced by nutrition and health care, as well as by inheritance. But dental formation is less dependent on behavioral factors than are dental aging and degeneration.

Formative Changes in Teeth

Tooth formation and eruption are very useful for determining the age of infants, children, and young adults. There are, of course, individual and population differences. The observer needs to allow for normal variation and note individual anomalies. Direct observation and dental radiographs should be sufficient tools.

Each of the following steps occurs, in sequence, in the formation of teeth. All can be seen on dental radiographs.

- Commencement of crown development. (The cusps form first.)
- Completion of crown development. (The enamel is complete.)
- Commencement of root development. (The C-E junction is visible.)
- Bifurcation of the root in multi-rooted teeth. (The floor of the pulp chamber is visible in molar teeth.)
- Eruption into the oral cavity. (The crown is no longer completely enclosed in alveolar bone.)
- Attainment of occlusion. (The cusps are level with the occlusal plane.)
- Closure of the root tip. (The outer walls of the tooth root curve toward each other and the sharp terminal edges thicken.)

Infant and Toddler—Deciduous Dentition

The illustrations on this page and pages 124–125 are adapted from Ubelaker 1978, Figure 62. Deciduous teeth are shaded, adult teeth are white.

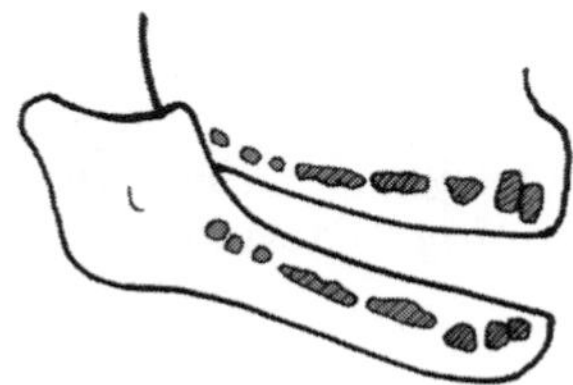

Birth ± 2 Months

No teeth have erupted, but the maxilla and mandible are packed with growing teeth.

- Crowns of the deciduous incisors are near completion.
- All other deciduous teeth are present.
- The crown of the first permanent molar is beginning to develop.

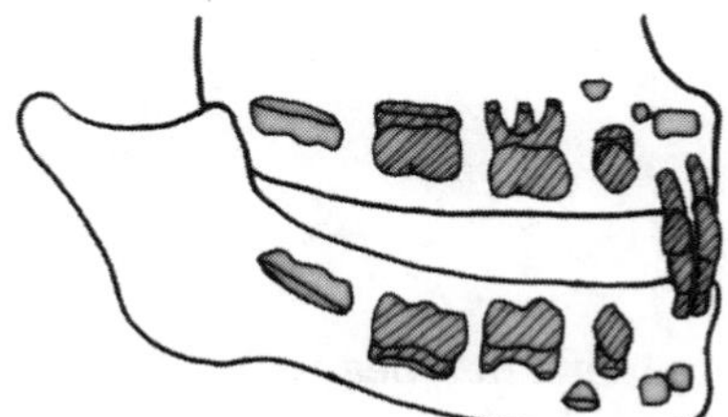

1 Year ±4 Months

The deciduous incisors have erupted.

- The first deciduous molar is ready to erupt.
- Crowns of the first permanent molar, incisors, and canine are beginning to develop.

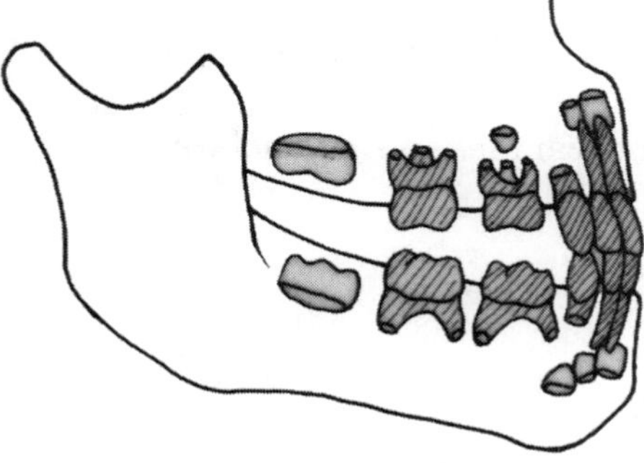

2 Years ± 8 Months

The deciduous dentition is completely erupted, but the roots are incomplete.

- The crown of the first permanent molar is near completion.
- The crown of the upper first permanent premolar has begun to develop.

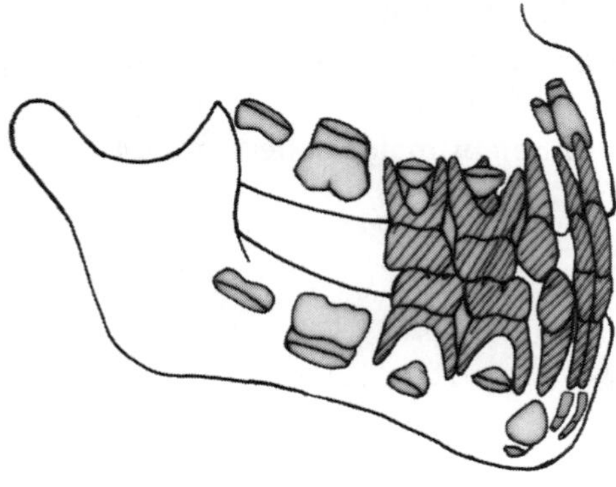

4 Years ± 12 Months

The deciduous dentition is complete including root tips.

- The crown of the second permanent molar is beginning to develop.
- All of the permanent teeth except the third molar are now growing in the developing mandible.

Child—Mixed Dentition

The deciduous dentition is shaded. The adult dentition is white.

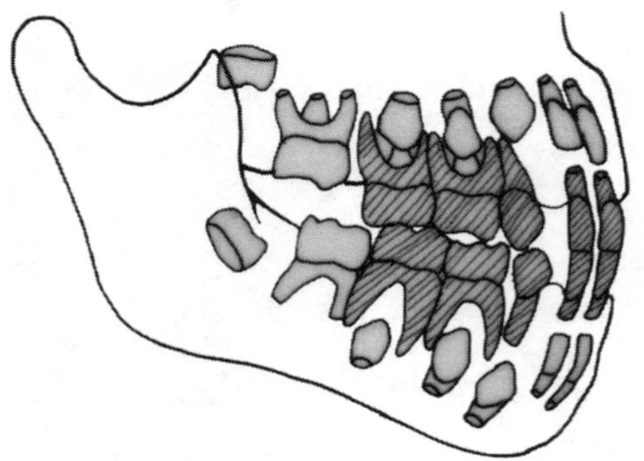

6 years ± 24 months

- The first permanent molar is erupting.
- The permanent incisors are ready to erupt.
- The second permanent molar is beginning to develop.

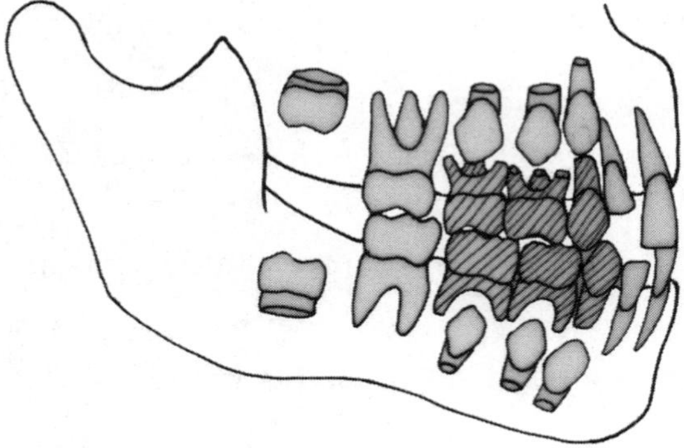

8 years ± 24 months

- Exfoliation of deciduous teeth has begun.
- Permanent incisors have erupted.
- The root tips of the first permanent molar are complete.
- The root of the second permanent molar is developing.
- The roots of the canine and premolars are developing.

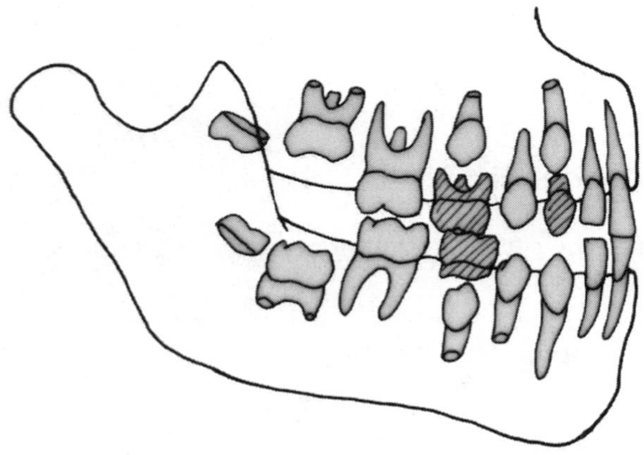

10 years ± 30 months

- Exfoliation and replacement is near completion. Only the upper canine and second deciduous molars remain.
- The root bifurcation of the second permanent molar is complete.
- The third permanent molar is beginning to develop.

TEENAGER AND ADULT—PERMANENT DENTITION

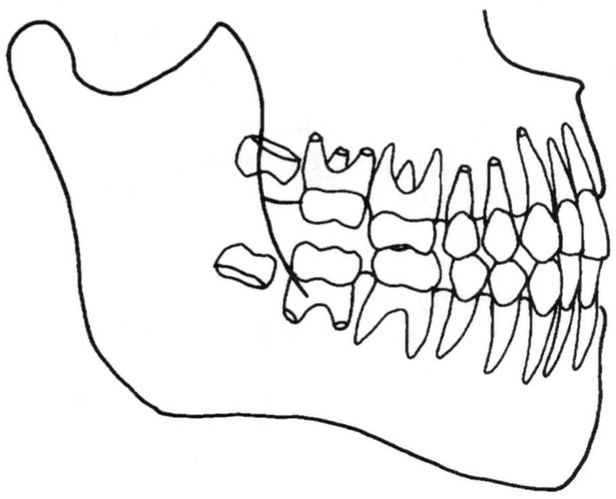

12 YEARS ± 30 MONTHS.

- No deciduous teeth remain.
- The second permanent molar has erupted.
- Many of the root tips are incomplete.
- The crown of the third molar is developing.

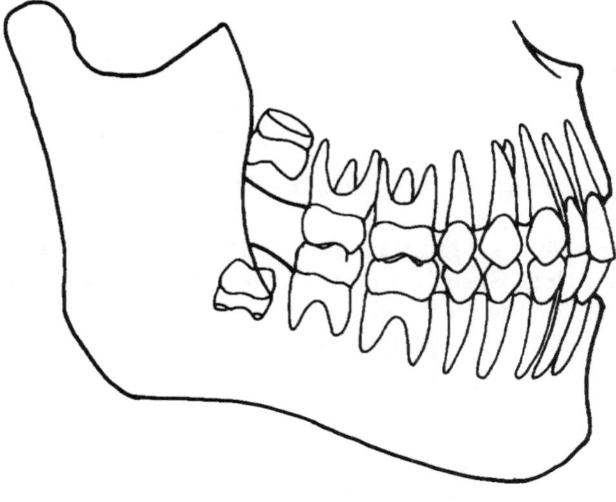

15 YEARS ± 30 MONTHS.

- The root tips of the erupted teeth are all complete.
- The root of the third molar is developing.

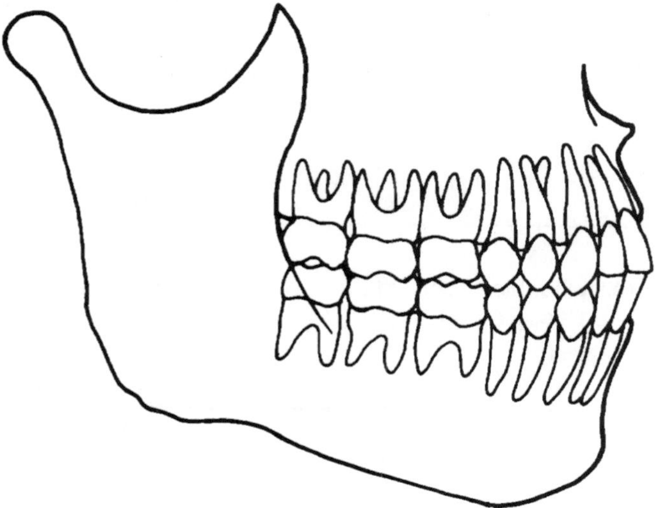

21 YEARS OR MORE—COMPLETE PERMANENT DENTITION

- All thirty-two teeth have erupted.
- All have reached occlusion.
- All root tips are fully formed.

Degenerative Changes in Teeth

Degenerative changes are much more complicated than formative changes. As with the rest of the body, degenerative changes are influenced by diet, nutrition, and general health. In the present world of processed food and long lifetimes, teeth are also influenced by individual behavior and professional dental care.

Some changes can be seen on dental radiographs, but ground sagittal sections of undecalcified teeth are recommended for viewing age-related changes. Each of the following changes occurs in the degeneration or aging of teeth.

- Attrition—loss of tooth crown due to abrasion
- Secondary dentin—deposition of minerals within the pulp chamber
- Periodontosis—apical migration of the periodontal attachment level
- Root transparency—sclerosis of the root dentin beginning with the apex
- Cementum deposition—thickening of the cementum layer
- Root resorption—resorption and flattening of the apex

Multifactorial analysis of age-related changes has produced the best age estimates to date. Gustafson first suggested this approach in 1950. It has been tested and modified several times since (Burns and Maples 1976; Maples 1978; Maples and Rice 1979). The method would probably be in more general use if the equipment were more easily obtained and the techniques were more accessible.

Age determination from teeth is highly recommended for commingled remains from the same population. Even if the exact age is not determined due to lack of a control sample for the particular population, it is still possible to separate the teeth into progressive age groups. This can aid in the process of identification through other sources.

Table 10.3 Equipment and Supplies for Producing Thin Sections of Teeth

Equipment
A Buehler Isomet Low-Speed Saw.
A microscope capable of 100x or near-100x magnification, with transmitted light (polarized light is also useful).
A table or counter with good lighting and water supply.
A fume hood is highly recommended for plastic embedding.
Supplies
Glass slides—either petrographic or histological.
A castable (cold) mounting compound such as Castolite by Buehler. It should be liquid, transparent, and clear. It should withstand temperatures of at least 100 degrees F (38°C).
Embedding cups. (Rubber cups for closing pipe ends work well.)
Mounting medium for glass slides (e.g., Permount).

Table 10.4 Scoring Information for Age-Related Data from Teeth

Score	Stage 0	Stage 1	Stage 2	Stage 3
(A) crown attrition	no attrition	attrition into enamel only	attrition into dentin	attrition into original pulp chamber
(S) secondary dentin	no secondary dentin	secondary dentin visible	secondary dentin filling 1/3 of the pulp chamber	secondary dentin filling most of the pulp chamber
(P) periodontosis	periodontal attachment at C-E junction	reduced periodontal attachment	periodontal attachment at the upper 1/3 of root	periodontal attachment at the lower 2/3 of the root
(T) root transparency	no transparency	beginning transparency	transparency of the apical 1/3 of the root	transparency of the apical 2/3 or more of the root
(C) cementum	thin, even cementum	increasing cementum	thick layer of cementum	heavy layer of cementum
(R) root resorption	no resorption and open apex	beginning resorption and closed apex	flattening of root apex, affecting only cementum	flattening of root apex, affecting both cementum and dentin

Source: Adapted from Gustafson, 1966.

Age Changes in Adult Teeth

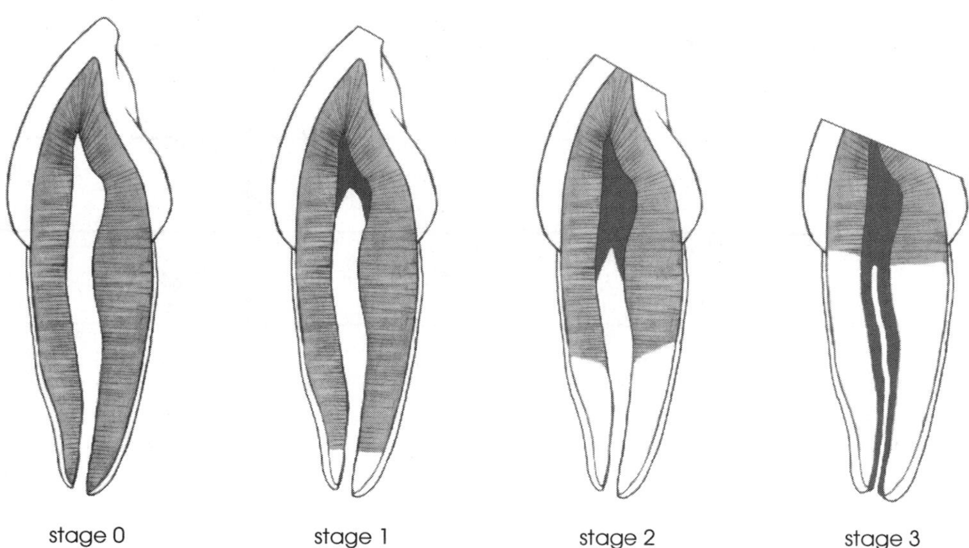

Table 10.5 Regression Formulae for Determination of Age from Teeth

Source	Position	Formula	Se*
Gustafson '50, '66	all	age = 11+4.56 (**A+P+S+C+R+T**)	±10.9
Maples '78	1	age = 3.89S+14.23T+15.28	±9.1
	2	age = 6.51**S**+12.55**T**+25.16	±9.6
	3	age = 18.67**S**+11.72**T**+21.94	±11.0
	4	age = 2.92**S**+15.25**T**+19.65	±12.2
	5	age = 4.79**S**+15.53**T**+17.99	±7.4
	6	age = 11.28**S**+ 5.32**T**+10.86	±11.1
	7	age = 6.99**S**+10.86**T**+19.31	±6.8
	8	age = 4.71**S**+12.30**T**+24.57	±12.0

Note: *se = standard error of the estimate

STEPS FOR AGE ESTIMATION FROM TEETH

1. Cut serial sections from the center of each tooth using a low-speed diamond sectioning saw. The sections should be thin enough to allow transmitted light (100 to 300 microns). It should be possible to locate and examine the microstructural features listed in Table 10.6.
2. Mount the tooth sections on glass slides for stability and maintenance.
3. Put an identification number on each glass slide.
4. Evaluate each of the age-related factors according to Table 10.6.
5. Apply the scores to the formulae and compare results with any and all other information available.

Table 10.6 Example of a Table for Tooth Section Data

Tooth #	A	S	P	T	C	R

Dentistry Terms

The terms listed in Table 10.7 are just a few of the terms used in dentistry. They can help to develop more effective communication between the anthropologist and the odontologist.

Table 10.7 Dentistry Terms

Term	Definition
amalgam	a restoration made of a metal in mercury solution (usually 67% Ag, 27% Sn, 5% Cu, and 1% Zn) One part alloy and 2 parts mercury are mixed and packed into the cleaned and sealed dental cavity. It hardens in about 24 hours.
bridge	a fixed or removable replacement for missing teeth, attached to natural teeth by wires or crowns
composite	a plastic resin restoration that mimics the appearance of enamel
crown	a permanent replacement for a natural crown, made of porcelain on metal, or metal alone (gold or other stable metal)
dental prosthesis	fixed or removable replacement of one or more teeth and/or associated oral structures; denture, bridgework, or oral appliance
denture	a complete or full d. replaces all of the natural dentition of the maxilla or mandible; a partial d. replaces one or more teeth and is retained by natural teeth at one or both ends
edentulous	toothless; a mouth without teeth
inlay	a prefabricated restoration (usually gold or porcelain) sealed in the cavity with cement
pulpectomy	removal of the entire pulp, including the root; commonly known as a "root canal"; the tooth is no longer living
radiograph, bite-wing	a film of posterior teeth produced by exposure of laterally-oriented intraoral film. The x-ray beam is angled between the teeth. The crowns are the main focus of the films.
radiograph, apical	a film produced by exposure of vertically-oriented intraoral film. The x-ray beam is angled from above maxillary teeth or below mandibular teeth to capture the complete tooth, including the apex.
radiograph, Panorex	a film of the entire oral cavity produced by immobilizing the head and moving the x-ray beam behind the head while film moves in synchronization in front of the face
restoration	any inlay, crown, bridge, partial denture, or complete denture that restores or replaces lost tooth structure, teeth, or oral tissues

Oral Disease

Key Term

pathogen Any microorganism or other substance causing disease.

As the major entrance to the interior of the body, the mouth admits many uninvited guests, otherwise known as **pathogens**. Even the healthiest of bodies usually shows some evidence of oral or dental disease. Oral diseases are extensive enough to fill entire books and require years of study. Here, however, the focus is only on the most common diseases that leave their mark in the oral tissues most likely to be found in skeletonized remains. Each of the following conditions should be reported. They all provide clues about the life history of the individual.

Dental Caries

The most common chronic disease in the modern world is dental caries or "cavities." It is caused by microbial invasion of the teeth. The organisms first demineralize the inorganic substance of the teeth, then destroy the organic substance. If not arrested, the sensitive nerve tissue at the center of the tooth is exposed and the entire tooth is consumed. The pulp chamber and the root provide free and easy access to the alveolar bone that supports the tooth, and soon the bone itself is also invaded and destroyed. Once inside the bone, the infection can proceed to the sinus cavities and even the brain. The pain is so great, however, that few people allow the disease to advance so far before finding a way to extract the tooth.

Dental caries is most common among modern populations with high carbohydrate diets (e.g., corn agriculturalists). The occurrence of caries is greatest in groups that have both high carbohydrate diets *and* drinking water with low mineral content. Modern societies counter this problem by adding stannous fluoride (or stannous hexafluoroziconate) to drinking water and toothpaste. Fluorine reduces the incidence of caries by making the tooth enamel harder and less penetrable.

Key Term

abscess A circumscribed collection of pus, the result of acute or chronic localized infection; a cavity formed by liquefactive necrosis within solid tissue.

Apical Abscess

An apical **abscess** is the result of microbial invasion of the tooth root. The abscess forms at the apex of the root and a cavity develops in the bone. The shape of the cavity is rounded and smooth-walled. This is a result of the fight to wall off the infection. The abscess will often drain by perforating the labial or buccal bony plate. (See illustration of periodontal disease on page 131.)

Calculus Accumulation

Calculus or "dental tartar" is the hard substance that forms around the neck of the tooth—in the area of the C-E junction. It is dental plaque that has undergone mineralization. In some individuals, dental calculus accumulates to the extent that it forms a "bridge" between teeth. In extreme cases, a tooth may be held in place only because it is attached to adjacent teeth by the calculus bridge. Occasionally, a calculus "collar" will grow into a calculus "crown," literally covering the entire tooth.

Periodontal Disease

Periodontal tissues support and anchor the tooth. Any disease in the periodontal tissues endangers the tooth also. Usually periodontal disease begins with simple plaque, followed by calculus formation. Calculus is rough and porous. It harbors bacteria easily. The result is irritation and inflammation of the surrounding gingival tissues.

Underlying alveolar bone is affected by the inflammation in the gingiva and the bone resorbs and remodels. The result is pocket formation around the teeth, more bacteria, more plaque, more calculus, more inflammation, and more bony resorption.

Eventually, the tooth root is exposed within the oral cavity and the tooth becomes unstable. Finally, the tooth has insufficient bone for support and it simply falls out. By this time, the alveolar bone is highly irregular in appearance and very little tooth socket is visible. See the illustrations of advanced periodontal disease below. Note the extreme alveolar bone loss. The existing bone is very porous and the tooth roots are exposed. During life, the remaining teeth were loose and near **exfoliation**. Apical abscesses had perforated both the labial and palatal bone. This is good evidence that the deceased individual was experiencing pain and halitosis (bad breath).

Key Term

exfoliation (of teeth) Loss of deciduous teeth after physiological resorption of root structure.

Evidence of Advanced Periodontal Disease in the Maxilla, Lateral View

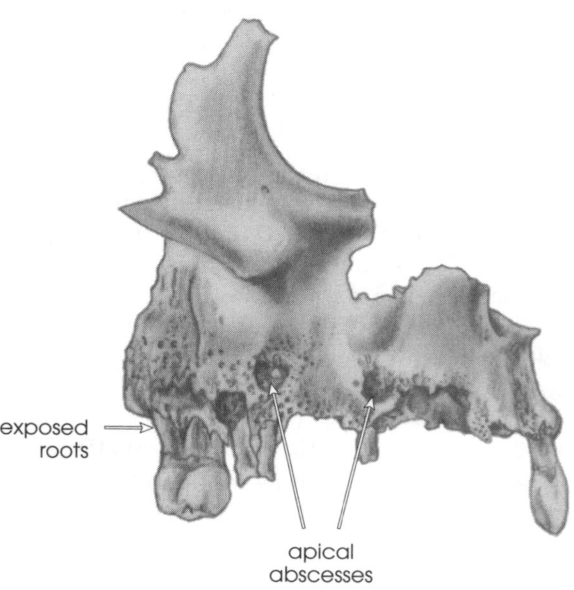

Evidence of Advanced Periodontal Disease in the Maxilla, Palatal View

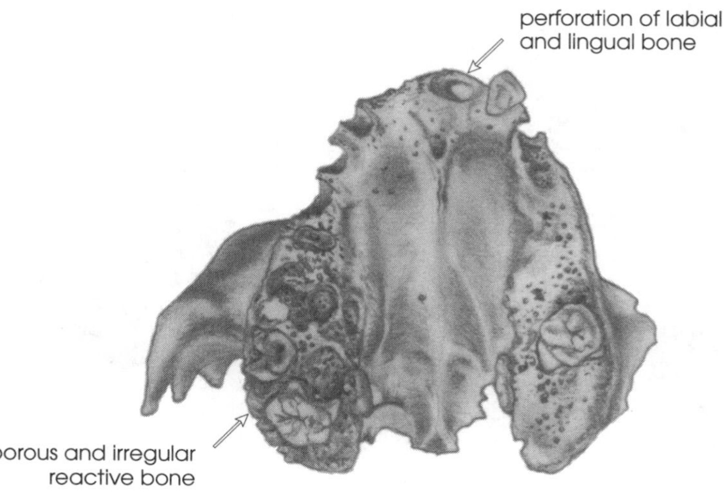

Dental Staining

Staining is not a disease, but it is mentioned here because it is one of the dental observations that may help in the identification of the remains. There are many reasons for staining. In fact, the staining may result from the burial conditions rather than life habits. If so, other parts of the skeleton, particularly the skull, should be generally consistent in color with the teeth.

If the staining occurred during life, it may be a trait common to all of the people living within a specific area or it may be characteristic of this one individual. As always, it is good to establish what is normal for a population before trying to recognize individual variation. Dental staining may be the result of something as simple as iron oxide in the local drinking water. It may also be caused by coffee or tea that is drunk by the majority of adults within the population. In such cases, unstained teeth would be of more interest than stained teeth.

Tobacco is an effective staining agent. If the deceased was a tobacco user, the pattern of staining may provide information about the type and extent of tobacco use. A cigarette smoker will have an overall staining that intensifies on the lingual surfaces. A person who uses chewing tobacco will have more stain in the place where the "wad" is habitually placed, typically the buccal surface of only one side.

The Effects of Long-Term Tooth Loss

Compare the two skulls in the illustrations below. They are approximately the same size and of the same sex and race. The lower halves of the faces are, however, very different. When teeth are extracted, the alveolar bone that supports the teeth is no longer under tension from the periodontal fibers. The only force becomes compression as a person "gums" their food. Therefore, the alveolar ridge resorbs. The maxilla and the mandible are shortened and the facial appearance changes drastically.

Normal European Male Skull with Teeth

The alveolar ridge fully supports the teeth. (Only the third molars are missing.)

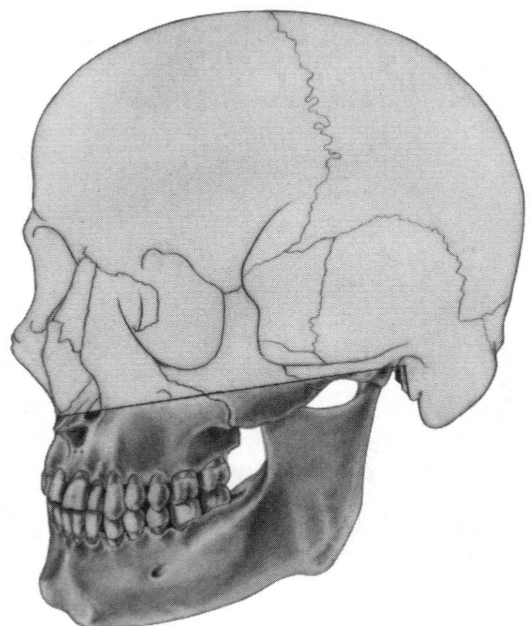

Normal European Male Skull without Teeth

The teeth were lost years before death. The maxilla and mandible remodeled to exclude the alveolar ridge.

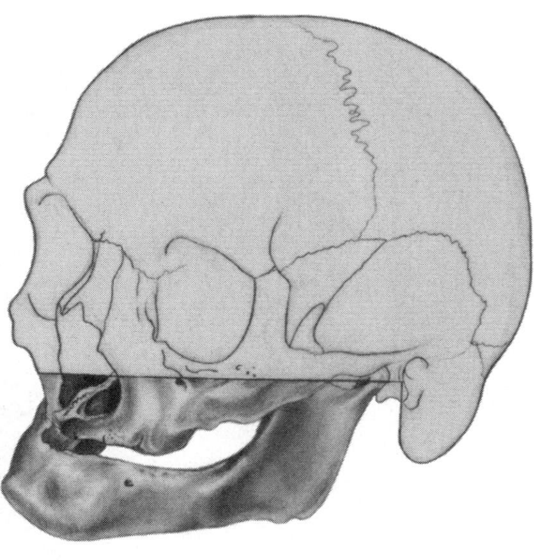

Dental Inventory Form

The chart shown with Table 10.8 is an example of a dental record chart. It is for general use in recording the dental condition of the victim. Use it to mark the location of the condition and provide a detailed description.

Devise a system of notation for each of the following conditions or use the abbreviations offered here. Always include a key with the chart.

Table 10.8 Dental Inventory

Condition	Abbreviation	Condition	Abbreviation
antemortem tooth loss	X-a	attrition level into the enamel, dentin, or secondary dentin	L-e, L-d, L-sd
postmortem tooth loss	X-p	exposed root level or extent of periodontal disease	P-0, P-1, P-2
fracture	F	apical abscess—location and perforation site	A
carious lesion	C	restorations—amalgam, gold, composite, crown, etc.	R

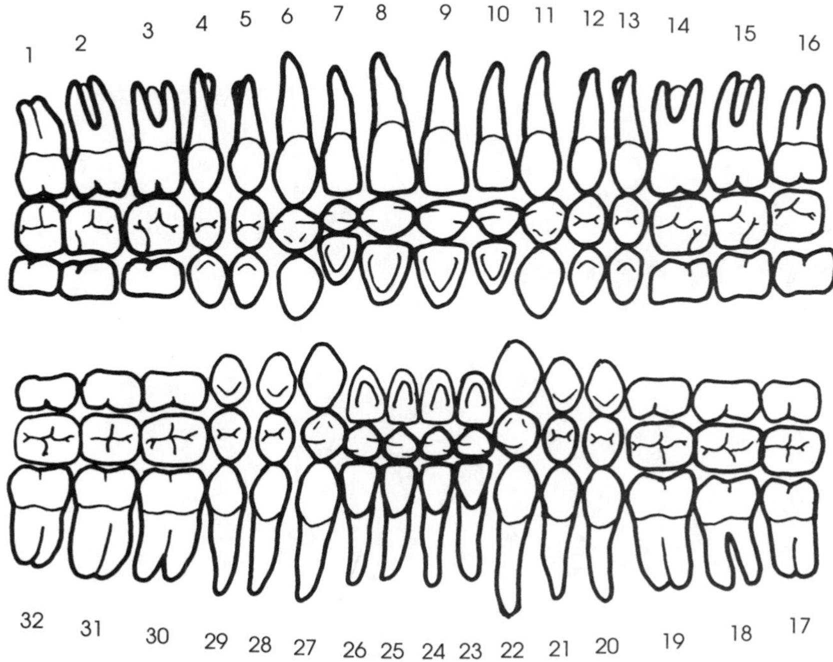

PART II

FORENSIC SCIENCE INTERFACE

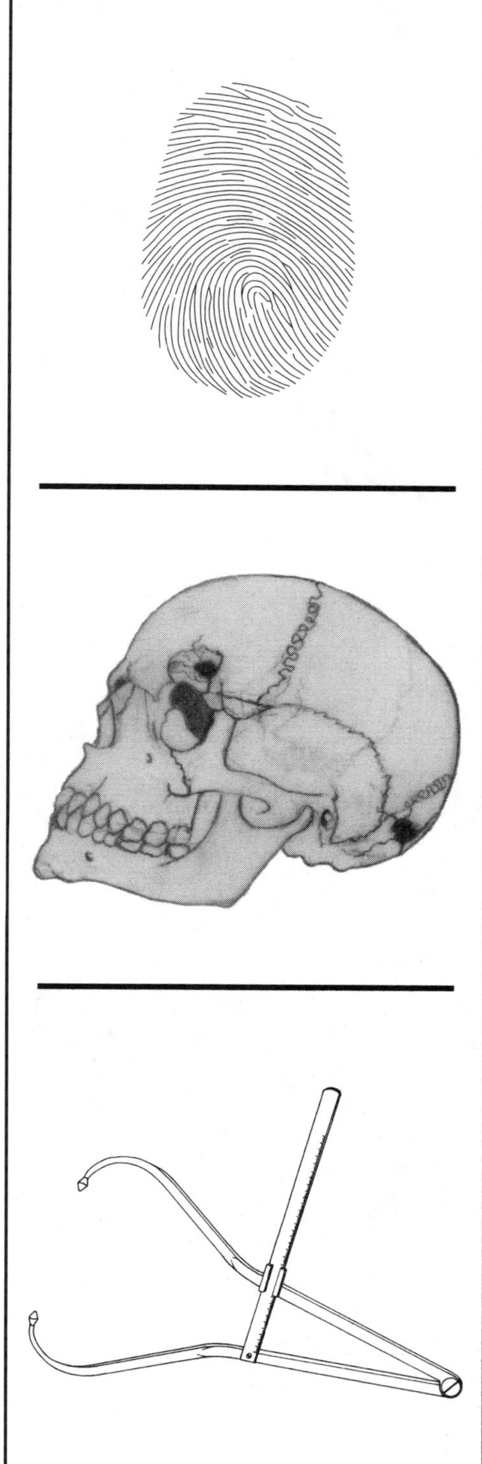

PART OUTLINE

CHAPTER 11

INTRODUCTION TO THE FORENSIC SCIENCES

CHAPTER OUTLINE

Physical Evidence
- What Is Evidence?
- What Evidence Is Used in a Court of Law?
- How Is Evidence Used?
- Challenges in the Use of Physical Evidence

Death Investigation Specialists
- Ballistic Specialists
- Crime Scene Investigators
- Criminalists
- Drug Analysts
- Fingerprint Specialists
- Forensic Anthropologists
- Forensic Pathologists
- Forensic Psychiatrists
- Questioned Document Examiners
- Serologists
- Toxicologists

Which Specialist—Forensic Pathologist, Forensic Anthropologist, or Crime Scene Investigator?
- No Visual Identification Possible
- Legal Consequence Unlikely

Physical Evidence

> **Key Term**
>
> **physical evidence** Physical data used to base judgment or establish proof.

In the United States, the high-profile trials of the 1990s have demonstrated that **physical evidence** is critical. The widely publicized trials of O. J. Simpson and Timothy McVeigh are prime examples. People can forget, lie, and distort the truth, but, in and of itself, physical evidence is incapable of deception. However, specialized education, training, and experience are required before physical evidence can be effectively utilized. It must be collected without contamination, analyzed correctly, and interpreted accurately.

What Is Evidence?

Evidence is information on which to base belief or reach conclusions. It is information that makes the truth clear to others whether or not they were present at the critical time or place. Evidence is also the term used for the statement produced before a court of law.

What Evidence Is Used in a Court of Law?

There are two major types of evidence—verbal evidence and physical evidence. Verbal evidence is oral testimony from a witness about his or her own observations. The person who gives verbal evidence is usually an eye witness or a character witness. Physical evidence is material that can be collected. analyzed, and interpreted by scientific method. The person who presents and interprets physical evidence in a court of law is an *expert witness*.

How Is Evidence Used?

When no human witness is available, physical evidence is used to interpret events. When an eye witness gives testimony, physical evidence is used to support or refute the verbal testimony. Physical evidence is also used to identify victims and suspects.

Typical Physical Evidence from a Crime Scene

- A human body or any part of a body
- Fingerprints
- Blood splatter or other body fluids
- Cigarette butts
- Clothing
- Drugs
- Fibers
- Footprints
- Hair
- Handwriting
- Personal effects such as jewelry, keys, wallet
- Projectiles
- Weapons

Typical Physical Evidence from a Human Burial

- Skeleton or decomposing human remains
- Fibers
- Clothing

- Hair
- Fingernails
- Personal effects such as jewelry
- Shovel marks in soil
- Mummified skin with friction ridges or tattoos
- Postmortem trauma (e.g., shovel marks or tooth marks)
- Perimortem trauma (e.g., gunshot wounds, knife marks, other tool marks)

Challenges in the Use of Physical Evidence

It may seem that physical evidence can simply be found and collected, but this is far from the truth. Evidence is useless if it is not handled properly from first sighting to final presentation. If evidence is to be convincing, it requires complete documentation, careful collection, proper handling, effective preservation, appropriate analysis, correct interpretation, and accurate reporting. Haste is the worst enemy of good evidence collection. It is better to step back from the scene and plan carefully than to rush in and handle something without correct training and preparation. All too often an enthusiastic but inadequately-prepared law enforcement official has become the inadvertent enemy of the judicial process. The following is an introduction to methods of handling physical evidence. A more thorough discussion of field methods is found in Chapter 13.

Documentation

Documentation of evidence begins at the moment of discovery. The evidence should be recorded photographically and in a written record before it is disturbed. (If the evidence is first discovered by a member [or members] of the general public, the person [or persons] should be located and interviewed.) Documentation continues at each stage of recovery, each time any procedure is performed, and each time that the evidence changes hands.

Collection

After a record is made of each item *in situ* (photos, map, and written description), the evidence can be collected. Make every effort to collect the evidence without alteration or contamination. Think before touching. The evidence may require the use of rubber gloves or other protective clothing.

Mark the packaging so that it can be located, identified, and matched easily with records. This usually requires plenty of labeling or tagging with indelible ink.

If the evidence is packaged well, tampering should be obvious. One way to accomplish this is to secure the package with one-use tape and then sign your name. Begin the signature on the tape and end on the package itself.

Custody

There must be a record of each and every person who handles the evidence. This record, also known as the "chain of custody" is the only way to maintain the value of the physical evidence. The integrity and credibility of the people who handle the evidence becomes the integrity and credibility of the evidence. The unbroken record also makes it possible to trace any alteration in the evidence. Without a documented chain of custody, the investigators may face accusations of evidence tampering. Such charges can make the best physical evidence and all of the painstaking analyses worthless.

PRESERVATION

It is important to maintain the evidence for future analysis by other scientists or with improved methods. Good preservation requires that the evidence maintenance be as stable as possible. Every type of sample has its own requirements, but "cool, dry, and away from sunlight" are almost always good guidelines. Antimicrobial agents may be useful in some cases and avoidance of over-drying is important in others. Use common sense and check with experts on specific substances.

ANALYSIS

Methods of analysis change over time, but it is important that the analysis be appropriate for the material and the resources. It is also important that the method be consistent with generally accepted methods within the specific scientific discipline. Use multiple, nonrelated methods whenever possible.

INTERPRETATION

Interpretation of the evidence must take into account the limits of the analytical method(s) being used. All methods for biological analyses have limits. The size of the sample, origin of the sample, and the composition of the sample population must be taken into account.

REPORTING

Reporting of results should be as simple and direct as possible. Refer to Chapter 14, "Professional Results," for a discussion of forensic reports.

DEATH INVESTIGATION SPECIALISTS

> **Key Term**
>
> **death investigation specialist** A person trained to collect or analyze one or more types of physical evidence in death investigation cases.

A wide assortment of specialists contribute to death investigation. They have come to be known by the collective name of **death investigation specialists** because of their common focus on evidence. They may be involved in collection of evidence, analysis, report writing, and/or verbal testimony, but they are all concerned with some aspect of evidence for legal purposes in death investigation cases.

Death investigation specialists come from police investigation training, medical training, or the physical and biological sciences. They are known as crime scene investigators, fingerprint experts, forensic photographers, or one of the many types of forensic scientists. Some of the specialists work directly with the body, others focus on the scene. Some specialists are more likely to be found in the field, others in the laboratory. Some spend a lot of time testifying in court, others submit their reports and are rarely called to court.

The following is a short list, in alphabetical order, of death investigation specialists and a brief description of the work of each. Each specialist is capable of far more than the basic description suggests. Years and breadth of experience are a specialist's most valuable resource.

BALLISTIC SPECIALISTS

Ballistic specialists are the firearms experts who are capable of recognizing and analyzing weapons and projectiles. They can determine if a weapon has been fired and match a projectile to the specific weapon that fired it.

Crime Scene Investigators

The scene investigations of recent deaths are usually carried out by police officers who specialize in processing crime scenes and gathering forensic evidence. Ideally, the scene investigators are the first on the scene. They must be able to recognize, photograph, organize, and collect evidence. The evidence can then be sent to a forensic laboratory for more thorough analysis with equipment not available at the crime scene.

Scene investigators are typically knowledgeable about fingerprints, footprints, hair, fibers, blood splatter dynamics, and weapons of all types. Most scene investigators call on coroners, medical examiners, or their investigators to deal with human remains.

Criminalists

The criminalist is the jack-of-all-trades in the forensic sciences. Many types of specialists are called criminalists. Usually the work of the criminalist focuses on the physical evidence from the crime scene, but not the body itself. Criminalists analyze glass, fibers, hair, paint, tool marks, residues, soil, and anything else that may reveal information with the help of microscopy, chromatography, spectrophotometry, mass spectrometry, neutron activation analysis, x-ray diffraction, and other methods of scientific analysis.

Drug Analysts

Drug analysts are the chemists that analyze and identify the wide variety of drugs and poisons available to man. They are usually excellent chemists with knowledge of pharmaceutical products as well.

Fingerprint Specialists

Fingerprint specialists collect latent prints, enhance prints for identification, classify fingerprints, and compare friction ridge patterns for identification. Most are now accustomed to computerized analysis of fingerprints.

Forensic Anthropologists

Anthropologists, both physical anthropologists and archaeologists, analyze and study the remains of ancient man and the sites of ancient and historic occupation. Their scientific methods have proved to be ideal for use in modern crime scenes, such as clandestine burials, and disaster situations.

Whenever the scene is obscured by dirt and the human remains are no longer visually recognizable, anthropological methods are ideal. The archeologist is usually responsible for the excavation of the site and the physical anthropologist is responsible for the analysis of the human remains.

Forensic Pathologists

The investigation of recent deaths is the work of medical doctors who specialize in pathology. Most pathologists work in hospitals. They evaluate diagnostic tests on living or dead patients and supervise laboratories. Some pathologists specialize still further in the field of *forensic* pathology. They are employed as medical examiners and are responsible for autopsies, analysis of trauma, and courtroom testimony.

Until the last few decades, a murderer was very likely to succeed if the victim was unrecognizable. But today, such a case is often solved with the combined efforts of forensic specialists from the disciplines of both medicine and anthropology.

Forensic Psychiatrists

Forensic psychiatrists study the mind of the criminal as well as the crime itself and the crime scene. They interview suspects and testify about competence, motives, and responsibility. Because of their understanding of the criminal mind, they are sometimes called upon to describe or "profile" the type of person capable of a particular crime.

WHY SHOULD A FORENSIC ANTHROPOLOGIST BE CONCERNED WITH THE METHODS OF OTHER FORENSIC SCIENTISTS?

Forensic science is multidisciplinary. No one specialist can ignore the work of the others any more than a plumber, an electrician, and a carpenter can avoid each other on a home building project without causing costly mistakes.

The success of an investigation may depend on the fact that one person knows when to call on another, that someone takes responsibility for knowing what each specialist is capable of doing, and that someone suggests the appropriate techniques at the right time.

Example 1: Questioned Documents

A box of bones, ragged clothing, and assorted garbage had gathered dust in the back of the state morgue for many months. There was little hope of identifying the incomplete remains found in an empty city lot, so other cases were given priority.

When I took custody of the box, I sorted the filthy contents and found three plastic hospital identification bracelets. They were badly weathered and no ink was visible, but I knew that documents examiners often use alternative light sources to reveal hidden ink, so I took the bracelets to the questioned documents laboratory. Within the hour, there was a tentative identification, and before the week was over, a positive identification by multiple radiographic comparisons.

The hospital bracelets were particularly important in this case because a clear description was not possible, and the deceased person had never been reported missing.

Example 2: Fingerprints

A police officer had been working on an unidentified person case. The pathologist told him to look for a missing woman in her mid-twenties, but no matches surfaced in six long months of searching. Finally, the officer decided to ask for help through another jurisdiction. I looked at the skeleton and said that he would have to start all over again and look for a teenaged male. I also noted that the remains included mummified fingers that could be printed.

Several more months and many bureaucratic obstacles later, the 18-year-old male was positively identified by fingerprint comparison. His remains were returned to his family in a foreign country for burial.

Questioned Document Examiners

Questioned document examiners are the scientists who analyze and compare writing of all types. They are handwriting experts. They know ink, paper, pens, pencils, typewriters, printers, and copy machines.

Serologists

Serologists are the chemists who extract essential information from body fluids. They report and testify about blood type, DNA comparisons, and the presence of sperm, saliva, and other biological fluids. Often they are called to analyze residues of fluids recovered from clothing or discarded items at crime scenes.

Toxicologists

Toxicologists are the chemists with the job of extracting drugs and poisons from body tissues and fluids. Typically, blood and/or urine samples are sent to the toxicologist if there is a question such as alcohol or drug overdose, carbon monoxide poisoning, or lead or arsenic poisoning. The toxicologist may also extract and identify a wide range of other foreign substances from tissue samples.

Which Specialist—Forensic Pathologist, Forensic Anthropologist, or Crime Scene Investigator?

As time progresses, physical evidence changes. If a scene is preserved, it is probably covered—usually with dirt. If anything remains of the body, it is most commonly the hard tissues of the skeleton and the teeth. The focus of an investigation changes from the typical crime scene and autopsy to excavation and skeletal analysis. The forensic specialists also change. The archaeologist replaces the crime scene investigator and the physical anthropologist replaces the forensic pathologist.

The biggest difficulty for the person in charge of an investigation is knowing when one specialist might be more effective than another. For the dead body, this question can be answered by taking a careful look at the processes at work on the time line of death and decay. There are two critical points. Neither point can be pinpointed by hours, days, or even years, because they are subject to both environmental and legal conditions.

No Visual Identification Possible

The first critical point on the time line occurs when simple visual identification of the body is no longer possible. This may be the result of decomposition, burning, or disarticulation. Beyond this point, the remains can no longer be recognized by relatives or friends.

Legal Consequence Unlikely

The second critical point on the time line is the loss of legal consequence. Beyond this point, it is unlikely (although not impossible) that identification will result in legal action. Most statutes of limitation are exceeded, the concerned relatives or friends are dead, or the person responsible for the death is dead. Discoveries of remains beyond this point are classified as historical or ancient deaths.

In Table 11.1, note which specialists investigate the scene and the body in each region of the time line. Multidisciplinary cooperation is most important in the years between loss of visual identification and loss of legal consequence.

Table 11.1 Choice of Specialist, Dictated by Time since Death

	Recent Death (Visual Identification Is Possible)	*The Years between Loss of Visual Identification and Loss of Legal Consequence*	*Ancient Death (Legal Consequences Have Diminished)*
The Scene	Scene Investigator	Scene Investigator and Forensic Archaeologist	Archaeologist
The Body	Forensic Pathologist and Forensic Odontologist	Forensic Anthropologist and Forensic Odontologist	Physical Anthropologist

CHAPTER 12

LABORATORY ANALYSIS

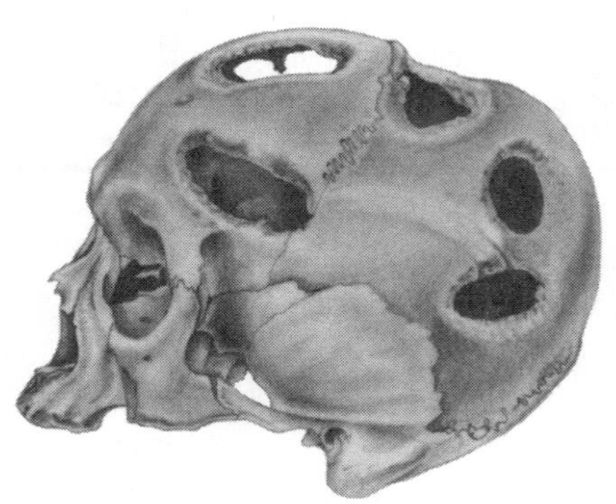

CHAPTER OUTLINE

Analysis

Key Term

analysis The examination and study of a whole item through the study of its component parts.

When the student is capable of recognizing every bone of the human skeleton, complete or fragmented, **analysis** can begin. The objective of a full skeletal analysis is information—the maximum amount of information that the bones will yield.

Identification of the deceased is only one of the desired results. A full skeletal analysis should also provide information about the life of the deceased, the circumstances surrounding death, and the fate of the remains since the time of death. The complete information has tremendous power. Collect it carefully and thoroughly.

When analysis begins, the information grows indiscriminately. It is the responsibility of the person examining the evidence to organize the information in such a way that the information can answer questions. This can be accomplished by keeping the questions in mind and recording information by category.

Try to maintain a sequence of analysis rather than attacking the evidence haphazardly. The sequence will increase both efficiency and the amount of information.

Organization of Analysis

Information Categories

- Description of the victim
- Identification of the victim
- Understanding the events of the time of death
- Estimation of the length of time since death
- Evaluation of any alteration of the remains since death

Sequence of Analysis

- Prepare the laboratory.
- Look over everything before beginning any cleaning.
- Analyze the associated physical evidence.
- Analyze the human remains (usually skeletal material).
- Collect samples for further analysis in other laboratories.

The Basics of Skeletal Analysis

- Age estimate
- Sex differentiation
- Racial identification
- Stature estimate
- Weight estimate
- Handedness, dominant side
- Trauma analysis
- Disease history
- Muscularity
- Evidence of habitual activity

MAKESHIFT LABORATORIES

I have used many structures for a laboratory (a barn, a garage, a schoolhouse, a hotel, several morgues, a hospital, etc.). Tables can be created from sawhorses and plywood. Lights can be rigged from the nearest power supply, or they can be battery-operated. Water can be a little trickier in some places, but there is nothing like a bucket. The hardest thing to arrange in some parts of the world is security. But determination and creativity usually win out.

Preparation for Analysis

The laboratory

The question is often asked, "What do I need to get started?" Some equipment and supplies are essential. Other items are optional. They are time savers, but the job can be accomplished without them. (See Table 12.1, which lists essential and optional equipment and supplies.)

The laboratory itself has several requirements. Security for the evidence and some degree of privacy for the work are both required. Tables or some other working surface is necessary. Good lighting and available water are also important.

Table 12.1 Equipment and Supplies to Get a Laboratory Started

Essential Equipment	Essential Supplies
sliding calipers or dial calipers (see illustration on page 147)	background cloth for photos
spreading calipers (see illustration on page 147)	photographic film
osteometric board or tree calipers	3x5 or 4x6 cards for labels
large tables or plywood on sawhorses	indelible ink pens
chairs or benches	rulers and grid paper
camera with macro lens	osteometric forms
extra lights and extension cords	soap and other cleaning supplies
	glue
Optional Equipment	**Optional Supplies**
glue gun (hot wax glue)	computer disks
label maker	paper for printer
hardware: computer and printer	paper or plastic cover for tables
software: spreadsheet, word processor, and Fordisc 2.0	chalk
chalk board	coffee or tea and cups
coffee pot or tea pot	

Sliding Calipers (Also Called Dial Calipers)

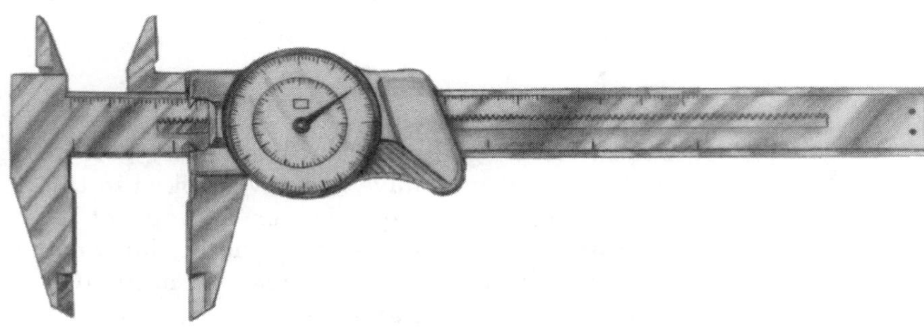

Spreading Calipers

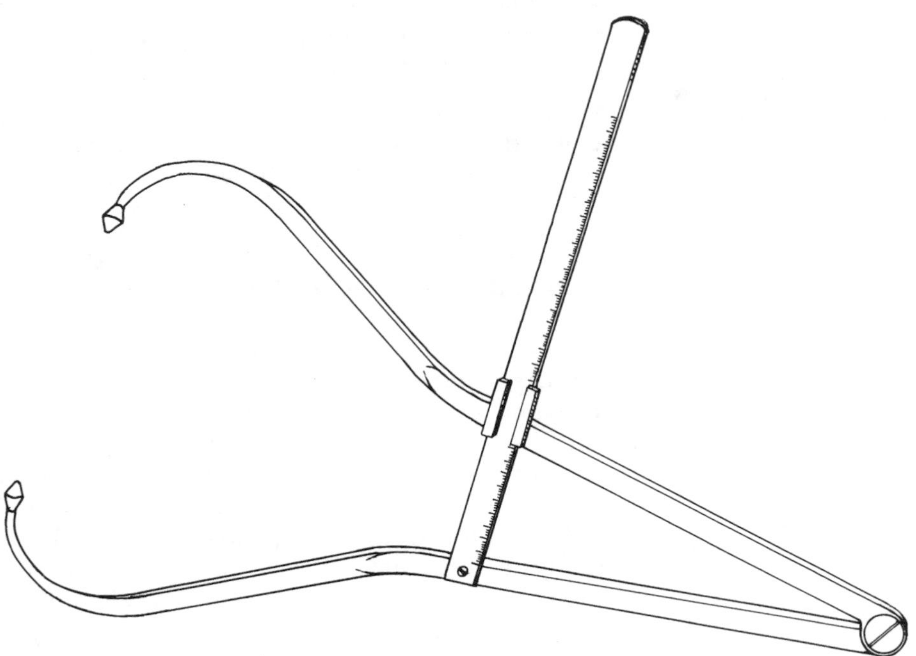

Overall Examination

This is the opportunity to thoroughly scrutinize and document the evidence. It is also the time to note gut reactions, strange smells, and other oddities before you begin to get used to them.

Examine Everything

Before cleaning the evidence, examine everything carefully. Look for any evidence that may have been overlooked in the field. Record all findings in note form, even suspicions or feelings of uneasiness about something. Usually no one else sees your notes, but you might wish to use them to review a case and bring new ideas to mind. (Occasionally a highly sensitive case will require that notes be turned over to the court along with the report. Be wary in such a case and avoid writing anything that might be misinterpreted.)

While examining the evidence, look for the following:

- Hair
- Fibers
- Stains from blood
- Stains from metal oxides
- Tool marks of any sort
- Tooth marks
- Anything that may seem out of place, such as sand in remains recovered from nonsandy soil

Preparation of Skeletal Material

Clean

Clean the bones carefully. Marks from knife blades, embedded metal fragments, and stains are more visible after cleaning, but great care must be taken to avoid altering or contaminating the marks. Numerous pathological conditions are also visible after exposure of the bone surface. Such evidence may be exceedingly fragile and easily lost or altered.

The type of cleaning depends on the condition of the bone and the type of analysis to be carried out. Any specimen that is to be used for DNA analysis or any other chemical analysis should be treated with special care. Contact the laboratory for preservation and packing instructions. Some DNA laboratories prefer to send their own containers for packing and shipping.

Stabilize

Now that the remains have been found, it is necessary to ensure that they will remain in good condition at least until they are re-interred or turned over to another party.

The correct stabilization method depends on the condition of the bone. Water soluble plastics such as Acrysol or Rhoplex (produced by Rohm and Haas Co., Philadelphia) work well for this purpose. They can be painted on with a soft brush or sprayed on. Several thin coats, each allowed to dry, are preferable to one thick application.

Check all teeth for stability within the sockets and overall integrity. Single-rooted teeth tend to fall out at inopportune moments. Loss or breakage is the result. Teeth are better maintained if they are left in the alveolar bone than out of the skull. The alveolar bone is also less likely to chip. A tiny drop of adhesive material in the correct tooth socket works to retain the tooth without harming it for future study.

Enamel dries over time and cracks more easily. Coat the teeth with a nonerosive, protective glaze if necessary. Also use care in packing and setting remains on tables. Skulls and teeth sustain less damage if they are placed upside down in ring-type cushions. These can be made of cork, foam, cloth, acid-free plastic wrap, or any other nonabrasive, nonreactive substance.

INVENTORY

Lay the bones out in anatomical order and fill out an inventory form. Use this opportunity to examine each and every aspect of each bone in detail. Note anomalies for future examination. It may be necessary to find comparative skeletal material, refer to textbooks, or discuss the case with colleagues before reaching any conclusions.

Table 12.2 Bone Preparation Chart

Condition of Bone	Detergent or Enzyme Use	Water Use	Tools	Preservation
fresh with decomposing flesh still well attached	enzyme detergent	yes, boiling	scalpel, forceps, firm brush	air dry, store in dry, cool place
greasy without flesh attached	enzyme detergent	yes, warm	firm brush	air dry, store in dry, cool place
intact, well calcified bone covered only by light soils	detergent but no soaking	yes, cold	light brush	slow air dry, store in dry, cool place
intact, poorly calcified porous bone	no detergent	no water, dry slowly if damp	soft brush or forced air	light mist coating of a water soluble, reversible substance such as Acrysol or Resinol
fragmented, poorly calcified porous bone	no detergent	no water, dry slowly if damp	very soft brush	light mist coating of a water soluble, reversible substance such as Acrysol or Resinol

THE MINIMUM NUMBER OF INDIVIDUALS (MNI)

Why bother to determine the minimum number of individuals (MNI)? MNI may be one of the only results possible. Under such conditions, MNI can be the one critical piece of physical evidence that supports or refutes verbal testimony.

EXAMPLE 1

During the Guatemalan civil war, villagers reported the location of a mass grave and requested an exhumation. Before the official exhumation could begin, someone else removed the remains in an attempt to destroy evidence of the massacre and discredit the testimony of the villagers.

We went ahead with the excavation and recovered bones from the hands and feet of the victims as well as several unfused epiphyses from a teenager. The skeletal analysis revealed an MNI of six, based solely on the left first cuneiform. None of the epiphyses were duplicated; therefore, only one of the six was confirmed to be teenaged.

The villagers had testified that five adult men and one teenaged boy disappeared just before the time that the area of recently disturbed earth was found in a nearby forest. The villagers' claims were supported by the physical evidence.

EXAMPLE 2

A cemetery relocation firm in the United States was contracted to move a large unmarked cemetery prior to redevelopment of the site. Since the number of graves was unknown, the contractor was to be paid by the number of graves moved rather than for the job as a whole.

Previous landowners estimated that the area contained approximately two thousand separate graves. The relocation firm, however, reburied more than four thousand boxes of bones! Suspicion was finally aroused, and I was asked to find a way to examine the work of the cemetery relocation firm.

I disinterred forty of the four thousand boxes and found the MNI to be eighteen. The skeletal elements were in good condition, but there was significant postmortem breakage. It is possible that more than eighteen individuals were present, but it is highly unlikely that forty individual graves were represented. The firm was charged with fraud.

SKELETAL ANALYSIS AND DESCRIPTION

Key Terms

formative changes The modifications that occur during the processes of formation, growth, and development.

degenerative changes The modifications that occur as a result of age, wear, and disease.

Now that the laboratory and the skeletal material are ready, each of the major description questions can be pursued with vigor.

AGE

Methods for determining age are covered in Part I. Refer back to specific skeletal sections, particularly the chapters on the skull, clavicles, ribs, vertebrae, pelvis, and teeth.

Over the years, analysts have relied on **formative changes**, such as dental eruption and epiphyseal union, and **degenerative changes**, such as dental wear, changes in tooth and bone histology, pubic symphysis modification, rib end growth, and general osteoarthritis. All of these methods have advantages and limitations.

Remember that no aging method is even close to 100 percent accurate. There are two sources of error: (1) individual variation as reported in the standard deviation of the method, and (2) difference between the sample population and the population of origin of the unidentified person. Unfortunately, the population origin of an unidentified body is usually unknown.

No one method should ever be used alone unless there is no choice. Choice of method is, of course, limited when incomplete or fragmentary remains are the only material available.

Always provide a range when estimating age. This is no time for demonstration of pride or games of chance. It is far better to give a 10 to 20 year age range and succeed in matching the missing person with other characteristics than a 3 to 5 year range and miss the identification entirely.

Sex

Sex is a little easier than age because there are supposed to be fewer alternatives. In truth, the human animal is not as neatly divided into typical males and typical females as most people tend to think. Normal sexual variation is best visualized as an overlapping set of normal curves with considerable tails on each curve. Many people are in the area of overlap and quite a few are located in the tails!

Typical Distribution Pattern for Sexual Differences

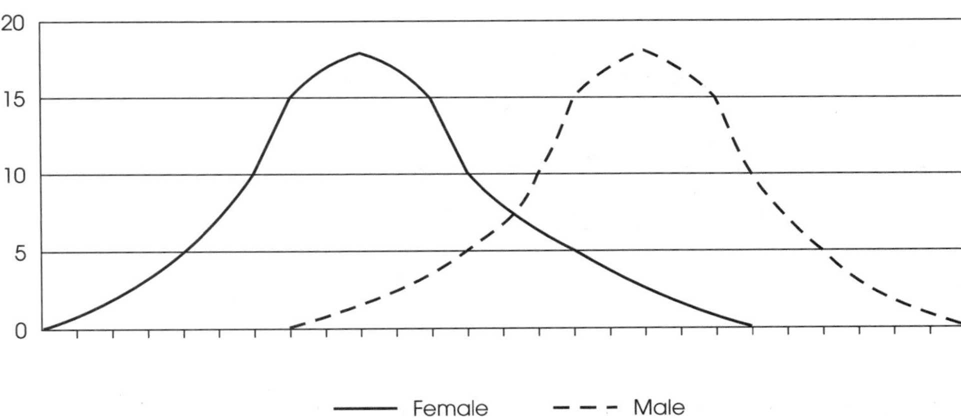

All sexual traits, even the form of the genitalia, can be confusing. This is just within the *normal* population. If the reader wishes to pursue this topic into the abnormal, a study of endocrinology is recommended. There is more than one way for a male to look like a female, and vice versa.

This is all reason to be cautious, but not reason to give up. Part of caution is knowing the skeletal traits of the typical male and female so well that *all* available information can be taken into consideration. Then, if the information is insufficient for a conclusion, say so.

Table 12.3 (on page 152) summarizes the basic sexual differences in the normal skeleton. The most reliable differences are in the pelvis.

Table 12.3 Sexual Differences in the Skeleton

The Bone	The Differences	Male	Female
	overall size	larger	smaller
	muscle attachments	larger	smaller
pubis	pubic length	short	long
	ventral arc	absent	present
	subpubic concavity	absent	present
	subpubic angle	narrow	wide
	ischiopubic ramus	wide	narrow, "stretched"
	parturition pits	absent	sometimes present
ilium	preauricular sulcus	absent	often present
	sciatic notch	narrow	wide
femur	femoral head diameter (Stewart 1979)	possible: 46.5–47.5 mm. probable male: >47.5 mm.	possible: 42.5–43.5 mm. probable female: <42.5 mm.
frontal	supraorbital ridge	prominent	absent
	frontal bossing	double boss	single central boss
temporal	mastoid process	large	small
	zygomatic process length	extends to the external auditory meatus and beyond	ends before the external auditory meatus
occipital	nuchal ridges	strong muscle attachment	slight muscle attachment
mandible	ramus	wide and sharply angled	narrow and less angled
	chin shape	square	rounded or pointed
rib	subperichondral ossification	marginal ossification	central foci of ossification
sternum	sternum length	the body is *more* than twice the manubrium length	the body is *less* than twice the manubrium length

Race

Race is both a biological and a cultural concept. It is confusing because it includes everything from skin color to family origin, nationality, ethnicity, religion, and more. The politically charged connotations of the very word, race, make racial analysis the most difficult aspect of human identification. (And the most easily misunderstood.) Obviously, the analysis of skeletal remains must rely on biological information. But the report must communicate to the many nonbiologists who inevitably interpret racial terms on a cultural basis. The challenge is effective communication.

Even within biological and cultural definitions, there is confusion. The biological information is complicated by the fact that there are no real racial boundaries. Any amount of genetic intermixture is possible. The detectable differences in human phenotypes are the result of minor genetic differences fixed by geographic isolation. Such isolation is dissolving as the world population grows, the gaps between groups disappear, and more and more people travel and relocate.

Most of the world recognizes race through the veil of culture. The lines between major racial groups are drawn differently by each cultural group. To some, skin color is all-important. To others, hair type, eye shape, nose size, or lip form is more important. Most of the recognizable racial traits are on the head, but body types and proportions vary as well.

Race is so complicated that it is tempting to try to ignore it altogether. Some choose to approach the subject only through euphemisms. The results are counterproductive or noncommunicative. No matter how difficult it is to define or determine, race is still important to the process of identification. People identify themselves and others by membership in specific racial groups (or racial mixtures). Race is as much a part of personal identification as is sex or age.

The analyst needs to find ways to cope with the difficulties of racial identification rather than avoiding them. This can be accomplished through thorough description and explanation. Describe the racial traits of the unidentified person by describing how the person looked. Explain the relationship between a specific trait and various racial groups. Allow room for interpretation and use the terminology that best communicates with the people that will be reading the report.

EXAMPLES OF USEFUL RACIAL DESCRIPTIONS

- "The inferior nasal border has the double-edged appearance known as *subnasal guttering.* This is a trait most commonly found within black populations or among people of African heritage."
- "The cranial traits such as the straight facial profile, the narrow nasal aperture, and long nasal spine are consistent with those of European-derived white populations."

CRANIAL TRAITS

Table 12.4 (on page 154) provides a list of nonmetric cranial traits that are common, but not ubiquitous, within each of the major racial groups listed.

Metric traits are also useful, particularly when used to compare the skull in question with a large database of measurements from other skulls. This is best accomplished through computer analysis. A word of warning is necessary—do not rely on metric analysis unless you have had the opportunity to check your measurement technique with an experienced physical anthropologist. When working alone, it is easy to misinterpret instructions. The results can be misleading and disastrous. (Illustrations and lists of cranial differences are also provided in Chapter 2.)

POSTCRANIAL RACIAL TRAITS

Many postcranial traits and measurements have been examined in relation to racial affinity. These include the curvature of the femoral shaft (Finnegan and Schulter 1975 and Gilbert and Gill, in Gill and Rhine 1990) and the intercondylar notch (Baker, Gill, and Kieffer, in Gill and Rhine 1990).

There is no end to the variation that can be examined, but it is imperative that controls be established on the population to be examined before any method is applied with confidence.

Table 12.4 Nonmetric Cranial Racial Traits

Elements of Difference	American Indians	European Whites	African Blacks
incisors	shovel-shaped incisors	blade-form incisors	blade-form incisors
dentition	not crowded, often well-sclerosed	crowded, frequently impacted 3rd molars	not crowded
zygomas	robust and flaring, with malar tubercle	small, retreating zygomas	small, retreating zygomas
zygomaxillary suture	angled	jagged or S-shaped	curved or S-shaped
profile	moderate alveolar prognathism	little prognathism, orthognathic	strong alveolar prognathism
palatal shape	elliptic	parabolic	hyperbolic
palatal suture	straight	Z-shape	arched
cranial sutures	complex, with Wormian bones	simple	simple
nasal bones	low "tented" nasals	high and arched with nasion depression	low, flat, shallow arch shaped
nasal aperture	medium	narrow	wide
nasal spine	medium, tilted	large, long	little or none
nasal sill	sharp	very sharp	"guttered"
chin	blunt median chin	square, projecting chin	retreating chin
ramus	wide ascending ramus	intermediate ramus	narrow ascending ramus
cranium	low, sloping	high	low, with postbregmatic depression
hair form	straight round cross section	wavy oval cross section	curly or kinky flat cross section

Source: Adapted from Gill 1995.

STATURE

Stature (height) is determined by measuring long bones and comparing the measurement with average measurements from large databases. The formulae vary by sex and race, so it is advisable to know the sex and race of the subject before beginning stature analysis.

Long bones are usually measured on an osteometric board. The large sliding calipers used by foresters for measuring tree diameters are also accurate. (Tree calipers are also more portable than most osteometric boards.)

MEASUREMENT SYSTEMS

It is easy to become confused when moving from one measurement system to another. People in the United States usually know just how tall a 5 foot 3 inch woman is, but they are confused if they are told that the woman is 160 cm tall. One system is adequate within any single group of people, but the international worker needs more.

Table 12.5 Quick Conversion Table for Stature Measurements

Feet and Inches	Inches	Centimeters
4′ 10″	58	147.3
4′ 11″	59	149.9
5′ 0″	60	152.4
5′ 1″	61	154.9
5′ 2″	62	157.5
5′ 3″	63	160.0
5′ 4″	64	162.6
5′ 5″	65	165.1
5′ 6″	66	167.6
5′ 7″	67	170.2
5′ 8″	68	172.7
5′ 9″	69	175.3
5′ 10″	70	177.8
5′ 11″	71	180.3
6′ 0″	72	182.9
6′ 1″	73	185.4
6′ 2″	74	188.0
6′ 3″	75	190.5
6′ 4″	76	193.0

MEASURING BONES

The formulae for stature calculations require that the bones be measured in centimeters. Most of the measurements are simple maximum lengths. This includes the measurement of the humerus, radius, ulna, femur, and fibula.

The tibia is a bit more complicated. It is measured from the superior articular surface of the *lateral* condyle to the tip of the medial malleolus. In other words, the intercondylar eminence is not part of the measurement. One way to avoid measuring the intercondylar eminence is by using an osteometric board with a hole or notch for the intercondylar eminence.

Stature Determination by Formulae

After measuring each bone according to the instructions in the previous pages, insert the measurement into the appropriate formulae below. For example, if the unidentified person is a white male, and the measurement of the humerus is 32.7 centimeters, the first formula is the correct one to use:

$$\text{stature} = (2.89 \times 32.7) + 78.10 = 172.6 \text{ cm.} \pm 4.57 \text{ cm. standard deviation}$$

The predicted height of the unknown person is 168.0–177.2 centimeters, 66.1–69.8 inches, or 5 feet 6 inches to 5 feet 10 inches. This may seem like a wide range. (The prediction interval from the femur would be a little narrower.) But think about the goal—identification. It is better to give a wide range and search a few more records for the missing person than to give too narrow a range and miss the chance at a successful identification.

Table 12.6 Stature Formulae

Race/Sex	Bone	Formula (cm.)	s.d.
African male	humerus	2.88 humerus + 75.48	± 4.23
	radius	3.32 radius +85.43	± 4.57
	ulna	3.20 ulna + 80.77	± 4.74
	femur	2.10 femur + 72.22	± 3.91
	tibia	2.19 tibia + 85.36	± 3.96
	fibula	2.34 fibula + 80.07	± 4.02
African female	humerus	3.08 humerus + 64.67	± 4.25
	radius	3.67 radius + 71.79	± 4.59
	ulna	3.31 ulna + 75.38	± 4.83
	femur	2.28 femur + 59.76	± 3.41
	tibia	2.45 tibia + 72.65	± 3.70
	fibula	2.49 fibula + 70.90	± 3.80
Asian male	humerus	2.68 humerus + 83.19	± 4.16
	radius	3.54 radius + 82.00	± 4.60
	ulna	3.48 ulna + 77.45	± 4.66
	femur	2.15 femur + 72.57	± 3.80
	tibia	2.39 tibia + 81.45	± 3.27
	fibula	2.40 fibula + 80.56	± 3.24
European male	humerus	2.89 humerus + 78.10	± 4.57
	radius	3.79 radius + 79.42	± 4.66
	ulna	3.76 ulna + 75.55	± 4.72
	femur	2.32 femur + 65.53	± 3.94
	tibia	2.42 tibia + 81.93	± 4.00
	fibula	2.60 fibula + 75.50	± 3.86
European female	humerus	3.36 humerus + 57.97	± 4.45
	radius	4.74 radius + 54.93	± 4.24
	ulna	4.27 ulna + 57.76	± 4.30
	femur	2.47 femur + 54.10	± 3.72
	tibia	2.90 tibia + 61.53	± 3.66
	fibula	2.93 fibula + 59.61	± 3.57
Mexican male	humerus	2.92 humerus + 73.94	± 4.2
	radius	3.55 radius + 80.71	± 4.04
	ulna	3.56 ulna + 74.56	± 4.05
	femur	2.44 femur + 58.67	± 2.99
	tibia	2.36 tibia + 80.62	± 3.73
	fibula	2.50 fibula + 75.44	± 3.52
Mexican female	femur	2.59 femur + 49.74	± 3.82
	tibia	2.72 tibia + 63.78	± 3.51

Source: From Trotter and Gleser 1952, 1977 and Genoves 1967

ERRORS INTRODUCED BY SELF-REPORTING, AND FAULTY MEMORY

Stature estimates are complicated by more than biological variation. The estimate may be accurate while the records of the missing person are entirely wrong. Many records of height are nothing more than self-reported estimates. Height tends to be exaggerated (or sometimes diminished) according to the wishes of the individual. Often missing person records are verbal reports by family and friends. It is not uncommon for people to have difficulty remembering the height of a person that they have not seen recently. Strangely enough, much-admired people and national heroes tend to "grow" after death!

CHANGES IN HEIGHT WITH ADVANCING AGE

Another problem is the loss of height with age. Most people do shorten with age. The intervertebral disks compress and the vertebra collapse, causing the gradual loss of a few centimeters. However, people seldom report themselves to be any shorter than they were at age 20.

HANDEDNESS

In a group of unidentified persons, the lone left-handed person might be more easily identified if he could be recognized and separated from the majority of right-handed people. Approximately 90 percent of the human population is predominantly right-handed. Among the remaining 10 percent, a great deal of variability exists. Some people are strongly left-handed. Others are ambidextrous; they are left-handed for some activities and right-handed for others.

The hand an individual prefers is in part genetically determined, but the precise ways in which genes affect handedness are unknown. It is not simple inheritance (i.e., two right-handed parents can have a left-handed child or the reverse).

The methods of recognizing handedness in skeletal remains are imprecise. The question is difficult to study in a skeletal population because there are seldom records of handedness as there are of stature, sex, and race. It is usually necessary to interview the family to obtain this information.

One thing is certain—the majority of skeletons are asymmetrical. The right arm is usually longer and the left leg is usually longer. It is generally accepted among anthropologists that the dominant arm tends to be longer. I prefer to obtain additional information from the skeleton to indicate uneven use of the upper limbs. The scapula and the humerus are the main bones of interest.

The two humeri can be compared for differences in the muscle attachment areas, particularly the deltoid tuberosity. The dominant side is expected to show slightly larger attachment areas. The humeri can also be compared at the elbow area where differences in osteoarthritic changes may indicate increased use on one side over the other.

The scapulae can be compared for differences in use patterns. On the dominant side, the glenoid fossa is more likely to demonstrate a dorsal bevel. This is probably the result of repeated reaching and wearing of the glenoid rim. The nondominant side is more likely to show a simple osteoarthritic rim on the dorsal margin of the glenoid fossa. Both beveling and lipping are progressive age changes, therefore the elderly show greater changes than youth.

Stewart's method (1979, 239–244) is recommended for clearly visualizing the glenoid bevel. It is summarized in the illustration on page 158.

Right and Left Scapulae, Lateral View, with Line across Glenoid Rim

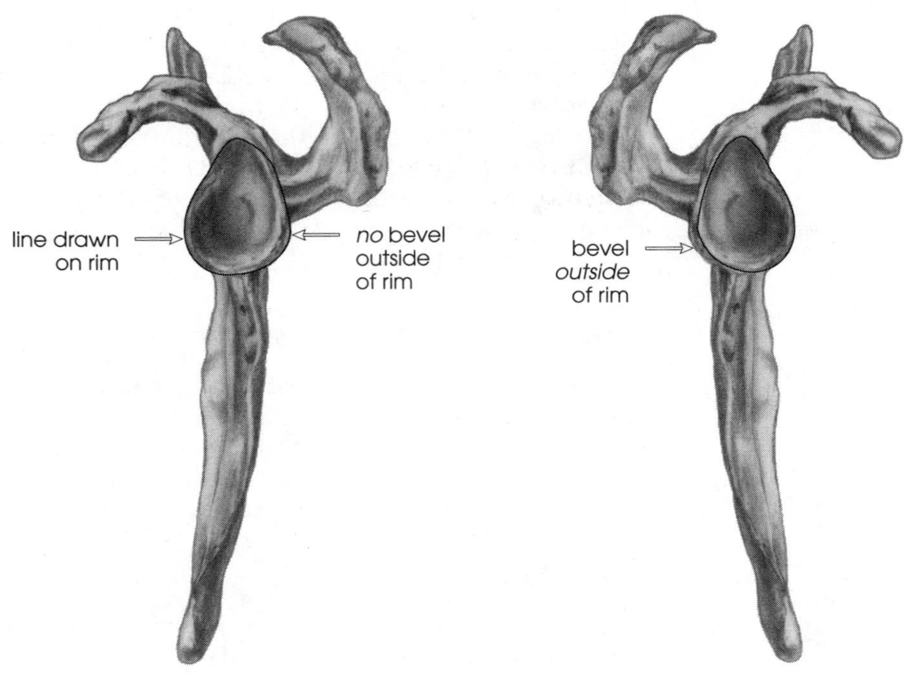

Are These the Scapulae of a Right- or Left-Handed Person?

First, make the rim of the glenoid fossa clearly visible by drawing the flat side of a long piece of chalk across the surface. (A long piece of lead removed from a mechanical pencil also works well.)

Next, hold the right scapula in your right hand and the left scapula in your left hand while looking at the glenoid fossae. Compare the dorsal rims of the left and right glenoid fossa. Look for a distinct bevel outside the dorsal rim of the glenoid fossa.

If one rim is beveled and the other is not, the person probably did more reaching with the arm on the beveled side. In other words, he *used* the arm more. The arm showing more use is usually the dominant arm and, by inference, the dominant hand.

Analysis of Trauma

Timing—When Did the Incident Occur?

In the analysis of skeletal remains, certain aspects of trauma take precedence over others. The standard questions like when, what, and where are redefined by the condition of the remains. When evidence of trauma is observed, the first question is, "When did it happen?" Did the traumatic event occur before death, at or around the time of death, or after death?

Antemortem Trauma

Antemortem trauma is very useful for identification purposes. Evidence of traumatic events during the life of the individual can be compared with medical records or testimony of friends and family.

An injury that occurs before death is one that shows signs of physiological response by the injured tissue. The wound will have healed or at least begun to heal. Bony surfaces will show signs of callus formation or the thickly rounded surfaces characteristic of bony remodeling.

Trephination

This amazing cranium is from an archeological site. The individual lived for many months (possibly even years) after the holes were cut into his skull. The edges of the holes are well-rounded. At the time of death, lamellar bone was continuing to develop over the exposed spongy bone. All of the holes are somewhat beveled toward the outer surface. If this were a example of modern cranial surgery, there would be small drill holes at the edges of the larger holes. Also the bony plates would be wired back into place. (Note also that the individual was edentulous. There are no alveolar sockets and little or no alveolar bone.)

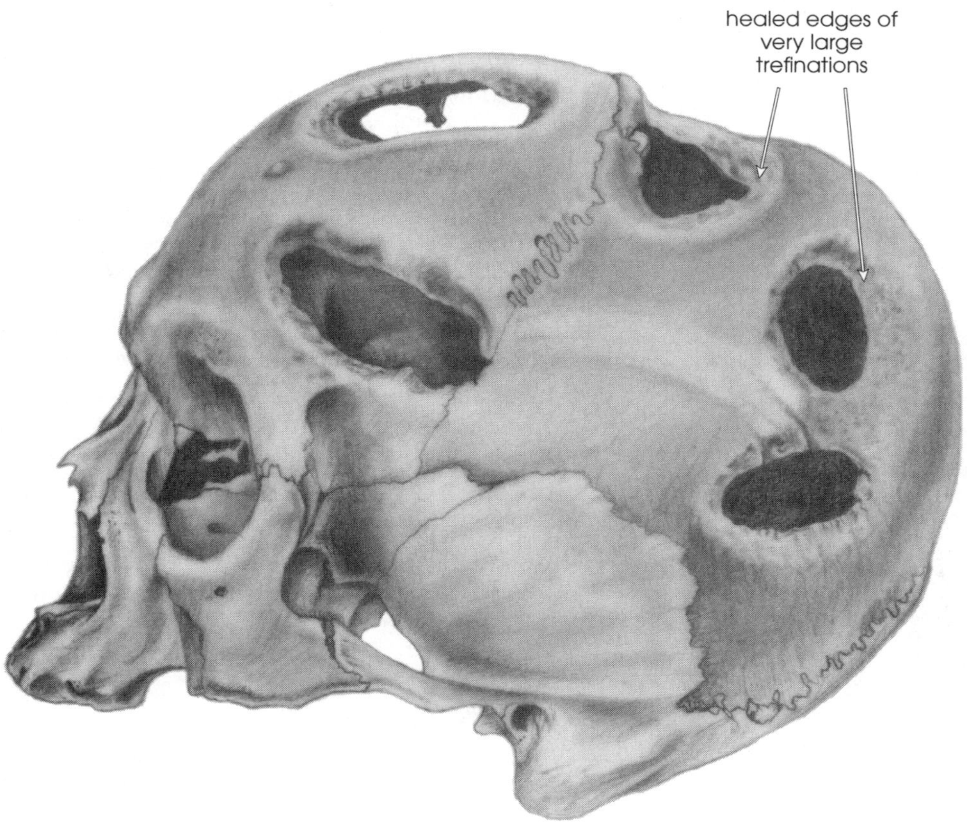

PERIMORTEM OR CIRCUMMORTEM TRAUMA

An injury that occurs around the time of death may provide valuable information about the cause or manner of death. The exact moment of death is not the issue. The trauma may have taken place immediately before, during, or after death.

Perimortem is characterized by no sign of healing, and it should be clear that the damage occurred in fresh bone, not dry bone. Any staining or weathering should be consistent with that of the surrounding bone.

POSTMORTEM TRAUMA

It is important to clearly separate perimortem trauma from postmortem trauma, because perimortem trauma has far greater forensic implications. Perimortem trauma may have been caused by a murderer, whereas postmortem trauma is more likely to have been caused by a hungry scavenger or a sloppy excavator.

Trauma that occurs long after death usually has a different appearance because bare dry bone breaks differently and marks differently than wet bone that is still covered by flesh. The outer surface of bone that has been exposed to dirt and weather is usually different from the protected inner surface. Therefore a recent mark will reveal an inconsistent color.

Classification—What Caused the Injury?

The evidence of trauma is highly variable. It is necessary to consider the specific effects of the traumatic source as well as the structural components of the location of impact. Major factors include size, shape, density, velocity, and angle of impact.

The following material focuses on analysis of the most common types of bone trauma—fractures, cutting wounds, and gunshot wounds.

Fractures

- Simple—a "clean" break with no skin penetration
- Compound—broken ends of bone protrude through an open wound in the skin
- Comminuted—the bone is broken into many pieces
- Compression—crushed bone (common in porous bone)
- Depressed—broken bone is pressed inward (as in a blunt force trauma to the skull)
- Impacted—one of the broken ends of a bone is forced into the cancellous bone of the other end
- Spiral—a ragged break caused by excessive twisting
- Greenstick—an incomplete break with one side bent inward and the other side broken outward (common in children, rare in adults)

Cutting Wounds

Each type of blade creates its own pattern of damage. Other tools such as hammers, screwdrivers, and ice picks also produce distinctive patterns. The student will benefit by experimenting with fresh bones obtained from a local butcher. Examine the marks made by every tool available. Use a low-power microscope or a magnifying glass to observe the finer patterns of the marks.

- Knives: The wound is small, clean, and sharp-edged. There is variation depending on the size, type, weight, and sharpness of the knife (e.g., a paring knife, a serrated bread knife, a large butcher knife). (See illustration on page 161.)
- Machetes: The wound is long, deep, and sharp-edged. (See illustration on page 161.)
- Other toolmarks: The wound is related to the form of the tool (e.g., handsaw, screwdriver, hammer, ice pick). (See illustration on page 161.)

Knife wounds are characterized by straight lines. Neat, clean, straight lines are seldom found in nature. They are usually formed by man-made tools.

In the illustrations on page 161, compare the saw marks on the cut surface of the femur with the illustrations of knife marks and machete marks.

Knife Wounds on Skull from Scalping

The marks were left by a butcher knife in an attempted scalping. The edges are clean, but they penetrate only the outer table of bone.

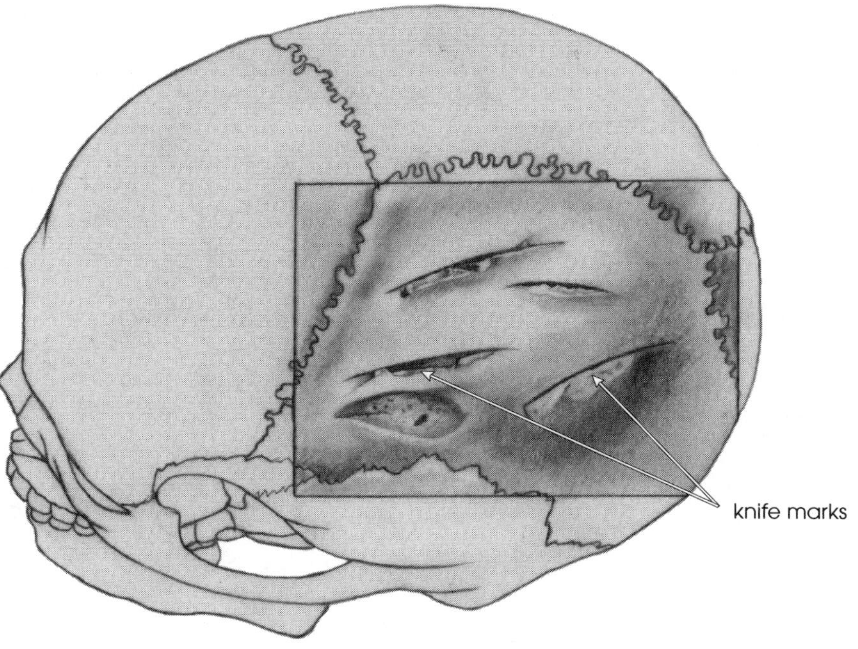

Machete Wounds in Skull

The wound left by a machete is long, deep, and sharp-edged. It can penetrate or decapitate.

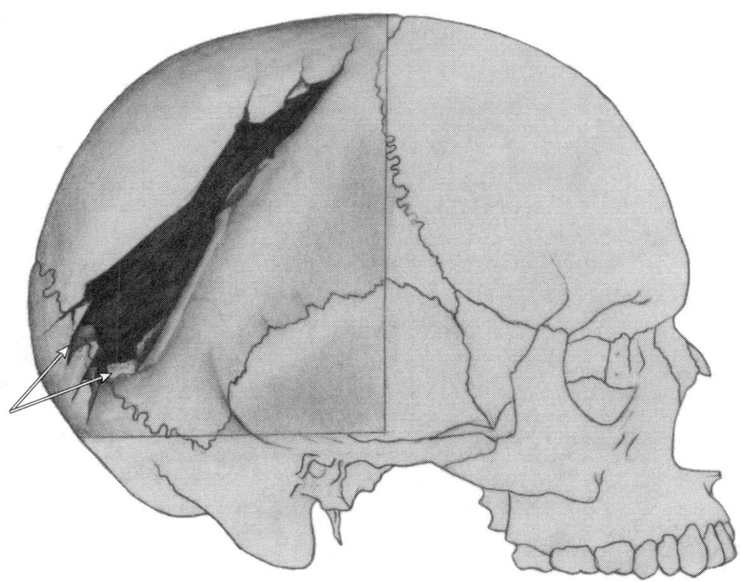

Hacksaw Marks on Femur

Marks from a hacksaw are repetitive and somewhat parallel.

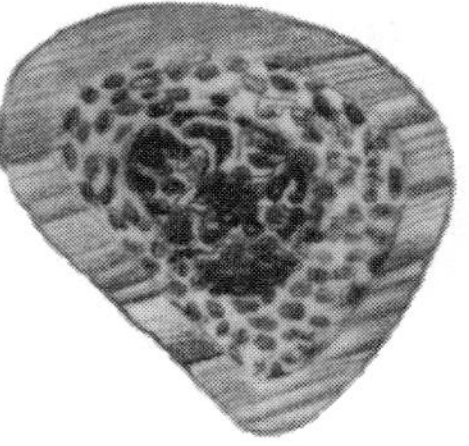

GUNSHOT WOUNDS

The type of weapon, type of projectile, range, and trajectory all have an effect on the resulting gunshot wound. Thorough analysis of gunshot wounds is best accomplished by experts with the most experience. (Big city medical examiners are usually a good choice.) It is, however, possible for even the novice to separate out the major characteristics of gunshot wounds and report them, without overstepping their expertise with the weapons themselves.

Separate the obviously high-power wounds from the low-power wounds by classifying the damage surrounding the point of penetration. Low-power weapons such as small pistols release less energy than high-power weapons. The resulting wound can be a simple hole, beveled larger in the direction that the projectile traveled. If the projectile exits the body, the exit wound is larger than the entrance.

High-power weapons such as rifles and machine guns release large amounts of energy. As the projectile enters the body, there is a sudden expansion or bursting effect. (In soft tissue, this is called temporary cavitation.) The resulting wound in bone takes on a "starburst" pattern.

Low-Power Gunshot Wound

With a low-energy gunshot wound there is less expansion and fewer cracks. In this particular case, the energy is also partially absorbed by the cranial suture.

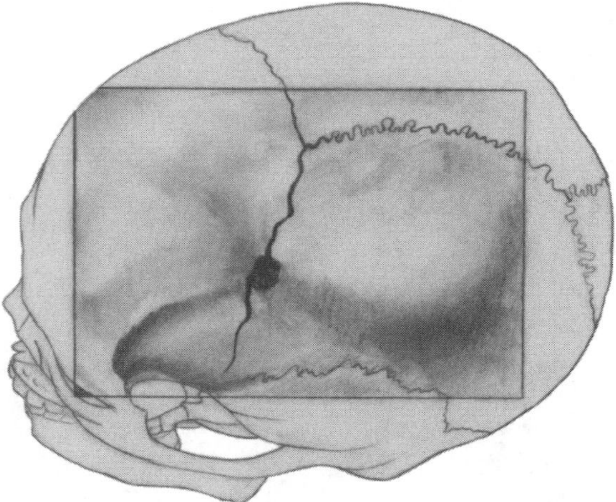

High-Power Gunshot Wound

With a higher-energy gunshot wound there is a "starburst" pattern of cracks. This is the result of rapidly expanding gases within the cranial vault.

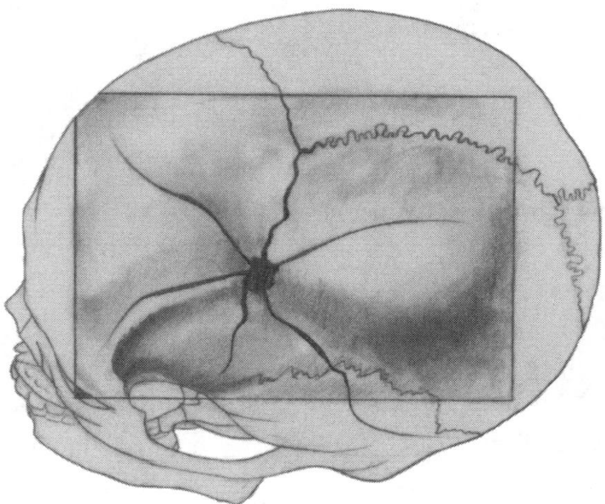

GUNSHOT WOUNDS—PROJECTILE TYPE

There is an enormous variety of projectiles available. Basically, they can be described by caliber, material, shape, and jacket. The combination produces different effects when striking living tissue.

The shape of the wound and the amount of tissue damage is related to the type of material (usually lead, but sometimes plastic or rubber), the shape of the projectile (with or without a hollow point), the presence or absence of a metal jacket, and the extent of the jacket (full or partial). Full metal jacket rifle bullets usually exit the body. Partial jacketed, hollow pointed bullets expand and often do not exit. Handgun bullets vary greatly in effect.

GUNSHOT WOUNDS—ENTRANCE AND EXIT CHARACTERISTICS

Wounds provide some information about the direction of fire and type of projectile as well as size and caliber of the weapon. But beware of trying to read too much from the wound. Unknown factors may have contributed to the pattern of injuries, and changes may have occurred since the time of death. *Use caution in interpretation!*

Bone does *not* accurately maintain the caliber of the projectile. The diameter of the wound may be larger because of the angle of entry, distortion of the projectile by intermediary targets, chipping bone edges, and many other factors. The diameter of the wound may even be slightly smaller because of shrinkage of the bone during drying.

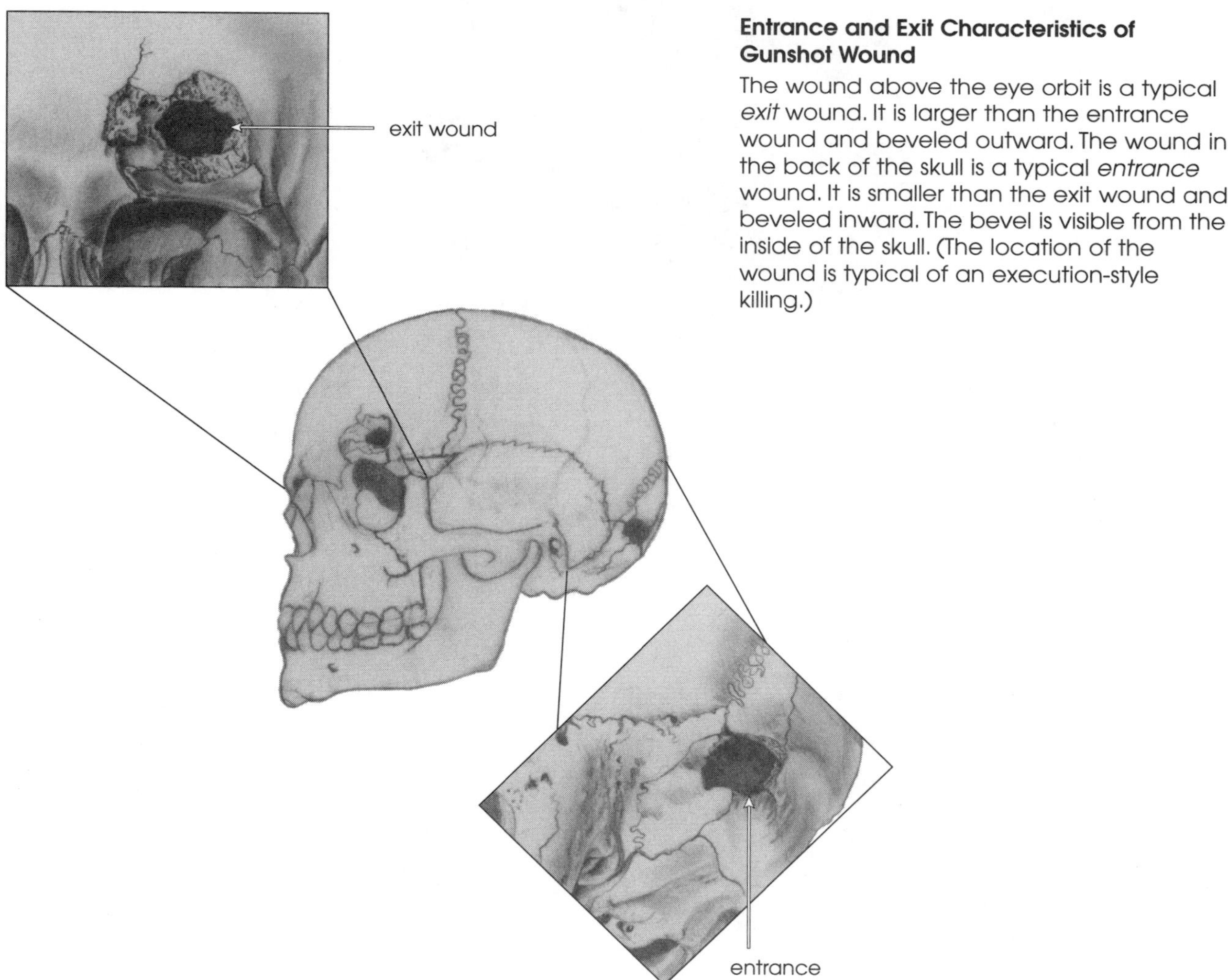

Entrance and Exit Characteristics of Gunshot Wound

The wound above the eye orbit is a typical *exit* wound. It is larger than the entrance wound and beveled outward. The wound in the back of the skull is a typical *entrance* wound. It is smaller than the exit wound and beveled inward. The bevel is visible from the inside of the skull. (The location of the wound is typical of an execution-style killing.)

SHOTGUN WOUND

Shotguns produce entirely different types of wounds. The size of shot and the range between muzzle and target affect the size and shape of the wound, the overall pattern of the wound, and the degree of injury.

Skull with Shotgun Wound

This skull was penetrated by two rounds from a .410 shotgun fired at close range. Note the *scalloped margins* and the small *"starburst" cracks*. There is only slight inward beveling of the entrance wounds. Shotgun pellets rarely exit the body.

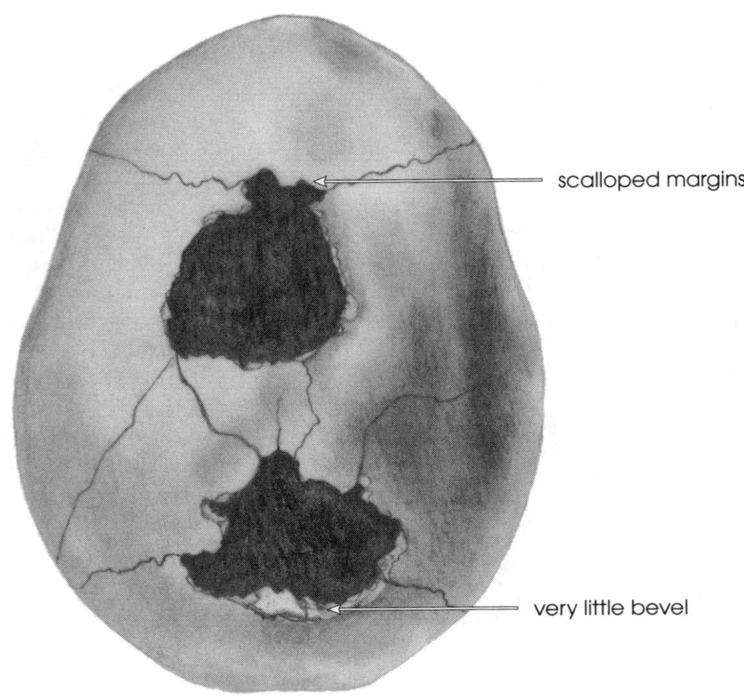

BLUNT FORCE INJURY

The illustration below shows a blunt force injury.

Skull with Blunt Force Trauma

This skull was penetrated by a carpenter's hammer with a strong arm swinging it. Note the presence of *concentric cracks* in addition to the occasional "starburst" crack. Fragments of bone are also bent inward because of more complete fracture of the outer table than the inner table of bone.

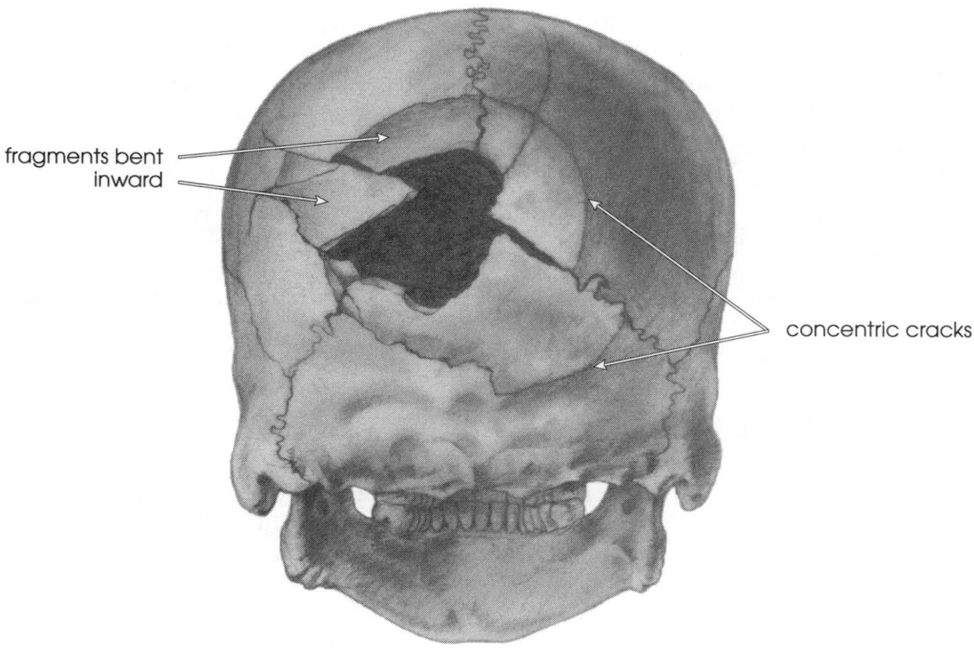

IS IT POSSIBLE TO CONFIRM RAPE OR TORTURE WITH SKELETAL ANALYSIS?

Rape is usually determined by vaginal swabs and evidence of genital bruising. Of course neither is possible with skeletal remains. However, other physical evidence may exist that is consistent with the conditions of rape and that may support verbal testimony from witnesses.

Example

An entire village of women and children were massacred in Guatemala during their recent civil war. One witness watched from a distance. She reported that the women were raped and beaten by the military before they were executed.

More than a decade later, the mass grave was carefully exhumed. The skeletons of the women were found with blouses still in place, but no skirts. (The blouses and skirts had been of the same fabric, so they would not have decayed at different rates.) Many of the victims exhibited circummortem fractures of zygomas, mandibles, and arms. This type of fracture is consistent with beating about the face and attempts to defend against a stronger opponent. While rape could not be proven after so many years, the physical evidence definitely supported the testimony of the witness.

The Stages of Bone Healing

The exact timing of healing depends on the extent of the injury as well as the age and health of the victim. But bone healing does follow a neatly predictable sequence of steps: blood clot, vascular bridge, infusion of cells, soft callus, bony callus, and remodeling.

1. Clot formation (time period: hours): Immediately following the injury, there is an infusion of blood into the tissue surrounding the break and a clot or hematoma forms.
2. Vascular bridge formation (time period: days): A vascular network is established through the clot. The vessels bridge the ends of the broken bone and provide a conduit for nutrients and cells.
3. Infusion of cells (time period: throughout the healing process): Osteogenic cells infuse into the vascular bridge and begin to differentiate into the variety of cells needed to build bone.
4. Soft callus formation (time period: weeks): Osteoblasts build a soft callus. This is an organic matrix on which minerals can be deposited. The soft callus begins to buttress the damaged area.
5. Bony callus formation (time period: 1–2 months): Osteoblasts continue to build by depositing minerals within the callus. The new woven bone buttresses the damaged area. A hard mass is palpable in the area of the break.
6. Bone remodeling (time period: years): Once the broken bone is stabilized by the bony callus, osteoclasts and osteoblasts commence to remodel the callus into lamellar bone, and osteocytes take over the long-term maintenance of the rebuilt Haversian systems. The bony callus becomes smoother and denser but remains visible in spite of remodeling.

Timing the Healing Process

There are so many variables in the process of bone healing that it is difficult to state the exact amount of time required for each step. Under ideal conditions, osteoclastic bone resorption and subperiosteal bone apposition is visible two weeks following the fracture and the bony callus has bridged the break by one month.

Healing is delayed if damage is severe or if bone approximation and immobilization are inadequate. Under such conditions, the body's effort to rebuild bone may finally fail. The proliferating cells differentiate into chondroblasts that produce a hyaline-like cartilage over the ends of the fractured bones and a pseudoarthrosis or false joint is formed.

Advanced age, poor nutrition, and disease can also slow the healing process. The entire process of repair is sabotaged and delayed by infection. If, however, immobilization is maintained and the infection subsides, repair resumes after the fragments of dead bone are reabsorbed.

Stages of Healing of a Radius

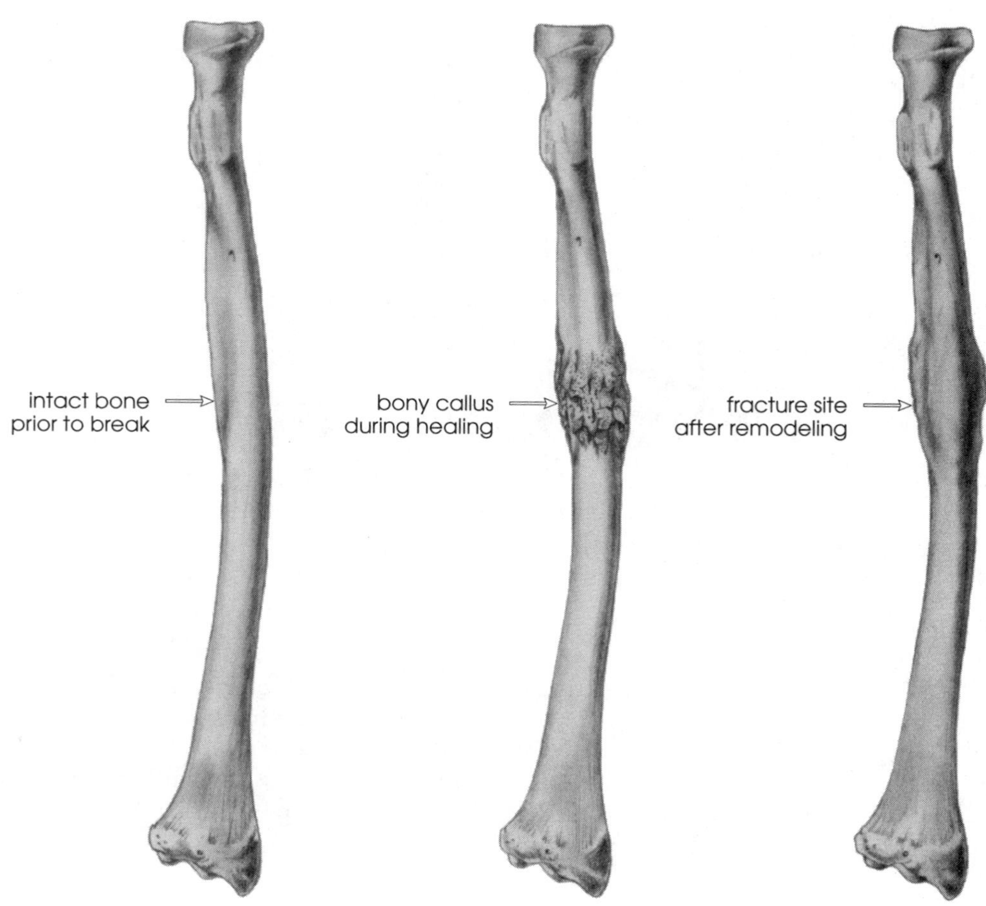

The amputated end of a bone remodels in response to change or loss of function. In general, this means that the sharp edges disappear and the terminal part of the bone becomes smoothly rounded.

The femur, however, is a weight-bearing bone. The individual whose bone is featured in the illustration below was a double amputee who used the stumps for modified walking. The result is function-specific remodeling. Note that a large resorption pit is apparent at the point of compression. This is a typical bony response to compression necrosis. The posterior surface of the amputated end of the femur is expanded into osteophytic processes. This modification provides greater surface area for muscle attachment. Remember that form follows function!

Bone Resorption and Remodeling Following Amputation

This is a remodeled femoral stump, years after above-the-knee amputation.

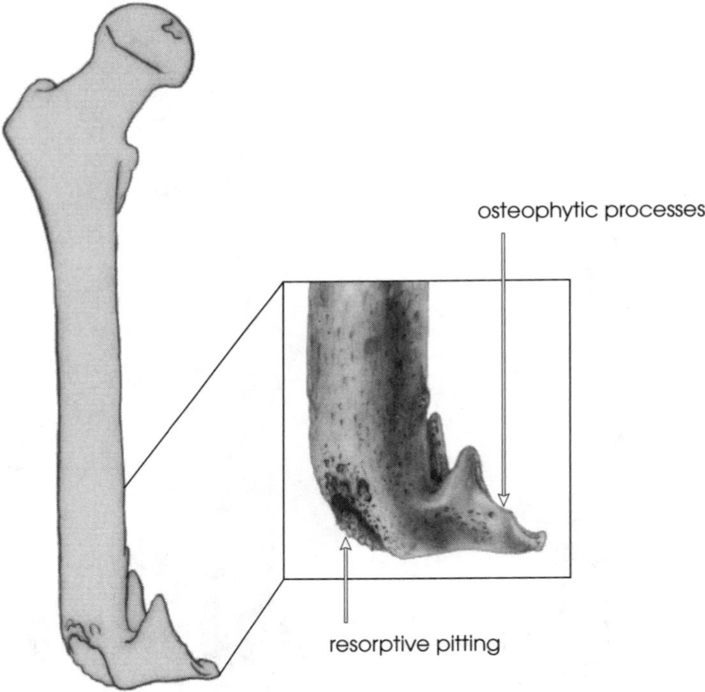

Disease Analysis

Bone diseases result from a number of factors including advancing age, inadequate nutrition, infection, or neoplasm. It is not always possible to separate the effects of disease from the effects of trauma, and analysis of disease from bone alone is challenging. It is advisable to explore the range of possibilities for a condition in relation to any known facts about the deceased person.

If nothing is known about the person, it may be necessary to offer a range of possible causes for the bony condition. Similar conditions can be produced by different agents. Also, the same events or pathogens are capable of producing different conditions in different individuals or at different times of their lives.

Age-Related Conditions

Osteoarthritis refers to a group of degenerative joint diseases. The most common is caused by progressive wear and tear on joints with age. The articular cartilage thins, bony projections proliferate at the edge of the articular surface, and, in later stages, striations appear on the face of the articular surface. Osteoarthritis can be accelerated inflammation caused by trauma or infection. Generalized osteoarthritis is more likely to be age-related. Osteoarthritis caused by disease is more likely to be localized. (See the illustration of osteoarthritis in the lower back in Chapter 4, page 66.)

Osteoporosis refers to a group of diseases in which bone reabsorption out-paces bone deposition. Bone becomes porous and light. It is a common condition of postmenopausal women and is the underlying cause of the typical "dowager's hump." Osteoporosis also leads to the bone breaks sometimes referred to as "old lady fractures"—easily broken wrists and hips. Such fractures are slow to heal and often leave misshapen bones in spite of careful splinting and casting.

Osteomalacia refers to a number of disorders in adults in which bones are inadequately mineralized. The lower limbs tend to bow because they are not strong enough to support body weight.

Paget's disease is characterized by excessive rates of bone deposition and reabsorption. The newly formed bone has an abnormally high ration of immature woven bone and little mature compact bone. It is also less mineralized than normal bone, thus it is soft and weak. It is a disease of the elderly, progresses slowly, and is seldom life-threatening. Paget's disease may effect only one bone, even a single vertebra. If the tibia is involved, it becomes saber-shaped. The legs may bow.

Nutrition and Metabolism

Rickets in children is analogous to osteomalacia in adults. The bones are inadequately mineralized and the limbs tend to bow. It is caused by inadequate amounts of vitamin D. Narrow tibia ("saber shins") can also be the result of rickets.

Porotic or spongy hyperostosis appears as lesions on the surface of the cranial vault and a "hair-on-end" trabecular pattern within the diploë of the cranial vault. It can be caused by anemia—usually iron deficiency anemia, or one of the congenital hemolytic anemias (e.g., thalassemia and sickle cell disease).

Cribra orbitalia is bilateral pitting of the orbital roofs of the frontal bone. (See the illustration on page 170.) It is produced by simultaneous bone lysis (pitting) and new bone formation (thickening). Like porotic hyperostosis, cribra orbitalia is related to anemia.

Enamel hypoplasia is seen as horizontal striations in tooth enamel. It results from inconsistent nutrition during formative years. Seasonal swings in food supply may cause regular enamel lines. Serious childhood illnesses may result in irregularly spaced lines.

Cribra Orbitalia

This skull is from a Peruvian man. His anemia was probably altitude-related.

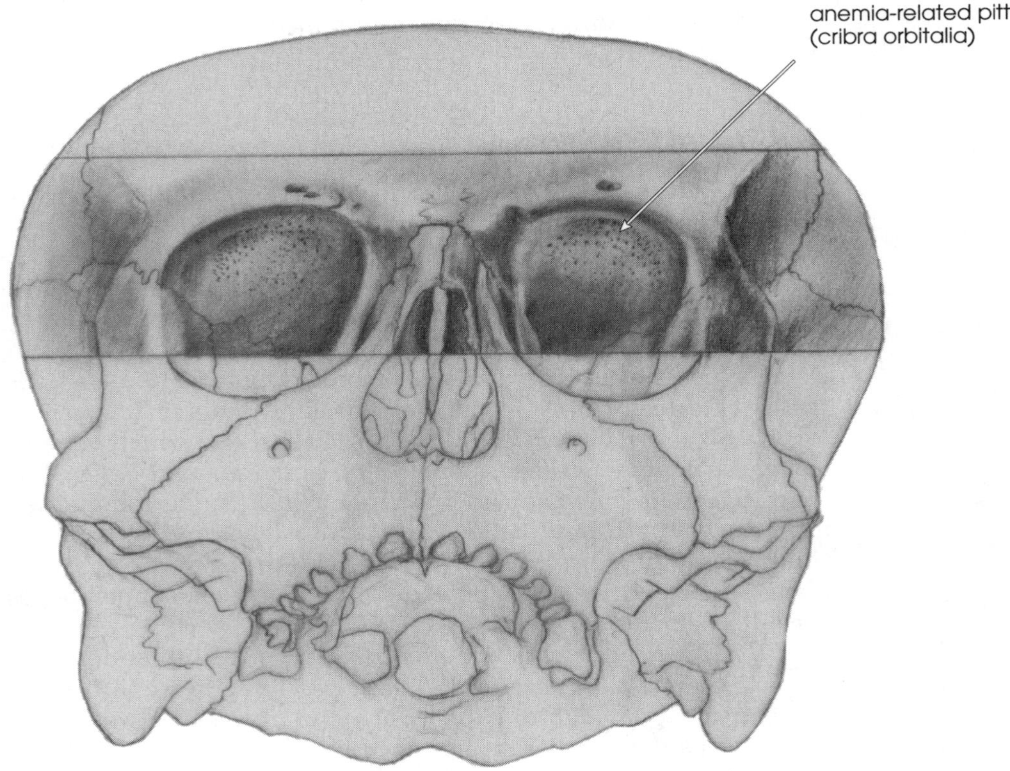

Bacterial Infections

Osteomyelitis is a general term for a bacterial infection of bone and bone marrow. It can enter from infections in surrounding tissues or through the blood stream. It can also follow a compound fracture.

Periostitis (or periosteitis) is a general term for a bone infection with involvement of the periosteum. (See the illustration on page 171.) The periosteum is the membrane enveloping the bone.

Syphilis is an infection caused by a specific species of bacteria, *Treponema pallidum*. The effects vary depending upon the age of acquisition. If the infection is established in the fetus, it is "congenital syphilis." The skull, radius, ulna, and tibia are usually involved. Saber tibia is one of the resulting deformations.

Sexually transmitted syphilis is "acquired syphilis." Skeletal effects include gummata of the medullary cavity or the periosteum. Primary sites include the frontal bone and the proximal ends of the tibia and humerus.

By the way, syphilis should not be dismissed as a disease of the past. According to scientists at the Center for Disease Control and Prevention (CDC) in Atlanta, syphilis is still present in the world (including in the United States). There is a new outbreak every seven to ten years. Syphilis responds well to antibiotic treatment, but there is no vaccine. Unfortunately, cultural inhibitions result in reluctance to seek immediate treatment. (St. Louis and Wasserheit 1998)

Skeletal tuberculosis is caused by the bacterium, *Mycobacterium tuberculosis*. Lesions caused by *M. tuberculosis* are most often found in the vertebral column (T6 to L3), the hip, and the knee.

Periostitis in the Distal Shaft of the Ulna

Here the surface of the distal shaft of the ulna is elevated and pitted by the reaction of the bone to a periosteal infection. The infection is localized. The rest of the bone shaft and the other bones of the body appear normal.

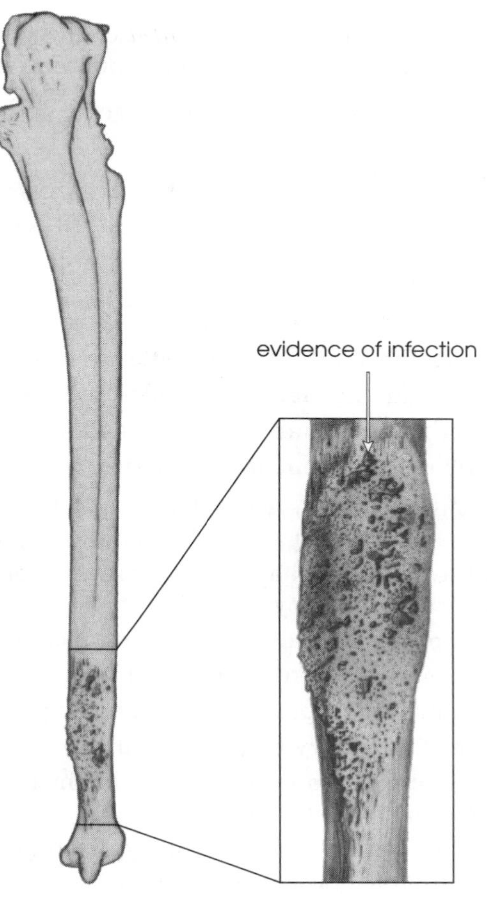

Leprosy is caused by *Mycobacterium leprae*, a member of the same bacterial family as tuberculosis, Mycobacteriaceae. The bones of the hands and feet are most affected in leprosy. The phalanges first appear to sharpen, then resorb into distorted stumps.

Neoplasms

An *osteoma* is a benign bone tumor. Osteomas are common, and many classification systems exist. But, basically, they are dense, circumscribed, nonproliferating, and symptomless. Osteomas may be caused by trauma or excess callus formation. Most osteomas occur on the inner and outer surfaces of the cranium and mandible, but some are found in the postcranial skeleton, particularly in areas prone to injury.

Osteosarcoma (osteoid sarcoma) is a highly malignant tumor containing bony tissue. It is formed by proliferation of mesodermal cells and is more commonly known as bone cancer. Osteosarcomas primarily affect young people between 10 and 25 years of age.

A Final Review of the Data

Before completing a skeletal analysis, go over the following checklist to be sure that all possible information has been considered.

1. **Age Changes:** Were *developmental* changes ongoing at the time of death? Were *degenerative* changes apparent at the time of death?
2. **Sexual Variation:** Consider the pelvis. *Is it long and narrow or short and wide?*
   - Pubis elongation
   - Subpubic angle
   - Ventral arc
   - Sciatic notch
   - Preauricular groove

   Consider the skull. Is it rugged or gracile?
   - Mastoids and nuchal area—male-female comparison
   - Supraorbital ridge and frontal—male-female comparison
   - Mandible—male-female comparison
3. **Racial Variation:** Consider the skull. What is the most prominent feature of the face—the mouth, the nose, or the cheeks? Examine each of the following features and assess them in relation to skulls of known racial identity:
   - Nasal aperture—width in relation to length
   - Nasal spine—present or absent, size
   - Nasal guttering—present or absent, degree
   - Degree of maxillary prognathicism
   - Zygomatic position in relation to the maxilla—on the same plane or posterior to that plane
   - Zygomatic suture form—S-shaped, Z-shaped, or straight
   - Dental arch shape—rounded or V-shaped

   Consider the teeth. Are there any obvious racial characteristics?
   - Shovel-shaped incisors—usually the maxillary centrals
   - Carabelli's cusp—on the maxillary first molars
4. **Stature Estimation:** Look over the entire skeleton for consistency. Are the limbs of the same general length? Is the bone density consistent throughout the skeleton? Is there evidence of scoliosis or anything else that would create inconsistency between long bone measurement and actual height?
   - Measure the long bones.
   - Use the most recent formulae or computer analysis. Fordisc 2.0 by Ousley and Jantz, University of Tennessee, is recommended because it is supported by a large modern database.
   - Account for incongruities when possible.
5. **Trauma:** Have you examined every bone for evidence of traumatic incidents? Can you separate antemortem, perimortem, and postmortem trauma? Can you explain anomalies in terms of the bone dynamics? Will radiographs be useful?
6. **Disease:** Is there any evidence of systemic disease, infection, or poor nutrition? Will radiographs or other analysis such as microscopy be useful?

THE BASICS OF HUMAN IDENTIFICATION

Once the skeletal description is complete, human identification is possible, but definitely not certain. Skeletonized human remains often are never identified. They are labeled "John or Jane Doe," boxed, cremated, and forgotten. The families of the dead live out their lives in the limbo between hope and grief. The murderers go undetected and unpunished. The problem is compounded by silence—the unidentified body doesn't complain, the family doesn't know to whom to complain, and the murderer certainly stays silent. Only the public can apply pressure, and the public is usually apathetic unless a serial murderer or a terrorist threatens the well-being of the entire community.

The major reason for this travesty is the common thought that skeletonized remains are unidentifiable except by dental records. This is not true. There are many methods for description and identification of skeletal remains. (See Table 12.7 on page 175.) Identification *is* dependent on preexisting records of the deceased individual. Valid records may, however, be written, photographic, radiographic, or within the memories of survivors.

It is not possible to know what part of the skeletal system will provide the key to identification. Therefore, careful analysis must follow careful retrieval. The result is large amounts of information from mere fragments of bone. The information leads to the possibility of identification as well as information about cause and manner of death, time since death, and events since death.

Even when the unidentified person is fully described, there will be no identification until information on a missing person is offered for comparison. It is, perhaps, like putting the best batter in the league at home plate. If the pitcher never throws the ball, there will be no hit.

To continue the baseball analogy, a hit does not mean a home run. There are three bases to pass on the way back to the home plate. Likewise, there are levels of identification, and they are usually passed in sequence. Tentative identification is the first step (first base). It can result from any available clue—clothing, jewelry, pocket contents, body location, etc.

A tentative identification leads to the search for more information. Some of the information collected on the missing person may result in an identification intermediate to tentative and positive. This is "identification by exclusion" or "identification by preponderance of evidence" (second and third base).

Positive identification (home base) results only from information that is exclusive to one and only one individual (e.g., fingerprints and radiographs, dental and others). Even DNA is less than perfect for identification if an identical twin exists.

PHOTO SUPERIMPOSITION

Photo superimposition, also known as video superimposition, can be a convincing method for identification when all else is lacking. It is accomplished by photographically superimposing a carefully positioned skull on a facial photograph.

Photo superimposition is most easily done with the use of two video cameras, but it can also be accomplished with as little as one camera, a piece of glass in a vertical stand, and two separate light sources.

Numerous points of reference should be visible on both the photograph and the skull. For example, it should be possible to match the following points and curvatures:

- Bridge of nose
- Length of nose

- Width of nose
- Distance between eyes
- Lip line
- Any visible teeth
- Chin—lowest point
- Chin—most forward point
- Angle of jaw
- Ear canal

Photo superimposition has been shown to be most successful for identification purposes if two photographs are used (Austin 1994). The photos should show the individual from different perspectives such as frontal and profile. A physical anomaly such as a broken nose is very useful if it is apparent in the photograph. Consult the references for video superimposition in the bibliography before attempting the method.

Other Useful Methods

There are many other useful methods in general use by forensic laboratories and under development by research laboratories. Most of these methods require highly specialized equipment. If the circumstances of the case require greater analysis and the funds are available, it is possible to send samples to specialized laboratories for the following analyses:

- Blood typing for exclusion of people as possible relatives
- DNA analysis (genetic analysis) of blood or tissue for information about genetic affinity between two or more people, and positive identification
- Element and isotope analysis for information about nutrition or disease
- Isotope analysis for information about the year of death
- Microstructural analysis of bone (sometimes called "histological analysis") for information about age at death
- Microstructural analysis of teeth for information about age at death (see Chapter 10)
- Ballistics analysis for identification of weapon and projectiles as well as matching of fired projectiles with weapons.
- Toxicology analysis of biological substances
- Hair and fiber analysis and comparison
- Fingerprint classification and comparison

More types of analyses are also possible. But remember, each provides only part of the total picture. The requirements of the specific case dictate the route to follow and the experts to seek.

It is wise to consult the prospective laboratory before collecting samples. Ask about their preferences regarding collection methods, preservation, packaging, and transport. Work with them to maintain the chain of custody and the integrity of the sample.

Table 12.7 Degrees of Identification

Type of I.D.	Basis for I.D.
tentative identification	clothing
	possessions
	location of body
	verbal testimony
identification by preponderance of evidence	anomalies known by family or friends, but without the existence of written records
	photo superimposition
identification by exclusion	"Everybody else is identified and there is no evidence that this is *not* the only person still missing."
positive identification	dental identification
	radiographic identification
	mummified fingerprints
	prosthetic identification
	DNA analysis
	unique skeletal anomalies

WHEN IS A "PERFECT" IDENTIFICATION NOT ENOUGH?

Convincing the investigator is not always enough. The jury and the family must be convinced also. Jurors may lack the education or experience to easily grasp the methodology used for identification. This can usually be overcome by introducing good teaching techniques in the courtroom.

The family is another problem entirely. In my experience, most families want answers. They want an end to the nightmare of not knowing what has happened to their loved one. But there are times when members of the deceased's family simply do not want to believe the evidence. They choose to turn their backs on the evidence and go on hoping that the loved one is still alive.

Example

One family in Georgia was notified of the identification of their missing grandfather. The identification was made by radiographic records. They said, "No, it couldn't be him. We won't bury some stranger!"

The missing man was found almost completely skeletonized, and the family didn't believe that he could have decomposed so quickly. (In fact, a body can be reduced to a skeleton within two weeks in a hot Georgia summer. A few days are adequate if animals have access to the body.)

In an effort to provide the family with information that they would be willing to accept, I filmed a superimposition of the skull with two separate photos (frontal and lateral views) of the missing man. The family was invited to a private viewing of the video in the medical examiner's office. Afterward, they quietly accepted the remains for burial and the case was closed.

WHEN IS DNA TESTING APPROPRIATE?

"Why not just use DNA for everything?" The answer is simple, but it takes a little time to understand the mechanisms involved. Genetic analysis is expensive and time-consuming. The few laboratories equipped to do such tests will usually not accept the case until the initial investigation is complete, a tentative identification has been made, and appropriate relatives have been located.

Usually, in skeletal tissues, mitochondrial DNA (mt-DNA) is the only type available. This is both good and bad. It is good in that the victim will have mt-DNA identical to his or her mother and siblings. A comparison sample is required from only one maternal relative. It is bad in that close relatives (siblings, maternal cousins, mother and child) are indistinguishable. In other words, mitochondrial DNA cannot stand alone as an identification method if there is any possibility that the body is that of a close relative. There must be some other indication of identification, some assurance that the victim has not been confused with any of the other people sharing the same mitochondrial DNA.

In a mass grave from a single village, it is highly likely that siblings, cousins, and other closely related individuals have been massacred together. Quickly packing a series of samples off to the lab will not solve the identification problem.

Example

A clandestine grave on a beach in Haiti revealed the decomposed remains of a young man. Reports suggested that he was one of many killed while trying to escape to boats during a massacre of civilians. No close relatives were reported missing in the same event.

Testimony of a survivor linked a badly rusted key from the victim's pocket to a house near the shore. The key fit. The tentative identification based on the key led to relatives who provided a matching description of the victim, including specific dental characteristics. The description and dental characteristics provided a probable identification that supported the decision to compare mt-DNA from an intact molar tooth with blood from maternal relatives of the disappeared man. The mt-DNA was identical and a positive identification was made.

CHAPTER 13

FIELD METHODS

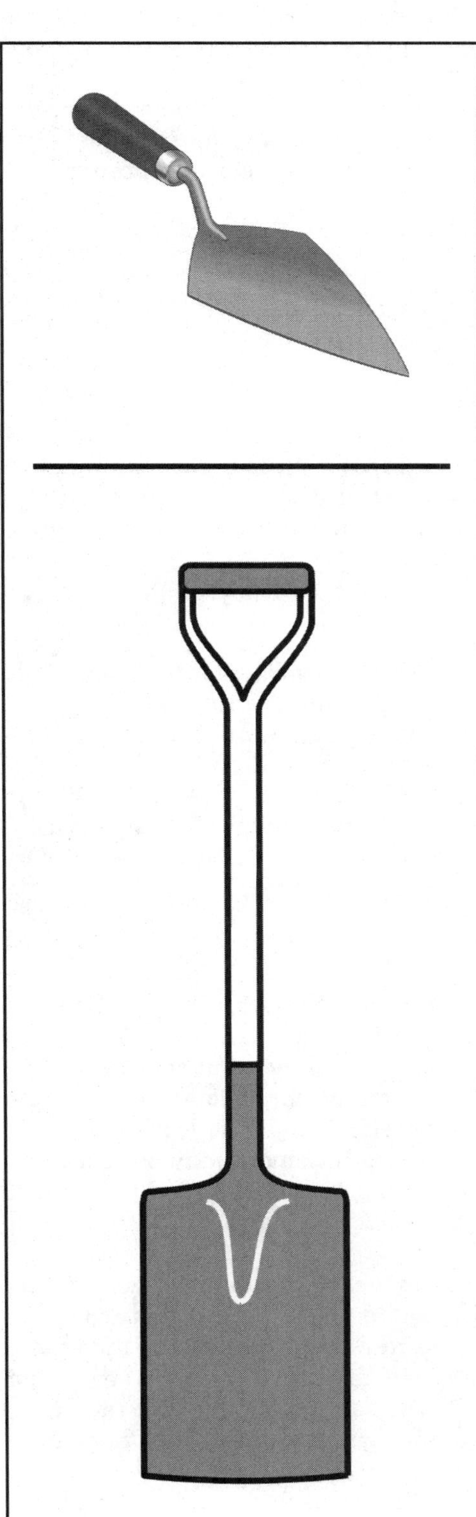

CHAPTER OUTLINE

Preparation for Fieldwork

Expectations

The unexpected is normal in field work. It can take the form of unusual weather, equipment breakdown, worker injury, illness, and more. Thorough preparation offers few thrills and little sense of adventure, but it requires creative thinking, and it is essential. The time spent in preparation is well rewarded in productivity.

If the work site is close to a modern city, it is possible to send for supplies. But most field work is far from supply sources, and most budgets are planned in advance of the work. Success depends on serious preparation together with on-the-spot ingenuity.

Is the Job Legally, Financially, Physically, and Technically Possible?

Legal Permission

Legal requirements vary from state to state and from country to country. It is imperative that anyone planning to excavate a human body be aware of the law and adhere to the appropriate legal procedures. For example, in Guatemala, the local judge must be present at all times during the excavation. To absent-mindedly begin without checking for his presence would jeopardize an entire project.

Funding

Funding should be adequate to assure completion of a thorough job. This includes everything from the planning stage through the final report.

The source of the funds is as important as the quantity. If the excavation is part of an investigation that reflects on a political entity, the political motivation of the funding source will affect the general reception of the report and the results of any subsequent legal proceedings. For this reason, private or international funds backed by general interests are often preferable to single-government funds.

Security and Storage

Security is an issue for the workers, the site, and the evidence. In the past, forensic anthropologists did not begin work until many years after the critical event. At that time, it was necessary to guard the evidence, but concern for the safety of the workers was minimal. Today, however, forensic anthropologists are working in active war zones and disaster sites subject to looting. Worker safety has become an important issue. Military advisement may be required.

The site itself should be treated as a crime scene. Use good judgement about the security required. It may be necessary to leave a night guard at the site during the excavation process.

The excavation record should include evidence of unauthorized disturbance. Photography provides a simple method for documenting disturbances. Establish and mark a specific point or several points from which the entire site can be observed. Take a photograph from the point(s) at the beginning and end of each work day. Use a tripod or the same photographer (a person of the same height) to ensure that the angulation is identical from one photograph to the next.

Plan to store all evidence—both human remains and other physical evidence—in a dry, secure area during all phases of the work. Refrigeration will be necessary if decomposition is a problem.

Never leave evidence unguarded or unlocked—even for lunch or coffee break. Lack of security damages the chain of custody. The error will return to haunt the witness when the time comes to testify about the legitimacy of the evidence.

Antemortem Information

Key Term

antemortem Before death.

There are two phases in the collection of **antemortem** information. The first phase precedes both field and laboratory work. It consists of gathering information from personal interviews, medical records, and state records.

The second phase follows the field and laboratory work. It consists of follow-up interviews and renewed searches. The goal is to fill in missing information and resolve any discrepancies between the descriptions of the missing persons and the descriptions of the unidentified remains.

The Interview

There are circumstances under which the personal interview is the sole means of obtaining information about the deceased. Plan ahead for optimal communication. Find local translators if possible. They are more likely to understand nuances in communication. Also, consider the following interview tools.

Questionnaires

Use standardized questionnaires that can be adapted to computerized database programs whenever possible. Programs for matching missing and unidentified persons are available in the United States from several organizations, including the National Disaster Medical System and the National Crime Information Center.

A sample questionnaire is included in the appendix. It is designed for use by families and friends of victims.

Visual Aids

Use visual aids wherever possible. Memory is enhanced and fewer translation errors and left-right errors occur when the interviewee can communicate without ambiguity by pointing or drawing.

If scars or amputations are mentioned, provide diagrams of faces or full body diagrams. The location of the identifying characteristic can be drawn on the diagram and included with the file.

When teeth are discussed, use full mouth dental casts or drawings of teeth. It is easier to point to the location of the missing or broken tooth than to try to describe it. If clothing is discussed, offer color charts and record the number of the color for each article of clothing. Color is notoriously difficult to communicate, even between people of the same culture and language group. Cloth samples can also be useful. Samples can be collected from a local tailor or dressmaker's shop. The samples should be representative of the types of cloth used in the area (e.g., several different weights and textures of cotton or wool).

Key Term

postmortem After death.

Medical Records

Almost *any* medical records may be useful, but radiographs are very useful for identification of skeletal remains. Positive identifications can be made from comparisons of antemortem and **postmortem** radiographs of almost any type.

Examples of Useful Medical Records

- Dental radiographs
- Cranial radiographs showing frontal sinuses
- Radiographs of broken or healed bones
- Radiographs of arthritic joints
- Any radiograph that demonstrates the trabecular pattern in calcified tissue.
- Written descriptions of physical problems

Photographs

A clear photograph can help to define distinctive traits of the missing individual. Photographs can be very useful for identification purposes when used with analytical skill *and* common sense. A *smiling* photo is particularly useful because the dentition can be observed directly in the skull. Anterior teeth may be missing, chipped, or out of alignment (crooked). A *profile* photo reveals the curvature of the forehead, brow, and upper part of the nose. The same curvatures can be observed on the frontal bones, the supraorbital ridge, and the nasal bones. A three-quarter view portrait photo or a photo with *side lighting* may reveal a trait such as a broken nose, a deeply cleft chin, or large frontal bossing.

Numbering System and Records

An unambiguous numbering system should be ready for use before work commences. If a numbering system is not already in effect, devise one and stick with it. A good numbering system does two things: It *identifies* the specific piece of evidence, and it *provides information* for the users.

Evidence Identification

Date

The date of recovery or the date of accession of the evidence should be included in the number. It is necessary to decide how much of the date is required—year, month, and/or day. In some cases, time of day is also important.

Organization

The name or abbreviation of the agency or institution responsible for recovery of the evidence: Initials or a specific code for the individual responsible for the recovery can be incorporated here.

SITE

The site name or an abbreviation of the site name: The systems employed by the law enforcement or military in a particular area may be useful because of the need to communicate with other organizations. If no other system is in effect in a particular area, grid coordinates can be used.

NUMBER

The identification code must include a unique number for the individual remains or piece of evidence. Ideally, the numbers are assigned in sequence of recovery. If, however, there are no numbers assigned at recovery, numbers must be assigned in order of examination in the laboratory.

EXAMPLES OF IDENTIFICATION NUMBERS

- 85-LAMAR-GBI-2059 (1985, Lamar County, Georgia Bureau of Investigation, the 2059th case of the year)
- EAFG/02-12-93/SJPL/E24 (Equipo Antropologia Forense de Guatemala, 2 December 1993, San Jose Pacho Lemoa, skeleton 24 from pit E)

Data Record Forms

Forms are provided in the appendix for specific categories of tasks. Use them as they are or use them as a starting point from which to develop forms that fit the specific needs of the work at hand. The major categories of forms include the following:

- Observation forms—for use in the field and laboratory
- Diagrams of skeletons and fleshed bodies—for the field and laboratory
- Inventory forms—for use in the laboratory after the remains are cleaned, sorted, and ready for examination
- Measurement forms—for use in the laboratory when numerical analysis is planned

Equipment and Supplies

As mentioned before, every project is different. There is no such thing as the "perfect field kit" for every situation. But that is no reason to be unprepared. Gather as much site information as possible and think through what may or may not be needed. Table 13.1 (on page 183) is a guide to equipment and supplies based on experience. Some items are essential and some are optional but nice to have on hand. Occasionally, the optional items prove to be essential. Each year brings new experiences and new ideas. Begin your own lists and use your own creativity.

Tools

Leaf rakes are useful for removing debris from the soil surface. However, if you choose to rake the area, watch the ground carefully while raking. Hair and other small, light evidence is easily caught up and removed within the leafy debris.

Shovels are essential, but not just any shovel will do. The type of shovel with a rounded end is easier to find, and it is usually a good tool for digging holes. But a standard, vertically excavated hole is not the objective; information is the objective. A sharp, square-edged shovel can *shave* the dirt *horizontally* and make stains, outlines, and interrelationships of features visible.

The most common hand tool is the trowel. It must be small enough to be easily manipulated and it must have a straight, sharp edge, not a rounded edge. Paint brushes are useful if the soil is dry. Dental tools and thin plastic scrapers are better if the soil is damp and sticking to the brushes. Dental tools can also used (with great care) when the earth around the remains is extremely hard (e.g. sun-baked clay).

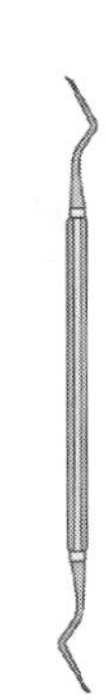

Table 13.1 Equipment and Supplies for Work in the Field

Essential Equipment	Essential Supplies
compass	wooden stakes
measuring tape	string
probe	paper bags
flat, square shovels	cardboard boxes
metal file for tool sharpening	indelible ink pens
trowels	pencils
saw	water-proof paper for mapping
paint brushes (large and small)	notebook
whisk broom	clipboard
plastic tools for close work	insect repellent
buckets	photographic film
screens (0.5, 0.25, 0.125 in. mesh)	
camera (with zoom and macro lenses)	
gauge for photographs	
calipers (small and large)	
canvas or heavy plastic sheets	
container for drinking water	
Optional Equipment	**Optional Supplies**
metal detector	flags for marking
root clippers	spray paint for gridding
leaf rake	4 x 6 cards for tags
small black board	chalk board and chalk
colanders	background cloth for photos
water sprayer/mister	gloves (cloth and plastic)
notebook computer	protective clothing
tripod for camera	plastic bags for temporary storage
folding tables, or saw horses and plywood	

Burial Location and Scene Investigation

The process of locating human remains is both a crime scene investigation and an archaeological site survey. In many cases, it is necessary to locate the grave within a given area. The verbal information about the site is often distorted by memory, or the site itself may be altered by the passage of time and the action of human or environmental factors. The movements of earth, wind, and water are enough to befuddle the clearest of memories. Add in the action of plants and animals, or the work of devious persons, and the picture may be quite different from expectations.

A questionnaire for information about burial sites is included in the appendix.

What to Look for

Surface Irregularities

There are numerous methods of locating graves. The appropriate method depends on the age and type of the grave and the environmental conditions. It may be possible to locate a grave visually. When a person becomes accustomed to the landscape, it is possible to recognize irregularities in both the vegetation and the ground surface.

Vegetation Changes

The plants over a burial are often out of synchronization with surrounding plants. This is due to disruption in the natural succession of plant species, changes in soil nutrients, or the introduction of foreign elements. Increased nutrients from a decomposing body and increased moisture within a burial depression result in more lush vegetation.

Sometimes, the plants over a burial are stunted or dying. This may be the result of decreased access to nutrients caused by impermeable synthetic burial cloths. It may also be caused by harmful chemicals introduced to the soil at the time of burial. In one rather unusual case, the murderer seeded the clandestine grave of his victim with grass seed—a strange sight in the middle of a brush thicket!

Changes in Soil Density

After completing a thorough visual search of the suspected area, a test of soil density provides additional information. This can be accomplished with a simple metal probe.

The fill dirt within a grave is more loosely compacted than surrounding soil. It is easy to differentiate in an otherwise undisturbed area. It is more difficult to differentiate in a disturbed area such as a plowed field, a construction site, or a dump site. Probing should be carried out in a regular pattern. When the edge of a grave fill is found, search for the outline of the disturbance and avoid probing through the middle of the pit. It is exceedingly annoying to find probe holes in essential pieces of evidence when the excavation begins.

Anything Else

Even if the location of the grave is known, a search of the entire area is necessary before beginning the excavation. Evidence on the ground surface is often destroyed or distorted by human activity after the excavation begins.

Look for any inconsistencies on the ground—footprints, tire tracks, damaged vegetation, spent cartridges, garbage, or discarded cultural materials.

Look above and below the ground surface. Rodents, carnivores, and birds are known to carry off both food items and nesting materials. Check animal burrows (carefully) and nests. Fibers or hairs become entangled on branches or tree bark. Stray bullets embed in tree trunks, embankments, and buildings.

Burial Classification

When the burial is found, begin the record of the grave by describing and classifying the type of grave. The burial classification is part of the complete description of the grave. It is useful in communicating the reasons for the methods used and the type of results expected.

Surface Burial or Below-Surface Burial

"Surface burial" sounds like a contradiction or an oxymoron, but it is, in fact, common usage. A surface burial is a "non-interment." The remains are left to decompose on the surface of the ground. It is not uncommon for surface burials to be disturbed or destroyed by carnivores and scavengers. The degree of disturbance is directly related to the size of the animals.

- Insects feed on soft tissues and cause little or no positional disturbance.
- Small animals such as rodents feed on both soft and hard tissues. They sometimes carry away the small bones of fingers and toes. Shiny items such as rings may be found in rodent nests.
- Scavenger birds feed on soft tissues in situ. They may also carry off smaller parts to perches. The bones may then be dropped from the perch. Birds are known to collect hair to use for nesting material.
- Large mammals such as dogs and pigs carry sections of bodies for long distances. They also do the most destructive damage to larger bones.

A "below surface burial" is a standard below-ground interment. The depth is of no importance in the classification. The body can be with or without clothing, shroud, coffin, casket, or vault.

There is one more common type of burial. "Above ground interments" are more consistent in features with the below ground interments than with surface burials. Above ground interments are practiced in areas close to the coast lines where the water table is high and water erosion is common. The body is protected, usually by a vault of stone or concrete. Decomposition takes place under protected conditions and the condition of the remains is likely to be quite good.

Individual or Commingled Burial

An individual burial is the burial of a single person in a single location, above or below the surface of the ground.

A commingled burial contains more than one person buried in the same location. It can be two persons such as mother and child buried in a single grave, or it can be a mass grave created by a bulldozer and containing thousands of intermingled bodies. The commingled remains may have been buried at the same time or at different times. A burial in the site of another primary burial is called an "intrusive" burial.

ISOLATED OR ADJACENT BURIAL

Isolated burials share no walls with other graves. Adjacent burials share at least one wall with another grave.

This classification is important when choosing an appropriate excavation method. Isolated graves can be excavated without concern about encroaching upon other graves, but adjacent graves, such as those within crowded cemeteries, require special excavation techniques. Since the wall of an adjacent grave is shared, disturbance of the wall disturbs the other grave as well. (Adjacent burials can be quite challenging.)

PRIMARY OR SECONDARY

The primary burial is the initial resting place of the remains. The secondary burial is *any* subsequent burial. The remains may be disinterred many times, but each new burial is called a secondary burial.

DISTURBED OR UNDISTURBED

An undisturbed burial is unchanged (except by natural processes) since the time of primary burial.

A disturbed burial is one that has been altered sometime after the time of burial. Sometimes the remains are not moved to a new place, but they are not in the original burial position, either. Disturbances may be caused by burrowing animals, grave diggers in the process of digging other graves, looters searching for bones or grave goods, or any number of other incidents.

Unmarked graves are often accidentally disturbed by excavation equipment or plows. Any graves can be disturbed on purpose if someone decides to move the remains elsewhere. All secondary burials are disturbed burials.

THE EXCAVATION/EXHUMATION

ASSIGNING DUTIES

Key Term

excavate To remove from a covering of earth.

Before a single shovel is lifted, assign auxiliary duties to specific team members. The entire team is usually involved in the **excavation** process, but several of the more reliable team members should also have one other duty to keep up with and be responsible for. The work will flow more smoothly and the result will be more complete.

RECORDER

The recorder maintains a chronological written record of the progress of the excavation. The recorder's accuracy affects everyone in the team, so the recorder's success is everyone's success.

It is useful to maintain two types of records:

- a simple log-type of record with date, times, persons present, and major activities.
- a detailed account of each and every phase of the work and field description of burials and evidence.

Example of a Typical Daily Log

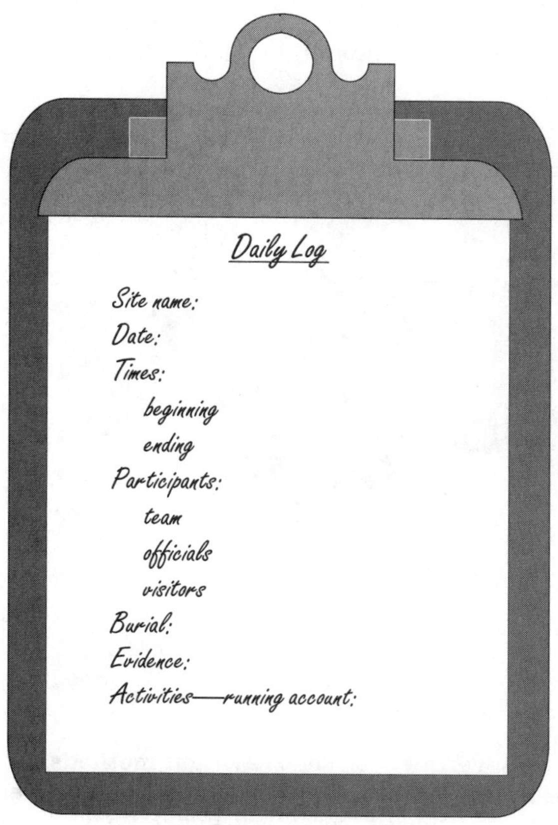

MAPPER

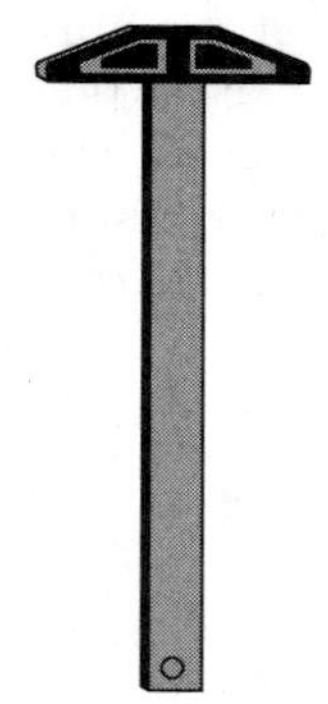

The mapper plans and maintains both two-dimensional and three-dimensional maps of the excavation as it progresses. First the site is measured and then a grid system is planned. The entire system is reduced and drawn. Any permanent features of the landscape are recorded. Natural features such as rivers, streams, large rocks and boulders, and large trees should be included, along with man-made features such as roads, walls, water towers, power lines, and buildings. Include as many things as possible for reference points.

The mapper also maintains a record of each feature or piece of evidence as it is found. Cooperation is requisite. The workers must stop whenever the mapper requests and provide measurements on all coordinates.

PHOTOGRAPHER

The photographic record is essential. The photographer has the task of maintaining the photographic record above all else. A professional photographer is recommended. If it is not possible to hire a professional, one person should be assigned the task of maintaining a photographic record above all other tasks. This includes photographing the site and the evidence and maintaining a log of date, time, and subject for each photo.

Other workers should be able to concentrate on their specific tasks and rely on the photographer to be alert and observant. In this way, neither the work nor the photographic record is compromised.

If the excavation lasts more than one day, the photographer should mark a permanent spot from which to photograph the site at the beginning and end of each work day. The twice-daily photographs serve as a record of any disturbance that may take place when the team is not in the area.

Excavation Methods

There are several effective excavation methods. The best method for the job depends on the *type* of burial (e.g., single, multiple, adjacent), the *location* of the burial (e.g., forest, cemetery, house floor), the *condition* of the soil (e.g., loose or well-packed, wet or dry), and the *depth* of the burial. Assess the conditions, establish priorities, and determine to be practical and flexible.

A model excavation is presented on the following pages (pages 189–194). It is a single grave in a remote setting. The area around the grave is previously undisturbed; the soil is firm and dry; and the depth of the burial is approximately one meter. The sketches represent a vertical cross section of the grave at the top of the skull. The uppermost layer is topsoil; the cross hatching is the grave fill dirt; the uncolored area is undisturbed subsoil; and the stippling beneath the skull is the organic stain resulting from seepage of decompositional fluids.

1. Remove the litter and vegetation:

- Begin by carefully removing the leaf litter and the surface vegetation (the top layer in the sketch). Watch for hair, clothing, or any items that may indicate the presence of man in the area.
- Scrape the soil surface horizontally with a flat shovel until the topsoil is removed and the coloration of the subsoil can be evaluated.
- Examine the soil for changes in coloration that can be associated with the mixing of topsoil and subsoil. When color differences are slight, a light spraying of water helps to darken organic matter and reveal color differences.

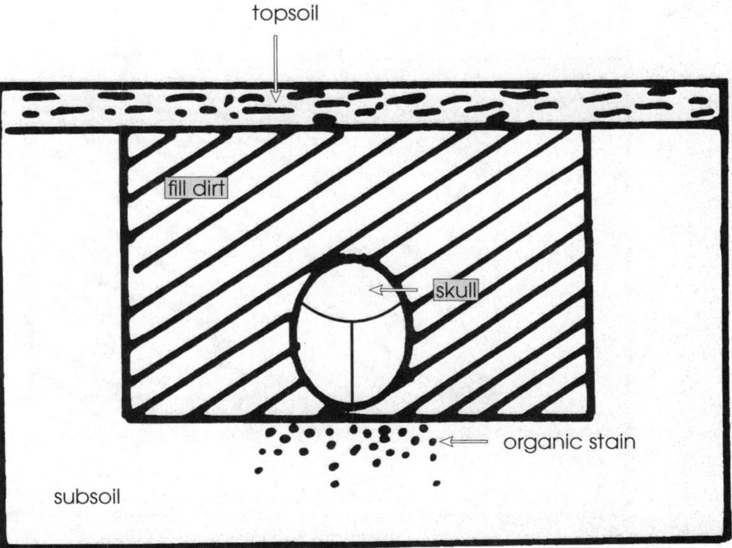

2. Stake out the work area:

- Stake out the exact area to be excavated and stretch a string close to the ground from stake to stake. The string should be positioned to provide straight lines to aid the mapper—avoid creating a hazard to trip the excavators.
- Map the area with reference to directional coordinates and major points of reference (e.g., large trees, buildings, fences). If GPS equipment and/or geological survey maps are available, include latitude and longitude.

3. Locate the grave outline:

- When the grave outline is fully visible, measure it, photograph it and map it. Then work carefully, removing the overburden of earth layer by layer.
- Sift the soil level by level. It is not unusual for evidence to be found in the backfill dirt. Cigarette butts, trash, weapons, projectile casings, cartridges, ropes, hair, and bits of clothing are just a few examples.
- Maintain constant control of the tools. They can cause considerable damage if metal meets bone on the level just out of sight.

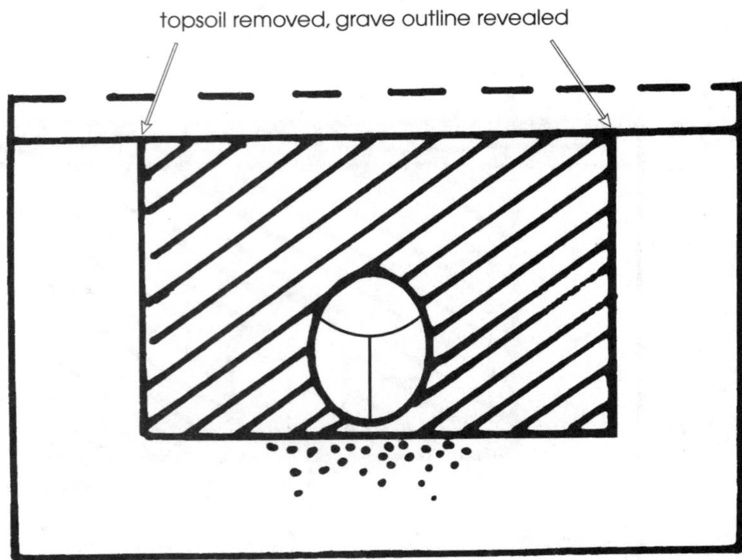

4. Work horizontally:

- Continue to orient the blade of the shovel so that the ground is scraped away horizontally, peeling off thin layers of dirt and maintaining a *flat* work surface.
- If you dig down into the soil as you would to plant a tree, you will damage the unseen body and lose the information provided by relative positions of evidence. Bullets, buttons, pocket contents, jewelry, and the small bones of hands and feet can be easily dislodged from meaningful positions and their information lost forever.
- If you are suspicious or curious because of changes in the density, color, or texture of the soil, change over from a shovel to a trowel to obtain finer control and sharper, cleaner soil surface. Like the shovel, the trowel must be used to cut the soil, not to smear it. This is best accomplished with a sharp edge and an angled approach.

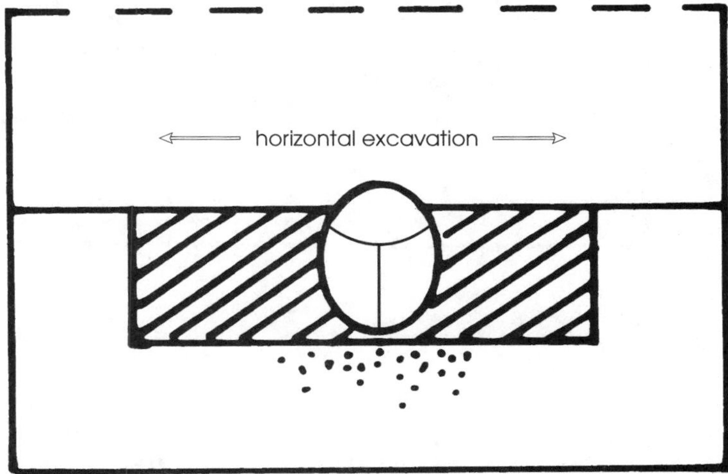

5. Stop and document:

- *Stop* as each find is discovered. Do not remove it unless it is blocking the progress of the excavation. Even then, only remove the find after it is exposed *in place* and completely documented.
- *Stop* when the body is first touched. Remove only enough dirt to determine the position of the body. Do not disturb or remove any portion of the body!

Key Term

pedestal To excavate around a feature, leaving the feature intact and above the floor of the excavation.

6. Pedestal the features:

- Circumscribe the body by digging on all sides to the lowest level of the body (approximately 30 cm.). This is similar to digging a ditch around the body. The result takes the form of a pedestal. Therefore, the common archaeological term for this method is **pedestaling**. *The object is to see what is going on before disturbing anything and to have room to work!* Pedestal any artifacts just as the body is pedestaled. The amount of pedestaling is limited by the burial terrain and conditions. If there is simply no room to dig around the body, do the best you can.

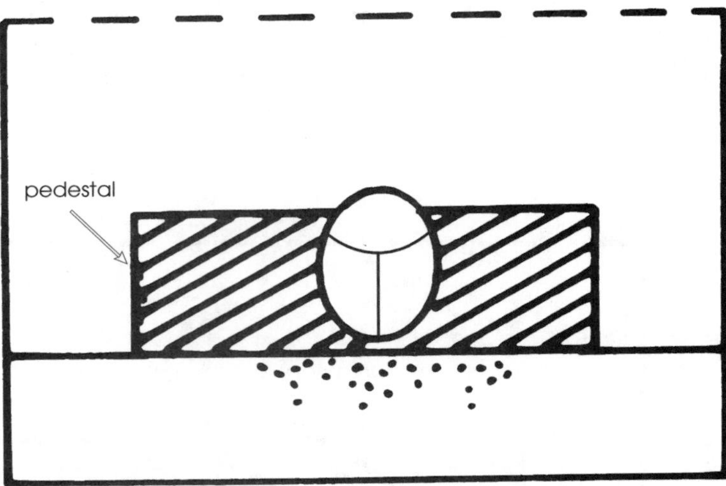

7. Expose everything without disturbing:

- Expose the remains and associated evidence by moving in laterally, using a soft brush and small tools. Do not use a brush on fabric, as it may destroy fiber evidence.
- Examine the soil around the skull for hair. Place this soil in a bag for laboratory study. Patience is essential. The remains may be fragile, and the interrelationships of elements may be easily disrupted. Document information before disturbing it.
- If the remains are from an adult female, be alert to the possibility of a fetal skeleton in the pelvic area!

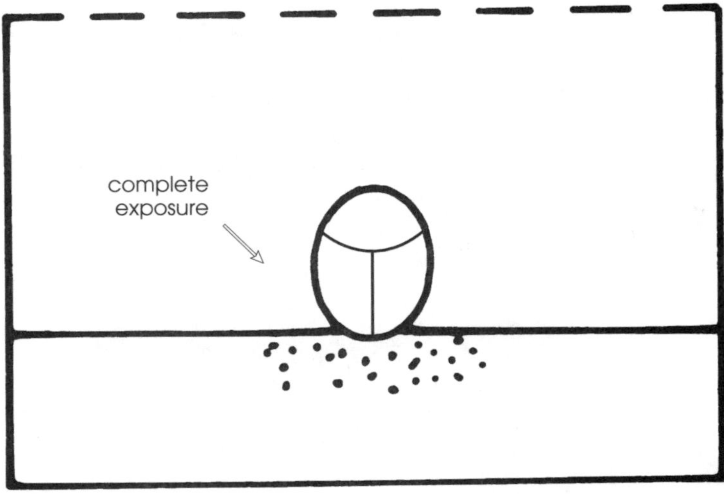

8. Stop and document:

- With the body and all associated evidence exposed and untouched, stop the excavation, photograph, map, and describe everything in writing.
- If there is any chance that the bones will break upon removal, measure the remains while in the ground. The measurements should be appropriate for estimation of stature.

9. Disinter the remains and all associated evidence:

- Remove the remains carefully and do a basic inventory of everything. Note the condition of the remains. Bag each hand and each foot separately. Include hair and fingernails if they are found. Take extreme care with facial bones. Check to see if teeth are loose and be sure none are lost.
- Remove and record all evidence associated with the remains. This includes such items as clothing, buttons, ornaments, weapons, bullets, hair pins, and eyeglasses. Some of the evidence may help identify the victim or the perpetrator. Some of the evidence may aid in the understanding of events around the time of death.

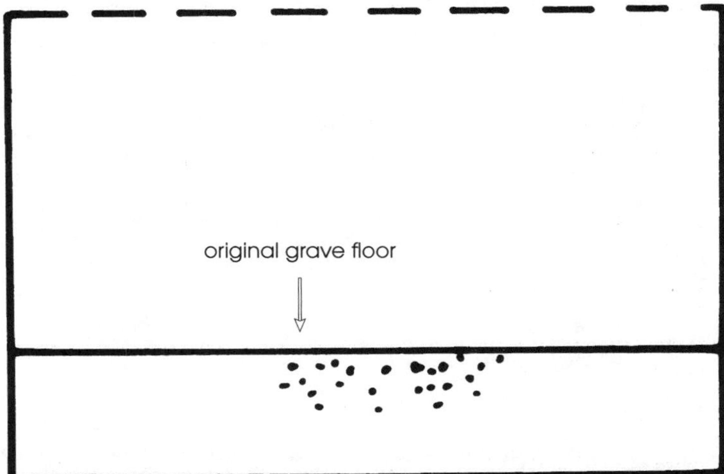

10. Continue until "sterile" soil is reached:

Key Term

necrophyte An organism that consumes dead organic matter; syn. saprophyte, necroparasite.

- Do not stop until "sterile soil" is reached. In other words, continue excavating the grave floor until unstained and undisturbed soil is reached. Screen everything. The area under the body is usually stained by decompositional fluids. The soil may be compact or loose, depending on both the original condition of the soil and the amount of animal activity since burial. It is not unusual for the level beneath the body to be tunneled through by necrophagous invertebrates (**necrophytes**).
- Watch for additional evidence. Hair, buttons, bullets, loose teeth, tooth restorations, coins, and jewelry are just a few of the items that may be recovered from beneath the body.

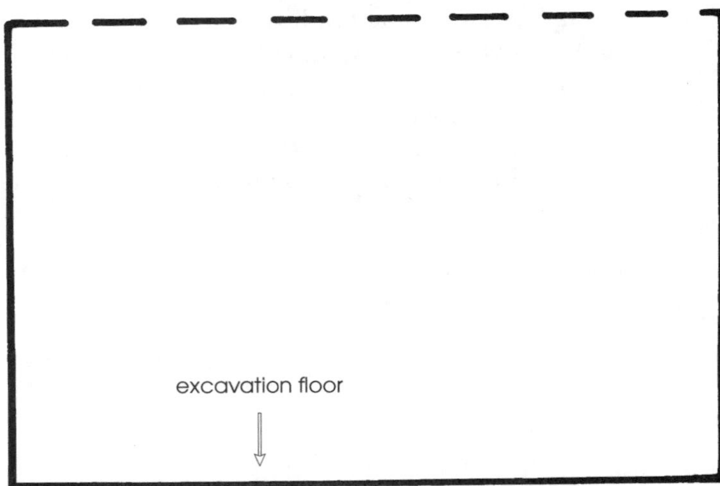

11. Pack carefully:

- Use paper bags and cardboard boxes to facilitate drying. Plastic bags encourage mold growth thereby causing further organic destruction.
- Mark evidence numbers clearly on all containers with indelible ink. Include the name of the site and the date if they are not part of the evidence numbers.

12. Finish the job:

- Backfill the excavation pit and clean up the site. Consider the local conditions and terrain, then burn, bury, or carry out all trash. You will leave the area, but the residents of the area will remember you by what you leave behind.

13. Final photographs:

- Photograph the area upon departure. The final photographs are the evidence of completion of a professional job. They also serve to protect the team from culpability for any subsequent vandalism.

WHICH IS MORE IMPORTANT—BIOLOGICAL OR NONBIOLOGICAL EVIDENCE?

When the remains of a human body are found unexpectedly, a frenzy usually follows. Questions come in sequence. "*Who* is it?" Then, later, "Okay, what happened?" Unfortunately, the physical evidence does not cooperate by presenting itself in the same sequence.

If the remains are ripped out of the ground and sent to the lab for identification, the relative position of nonbiological evidence is lost. At the same time, the value of the nonbiological evidence is reduced or completely lost. Worst of all, there is little chance of determining what is significant and what is clutter.

The nonbiological evidence must be treated with the same care as the biological evidence (usually the body). The nonbiological evidence may be all we have to answer the question, "Okay, what *happened*?"

Example

In Iraqi Kurdistan, a skeleton was exposed in an unmarked grave on a military base. It was necessary to know if the grave preceded the military base or if it contained one of the many "disappeared" of the war.

Information existed in the very method of burial. Muslim burials are conducted by the family. The women wash the body and wrap it in a simple shroud without clothing. The men bury the body on its side facing Mecca. A body found buried on its back or with clothing would not have been buried by the family.

The skeleton in question had been buried on its side facing Mecca. No clothing was apparent. However, careful examination revealed a double thread on both sides of both legs. The fabric of the pants, probably wool, had decomposed with the soft tissues of the body. The cotton-polyester thread of the pants seams remained in place. The victim was not buried by his family, hence he was most probably one of the Kurds executed on the military base. (The top of the skull contained a bullet entry wound.)

The information provided by simple dirt-stained threads proved invaluable.

Evidence Management

Evidence management is critical. The best evidence is invalidated by improper handling. Much can be learned by trial and error, but not this. Most people don't shoot themselves in the foot to learn about gun safety, and most don't want to lose a case to learn about evidence management. So take a deep breath, slow down, and think. Evidence management is part of the job.

Chain of Custody

Each and every piece of evidence, biological or cultural, must be documented in order to maintain its value as evidence. Documentation should include all of the names of the people who come in contact with the evidence. This includes who found it, who collected it, who was responsible for storage, who examined it, and anyone helping along the way.

If custody of the evidence changes, the written record must reflect the change. Both the person giving up the evidence and the person receiving the evidence are responsible for the accuracy of the written record.

Numbering System

The numbering system was discussed in the planning stage. It was devised and accepted by the group of workers, and it may have seemed perfect at the time. It is now time to check and see if it is really working as planned.

Boxing and Storage Systems

The boxing system and the storage systems should be reassessed also. Are they working as well as planned? If not, is there a present remedy or is there an idea that will aid in planning for the future?

Quality Check

How can you be confident that you are doing a good job? Use the following checklists to check your work for quality.

Items to Recognize and Recover

- All fifty-four hand bones, left and right separated
- All fifty-two foot bones, left and right separated
- The hyoid, all three parts
- The coccyx
- All teeth, including single-rooted teeth
- Infant or fetal skeletons
- Epiphyses of sub-adults
- Broken bone fragments
- Hair, fibers, fingernails, and artifacts

Completion of Written Documentation

- Write notes in narrative style.
- Number features consecutively.
- Map location of features, include scale.
- Sketch positions of features.
- Inventory and measure features.
- List all participants.
- Include source material where necessary.
- Sign and date report.

Reconstruction of the Entire Scene from the Photographic Documentation

- Photograph each item with and without numbers.
- Vary lighting and lens settings.
- Photograph each item in situ and in the lab.

- Photograph the entire scene with visible points of reference.
- Using a zoom lens, take several photos in sequence from the same position. This serves to orient observers to the scene and focus in on specific objects.
- Photograph smaller contextual areas with an arrow indicating north.
- Photograph close-ups with scale and labels.
- Use fill-flash to decrease shadows and natural light to increase shadows.

CHAPTER 14

PROFESSIONAL RESULTS

CHAPTER OUTLINE

Professionalism is about expectations—high expectations. A professional is a person who can and does produce results of the highest quality possible. A professional is fully aware of the standards of his or her profession and lives by those standards, whether work is in progress or not.

Record Keeping

There can be no professional report without accurate notes and records. Often, there is only one opportunity to collect information before it is destroyed. The very process of gathering data can alter it. For these reasons, it is important to record everything. Keep records as if your professional reputation depends on them—as indeed it does.

Each of the following categories of information is essential.

Background Information

- Name of the person responsible for the report
- Title, address, telephone number

Significant Dates

- Date of initial contact
- Date(s) of recovery
- Date of entry into official records
- Date(s) of examination
- Date of report

Chain of Custody

- Who gave the evidence to you? When and where?
- Did you sign for it?
- To whom did you release it? When and where?
- Did you request a signature?

Notes

Keep notes of *all* findings. Do not try to decide what is important and what is not important during the work itself. Instead, record everything. Wait until later to decide what belongs in the final report and what may be extraneous observation.

Report Writing

When writing reports, you should write as if amnesia were a foregone conclusion. The case report becomes the permanent record of the investigator's work. It should reflect the knowledge about the case, specific findings, conclusions, support for the conclusions, and recommendations. It must communicate clearly and accurately if it is to be of any use. This is especially important in international or multicultural cases.

A practical format for written case reports includes each of the following sections: case background, general condition of the evidence, inventory, anthropological description, other observations, conclusions, recommendations, signature and date, and appendices of maps or photos if they are useful for accurate communication.

Case Background

In narrative form, give a brief history of the case. Include names, dates, places, and history as you understand it. Be very careful to differentiate information based on your own experience and observations from information based on statements from others.

General Condition of the Evidence

In narrative form, describe the overall condition of the evidence. This includes all human remains as well as any associated physical evidence.

- Is the bone wet, dry, greasy, or ...?
- Is the bone well calcified and strong, demineralized and friable, or ...?
- What type of dirt is adhering to the evidence?
- Is it sun-bleached, stained, or both?

Append any charts and forms that will help convey information about the condition of the evidence.

Inventory

Inventory the remains and all other physical evidence received in association with the remains.

- Bones (percent of total skeleton, color, degree of decomposition, etc.)
- Teeth (number, color, wear, etc.)
- All other items received (e.g., hair, nails, clothing, shoes, bullets, casings, vegetation)

Anthropological Description

- Sex: based on what evidence—pelvic or skull morphology, size, or muscularity?
- Race: based on what evidence—skull morphology, hair, dental traits, or ...?
- Age at death: based on what information—epiphyses, pubic symphysis, rib morphology, osteoarthritis, or ...?
- Stature: based on what evidence and which bone measurements?
- Handedness: based on what evidence—glenoid beveling, arm length, or muscle attachment areas?

Other Observations

- Evidence of *antemortem* disease and injury: Describe the evidence both verbally and graphically. Use diagrams to indicate the location of the evidence and photograph the evidence.
- Evidence of **perimortem** trauma: Describe the evidence verbally and graphically. Use diagrams to indicate the location of the evidence and photograph the evidence.

Key Term

perimortem Around the time of death; syn. circummortem.

- Evidence of *postmortem* trauma: Describe the effects of burial, reburial, disinterment, carnivore activity, and anything else that may have happened to the remains after death. As much as possible, differentiate postmortem effects from antemortem or perimortem effects.

Conclusions

In clear, easy to read narrative form, summarize the description of the individual, the possible time of death, the cause of death, and any other significant findings. Do not say anything you cannot defend with data unless it is qualified as an opinion.

Recommendations

If it is advisable to perform tests beyond the scope of your laboratory, state your recommendations clearly. Add any additional information that may be useful to the final resolution of the case.

Signature and Date

After completing the report, sign and date it.

Appendix

Clearly number and initial all diagrams, drawings, maps, and photographs that are referenced in the report. Include them at the point of reference or append them to the end of the report.

Basic Ethics

Key Term

ethics Moral principles and practice.

Ethics can be discussed at great length for each and every aspect of human life. It is standard procedure for each professional organization to provide a code of ethics for its members. (The Code of Ethics and Conduct of the American Academy of Forensic Sciences can be found in the back section of the annual Membership Directory. It is Article II of the Bylaws.)

Most codes of ethics are firmly based in three fundamental requirements—respect, honesty, and confidentiality. In fact, most ethical problems result from disregard for one or more of these three fundamentals.

Respect

Any work in the forensic sciences or human rights requires respect for one's fellow man. The work involves highly personal, emotional, and religious aspects of life. It cannot be approached callously.

Honesty

Honesty is basic to any type of scientific endeavor. It is also the foundation of the application of forensic science to human rights. There are plenty of situations that call for silence, but there is never a time to lie.

Honesty includes the willingness to admit ignorance, mistake, or failure. It is unquestionably counterproductive to yield to shame or to fabricate excuses.

CONFIDENTIALITY

Confidentiality is essential. This means not talking about cases until the legal process is complete and general permission is given. Silence applies not only to news media, but also to close friends and relatives.

People never fail to be amazed when they hear their own words come back to them distorted. If you wish to maintain integrity, don't talk about a case prior to the formal release of the report or the completion of the judicial process. Let the written report, released by the authority in charge of the case, do the talking for you.

COURTROOM TESTIMONY

There are many books written on the subject of appropriate courtroom testimony (e.g., Matson 1994; McKasson and Richards 1998). Basically, the experts advise that you be well prepared, honest, and respectful. They recommend directing answers to the jury and refusing to be misled by verbal examination or cross examination.

The following material is a short exposition from the advice of the experts.

WHAT DOES IT MEAN TO BE "WELL PREPARED?"

- Know your own credentials. You must be "qualified" as an expert witness before there is any chance for your testimony to be heard. It is necessary to be articulate and convincing about the details of your training and experience.
- Discuss all issues with the attorney prior to the hearing of the case—*including* possible weak points.
- Review your findings and reports. Sometimes the case will come to court months or even years after the work is completed. A thorough review of the material is necessary.
- Have visual aids prepared for the jury. Communication is far more effective if it is visual as well as verbal.

HOW IS HONESTY PRESENTED BEYOND THE "SWEARING IN?"

- Report findings accurately. Never go beyond the limits of the evidence or your experience. If you do not know an answer, say so. Do not guess.
- Keep in mind that the scientist represents the physical evidence. He or she does not represent the people on either side of the case. The scientist may be a witness for the prosecution or for the defense, but that does not change the fact that he or she speaks for the data.

HOW DOES A WITNESS "SHOW RESPECT?"

- Dress appropriately. If there is some question about what is appropriate, ask the attorney for instructions.
- Use proper language. Courtrooms are usually conducted in a formal manner. Any informality whatsoever is seen as disrespect.
- Speak to the person or persons with decision-making authority. If a jury is present, address the answers to the jury, not the attorney

who asked the question. If the decisions are to be made by the judge, speak to the judge.

- Request permission of the judge to step down from the witness chair, even if leaving the chair is required for the presentation of testimony.
- Request permission of the judge to elaborate or clarify a point if it is necessary for accurate communication. The testimony may have been curtailed prematurely or led off track, but the expert witness still has the responsibility to convey information accurately and completely.

THE SCIENTIST AND PHYSICAL EVIDENCE

The scientist is the voice of the physical evidence. By speaking for the evidence, the scientist represents the physical evidence—*not* the victims or the perpetrators—*not* the law or the courts.

CHAPTER 15

HUMAN RIGHTS APPLICATIONS

CHAPTER OUTLINE

THE SCIENTIST AND VICTIMS' RIGHTS

Tradition has vested the profession (of forensic science) with a solemn authority to speak for victims. The dead cannot perjure themselves; only human failure to listen and interpret the evidence can dishonor their final testament (Snow, Stover, and Hannibal 1989).

The Role of the Scientist in Human Rights Work

Think back over international events of the past year. Is there any question about the widespread lack of protection for human rights? Two things are obvious: There are no easy solutions, and there will never be solutions without information and evidence. This is where the scientist is not only useful, but essential.

The work begins with acknowledging the relationship between science and human rights. Scientists make a unique contribution to human rights through the application of scientific methods and techniques to the investigation of human rights violations.

Evidence

Legal prosecution requires evidence. Evidence is "the data on which a judgement can be based or proof established" (American Heritage Dictionary 1983).

In human rights cases, evidence is often based solely on verbal testimony from victims or witnesses. There is no doubt about the importance of verbal testimony. But verbal evidence can be far more effective if it is corroborated by physical evidence.

Physical evidence has even greater value when there is conflict among testimonies from several parties. The physical evidence can be used to support, contradict, or further explain.

The most critical need for physical evidence is when no verbal evidence exists. Either the events in question were not witnessed by any living person, or the witnesses are unwilling to testify. In such circumstances, the physical evidence is the only path to truth.

Scientific analysis is required for evaluation of physical evidence. The scientist expects to care for the evidence and become its voice. A well-trained forensic scientist will maintain a careful chain of custody, preserve the security of the evidence, explain the methods used for analysis, report any and all results, and testify about method, results, and conclusions within a court of law.

Professional Committees

Involvement in human rights issues often begins with participation in professional committees. In the United States, numerous professional organizations have formed committees to investigate human rights issues related to their disciplines.

Physicians, lawyers, mathematicians, psychiatrists, psychologists, political scientists, civil engineers, and linguists are among the scientists

THE SCIENTIST AND HUMAN RIGHTS

The application of the forensic sciences to human rights investigations can be crucial in proving that such violations occurred and in obtaining judicial redress for criminal activity (Hannibal 1992, 10).

who have formally committed to aiding human rights causes. Many of these professional committees participate in letter-writing campaigns to encourage governments to intercede on behalf of colleagues in other countries. Some of the professional committees assign members the tasks of analyzing data, reviewing reports, and testifying in courts of law or before commissions of inquiry.

Interdisciplinary committees also exist. The Union of Concerned Scientists and the American Association for the Advancement of Science's Committee on Scientific Freedom and Responsibility are prime examples. The AAAS Committee, formed in 1976, examines the rights and responsibilities of scientists around the world and focuses on areas of conflict involving scientific freedom and responsible scientific conduct in today's society.

The Minnesota Lawyers International Human Rights Committee recognized a major need for information in international death investigation. They organized a group of forensic scientists in 1986 to write the document that became known as the "Minnesota Protocol." It was designed to serve as an aid to death investigation throughout the world. The Minnesota Protocol was adopted by the United Nations in 1991 and was republished in numerous languages under the title, *Manual on the Effective Prevention and Investigation of Extra-Legal, Arbitrary and Summary Executions*. This is a rather long title, but it is nevertheless a good start toward worldwide use of forensic science in human rights cases.

Human Rights Work Compared with Standard Forensic Work

For the professional forensic scientist, human rights work is basically the same as everyday work. Most of the differences are expected. The perpetrators of the crimes are the people in authority, many cultural assumptions just don't apply, and the scale of the work is far greater. One unexpected difference is the lack of support disciplines. The scientist often takes the availability of resources and other scientists for granted. He or she finds that it is necessary to become a jack-of-all trades in many other parts of the world. It is a "roll up your sleeves and get the job done" kind of work.

Within the United States and most other industrialized countries, the Universal Declaration of Human Rights is largely upheld by domestic law. Therefore, on home soil, human rights tend to be identified with law enforcement and forensic investigations. In many other parts of the world, however, human rights are not upheld by civil or criminal law. The only recourse for action is through the application of international or "universal" human rights covenants. Under such conditions, the only people available to enforce human rights covenants are the people employed by private and international human rights organizations.

INTERNATIONAL HUMAN RIGHTS WORK

With his famous facility for sizing up a problem, Clyde C. Snow exposed one of the major differences between forensic work in the United States and international human rights work. Dr. Snow was in Bolivia to analyze skeletal remains from the cemetery of a work camp. The dead were all street kids, petty thieves, and vagrants. They had never been formally charged, tried, or sentenced, but they had been imprisoned and forced to work until they died.

After examining the remains, Snow commented, "Back in 1979, I was pulled into a case where I had to identify a bunch of boys killed by a psychopath in Chicago. I never imagined that ten years later I'd be down here doing pretty much the same thing. But there's a big difference in this case. Camacho (the camp commander) and his men murdered those kids with the power of the state behind them. Now for me, that's the worst crime of all" (Joyce and Stover 1991).

I used to feel comfortable describing my work as disinterment and analysis of human remains. In other words, I considered physical evidence to be my entire sphere of work. I would give the investigating officers my recommendations for useful verbal evidence, but I would not become involved in that part of the investigation. Then I began to work on human rights missions and realized that there was no one trained to do the other half of the job. I was not going to succeed with my work if I did not become far more involved in collection of verbal evidence.

Mercedes Doretti of the Argentinean Forensic Anthropology Team (EAAF) describes the process in three parts: interviews, excavation, and analysis. The interviews consist of careful, organized collection of verbal evidence about the event, the site, and the missing people. The flow chart below (which also appears on page 5 in the "Introduction to Forensic Anthropology" chapter) is one that we both agree on. It gives a picture of the process of gathering all types of evidence and utilizing it to reach useful conclusions.

The Merging of Verbal Evidence and Physical Evidence
Verbal evidence and physical evidence are brought together to produce useful conclusions in a criminal investigation.

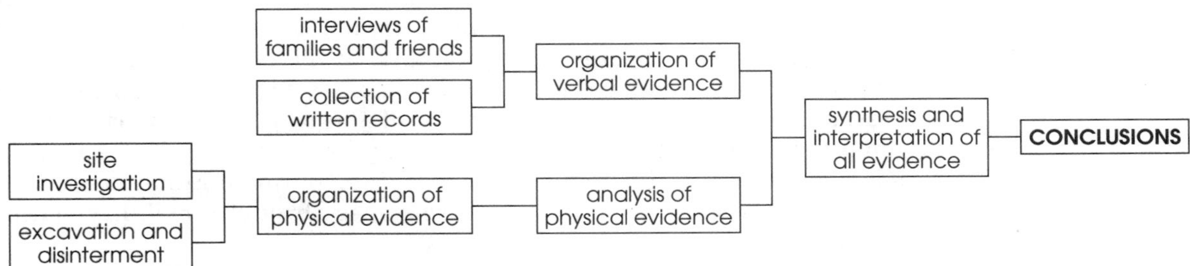

The Contribution of Forensic Anthropology

Forensic anthropologists, both physical anthropologists and archaeologists, contribute to human rights primarily by aiding in death investigation work. They join with physicians, odontologists, radiologists, and criminalists in revealing evidence of mass murder, genocide, torture, summary execution, and political "disappearances."

Forensic anthropologists are best utilized in cases requiring disinterment, personal identification, and trauma analysis. These cases require careful archaeological excavation in order to expose the body and associated evidence.

The entire site must be treated as a possible crime scene. Archaeological methods ensure that physical evidence is preserved and the greatest amount of information is obtained from the site. Adequate information from the excavation increases the probability that the dead can be identified. It also increases the chance that the events surrounding the death can be interpreted accurately and completely.

The very nature of human rights work requires sensitivity to cultural and linguistic differences. It also requires cultural flexibility. Anthropologists are ideally trained for this work. Most anthropologists have a broad-based education that includes training in cultural anthropology and linguistics as well as archaeology and physical anthropology. Anthropological training leads to an understanding of the effects of cultural differences and nuances.

For example, it is necessary to be able to recognize normal burial customs before it is possible to assess what may be abnormal. In the United States, we bury our dead in full clothing lying face up in coffins or caskets. If a body were found buried on its side without clothing or coffin, criminal activity would be suspected. In Islamic countries, however, the custom is to bury the dead on their sides, facing Mecca, wrapped only in a cotton shroud that deteriorates quickly. Under such cultural conditions, criminal activity is suspected if the body is found clothed or facing in a direction other than toward Mecca.

Anthropological training is also useful in conducting interviews with families and acquaintances to obtain antemortem information. Many things do not translate, no matter how expert the translator. Color is one example. It is far better to use a color chart, point to the color, and record it by number than to try to translate it from one language to another. The use of left and right in relation to the body can also be difficult. Pictures and diagrams serve to facilitate orientation to parts of the body.

Knowledge of local laws is necessary if a forensic team is going to function without incident within another country. In Guatemala, for instance, the local judge must be present during an exhumation. To absent-mindedly begin work without checking to be sure he is present would be to break the law and endanger an entire project.

A human rights worker must be willing to accommodate local customs. These can be disconcerting to anyone solely accustomed to police procedures within the United States. For example, it is not unusual in a Latin American country to have religious ceremonies conducted alongside a disinterment in progress. In many parts of the world, it is normal to have whole families in attendance and grieving loudly throughout an exhumation. The unexpected is to be expected in international human rights work. In this highly variable world, success comes through flexibility, patience, and persistence.

A group of Cakchiquel Indians present during an exhumation of a mass grave containing bodies from a 1982 massacre. The citizens of this Guatemalan community requested the exhumation in an attempt to locate missing family members and provide them with a proper burial. (*Lancerio López*)

A Cakchiquel Indian child watching the exhumation of members of her family from a mass grave near Patzun, Guatemala. (*Lancerio López*)

An exhumation in progress near Chajul, El Quiche, Guatemala. In human rights cases, the process of exhumation is usually carried out in the presence of the victims' families. Sometimes the families provide part of the physical labor. This is different from standard medico-legal procedure in the United States. The reason lies in the different order of priorities. (*Lancerio López*)

Scientific Human Rights Missions

The first well-publicized use of forensic anthropology in a human rights mission occurred in 1984. A group of scientists from the United States were asked to evaluate the possibility of identifying victims of the Argentinean "Dirty War" (1974–1983). Clyde Snow was the forensic anthropologist who traveled to Argentina as a consultant.

The request for help was initiated by the Abuelas of the Plaza de Mayo. The Abuelas are a group of grandmothers (and mothers) of the "disappeared." To this day they march once a week on the Plaza de Mayo in Buenos Aires, wearing white kerchiefs on their heads and carrying signs about their missing loved ones. In their quiet way, they have been a powerful force. They will not let their country forget its digression from sanity and morality.

The mission to Argentina was organized by Eric Stover, who was at that time the director of the Science and Human Rights Program of the American Association for the Advancement of Science. When the Argentinean mission was initiated, Snow and Stover could not have known what far-reaching effects their work would achieve.

Many Argentinean victims were identified, and a team of Argentineans, the *Equipo Argentino de Antropologia Forense* (EAAF), was formed in the process. Snow returned to Argentina many times during the excavations and training. He supervised the excavations, trained the team, and testified as an expert witness in Argentinean courts of law. He went on to provide technical support and encouragement to the EAAF for many years.

The EAAF established its own precedents by reaching out to provide technical aid to numerous other countries from Latin America to Africa. One of their many successes was the excavation at El Masote in El Salvador. The El Masote evidence was utilized by the Salvadorean Truth Commission, and the work received international publicity. The Argentinean team is now very much in demand because of their knowledge and experience.

At the time of this writing, there are many organizations organizing and facilitating scientific human rights missions. AAAS continues to work in Latin America while expanding the work to the Middle East, Africa, and Asia. Among other projects, the AAAS is helping human rights organizations and truth commissions to establish effective computer-based data management systems.

Several other human rights organizations have also supported scientific work. Human Rights Watch organized a mission to Iraqi Kurdistan after the Gulf War of 1991. The Carter Center of Emory University organized a mission to Ethiopia in 1992. Physicians for Human Rights had led missions to nearly thirty countries as of 1994 (Kirschner 1994).

A mission to the former Yugoslavia in 1993 was the first to be funded by the United Nations. It set a precedent that further validates and promotes the use of forensic anthropology in human rights work.

The blindfold is still in place on the skull of a teenaged boy who was executed with many of his friends in the city of Erbil, Iraq. The boys' only crime was that they were Kurds. The city's Iraqi leader executed the boys in order to gain greater control over the Kurdish population.

Prior to the arrival of the anthropologists, the Kurds of Erbil, Iraq, had dug up unidentified remains, removed the clothing, reburied the remains, and anchored the clothing to the graves with rocks. People of the community visited the grave sites to view the clothing in hopes of recognizing something belonging to a lost loved one.

Participants in International Missions

Human rights missions require the efforts, talents, and resources of a wide assortment of individuals and organizations. Participants include the families of the victims, activists within the country, human rights organizations, nonprofit funding agencies, governmental officials and commissions, scientists, laborers, students, and many others.

Nongovernmental Organizations (NGOs)

Human rights missions usually begin with requests from families of the dead and disappeared. The families have the most immediate interest in the problem, and they are in a good position to judge the political climate of the country. Families can sometimes become more effective in their quest for help when they join or form nongovernmental organizations. Human Rights NGOs are composed of a diverse group of activists: relatives of victims, leaders from the community, religious leaders, lawyers, teachers, doctors, journalists, students, and other concerned citizens.

Truth Commissions and Commissions of Inquiry

Truth commissions (also called commissions of inquiry) are bodies established by individual governments, nongovernmental organizations, or international authorities. They are becoming increasingly popular during times of governmental transition because of their effectiveness in slowing or ending the cycle of violence (Hayner 1994).

The truth commission has a limited period of authority and a stated task. Usually the task is defined as a report on human rights abuses by a former government. Truth commissions gather information, write a report, and make recommendations for appropriate action such as justice, amnesty, or protection.

The truth commission gathers verbal testimony and written records. However, they are not usually prepared to gather physical evidence. Fortunately, they often have the authority to hire or request scientists and investigators to aid with the physical evidence.

Intergovernmental Institutions

Intergovernmental institutions such as the United Nations Commission on Human Rights, with the recently established position of High Commissioner for Human Rights, become involved in much the same way as the truth commissions. Other important intergovernmental groups include the following:

- The Organization of American States, Inter-American Commission of Human Rights
- The Organization of African Unity, African Commission—the monitoring body for the African Charter on Human and Peoples' Rights
- The Council of Europe, European Court of Human Rights, and European Commission of Human Rights

Human Rights Groups and Organizations Interested in Science and Human Rights

International human rights groups maintain a low profile, but they play a vital role in the actualization and facilitation of human rights missions. These organizations listen to requests for help and analyze problems from all possible angles. They consider the social and political climate of the county and search for practical solutions.

Human rights groups are in an ideal position to maintain databases of information that enable them to locate the right professionals for specific jobs. They are capable of information research that makes it possible to estimate costs, locate appropriate funding, and set up accounting procedures.

Groups such as the following perform the extremely valuable service of publishing results and encouraging effective and wide-spread publicity:

- Amnesty International, London, U.K.
- American Association for the Advancement of Science, Science and Human Rights Program, Washington, D.C.
- Physicians for Human Rights, Boston, MA
- Human Rights Watch, New York, NY

Philanthropic Agencies and International Funding Agencies

Funding agencies are essential. Unfortunately, the credibility of the final report can be colored by the reputation of the agency that funded the work. It is, therefore, important that funds used for international human rights missions be free of any appearance of political or economic motive. For this reason, single-government funding is usually avoided. Private or international funding is preferred.

Information on funding can be obtained through the Human Rights Internet and the International Centre for Human Rights and Democratic Development in Canada. (See "Human Rights Internet" in the Bibliography.)

Technical Resources

There are many scientists who are well qualified to contribute effectively to human rights missions. The composition of the ideal group of investigators varies according to the country and the condition of the evidence. In lesser-developed countries, it is not uncommon for the victims to have few or no medical records. The comparative identification methods employed by radiologists and dentists in the United States are of limited use. It is more important to be able to describe and document individual anomalies and effects of antemortem trauma. This type of information can then be compared with antemortem descriptions from family interviews.

A basic multidisciplinary group includes an anthropologist, a criminalist, an odontologist, a pathologist, a photographer, and a skilled interviewer. Other specialists may be added to the team according to the specific requirements of the case.

An exhumation in progress near Chajul, El Quiche, Guatemala. The forensic anthropologists of the Guatemala Archbishop's Human Rights Office (ODHAG) Exhumation Project demonstrate excellent teamwork as they complete the exhumation, record and photograph all evidence, and extract the remains for laboratory analysis. They also spend time with the families of the victims, discussing items of clothing and any items not covered in the pre-exhumation interviews. In addition to doing the exhumation work, the team members must be continuously respectful of religious rituals and expressions of grief. (*Lancerio López*)

Most professional forensic anthropologists are physical anthropologists with extensive experience in human skeletal analysis. Some are professional archaeologists with experience in a wide variety of burial recovery procedures. Anthropological training is ideal background for work that involves locating and identifying the dead in difficult and unusual circumstances. The practicing forensic anthropologist is accustomed to extracting information from incomplete, damaged, or commingled remains. They regularly work with disarticulated remains as well as burned or cremated remains. Forensic anthropologists are trained in the analysis of skeletal evidence of trauma, consistent with violent or suspicious death. Some are also experienced at dealing with the special problems presented by mass burials.

There is considerable work for the anthropologist beyond the recovery and identification of human remains. International work requires cultural flexibility and the ability to handle isolated working conditions. Teaching and writing skills are important.

Cultural anthropologists can be helpful if they have experience with the specific culture and language. Most antemortem records must be collected by verbal interview of survivors. In fact, clear communication with survivors is often the *only* way to obtain reliable identifications. Such interviews can become exceedingly complex in intercultural situations.

Multinational Forensic Teams

When the problem is identified and defined, and the facilitators have set up a plan of action and located funds and professionals, it is time to find workers. It isn't enough to send professionals to the requesting country. Local workers and students are needed to provide muscle power and to begin the process of learning techniques and methods. A successful mission achieves more than just short-term goals. Technology transfer is the long-term goal. Through technology transfer, the local people are eventually able to help themselves and take control of their own destiny.

Local workers tend to select themselves. Citizens who take an interest in the work begin to demand more information, and become excellent students. In the case of unidentified dead, the people of the country live with the problem. They have a more immediate and personal interest in the solutions than does the average academic student. As a result, they are willing to work long hours to attain the necessary knowledge.

Argentina, Guatemala, Chile, and the Philippines have developed national forensic anthropology teams. The Argentinean team and the Guatemalan teams are probably the most active today. Both teams have moved beyond the boundaries of their own countries to provide help to countries in similar situations.

Columbia, Costa Rica, and Chile have worked on building national forensic teams, and there may be support for development of teams in Iraqi Kurdistan, Ethiopia, and Haiti in the future.

Planning Scientific Missions

There are many variables in forensic work, and it is always wise to expect the unexpected. Details can defeat a mission if not adequately handled at the very beginning. Experience teaches best those who come prepared, and good planning requires research. The major subjects for consideration are the following:

- Governmental permission
- Permission of religious authorities, if necessary
- Permission of the land owner or cemetery officials
- Coordination with local organizations
- Contact with academics (colleges, universities, police academies, museums)
- Budgeting and funding
- Specialists and laborers
- Equipment and supplies
- Laboratory and storage areas
- Living arrangements
- Travel arrangements
- Weather conditions
- Press interests
- Safety and security

Several of these subjects are covered in the following sections. There is much more to be considered, but the decisions are dependent upon the specific assignment. (More information on planning scientific missions can be found in Chapter 13, "Field Methods.")

Written Permission

Governmental permission is essential. It is necessary to research the relevant law and procedures within the host country and follow proper channels in obtaining permissions. This takes time because the procedures vary from one country to another and depend upon the structure of the government and the controlling authority. Permissions are particularly complicated if there is no consensus regarding competent authority. The mission may be deemed premature in such a case.

Two matters are in conflict: The worst human rights abuses occur in times of power struggles, and crime scenes grow cold over time. But the tradeoff is straightforward—a large amount of illegally obtained information that can never be presented in court versus a lesser amount of legally obtained information that can be used for long-term goals.

Other types of permission are required in special situations. It is advisable to have the permission of religious authorities when sanctified ground is involved. Some circumstances also require permission of the family. Legal council can be very helpful in this process.

Budgeting and Funding

The funding source is important. Large foundations known for their human rights contributions are the major funders. International funds from the United Nations were used for a mission to the former Yugoslavia in 1994. If the world continues to focus on the goal of peacekeeping, international funds may be the ideal source for the future. Of course, no funds will be forthcoming if the budget is not well thought out. So begin with planning the budget.

Specialists and Laborers

Assembling a suitable group of workers is the next difficult task. Professionals are chosen first for their training and experience. They are then screened according to their availability in relation to the window of opportunity afforded by the invitation, the permissions, the funding, and the availability of other team members. Prospective workers and team members may also be evaluated for general adaptability. It is necessary to be capable of functioning within a team and foregoing the comfort of a familiar culture and language. It is also important to be innovative and capable of working without modern equipment or conveniences.

Laboratory and Storage Areas

The laboratory area can take many different forms depending on the weather conditions. The most important aspects of the laboratory are large work tables, good lighting, a water source, and a shelter from public view.

The storage area is far more difficult to establish because it must be dry, reasonably cool, and well locked. Never underestimate the need for security. A breach of security can never be repaired.

Living Arrangements

Good living arrangements are important for the health and morale of the team. Productivity will suffer if health and morale are not considered.

Weather Conditions

Know what to expect—temperature, rainfall, humidity, wind conditions. There are times of the year during which the likelihood of success is extremely small. Be practical; don't waste valuable funds on poor chances.

Press Interests

It is important to have a plan for the arrival of the press. Otherwise you may find yourself reading about your work in a publication—complete with shockingly incorrect quotes from a semi-informed source.

Expect the press. Prepare the entire crew about what is open information and what is closed. Partial data can be seriously misleading. It is necessary to wait for all the data to be collected and the analysis to be completed before allowing results to be discussed publically or to be published.

Safety and Security

Consider the personal safety of workers, families, and any others who may be called to give testimony. It is not possible to guard everyone or guarantee safety to anyone, but it is possible to be alert to danger and use common sense. Take the following precautions, for example:

- Choose to work during daylight hours.
- Travel in groups of two or more.
- Live by the law of the land.

- Maintain cordial relations with local citizens and officials.
- Maintain communications with home.
- Establish contact with the local embassy.
- Have a plan for withdrawal if necessary.

Types of Missions

There are many types of human rights missions, but those involving forensic anthropology usually fall into four types or phases. The first is the exploratory mission. It is followed by any number of major excavation missions, training missions, and ultimately, follow-up missions, or general support missions.

The Exploratory Mission

The purpose of the first trip is to explore and develop information. Before any future work can be planned, it is necessary to meet people face to face, view the site or sites, and evaluate the local facilities. It is sometimes advisable to dig a test pit or carry out a preliminary excavation at this time.

An exposed clandestine burial near Patzun, Chimaltenango, Guatemala. Items of clothing decompose at different rates. In this case, the boots will outlast most of the other fabrics. (*Lancerio López*)

MEET THE PEOPLE

In the exploratory mission, the first job is to meet the people. It is essential to have the support and cooperation of local nongovernmental organizations, governmental officials, relatives, and witnesses. This is also a good time to begin the process of locating volunteer workers. In this type of work, motives are as important as education and experience, and it takes time to evaluate motives.

VISIT THE SITE

The next job is visiting the site or sites and evaluating them on the basis of probability of success. Success is based on ease or efficiency of excavation, likelihood of finding complete remains, and availability of antemortem information.

EVALUATE LOCAL FACILITIES

After the site is selected, space for processing and storing the remains must be located. A laboratory as such is not necessary, but security is very important. It is possible to work under a wide variety of conditions so long as there is light, water, a surface to work on, and a secure storage area.

A mass grave near San Jose Rio Negro, Alta Verapaz, Guatemala. Most clandestine graves are found near the surface because they were dug with hand shovels, and speed was the main objective. However, military operations often have heavy equipment at their disposal. Graves such as this one were dug by a bulldozer and are much deeper and larger than hand-dug graves. Bodies are even more likely to be thrown in and heaped in a haphazard fashion. Every aspect of this type of exhumation is challenging. (*Lancerio López*)

The exploratory mission is also a good time to consider the logistics for maintaining a crew of workers. This involves determining the availability of transportation, food, potable water, and shelter.

ASSESS THE WORK

If a preliminary excavation is deemed necessary or useful, a limited excavation is carried out. It can consist of a small site or a test pit or trench in a larger site. The preliminary excavation accomplishes several things at once. Physical evidence of the condition of the remains is obtained, excavation methods are demonstrated for the local volunteers, and professional credibility is established for the officials. Physical work is more effective than words to establish trust.

WRITE THE REPORT

A formal report is prepared after the exploratory mission. The report is used to publish the preliminary information, to review the initial planning effort, to plan for future work, and to enlist support.

The Major Excavation Mission

Major excavation missions have been carried out in many parts of the world. Many missions have been to Argentina and Guatemala, followed by Bolivia, Brazil, Croatia, El Salvador (Danner 1993), Ethiopia, Honduras, and Iraqi

Family of victims gather at an archaeological excavation and exhumation conducted by the Exhumation Project of the Guatemala Archbishop's Human Rights Office (ODHAG). Members of the village aid in the preliminary work of the exhumation. The area occupied by the skeletal remains is being pedestaled. From this point on, the work will progress more slowly with exclusive use of hand tools.

Human skeletons are carefully exposed by members of the ODHAG Exhumation Project. Anthropologists search the remains for physical evidence *in situ* before allowing anything to be removed from the ground.

Kurdistan (Stover 1992). Each of these major excavation missions involved extensive data collection—data from antemortem records and data from the excavation itself. Victims were identified, cause and manner of death were ascertained, and results were published. The missions also served to further governmental cooperation, develop citizen support, and initiate training of workers.

If the preliminary work has been carried out well, the major excavation will yield a large quantity of information. It will also serve to begin the training of workers who may later serve as the nucleus for a local team.

Careful excavation is essential (see Chapter 13). No one knows in advance which skeletal element is going to provide the critical piece of information—either for individual identification or determination of the cause or manner of death. Identifications have resulted from finding nothing more than the stump of an amputated finger tip, a benign tumor on a toe, or the bones of an unusually arthritic neck.

Any skeletal element lost or ignored lessens the probability that the individual will be identified. If the work is of professional quality, each individual is exposed, mapped, and photographed before being removed from the ground. The left and right hand and the left and right foot are bagged separately so that the phalanges can be differentiated. Fragmented bones are bagged separately, and all of the bones from a single individual are boxed separately.

An adult has 206 bones. A child has even more. It is not unusual for an inexperienced excavator to leave behind small bones from the hand and foot, the hyoid, the coccyx, single-rooted teeth, and epiphyses. Inexperienced excavators usually do not recognize a baby or a fetus as human, but they include large animal bones thinking they may be human.

Following the excavation, there must be time and space for analysis of the remains. These must be cleaned and described. The analysis opens the door for personal identification as well as providing information about the cause and manner of death and the circumstances surrounding the time of death. All information is recorded in both written and photographic form with the expectation that the remains will be released to the families as soon as possible. The records must be complete enough to stand alone.

The work is not done until the results are reported in a form that can be used by the nonscientist. The final reports should be released to the following groups:

- The human rights agencies serving as facilitators for all of the groups involved
- The government agencies granting permission for the work to take place
- The families, if they so request

The Training Mission

There are two major types of training missions. The first consists of introductory lectures to develop interest and support. The second is professional training in the methods of forensic anthropology.

Introductory Lectures

The introductory lectures are created for a diverse group of people, including human rights workers, prosecutors, judges, and doctors. This is the group of people that has the power to act on the results of the work. It is important that they understand enough about the science of forensic anthropology to appreciate its utility. They need to know when to call on the expertise of a forensic anthropologist, and they must be able to evaluate the resulting reports.

Basic Training Courses

Formal training courses are developed for persons with sufficient understanding of human anatomy and biology to begin an intensive study of forensic anthropology—including both the field aspect (excavation of human remains and artifacts) and the laboratory aspect (study of human osteology, analysis of skeletal remains, and human identification). Training can be accomplished in a natural progression when it is coordinated with excavations.

The work in Argentina and Guatemala provide good examples. The preliminary excavations were undertaken by archaeologists and physical anthropologists from the United States. Local students assisted in the work and learned the techniques of skeletal excavation while on the job. The skeletal material from the excavations was then used for formal training courses in human osteology. A full skeleton was available for pairs of students, and a complete report was required of each student. The best of the students became the nucleus of each national forensic team.

This class at Rafael Landivar University in Guatemala City is one of many in the 1990s providing an opportunity for Central Americans to study the details of human identification from fragmented, long-buried skeletal material. Most of the registrants are upper-level university students in anthropology and archaeology, but the class also includes practicing pathologists, lawyers, and other professionals intent on increasing their qualifications in the area of forensic science.

Training requires many practical considerations, such as classroom space, books (and translations), and teaching and reference materials (pictures, charts, forms, casts, etc.). The classroom can be established in a variety of places. Classes have taken place in hospitals, hotels, grammar schools, and universities. As long as large tables, chairs, blackboards, and locked storage are available, almost any place with a roof will do.

APPRENTICESHIP PROGRAMS

Most forensic scientists work through apprenticeship programs after completing their formal education. They are not expected to leap from the classroom desk to the expert witness' chair. There is no reason to expect newly formed forensic teams to operate on a more accelerated timetable. It may be useful for team members to visit and work in other countries as part of their training.

CONTINUING EDUCATION

Advanced short courses can also be useful. Special topics include the study of fetal and infant remains, professional dental restorations and charting, evidence of disease or surgery, analysis of trauma, histological techniques, and DNA analysis.

It is also wise to include an overview of information available from the full range of forensic sciences. All the speciality areas—pathology, radiology, odontology, fingerprints, toxicology, serology, criminalistics, ballistics, blood splatter analysis, footprint analysis, personality profiling, accident reconstruction, questioned documents, etc.—can be useful to each other at different times and under different circumstances.

Follow-up and Conclusion to the Missions

There are many reasons for continuing to provide support after the formal training is complete. Few scientists work well in isolation. Communication with others working in the same field and related fields is essential. A new group of scientists isolated in a troubled country cannot expect smooth sailing. They have even greater need for worldwide friends to call on for help. As they encounter new types of cases, they need to be able to call on the experience of others for advice and discussion. They may also need supporting testimony, help in locating funding, aid in publishing reports, or help in locating and purchasing equipment and books.

The time to conclude support is the time at which no more help is desired or requested. If the team formation has been successful, the mature team will become an active part of a wide network. The team will be capable of both locating support and giving support.

Results of Missions

When forensic anthropology is applied to human rights problems, there are two major results and three levels of effect. First, the dead are often identified. Second, physical evidence is collected for use in legal prosecution. The

A single burial exposed near Chajul, El Quiche, Guatemala. The osteological evidence indicates a female with typical Mayan features. The clothing is distinctive for Mayans of the Quiche region. (*Lancerio López*)

effects reach out to three groups of people—the families of the dead who had been condemned to suffer in ignorance, the leaders of the nation who may have allowed or perpetrated the atrocities, and the citizens of the world who otherwise might have silently looked the other way.

Human Identification

Identification of the dead is of immediate importance to the families. Knowledge of the fate of their loved ones and the opportunity to complete funeral rituals provide a measure of psychological closure for the families. A further consequence is empowerment of the survivors. Many do not realize it, but survivors are also victims, and they benefit from funeral parades and other rituals. The funeral is a public affair. It may even take place in the face of former persecutors. The process itself enables the living victims to become activists.

Physical Evidence

Physical evidence is collected to be used in the death investigation process. The physical evidence documents war crimes and other human rights abuses. It is useful in the legal prosecution of the persons responsible for torture, murder, or extra-legal execution.

International Publicity

International participation in human rights activities results in international publicity. Information is obtained from direct interviews, technical reports, popular articles, and oral presentations. Publicity helps to build pressure for change through censorship by the international community and increased global support for human rights. Evil may perpetuate itself in the dark, but it is inhibited under a world spotlight.

The Future

There is one thing certain—there is no dearth of work. Atrocities are committed throughout the world, and one corner of the world can no longer slaughter its people while the other corner goes on about its business. The Internet alone carries casual discussions around the world in seconds. Neighbors may still be ignored, but it is harder and harder to be unaffected by them.

Guatemala is an example. It sits just on the other side of Mexico from the United States. According to a report from News Release of the Indigenous Peoples of Guatemala, in forty years of civil war, "more than 150,000 people have been killed by the army, and 45,000 have disappeared" (Kowalski 1994). How can the neighbors of Guatemala not be affected?

Other countries around the world are suffering the same fate. Amnesty International (1994) reports that "the toll of the dead and 'disappeared' runs into the thousands in the former Yugoslavia, several of the republics of the former USSR, Somalia, and Zaire." Ethiopia, Haiti, and Sri Lanka are suffering similar problems.

It is hard to believe that the Universal Declaration of Human Rights was written a half century ago. The world remains a long way from embracing these essential freedoms. But hope exists as long as there are people willing to devote time, energy, talent, and knowledge to the struggle. Progress requires hard work and vigilance from all who have the strength and ability to contribute.

APPENDIX

FORENSIC FORMS

APPENDIX OUTLINE

UT Forensic Data Bank (FDB) Forms
- Forensic Case Information
- Forensic Inventory
- Forensic Morphological Observations
- Forensic Measurements
- Deciduous Dental Record
- Dental Chart

Argentinean Forensic Anthropology Team (EAAF) Forms
- Victim Information (Antemortem Form)
- Burial Site Information

Forensic Anthropology Training Manual Forms
- Bone Inventory Form
- Full Skeletal Diagrams
- Cranial Diagrams (Frontal, Posterior, Lateral)
- Cranial Diagrams (Basilar, Coronal)
- Axial Diagrams
- Innominate Diagrams
- Dental Diagrams
- Dental Inventory
- Osteology Quiz Form
- Interview Questionnaire for Families of the Missing

The forms in this Appendix are provided for general use and guidance. Use them to facilitate your work, but do not be limited by them. The perfect form will not be found—the circumstances and materials of each case are too variable. I recommend that you have a variety of forms available and remain flexible. Keep standard forms on the shelf for general cases and plan to design new forms for major cases.

UT Forensic Data Bank (FDB) Forms

The Forensic Data Bank (FDB) forms[1] were designed for recording data to be included in the database of human skeletal measurements at the University of Tennessee. They are reprinted here (on pages 229–234) to encourage contributions to the FDB. They are also very useful in the process of learning proper skeletal analysis because they clearly demonstrate the range of information that should be collected.

The FDB was started in 1986 with a grant from the National Institute of Justice. Prior to the development of the FDB, methods in forensic anthropology were based on information from the Terry and Hamann-Todd collections: "The data were initially used to test forensic methods developed from populations composed primarily of nineteenth-century indigents" (*FORDISC 2.0 User's Guide*, p. 28). These collections are clearly inconsistent with modern populations; therefore, they are inadequate for application to modern forensic cases.

FORDISC[2] is a set of new statistical methods based on data from more recent populations. FDB data have been useful in detecting and analyzing secular changes in human populations. If the data are continuously updated by the contribution of information from modern cases, this methodology can continue to be useful in the rapidly changing populations of the United States. It can also become more useful within relatively unknown populations if information is contributed from other countries.

These forms are reprinted with permission, and gratitude is extended to Dr. Richard Jantz for use of the forms. Copies of completed forms should be returned to:

Dr. Richard L. Jantz
Forensic Anthropology Center
Department of Anthropology
University of Tennessee
Knoxville, TN 37996-0720

[1]The forms are printed by FORDISC 2.0. They can also be found in the manual *Data Collection Procedure for Forensic Skeletal Material* by P. M. Moore-Jansen, S. D. Ousley, and R. L. Jantz, 1994, University of Tennessee, Report of Investigations, No. 48, Knoxville, TN.

[2]FORDISC 2.0 is an interactive DOS computer program that uses discriminant function analysis of skeletal measurements to classify unknown human remains by sex, stature, and race.

Forensic Case Information

COLLECTION ID/CASE #:________________ I.D. NAME:____________________

CURATOR/ADDRESS:____________________ MEANS OF I.D.:____________________

RECORDER:________________ DATE:______ POSITIVE IDENTIFICATION?_____ DATE:______

——————GENERAL INFORMATION (Pages 3-6)——————

		Source			Source
1. SEX:	____	________________	7. DATE OF BIRTH:	________	________
2. RACE:	____	________________	8. PLACE OF BIRTH:	________	________
3. AGE:	____	________________	9. OCCUPATION:	________	________
4. STATURE:	____	________________	10. BLOOD TYPES:	______	__________
5. WEIGHT:	____	________________	11. BIRTHS:	______	__________
6. HANDEDNESS	____	________________	12. PREGNANCIES:	______	__________

13. DATE REPORTED MISSING: ____________

14. DATE OF DISCOVERY: ____________

15. DATE OF DEATH: ____________

16. TIME SINCE DEATH: ____________

17. MANNER OF DEATH: ____________

18. DEPOSIT/EXPOSURE:____________

____

____

19. DEPTH IN CM (if buried): _____

20. EST. PERIOD OF DECAY: ________

21. NATURE OF REMAINS:____________________________________

22. PLACE OF DISCOVERY (Area):____________________________________

____

23. STATE:______ 24. COUNTY:____________ 25. MUNICIPALITY:____________

26. MEDICAL HISTORY:____________________________________

____

27. CONGENITAL MALFORMATIONS:____________________________________

____

28. DENTAL RECORDS (specify):____________________________________

____

29. BONE LESIONS (Antemortem):____________________________________

____

30. PERIMORTEM INJURIES:____________________________________

____

31. ADDITIONAL COMMENTS: ____________________________________

____

____

____

COLLECTION ID/CASE #:__________________ **CURATOR/ADDRESS:**______________________

---------------------------**SKELETAL INVENTORY (Page 7)**---------------------------

32. INVENTORY: Codes: 1 - present complete   4 - antemortem loss
2 - present fragmentary   5 - unerupted (dentition)
3 - absent (postmortem)   6 - congenitally missing

Cranium:_____

	Left:		Right:		Left:		Right:
Frontal:		_____		Maxilla:	_____		_____
Parietal:	_____		_____	Nasal:	_____		_____
Occipital:		_____		Ethmoid:		_____	
Temporal:	_____		_____	Lacrimal:	_____		_____
Zygomatic:	_____		_____	Vomer:		_____	
Palate:	_____		_____	Sphenoid:		_____	

Mandible:_____

	Left:	Right:		Left:	Right:
Body:	_____	_____	Ramus:	_____	_____

Dentition:_____

	Left:	Right:		Left:	Right:
Max. I1:	_____	_____	Mand. I1:	_____	_____
Max. I2:	_____	_____	Mand. I2:	_____	_____
Max. C:	_____	_____	Mand. C:	_____	_____
Max. P1:	_____	_____	Mand. P1:	_____	_____
Max. P2:	_____	_____	Mand. P2:	_____	_____
Max. M1:	_____	_____	Mand. M1:	_____	_____
Max. M2:	_____	_____	Mand. M2:	_____	_____
Max. M3:	_____	_____	Mand. M3:	_____	_____

Postcranium:_____

	Left:		Right:		Left:		Right:
Hyoid:		_____		Thoracic 1-12:		_____	
Clavicle:	_____		_____	Lumbar 1-5:		_____	
Scapula:	_____		_____	Sacrum:		_____	
Humerus:	_____		_____	Ilium:	_____		_____
Radius:	_____		_____	Pubis:	_____		_____
Ulna:	_____		_____	Ischium:	_____		_____
Hand:	_____		_____	Femur:	_____		_____
Manubrium:		_____		Patella:	_____		_____
Sternal Body:		_____		Tibia:	_____		_____
Ribs:	_____		_____	Fibula:	_____		_____
Atlas:		_____		Calcaneus:	_____		_____
Axis:		_____		Talus:	_____		_____
Cervical 3-7:		_____		Foot:	_____		_____

--------------------------------**RESEARCH MATERIALS**--------------------------------

33. SKELETAL MATERIALS: ______________________________
34. DENTAL CASTS: ______________________________
35. HISTOLOGICAL SECTIONS: ______________________________
36. RADIOGRAPHS/PHOTOS: ______________________________
37. OTHER (hair, etc.): ______________________________

Forensic Morphological Observations

COLLECTION ID/CASE #:____________________ I.D. NAME:______________________________

CURATOR/ADDRESS:________________________ RECORDER:____________________ DATE:______

EPIPHYSEAL CLOSURE (Pages 8-9)

Codes: 1 - No Union 2 - Partial Union 3 - Complete Union

38. BASILAR SUTURE: ____
39. MEDIAL CLAVICLE: ____
40. ATLAS-ANTERIOR: ____
41. ATLAS-POSTERIOR: ____
42. AXIS-ANTERIOR: ____
43. AXIS-POSTERIOR: ____
44. CERV. VERT. RIM: ____
45. THOR. VERT. RIM: ____
46. L5 BODY-ARCH: ____
47. LUMB. VERT. RIM: ____
48. SACRUM (1/2): ____
49. SACRUM (S2/3): ____
50. SACRUM (3/4): ____
51. INNOM. PRIM. ELEM. ____
52. ISCH. TUBEROSITY: ____
53. ILIAC CREST (ANT 1/3): ____
54. PROX. HUMERUS: ____
55. MED. EPIC. HUM.: ____
56. PROX. RADIUS: ____
57. DISTAL RADIUS: ____
58. PROX. ULNA: ____
59. DISTAL ULNA: ____
60. FEMUR HEAD: ____
61. GR. TROCH. ____
62. DIST. FEMUR: ____
63. PROX. TIBIA: ____
64. DISTAL TIBIA: ____

CRANIAL SUTURE CLOSURE (Pages 10-12)

Ectocranial

0: open 1: up to 50% 2: >50% 3: obliterated

Endocranial

1: open 2: partial 3: obliterated

	L	R
65. MIDLAMBDOID:	____	____
66. LAMBDA:	____	
67. OBELION:	____	
68. ANTERIOR SAGITTAL:	____	
69. BREGMA:	____	

	L	R
70. MIDCORONAL:	____	____
71. PTERION:	____	____
72. SPHENOFRONTAL:	____	____
73. INF. SPHENOTEMP:	____	____
74. SUP. SPHENOTEMP:	____	____

75. SAGITTAL: ____
76. LAMBDOID(L): ____
77. LAMBDOID(R): ____
78.CORONAL(L): ____
79. CORONAL(R): ____

RIB END CHANGES (Pages 13-22)

	Left	Right
80. RIB NO.: _____	Phase: _____	Phase: _____

PELVIC CHANGES (Pages 23-45)

	Left	Right
81. TODD (1920)/(1921):	______________________	______________________
82. SUCHEY-BROOKS (Suchey and Katz 1986):	______________________	______________________
83. McKERN AND STEWART (1957):	I:____ II:____ III:____	I:____ II.____ III.____
84. GILBERT AND McKERN (1973):	I:____ II:____ III:____	I:____ II:____ III.____
85. AURICULAR SURFACE:	______________________	______________________
86. DORSAL PUBIC PITTING:	1. ABSENT: ____ 2. TRACE-SMALL: ____ 3. MODERATE-LARGE:____	1. ABSENT: ____ 2. TRACE-SMALL: ____ 3. MODERATE-LARGE:____

Forensic Measurements

COLLECTION ID/CASE #:____________________ **RECORDER:**____________________ **DATE:**______

CRANIAL MEASUREMENTS (Pages 52-60)

Measurement		Measurement	Left	Right
1. MAXIMUM LENGTH (g-op):	___	13. NASAL HEIGHT (n-ns):	___	
2. MAXIMUM BREADTH (eu-eu):	___	14. NASAL BREADTH (al-al):	___	
3. BIZYGOMATIC BREADTH (zy-zy):	___	15. ORBITAL BREADTH (d-ec):	___	___
4. BASION-BREGMA (ba-b):	___	16. ORBITAL HEIGHT (OBH):	___	___
5. CRANIAL BASE LENGTH (ba-n):	___	17. BIORBITAL BR. (ec-ec):	___	
6. BASION-PROSTHION L. (ba-pr):	___	18. INTERORBITAL BR. (d-d):	___	
7. MAX.-ALVEOLAR BR. (ecm-ecm):	___	19. FRONTAL CHORD (n-b):	___	
8. MAX.-ALVEOLAR L. (pr-alv):	___	20. PARIETAL CHORD (b-1):	___	
9. BIAURICULAR BREADTH (ALB):	___	21. OCCIPITAL CHORD (l-o):	___	
10. UPPER FACIAL HGT. (n-pr):	___	22. FORAMEN MAGNUM L. (ba-o):	___	
11. MIN. FRONTAL BR. (ft-ft):	___	23. FORAMEN MAGNUM BR (FOB):	___	
12. UPPER FACIAL BR. (fmt-fmt):	___	24. MASTOID LENGTH (MDH):	___	___

MANDIBULAR MEASUREMENTS (Pages 61-63)

Measurement	Left	Right	Measurement	Left	Right
25. CHIN HEIGHT (gn-id):	___		30. MIN. RAMUS BREADTH:	___	___
26. BODY HEIGHT at MENTAL FOR:	___	___	31. MAX. RAMUS BREADTH:	___	___
27. BODY THICKNESS at M. FOR:	___	___	32. MAX. RAMUS HEIGHT:*	___	
28. BIGONIAL DIAMETER (go-go):	___		33. MAND. LENGTH:*	___	
29. BICONDYLAR BR. (cdl-cdl):	___		34. MAND. ANGLE:*	___	

* Record only if mandibulometer is used.

POSTCRANIAL MEASUREMENTS (Pages 64-76)

CLAVICLE: Epiph. P/A:	Left	Right
35. MAXIMUM LENGTH:	___	___
36. SAGITTAL DIAM. at MIDSH:	___	___
37. VERTICAL DIAM. at MIDSH:	___	___

SCAPULA: Epiph. P/A:	Left	Right
38. HEIGHT:	___	___
39. BREADTH:	___	___

HUMERUS: Epiph. P/A:	Left	Right
40. MAXIMUM LENGTH:	___	___
41. EPICONDYLAR BREADTH:	___	___
42. MAX. VERT. DIAM. of HEAD:	___	___
43. MAX. DIAM. at MIDSHAFT:	___	___
44. MIN. DIAM. at MIDSHAFT:	___	___

RADIUS: Epiph. P/A:	Left	Right
45. MAXIMUM LENGTH:	___	___
46. SAGITTAL DIAM. at MIDSH:	___	___
47. TRANSV. DIAM. at MIDSH:	___	___

ULNA: Epiph. P/A:	Left	Right
48. MAXIMUM LENGTH:	___	___
49. DORSO-VOLAR DIAMETER:	___	___
50. TRANSVERSE DIAMETER:	___	___
51. PHYSIOLOGICAL LENGTH:	___	___
52. MIN. CIRCUMFERENCE:	___	___

SACRUM: No. Segments:	___
53. ANTERIOR HEIGHT:	___
54. ANTERIOR SURFACE BREADTH:	___
55. MAX. BREADTH (S-1)	___

INNOMINATE: Epiph. P/A:	Left	Right
56. HEIGHT:	___	___
57. ILIAC BREADTH:	___	___
58. PUBIS LENGTH:	___	___
59. ISCHIUM LENGTH:	___	___

FEMUR: Epiph. P/A:	Left	Right
60. MAXIMUM LENGTH:	___	___
61. BICONDYLAR LENGTH:	___	___
62. EPICONDYLAR BREADTH:	___	___
63. MAX. DIAM. of HEAD:	___	___
64. A-P SUBTROCH. DIAMETER:	___	___
65. TRANSV. SUBTROCH. DIAM:	___	___
66. A-P DIAM. MIDSH:	___	___
67. TRANVS. DIAM. MIDSH:	___	___
68. CIRCUMFERENCE AT MIDSH:	___	___

TIBIA: Epiph. P/A:	Left	Right
69. CONDYLO-MALLEOLAR LEN:	___	___
70. MAX. PROX. EPIPH. BR:	___	___
71. MAX. DIST. EPIPH. BR:	___	___
72. MAX. DIAM. NUTRIENT FOR:	___	___
73. TRANSV. DIAM. NUTR. FOR:	___	___
74. CIRCUM. AT NUTR. FOR:	___	___

FIBULA: Epiph. P/A:	Left	Right
75. MAXIMUM LENGTH:	___	___
76. MAX. DIAM. at MIDSHAFT:	___	___

CALCANEUS: Epiph. P/A:	Left	Right
77. MAXIMUM LENGTH:	___	___
78. MIDDLE BREADTH:	___	___

DECIDUOUS DENTAL RECORD

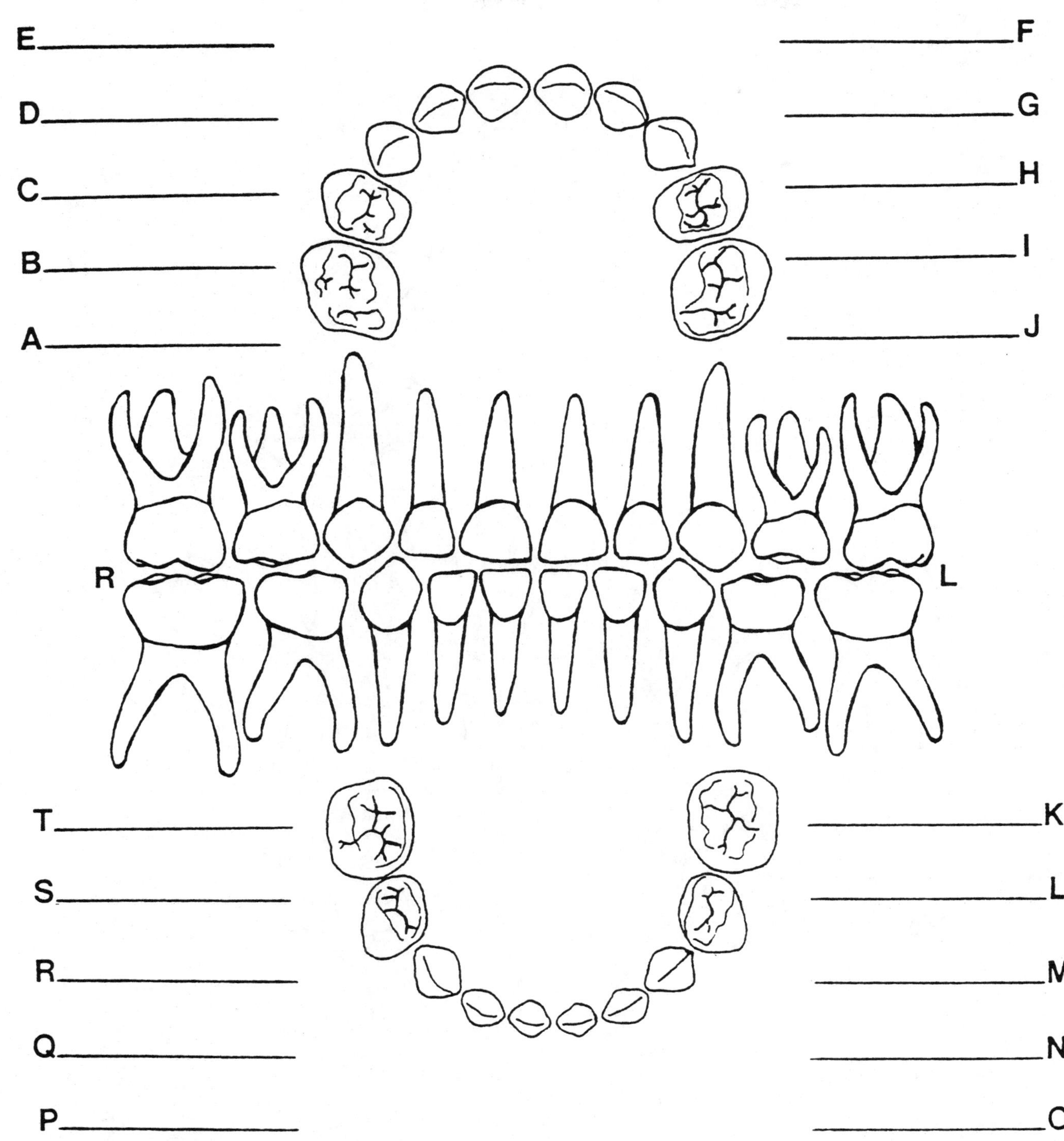

DENTAL CHART

Case No.: __________ Date: __________

8 ____________________ 9
7 ____________________ 10
6 ____________________ 11
5 ____________________ 12
4 ____________________ 13
3 ____________________ 14
2 ____________________ 15
1 ____________________ 16

RIGHT LEFT

32 ____________________ 17
31 ____________________ 18
30 ____________________ 19
29 ____________________ 20
28 ____________________ 21
27 ____________________ 22
26 ____________________ 23
25 ____________________ 24

ARGENTINEAN FORENSIC ANTHROPOLOGY TEAM (EAAF) FORMS

The Argentinean Forensic Anthropology Team (EAAF) forms (on pages 236–244) were developed by the Argentinean Forensic Anthropology Team for use in international human rights projects. The EAAF (*Equipo Argentino de Antropologia Forense*) was established in 1985 when Dr. Clyde C. Snow began training Argentine medical and anthropology students in methods for exhuming and identifying skeletal remains.[1] The Argentinean team first worked in their home country to recover and identify the "disappeared" from the period of the military coup. Their success, dedication, and outstanding teamwork soon led to worldwide requests for help.

Most of the present-day work of the EAAF is carried out in third world countries besieged by war or outright genocide. As a result of the work itself, the EAAF has developed methods distinct from those used by forensic scientists in the United States. In the countries requiring their help, medical records are scarce and oral records are essential. In addition, there are few support personnel to search for records or carry out interviews. Virtually all of the information about the graves and the victims must be obtained by the team members themselves as part of the work process. The team interviews families and friends both before and after the exhumations and forensic examinations.

Thanks are given to Mercedes (Mimi) Doretti and the rest of the Argentinean team for use of the EAAF forms.

[1]For the full story on the origin of the Argentinean Team, see Joyce and Stover 1991.

Victim Information (Antemortem Form)—Page 1

Witness:______________________________ Date:__________

Relation to the victim:______________________________

Address: ______________________________ Telephone: __________

City: ______________ State:__________ Zip Code: __________

Information about the Victim

First and last name:______________________________

Nickname:______________________________

Sex:______________________________

Age (at last time seen alive): ______________________________

Date and place of birth:______________________________

Nationality: ______________________________

Last resident address:______________________________

Single/Married: ______________________________

Sons:______________________________

Profession: ______________________________

Place of work: ______________________________

Associations to political parties, unions, student associations, others:______________

____

Date and place(s) of detention/kidnapping/execution/murder: ______________

____

____

____

____

His or her detention/kidnapping/execution/murder is related to other people: _____Yes _____No

If Yes, please record the names of the other people, explain their relation to the victim, and indicate if they were detained/kidnapped/executed/murdered together: ______________

____

____

____

____

Eyewitnesses to his or her detention/kidnapping/execution/murder: ______________

____

____

____

____

Victim Information (Antemortem Form)—Page 2

Physical Information about the Victim

I. General Physical Characteristics:

Physical complexion (size of clothing): ______________________________

Thorax: broad ____________ regular ____________ narrow ____________

Stature: exact ____________ approximate ____________ weight ____________

Laterality (handedness): ______________________________

Beard (color and shape): ______________________________

Mustache (color and shape): ______________________________

Glasses: ______Yes ______No

Smoker: ______Yes ______No

If yes, cigarettes, cigar, or pipe: ______________________________

How much: ______________________________

Blood group: ______________________________

Ethnic group: ______________________________

Identifying skin traits (e.g., tattoos, scars, birthmarks, spots, etc.): ______________________________

____

Describe dimension and characteristics of identifying skin traits: ______________________________

____

Hair texture (e.g., straight, curly, crisp, etc.): ______________________________

Hair color (e.g., blonde, brown, black, red, gray, etc.): ______________________________

Dyed hair: ______Yes ______No

Hair type (e.g., thick, thin, average, etc.): ______________________________

Hair amount (e.g., abundant, average, sparse): ______________________________

II. Skull:

Shape and characteristics of the head (e.g., dolichocephalic/brachycephalic, supraorbital arches, etc.):

____

____

Shape of the nose: ______vertical ______ straight ______eaglelike (curved)

______horizontal ______narrow ______broad

Shape of the chin: ______________________________

III. Antemortem Lesions:

Congenital deformations (e.g., harelip, cleft palate, extra vertebrae or ribs, spina bifida, etc.):

Fractures:

1. Type of fracture and circumstance in which the fracture occurred (e.g., accident, beating, gunshot wound, knife wound, etc.):
2. Date fracture occurred:
3. Did a doctor see it?:
4. If yes, name of the doctor and hospital/clinic and description of diagnosis and treatment:
5. Are there X-rays?:
6. Was the fracture plastered?:
7. Consequences of the fracture:
8. If the victim did not receive any medical attention or the witness does not remember the diagnosis, please indicate the location of the fracture and treatment as precisely as possible:

Professional or acquired deformations:

1. Type (e.g., pain in the lumbar area, lumbalgia, disk hernia, deformation in hand and/or foot, etc.):
2. Did the victim go to a doctor?
3. If yes, name of the doctor and hospital/clinic and description of diagnosis and treatment:
4. Are there X-rays?:
5. If the victim did not receive any medical attention, please indicate the location of the problem as precisely as possible:

Lesions in joints (e.g., twists, dislocations, etc.)

1. Type of lesion and circumstance in which the lesion occurred:
2. Date lesion occurred:
3. Did a doctor see it?:
4. If yes, name of the doctor and hospital/clinic and description of diagnosis and treatment:
5. Are there X-rays?:
6. If the victim did not receive any medical attention or the witness does not remember the diagnosis, please indicate the location of the lesion and treatment as precisely as possible:

Serious diseases and / or diseases with consequences to the bones (e.g., poliomylitis, tuberculosis, osteoporosis, malnutrition, starvation, rickets, arthritis, pneumonia, peritonitis, osteomyelitis, mastoiditis, sinusitis, etc.):

1. Type of disease:____
2. Date symptoms first appeared:____________________________________
3. Did the victim see a doctor?: ____________________________________
4. If yes, name of the doctor and hospital/clinic and description of diagnosis and treatment: __________

____

____

5. Are there X-rays?: ____
6. If the victim did not receive any medical attention or the witness does not remember the diagnosis, please indicate the nature and location of the problem as precisely as possible:________________

____

____

External elements of the body (e.g., pace maker, plastic or metal prosthesis, nonorganic heart valve, orthopedic prosthesis, intrauterine device, etc.): ____________________________________

____

____

If the victim is a woman, indicate number of pregnancies and births:____________________

Indicate name of doctor/hospital/clinic that may provide physical information about the victim: _______

____

____

IV. Dentition:

1. Complete dentition? ______Yes ______No ______Don't Know

If the victim had lost dental pieces, indicate which ones. If the witness does not remember the exact location and name of the missing teeth/tooth, indicate upper or lower maxilla, right or left side, anterior or posterior area: ____

____

____

____

____

2. Erupted third molars? _______Yes ______No ______Don't Know

Indicate the situation of each of the four third molars: ____________________________

____

____

____

3. Fractured dental pieces: ______Yes ______No ______Don't Know

Follow the guide from point 1:

4. Description of size and shape of the central and lateral upper and lower incisors:________________

____

____

5. Size of the teeth: ______small ______average ______big

6. Color of the teeth (indicate if the victim had stains in his or her dentition; stains can be the result of smoking, of certain pharmaceuticals—e.g., Tetracycline during the calcification of the enamel, potable water with excess of fluoride, etc.): ________________________

____

____

7. Bruxism (grinding/clenching of the teeth while sleeping): ______Yes ______No ______Don't Know

8. Congenital abnormalities:

   a. Number:

      missing teeth; indicate location: ________________________

      Extra numerary teeth; indicate location: ________________________

   b. Shape and volume:

      Macrodontia (big); indicate location: ________________________

      Microdontia (dwarf); indicate location: ________________________

   c. Position:

      Rotation (e.g., distal, mesial, facial, lingual, etc.); indicate the tooth:________________

____

____

____

   d. Interincisal Diastema: ______Yes ______No

9. Indicate name of dentist/hospital/clinic that may provide the victim's dental information: __________

____

____

10. Dental chart: See separated page with chart.

11. Genealogical tree: ________________________

____

____

____

____

____

____

Victim Information (Antemortem Form)—Page 6

I.D./Case Number: ______________________ I.D. Name: ______________________________

Address: ______________________________ Recorder: ____________________ Date: __________

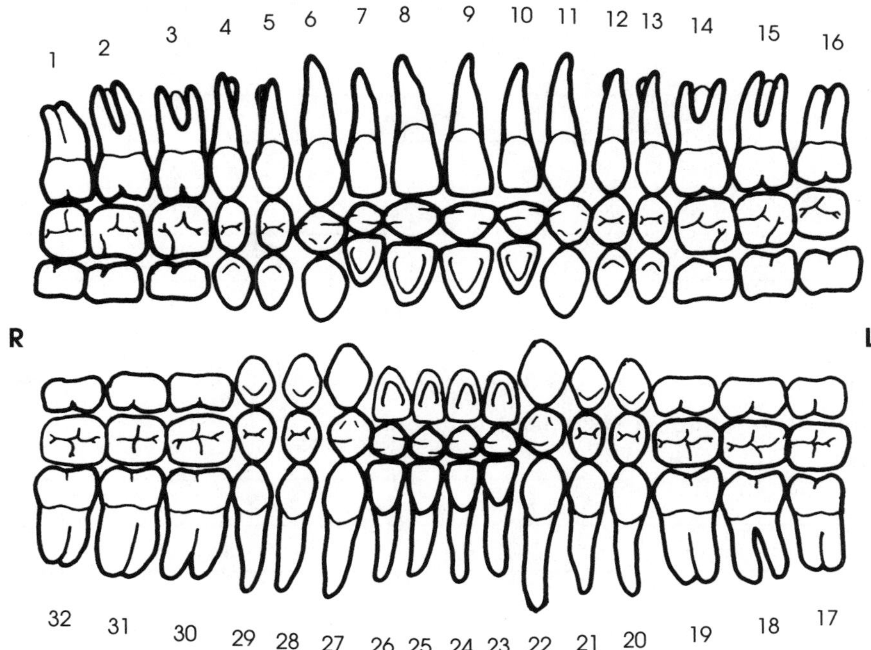

Codification

AX = absent antemortem
PX = absent postmortem
IX = absent perimortem
F = filling
B = bridge
MJ = metal jacket
GJ = golden jacket
PJ = porcelain jacket
AJ = acrylic jacket
RC = root canal
AB = abscess

PP = partial protesis
CP = complete protesis
C = caries
H = hypoplasia
P = periodontitis
D = diastema
S = supernumerary
Mi = microdontia
Ma = macrodontia
r = rotation

Burial Site Information—Page 1

1. Name the city/village and state in which the burial site is located:

2. Location of the burial site (e.g., at the local cemetery; at the sugar cane factory, mine, or well; on a barren land; close to a military base or detention center, etc.):

3. Do we have the exact or approximated location of the burial site? Please describe the location as precisely as possible and draw a map or sketch of the burial site:

4. Do we have an eyewitness or eyewitnesses of the burial of the bodies? If yes, describe in detail how the burial was done: Who brought the bodies? How was the grave dug? Did the eyewitnesses participate in the burial? Are the eyewitnesses related to the victim? If yes, in what way (relatives, neighbors, friends, members of the same political party or union or church, etc.)?:

Burial Site Information—Page 2

5. Were the victims killed at the burial site, or close to the burial site, or in a different place (their bodies later dumped into the grave)?:

____

____

____

____

6. Type of grave—individual or multiple/mass grave (more than one body):

____

____

____

____

7. Dimensions of the burial site (approx.): ______________________

8. Depth of the grave (approx.): ______________________

9. Features of the terrain (e.g., dry; wet; covered with water; covered with grass, bushes, trees, etc.). Does the rainy season affect the terrain?:

____

____

____

____

10. Information about the victim(s):

a. Number of victims (specify whether exact or approximated number): ______________

b. List of names of the victims (specify whether or not you are sure of the names; if you don't know the names, do you know if they belonged to a particular political, social, or religious organization?):

____

____

____

____

____

____

____

____

(Use another page if necessary.)

c. Are the relatives of the victims available? Please indicate the names of the relatives of the victims who can be contacted to obtain antemortem information:

(*Use another page if necessary.*)

11. Alleged cause of death:

12. Reason why this burial site was selected to be exhumed:

Forensic Anthropology Training Manual Forms

This final group of forms (on pages 246–256) provides alternatives for inventory of skeletal remains and an alternative questionnaire for families and friends of the missing. The series of diagrams are included for general use, including recording the location of trauma or anomalies. The diagrams can be used as the basis for illustrations to accompany the written report.

I would be grateful for suggestions for additions and improvements. Please send your comments, recommendations, and examples of forms to:

Dr. K. R. Burns
Department of Sociology, Anthropology, and Social Work
University of North Carolina at Charlotte
9201 University City Blvd.
Charlotte, NC 28223-0001

Bone Inventory Form

			R	L		R	L	Notes
Cranium		Hamate			Clavicle			
Mandible		Scaphoid			Scapula			
Manubrium		Capitate			Humerus			
Sternum		Triquetrium			Radius			
Atlas		Gr. Multang.			Ulna			
Axis		Ls. Multang.						
C3		Lunate			Innominate			
C4		Pisiform			sciatic notch			
C5		Metacarpal 1			iliac crest			
C6		Metacarpal 2			pubis shape			
C7		Metacarpal 3			symph. phase			
T1		Metacarpal 4			Femur			
T2		Metacarpal 5			femur head			
T3		Phalanges (#)			Patella			
T4					Tibia			
T5		Talus			Fibula			
T6		Calcaneus						
T7		Navicular			Rib 1			
T8		Cuneiform 1			Rib 2			
T9		Cuneiform 2			Rib 3			
T10		Cuneiform 3			Rib 4			
T11		Cuboid			rib phase			
T12		Metatarsal 1			Rib 5			
L1		Metatarsal 2			Rib 6			
L2		Metatarsal 3			Rib 7			
L3		Metatarsal 4			Rib 8			
L4		Metatarsal 5			Rib 9			
L5		Phalanges (#)			Rib 10			
Sacrum					Rib 11			
Coccyx					Rib 12			

Full Skeletal Diagrams

Anterior

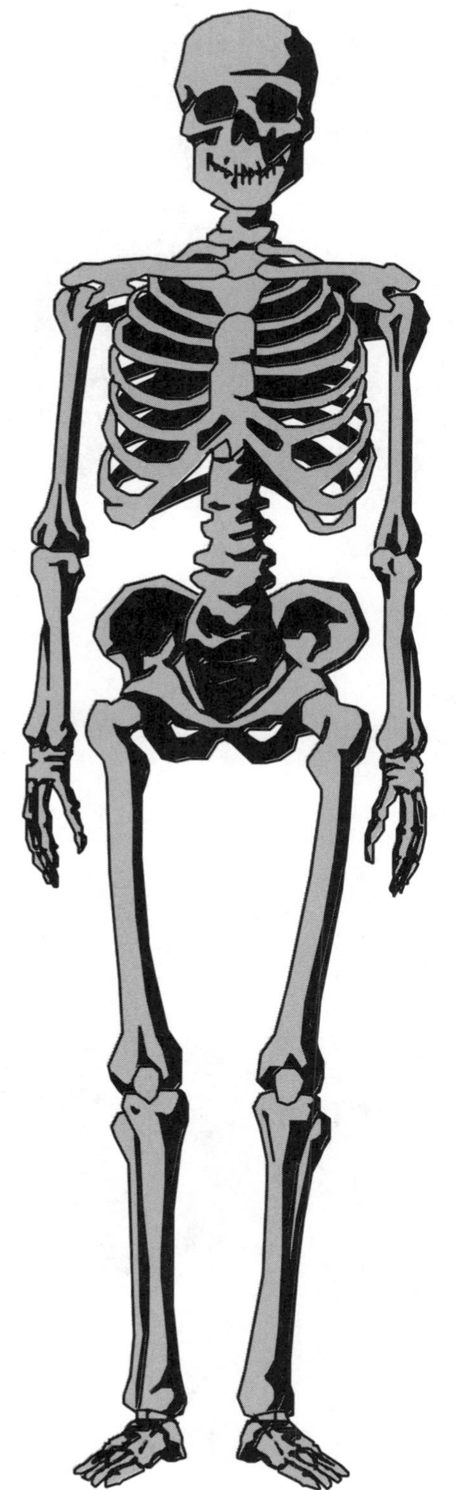

Posterior

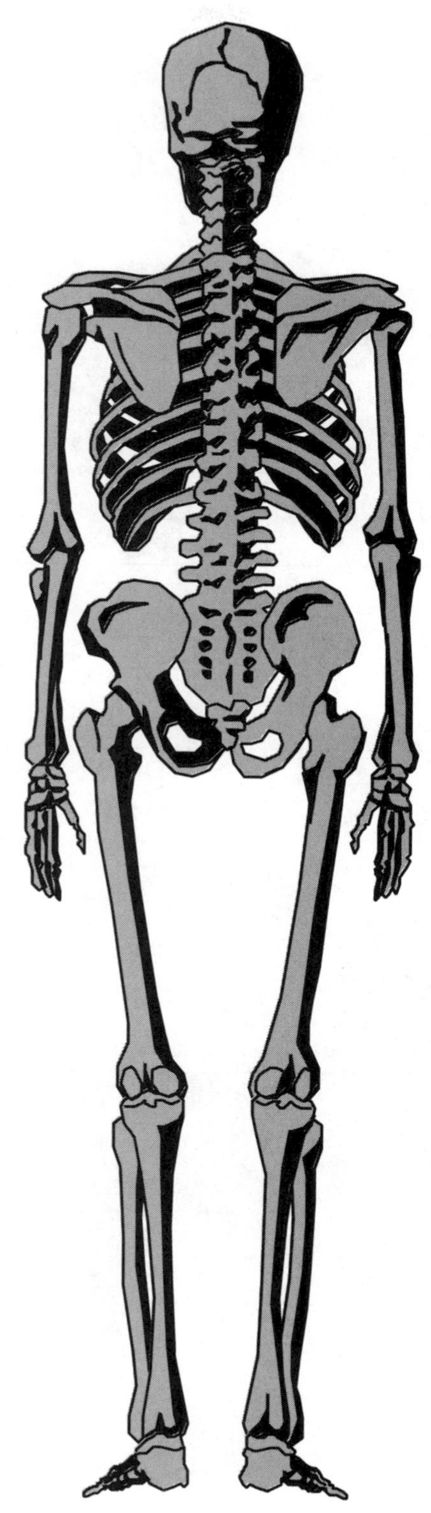

Cranial Diagrams

Frontal

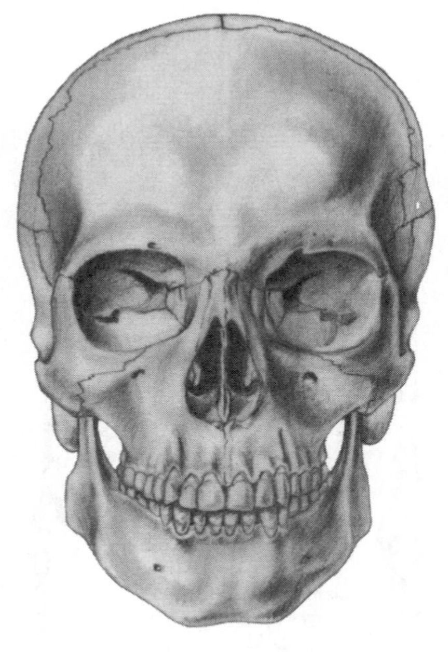

Posterior

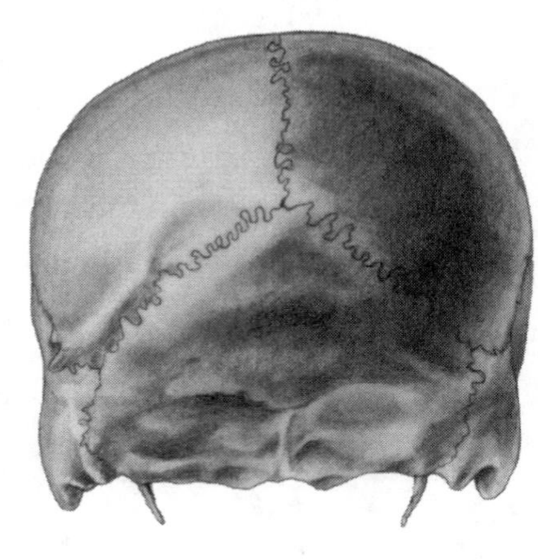

Left Lateral

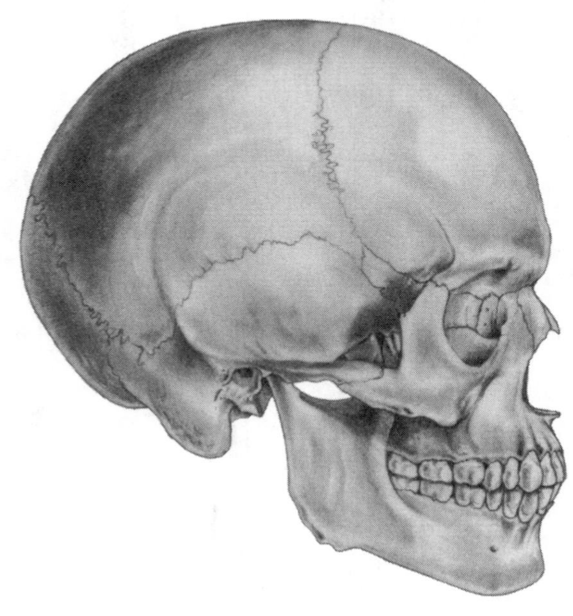

Right Lateral

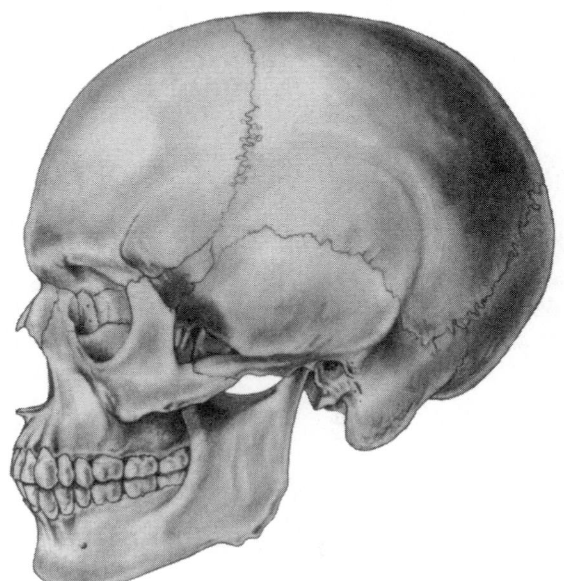

Cranial Diagrams

Internal Basilar

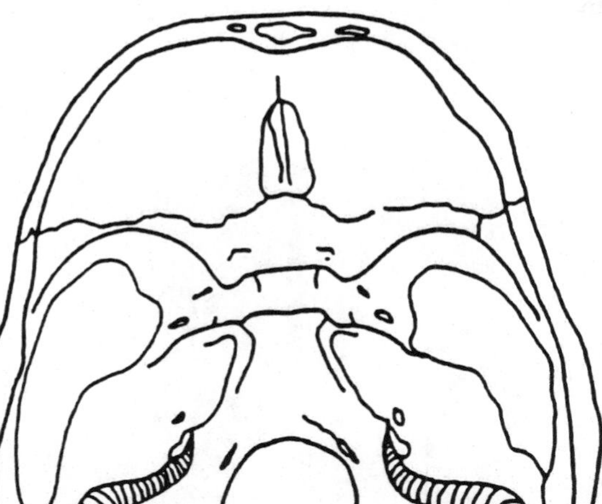

External Basilar

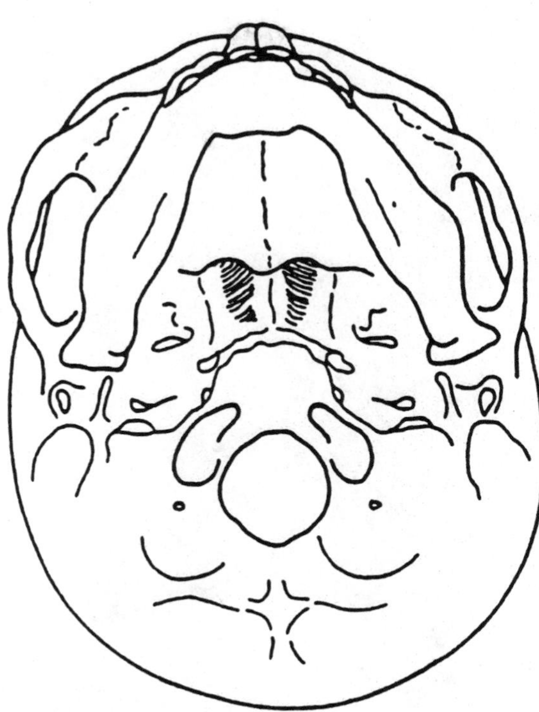

Internal Coronal

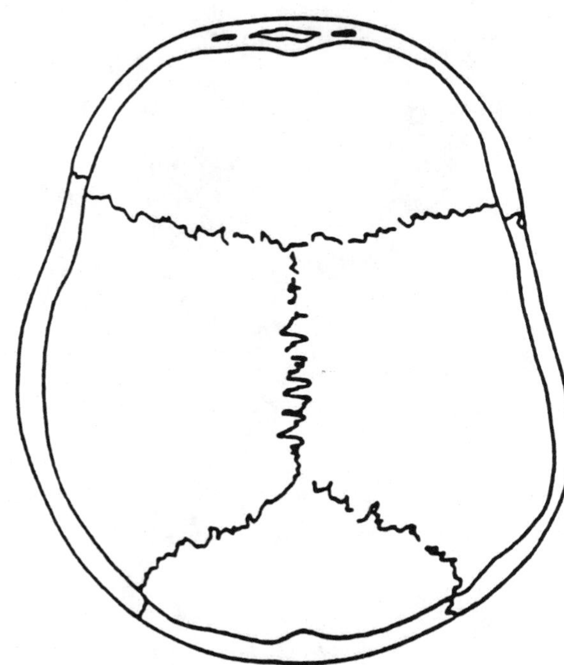

External Coronal

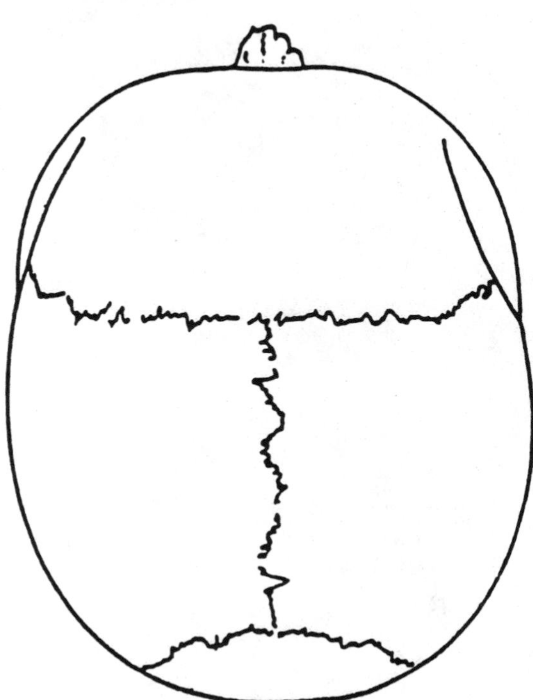

Left Lateral

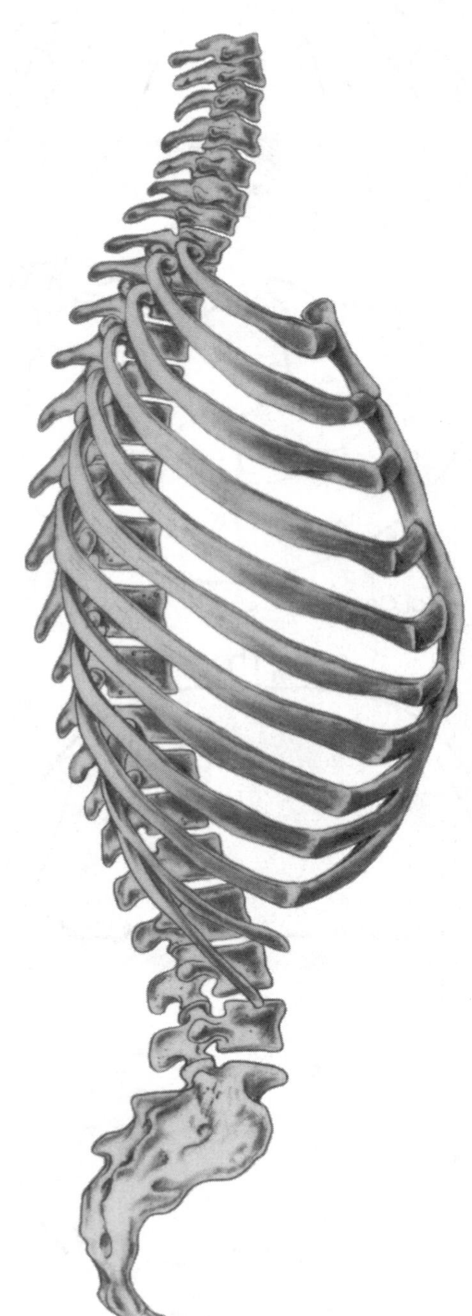

Right Lateral

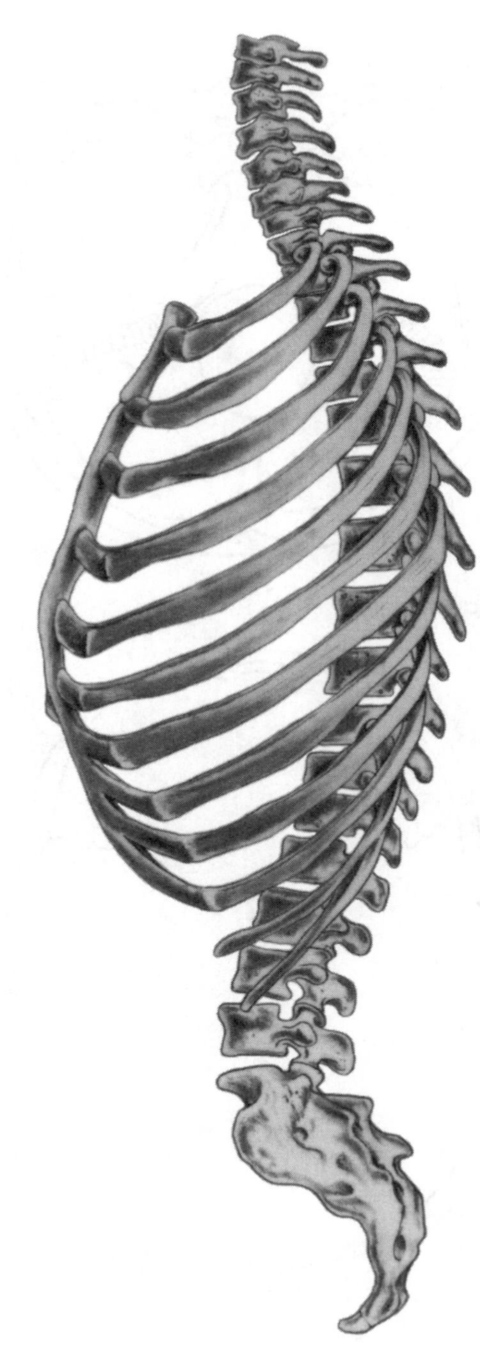

Innominate Diagrams

Observations:

Sciatic Notch Shape ______________

Pubis Shape ______________

Parturation "scarring" ______________

Pre-auricular sulcus ______________

Illiac Crest:

No Union ______________

Partial Union ______________

Complete Union ______________

Pelvic Measurements for Taylor and Dibennardo (1984) Sex Discrimination:

Notch Height (A-B) ______________

Notch Position (B-C) ______________

Acetabular Diameter (E-F) ______________

Left Lateral and Medial

Right Lateral and Medial

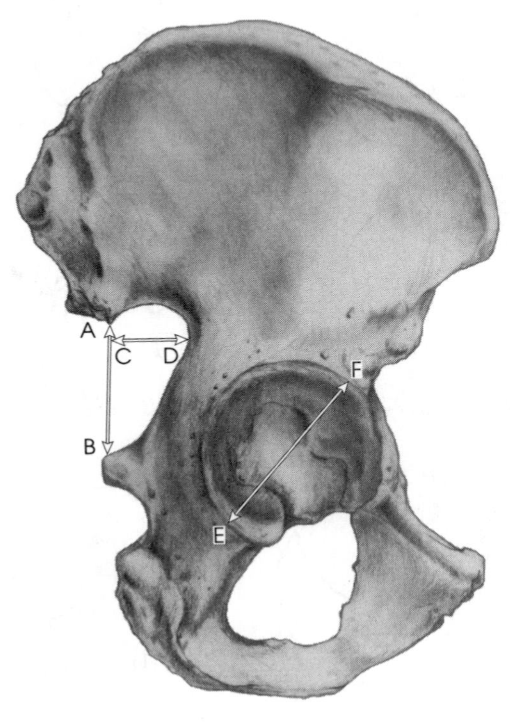

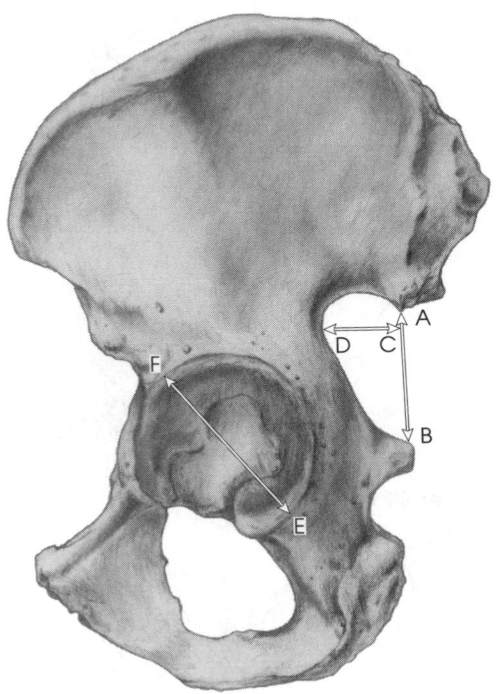

Deciduous Dentition

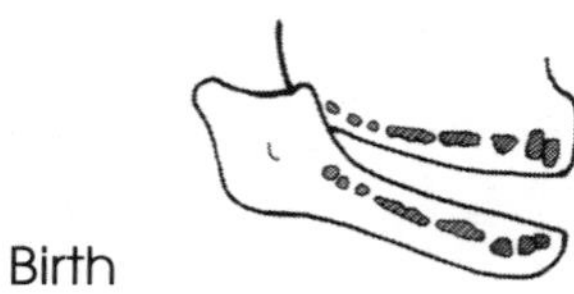
Birth

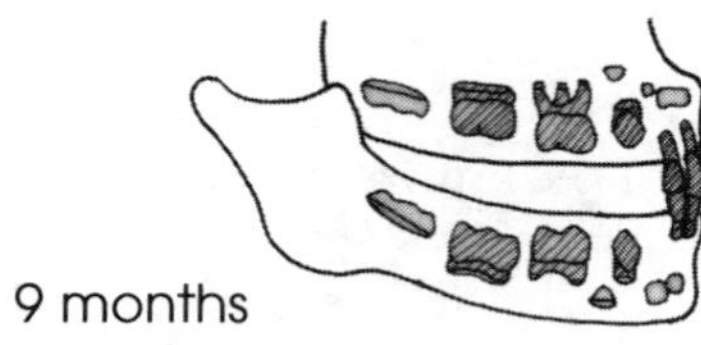
9 months

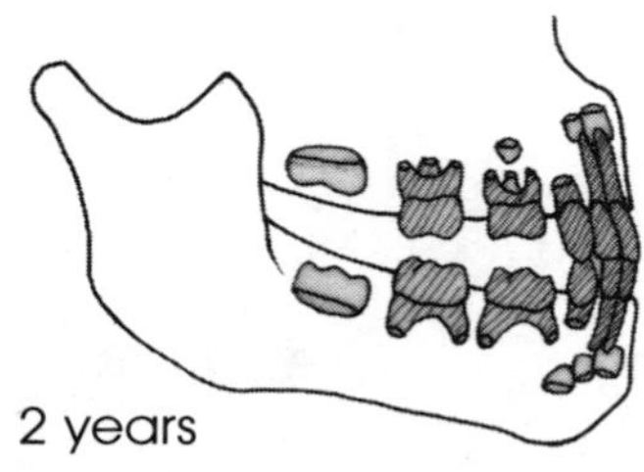
2 years

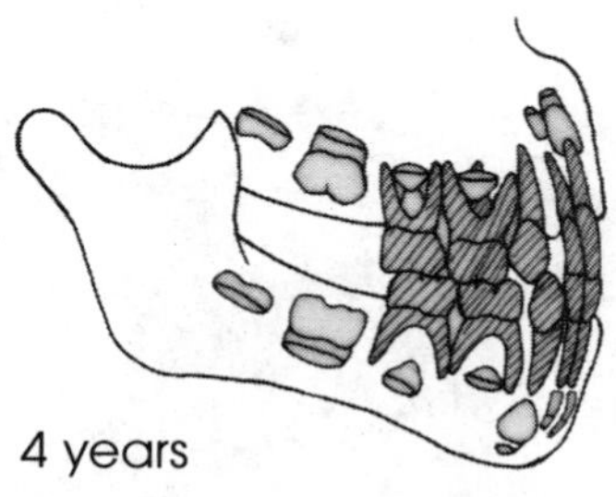
4 years

Mixed Dentition

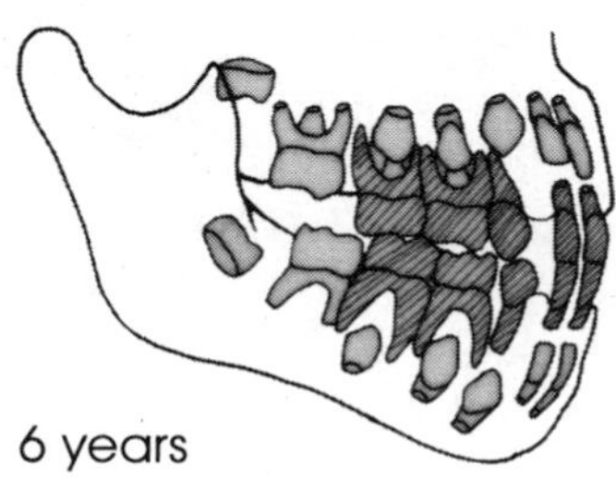
6 years

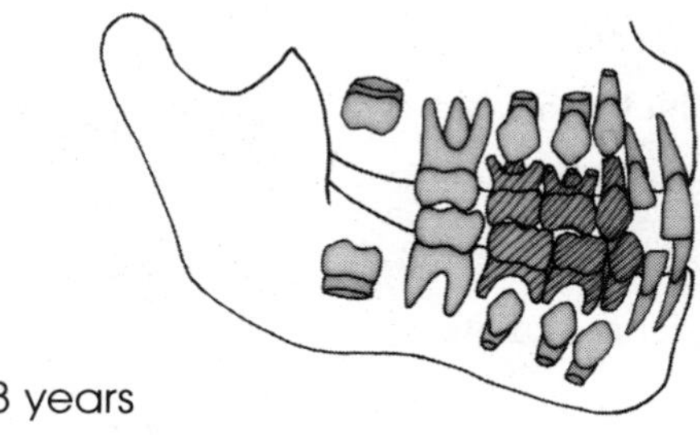
8 years

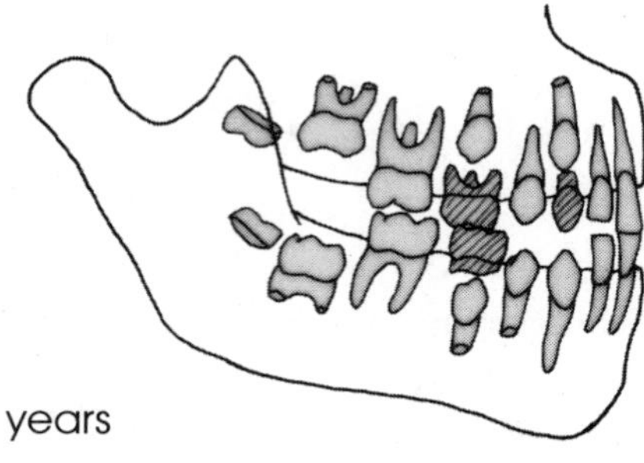
10 years

Permanent Dentition

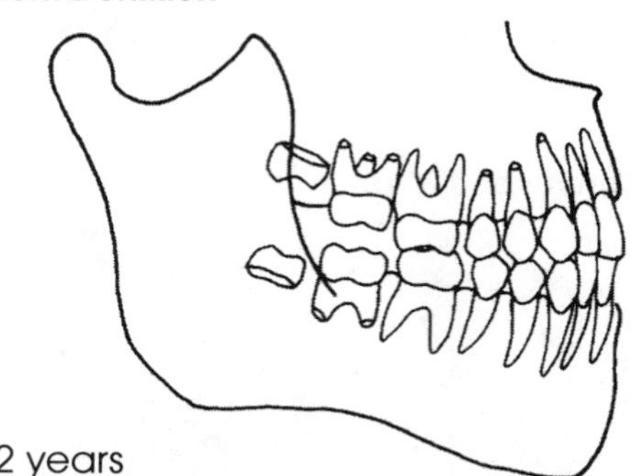
12 years

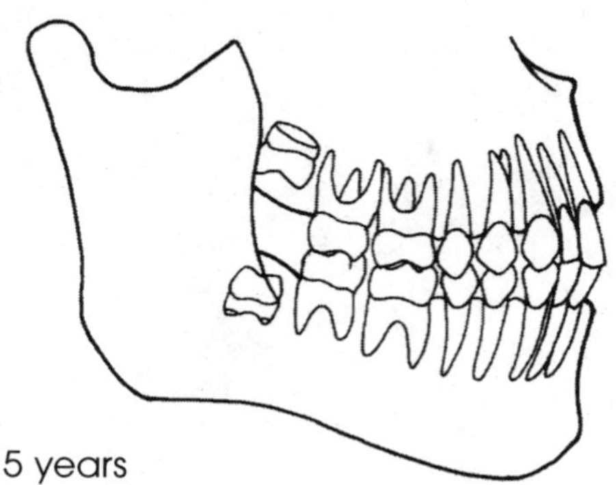
15 years

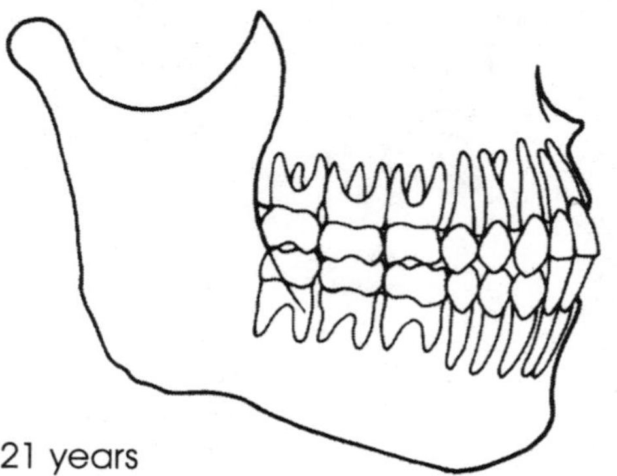
21 years

Dental Inventory

Key

Caries ....Shade the lesion

Apical abscess................................Circle the root

Antemortem loss ....X the tooth and mark AM

Postmortem loss ....X the tooth and mark PM

No attrition ....Mark with the number 0

Worn enamel only ....Mark with the number 1

Primary dentin exposed.................Mark with the number 2

Reparative dentin exposed ....Mark with the number 3

Only root remaining.......................Mark with the number 4

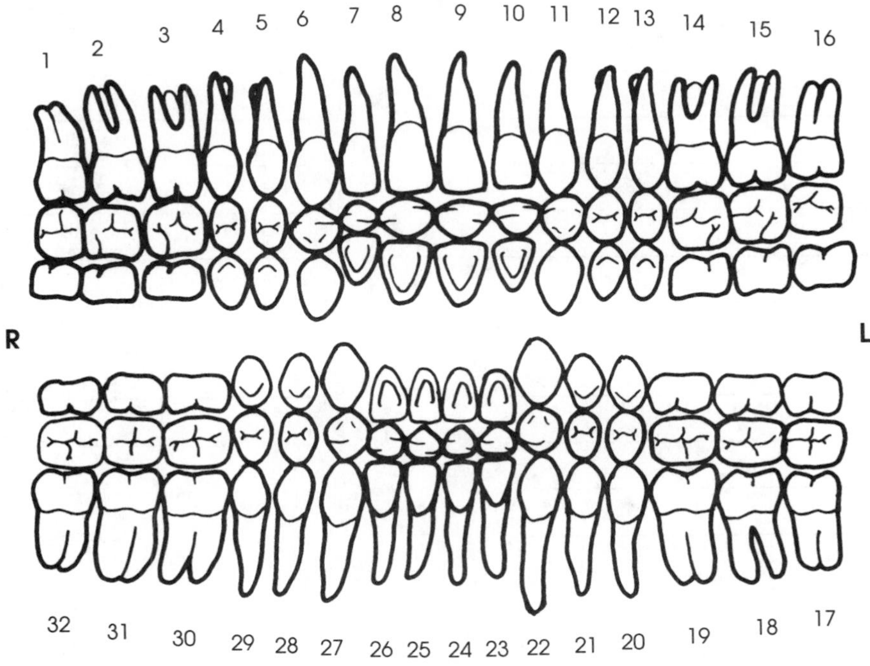

Osteology Quiz Form

Name: ______________________________ Date: ____________

Do not begin with #1 unless you are sitting at #1! Circle the number at *your* first station and begin your answers at that point on the paper.

Questions:

a. What bone is it?

b. What side is it from (right, left, or medial)?

c. Name the structure indicated by the arrow *or* answer the printed question.

1. a. ____________________
   b. ____________________
   c. ____________________
2. a. ____________________
   b. ____________________
   c. ____________________
3. a. ____________________
   b. ____________________
   c. ____________________
4. a. ____________________
   b. ____________________
   c. ____________________
5. a. ____________________
   b. ____________________
   c. ____________________
6. a. ____________________
   b. ____________________
   c. ____________________
7. a. ____________________
   b. ____________________
   c. ____________________
8. a. ____________________
   b. ____________________
   c. ____________________
9. a. ____________________
   b. ____________________
   c. ____________________
10. a. ____________________
    b. ____________________
    c. ____________________
11. a. ____________________
    b. ____________________
    c. ____________________
12. a. ____________________
    b. ____________________
    c. ____________________

INTERVIEW QUESTIONNAIRE FOR FAMILIES OF THE MISSING—PAGE 1

Provide all information possible. Fill in the blank or check the correct box where applicable.

INFORMATION ABOUT THE DISAPPEARANCE

Fill in the blanks with the appropriate information.

1. How long has this person been missing? ______________________________
2. Did you see the body? ______________________________
3. Did someone else report the death to you? ______________________________

INFORMATION ABOUT CIRCUMSTANCES OF DEATH

Witness should answer Yes or No and describe the type of weapon and location of wounds.

Type of Injury	Yes	No	Type of Weapon	Location of Wounds
4. Gunshot			*(e.g., handgun, AK47)*	
5. Garrote			*(e.g., rope, wire)*	
6. Stabbing			*(e.g., stiletto, machete)*	
7. Beating			*(e.g., baton, fists)*	
8. Other				

CLOTHING WHEN LAST SEEN

When colors are part of the description, the interviewer should use a color chart. Let the witness point to the correct color, and then record the color number.

Description and Color

9. Shirt or blouse ______________________________
10. Pants or skirt ______________________________
11. Type of shoes ______________________________
12. Jewelry or ornaments ______________________________

BASIC PHYSICAL DESCRIPTION

Fill in the blanks with the appropriate description.

13. Age (*If age is unknown, list as elderly, adult, adolescent, child, or infant.*) ______________________________
14. Sex (*male or female*) ______________________________
15. If female, did she bear children? (*yes, no, or unknown*) ______________________________
16. Race/Color/Ethnicity ______________________________
17. Possible mixed race? (*yes, no, or unknown*) ______________________________
18. Height (*If height is unknown, interviewer should ask for a comparison with a living person and record the results accordingly—e.g., If the missing person is said to be "just a little taller" than his 170 cm. cousin, list height as "slightly greater than 170 cm."*)

    ____
19. Musculature (*strong, average, or frail*) ______________________________
20. Habitual posture (*erect, hunched, or favoring one side*) ______________________________

Interview Questionnaire for Families of the Missing—Page 2

Dental Description

Interviewer should use a dental chart or dental casts and let the witness point to the correct tooth.

21. Were any teeth missing or extracted? (*yes, no, or unknown*) ____________________

22. If teeth were missing, which ones? (*Interviewer should use a dental chart and list the tooth numbers.*) ____________________

23. Were the teeth stained? (*yes, no, or unknown*) ____________________

24. Did the person smoke or chew tobacco? (*yes, no, or unknown*) ____________________

25. Did a dentist repair any teeth? (*yes + which ones, no, or unknown*) ____________________

26. Did the person wear dentures? (*yes, no, or unknown*) ____________________

27. Did the person complain of dental pain? (*yes, no, or unknown*) ____________________

28. Did the person have bad breath? (*yes, no, or unknown*) ____________________

Description of Antemortem Trauma

Interviewer should use an anatomical chart so that the witness can point at the body rather than trying to recall right or left. Record the information directly on the chart.

29. Did the person break any bones during life? (*yes + at what age, no, or unknown*)

____

30. If so, did he or she receive medical care? (*yes + at what age, no, or unknown*)

____

31. Did the person walk with a limp? (*yes or no*) ____________________

32. Can anyone remember a fall, an accident, or any unusual event? (*yes + nature of accident and at what age, no, or unknown*)

____

33. If there was an injury, what was the medical treatment? (*e.g., radiograph, sling, orthopaedic brace, plaster cast, surgical pin or wire, bone graft*)

____

34. Did the person complain of pain in a specific part of the body? (*yes + which body part (e.g., ear, jaw, shoulder, back, elbow, wrist, fingers, knees) or no*)

____

Records of Victim

The interviewer should collect medical records and photographs. Remember that more than one photographic view is recommended and a smiling image is preferred.

Record Type	Records Provided by (Name, Address, Phone Number)
35. Dental	
36. Medical	
37. Radiographs	
38. Photographs	

Glossary

acetabular fossa The central, nonarticular surface deep within the acetabulum.

acetabulum The articular surface for the rotation of the head of the femur; the point of fusion for the three pelvic bones.

acoustic meatus The internal or external opening of the ear canal; also called the auditory meatus.

acromion process The larger, more posterior of the two scapular processes; with the articular facet for the clavicle.

ala A wing-like structure (e.g., ala of sphenoid).

alveolar process The ridge of the maxilla or mandible that supports the teeth.

alveolus dentalis The tooth socket in which teeth are attached by a periodontal membrane.

amalgam A restoration made of a metal in mercury solution (usually 67 percent Ag, 27 percent Sn, 5 percent Cu, and 1 percent Zn). One part alloy and two parts mercury are mixed and packed into the cleaned and sealed dental cavity. It hardens in about twenty-four hours.

anatomic crown The portion of a natural tooth that extends from the cementoenamel junction to the occlusal surface or incisal edge.

anterior crest The shin; the anterior-projecting ridge of the tibia.

anterior superior iliac spine The larger, more anterior projection of the ilium.

anterior inferior iliac spine The small projection between the anterior superior iliac spine and the acetabulum.

apophysis A prominence formed directly upon a bone; an outgrowth of bone with an independent center of ossification (e.g., the basilar apophysis of the occipital bone).

arch Any vaulted or arch-like structure (e.g., palatal arch, dental arch, vertebral arch).

articular facet Any bony surface that articulates with another bony surface (superior articular facet of the vertebra).

articular process Any projection that serves to articulate.

auditory meatus The internal or external opening of the ear canal; also called the acoustic meatus.

auricular surface Ear-shaped roughened surface for the sacroiliac joint. The ilium and the sacrum both have auricular surfaces.

axillary border The lateral border of the scapula.

body of scapula The main part of the scapula (a thin triangular plate of bone).

body of rib The main part of the rib.

body of sternum The main part of the sternum, the corpus sterni, fused from the four central centers of ossification.

boss A rounded eminence or tuberosity (e.g., a frontal boss).

bridge A fixed or removable replacement for missing teeth, attached to natural teeth by wires or crowns.

calvaria Skullcap; the upper, dome-like portion of the skull.

capitulum The articular surface for the head of the radius on the distal end of the humerus.

Carabelli's cusp An extra cuspid on the mediolingual surface of upper molars; more common within the Caucasian race.

caries, dental A localized, progressively destructive disease beginning at the external surface with dissolution of inorganic components by organic acids produced by microorganisms.

cementodentinal junction The surface at which cementum and dentin meet (C-D junction).

cementoenamel junction The line around the neck of the tooth at which cementum and enamel meet (C-E junction).

cementum A porous layer of calcification covering the tooth root. The cementum provides a site for periodontal fibers to anchor.

centrum The body of the vertebra, especially the body without epiphyseal rings.

cervix (neck) The slightly constricted part of the tooth between the crown and the root.

clavicular notch The articular facets for the clavicles, located on either side of the jugular notch of the manubrium.

clinical crown The portion of the tooth visible in the oral cavity.

composite A plastic resin restoration that mimics the appearance of enamel.

conoid tubercle The bump on the posterior superior edge of the lateral end of the clavicle.

coracoid process The smaller, more anterior of the two scapular processes.

coronoid process The smaller of the two processes at the proximal end of the ulna (anterior).

costal notch The seven pairs of notches for joining of the costal cartilage with the sternum.

costal pit Articular surface for the rib on the vertebral body and the transverse process.

cranium (1) Skull; bones of the head collectively. (2) In a more limited sense, the bony brain case without the face or jaw.

crown The enamel-capped portion of the tooth that normally projects beyond the gum line; a permanent replacement for a natural crown, made of porcelain on metal or metal alone (gold or other stable metal).

cusp A conical elevation arising on the surface of a tooth from an independent calcification center.

cusp pattern The recognizable alignment of cusps on a particular tooth type.

deltoid tuberosity The attachment area for the deltoid muscle on the anterior surface of the humerus.

dens A tooth-like projection; an abbreviated name for the *dens epistropheus*, also called the odontoid process of the atlas.

dental prosthesis Fixed or removable replacement of one or more teeth and/or associated oral structures; denture, bridgework, or oral appliance.

dentin The main mass of the tooth; 20 percent is organic matrix, mostly collagen with some elastin and a small amount of mucopolysaccharide; 80 percent is inorganic, mainly hydroxyapatite with some carbonate, magnesium, and fluoride; structured of parallel tubules.

dentinal tubule The tubules extending from the pulp to the dentinoenamel junction; odontoblastic processes extend into the tubules from the pulp surface.

dentinoenamel junction The surface at which the dentin and enamel meet (D-E junction).

denture A complete or full denture replaces all of the natural dentition of the maxilla or mandible; a partial denture replaces one or more teeth and is retained by natural teeth at one or both ends.

dorsal plateau The convex inner surface at the dorsal margin of the pubic symphysis; one of the first areas of modification in the aging pubic symphysis.

dorsal tubercles The bumps on the dorsal surface of the distal end of the radius.

dorsal surface The posterior surface; the back.

edentulous toothless; a mouth without teeth.

enamel The dense mineralized outer covering of the tooth crown; 99.5 percent inorganic hydroxyapatite with small amounts of carbonate, magnesium, and fluoride, and 0.5 percent organic matrix of glycoprotein and keratin-like protein; structured of oriented rods consisting of rodlets encased in an organic prism sheath.

epiphyseal ring The secondary centers of ossification that fuse to the superior and inferior surfaces of the vertebral centrum.

epiphysis (pl. epiphyses) A secondary center of ossification that fuses to the primary center when growth is complete.

false rib Ribs 8, 9, or 10, which do not join directly to the sternum. They are attached to the sternum via the seventh rib cartilage.

femoral head The ball-shaped upper extremity of the femur; the femoral head articulates within the acetabulum of the innominate; the proximal epiphysis of the femur.

fibular articular surface The facets on the superior and inferior of the lateral side of the tibia providing articulation for the ends of the fibula. The superior facet is a flat oval. The inferior facet is a notch.

fibular head The knob-like portion of the proximal end of the fibula.

floating rib Ribs 11 and 12, which do not attach to the sternum or to any other rib.

foramen (pl. foramina) A round or oval aperture in bone or a membranous structure for the passage or anchorage of other tissue; any aperture or perforation through bone or membranous structure (e.g., sternal foramen or foramen magnum).

fovea capitis The pit in the femoral head providing attachment for the *ligamentum teres*.

gingiva The "gums"; the dense fibrous tissue covered by mucous membrane that envelops the alveolar processes of the upper and lower jaws and surrounds the necks of the teeth.

glenoid cavity or fossa The articular surface on the scapula for the head of the humerus.

greater trochanter The larger and more superior of the two protuberances between the neck and the shaft of the femur; a separate center of ossification.

greater sciatic notch The large indentation on the posterior border of the innominate; the superior border is formed by the ilium and the inferior border is formed by the ischium.

greater tubercle The larger of the two tubercles on the proximal end of the humerus. The greater tubercle is lateral to the lesser tubercle.

groove, costal The groove on the inferior edge of the inner surface of the rib.

humeral head The proximal articular surface of the humerus; it is half ball-shaped (hemispherical) and *has no fovea*.

iliac fossa Smooth, depressed inner surface of the ilium.

iliac tuberosity The posterior, inner thickening of the ilium, superior to the auricular surface iliac crest superior edge of the ilium.

inferior articular process One of the two processes on each vertebra that articulates with the superior articular process of the next inferior vertebra.

inlay A prefabricated dental restoration (usually gold or porcelain) sealed in a dental cavity with cement.

innominate The hip bone; one side of the pelvis; a composite of three bones that fuse at puberty—the ilium, ischium, and pubis. The innominates meet at the pubic symphysis anteriorly and join the sacrum posteriorly.

intercondylar fossa The depression between the two condyles on the posterior surface of the distal end of the femur.

intercondyloid eminence The bony projection between the two condylar platforms of the tibia.

interosseous crest The somewhat sharp edge on the bone shaft directed toward an adjacent bone and serving for attachment of an interosseous ligament. (An interosseous crest occurs on the radius and ulna and on the tibia and fibula.)

intertubercular groove The groove between the greater and lesser tubercles of the humerus.

ischial tuberosity The large, roughened eminence of the ischium inferior to the acetabulum.

ischial spine The process on the posterior border of the ischium bounded by the greater and lesser sciatic notches.

ischiopubic ramus The bridge between the ischium and the pubis.

jugular notch The medial, superior notch on the manubrium.

lateral condyle The lateral of the two distal femoral condyles; the lateral of the two proximal articular surfaces of the tibia.

lateral articular facet The articular surface that articulates with the anterior part of the lateral condyle of the femur. The patella articulates with the lateral and medial articular facets of the femur.

lateral epicondyle The bulbous area on the lateral side above the distal condyle of the humerus; the origin of the extensor muscles of the hand.

lateral malleolus The laterally rounded portion of the distal end of the fibula; the outer "ankle bone."

lesser trochanter The smaller and more inferior of the two protuberances between the neck and the shaft of the femur; a separate center of ossification.

lesser sciatic notch The indentation on the posterior border of the ischium bounded by the ischial spine and the ischial tuberosity.

lesser tubercle The smaller of the two tubercles on the proximal end of the humerus.

line A thin mark distinguished by texture or elevation—often the outer edge of a muscle or ligament attachment (e.g., the temporal line on the frontal and parietal bones).

linea aspera The muscle attachment line on the posterior surface of the femoral shaft.

malleolar fossa The hollow on the posterior surface of the distal end of the fibula.

manubrium The superior-most section of the sternum.

medial articular facet The articular surface that articulates with the anterior of the medial condyle of the femur; part of the patellar articulation.

medial condyle The medial of the two distal femoral condyles; the medial of the two proximal articular surfaces of the tibia.

medial epicondyle The bulbous area on the medial side above the distal condyle of the humerus; the origin of the flexor muscles of the hand.

medial epiphysis The epiphysis on the sternal end of the clavicle. (The clavicle has no lateral epiphysis.)

medial malleolus The projection on the distomedial end of the tibia; the inner "ankle bone."

metopic suture A midline suture of the frontal bone; the result of nonunion of left and right centers of ossification.

neck The area of a shaft immediately adjacent to a head (radius, humerus, femur, rib).

nutrient foramen A major vascular opening between the exterior of a bone and the medulla; notable foramina are on appendicular bones, mandible, and parietals.

obturator foramen The large opening bordered by the pubis, the ischium, and the ischiopubic ramus.

olecranon fossa The large depression on the posterior surface of the distal humerus for the olecranon process of the ulna.

olecranon process The larger processes at the proximal end of the ulna (posterior); the bony part of the elbow.

parturition pits Fossae on the inner surface of the female pubic bone.

periapical Around the tip of the tooth root.

periodontal ligament The fibrous tissue anchoring the tooth by surrounding the root and attaching to the alveolus.

periodontal disease Inflammation of the tissues surrounding the teeth resulting in resorption of supporting structures and tooth loss.

periodontosis Lowering of the attachment level of the periodontal ligament (associated with periodontal disease or general aging).

pits and fissures The depressed points and lines between cusps of premolar and molar teeth.

popliteal line On the superior and posterior surface of the tibia, a curved roughened attachment surface.

posterior inferior iliac spine The more inferior projection of the ilium adjacent to and superior to the greater sciatic notch.

posterior superior iliac spine The more superior of the posterior projections of the ilium.

preauricular sulcus Groove adjacent to the articular surface of the ilium; related to the trauma of childbearing.

primary dentin The dentin that forms as the root is completed in the growing tooth; tubular dentin.

process Any bony projection.

process, transverse Lateral vertebral processes, some of which articulate with ribs.

process, spinous The process that projects toward the dorsal surface of the back.

promontory; promontorium A raised place; the most ventral prominent median point of the lumbosacral symphysis; the most anterosuperior point on the sacrum.

pubic ramus The bridge of bone between the acetabulum and the pubic symphysis; the superior border of the obturator foramen.

pubic symphysis The medial surface of the pubic bone where the two innominates are joined together by fibrocartilage.

pubic tubercle A small projection at the anterior extremity of the crest of the pubis ca. 1 cm. from the symphysis.

pulp chamber The central cavity of the tooth surrounded by dentin and extending from the crown to the root apex.

pulp (of tooth) The soft tissue in the central chamber of the tooth, consisting of connective tissue containing nerves, blood vessels, lymphatics, and, at the periphery, odontoblasts capable of dentinal repair.

pulpectomy Removal of the entire pulp, including the root; commonly known as a "root canal"; after a pulpectomy, the tooth is no longer living.

radial nerve groove The diagonal groove on the posterior surface of the shaft of the humerus.

radial tuberosity The bump distal to the neck of the radius; one insertion of the biceps muscle.

radial notch The concavity for the radius on the lateral side of the proximal end of the ulna.

radial head The *proximal* end of the radius; the articulation with the capitulum of the humerus and the radial notch of the ulna.

radiograph, apical A film produced by exposure of vertically-oriented intraoral film; the x-ray beam is angled from above maxillary teeth or below mandibular teeth to capture the complete tooth, including the apex.

radiograph, bite-wing A film of posterior teeth produced by exposure of laterally-oriented intraoral film; the x-ray beam is angled between the teeth; the crowns are the main focus of the films.

radiograph, Panorex A film of the entire oral cavity produced by immobilizing the head and moving the x-ray beam behind the head while film is exposed in synchrony in front of the face.

reparative dentin Calcification of dentinal tubules immediately beneath a carious lesion, abrasion, or injury.

restoration, dental Any inlay, crown, bridge, partial denture, or complete denture that restores or replaces lost tooth structure, teeth, or oral tissues.

rib neck The constricted part below the rib head on upper ribs (not obvious on lower ribs).

rib head The vertebral end of the rib.

rib tubercle The center of ossification below the neck; part of the tubercle articulates with the vertebral transverse process.

rib, sternal end The open end of the rib that connects to the sternal cartilage; useful for aging purposes.

root, anatomical The portion of the root extending from the cementoenamel junction to the apex or root tip.

root (of tooth) The cementum covered portion of the tooth usually below the gum line. (The root may become exposed in advanced periodontal disease.)

root, clinical The imbedded portion of the root; the part not visible in the oral cavity.

scapular notch The notch on the superior border of the scapula.

scapular spine The long thin elevation on the dorsal surface of the scapula that ends laterally as the acromion process.

sclerotic dentin Generalized calcification of dentinal tubules as a result of aging.

secondary dentin Calcification within the pulp chamber; secondary dentin forms after the tooth has erupted due to irritation from caries, abrasion, injury, or age.

semilunar notch The proximal articular surface of the ulna for the trochlea of the humerus; it is bounded by the olecranon and coronoid processes.

septal aperture The olecranon foramen of the ulna—infrequent appearance, more common in females.

shaft The diaphysis of a long bone, especially humerus, radius, ulna, femur, tibia, fibula.

shovel-shaped incisors Central incisors formed with lateral margins bent lingually, resembling the form of a flat shovel or a snow shovel; common within the Mongoloid race (e.g., American Indians).

skull All the bones of the head as a unit.

sternal foramen An anomalous foramen in the sternal body.

sternal-end ossification Osteophytic growth from the rib end into the sternal cartilage; cartilaginous calcification. It increases with age and varies with sex.

styloid process A pointed process of bone. Styloid processes exist at the distal ends of the radius and ulna and at the proximal end of the fibula; there is also a large styloid process on the temporal bone.

subpubic concavity A depression on the inferior border of the female pubic bone; a structural byproduct of elongation of the female pubis.

subpubic angle The inferior angle formed when the two pubic bones are approximated. The angle is larger in females.

superior articular process On the vertebra, one of the two processes that articulates with the superior vertebra.

suture The interface of two bones of the skull (e.g., basilar, coronal, lambdoidal, sagittal, and squamosal sutures).

symphysial rim The margin of the pubic symphysis; the edge of the symphysial face; one of the later areas of modification in the pubic symphysis.

transverse foramen The aperture in the transverse process of the cervical vertebrae.

trochlea The articular surface for the ulna on the distal end of the humerus.

true rib Ribs 1–7, which attach *directly* to the sternum via cartilage.

ulnar head The distal end of the ulna.

ulnar notch The facet for the ulna on the medial side of the distal end of the radius.

ventral arc A slightly elevated ridge of bone that crosses the ventral surface of the female pubis at an angle to the inferior corner.

ventral rampart The concave outer surface of the margin of the pubic symphysis; this part develops a steep bevel in the middle phases of Todd's aging sequence.

vertebra (pl. vertebrae) A single segment of the spinal column; there are seven cervical vertebrae, twelve thoracic vertebrae, five lumbar, five sacral (fused to form the sacrum), and four coccygeal (often fused to form the coccyx and sometimes fused to the sacrum).

vertebral foramen The aperture between the vertebral arch and the vertebral body for the passage of the spinal cord.

vertebral border The medial border of the scapula.

vertebral body The centrum and its epiphyseal rings; the arch and the body fuse at 3–7 years of age.

xiphoid process The inferior projection of the sternum.

zygomatic arch The arch resulting from the meeting of processes from the zygomatic and temporal bones.

zygomatic process Part of the maxilla or part of the temporal extending toward the zygomatic bone.

Bibliography

Albert, A. M., and W. R. Maples. 1995. Stages of epiphyseal union for thoracic and lumbar vertebral centra as a method of age determination for teenage and young adult skeletons. *Journal of Forensic Sciences* 40: 623–633.

Amnesty International. 1994. *"Disappearances" and Political Killings: Human Rights Crisis of the 1990s, a Manual for Action*. Amsterdam: Amnesty International.

Amnesty International. 1981. *"Disappearances," a Workbook*. Amsterdam: Amnesty International USA Publications.

Amnesty International. 1993. *Getting Away with Murder: Political Killings and "Disappearances" in the 1990s*. Amsterdam: Amnesty International Publications.

Austin-Smith, D., and W. R. Maples. 1994. The reliability of skull/photograph superimposition in individual identification. *Journal of Forensic Sciences* 39: 446–455.

Averill, D. C. 1991. *Manual of Forensic Odontology*. American Society of Forensic Odontology, AAFS, P.O. Box 669, Colorado Springs, CO, 80901-0669.

Bass, W. M. 1989. *Human Osteology: A Laboratory and Field Manual of the Human Skeleton*, 3rd ed. Columbia, MO: Missouri Archaeological Society.

Bogin, B., T. Sullivan, R. Hauspie, and R. B. MacVean. 1989. Longitudinal growth in height, weight, and bone age of Guatemalan ladino and Indian schoolchildren. *American Journal of Human Biology* 1 (1): 103–113.

Brooks, S. T. 1955. Skeletal age at death: The reliability of cranial and pubic age indicators. *American Journal of Physical Anthropology* 13: 567–597.

Buergenthal, T. 1994. The United Nations Truth Commission for El Salvador. *Vanderbilt Journal of Transnational Law* 27 (3): 497–544.

Buikstra, J. E., and D. H. Ubelaker. 1994. *Standards for Data Collection from Human Skeletal Remains*. Arkansas Archeological Survey Research Series No. 44.

Burns, K. R. 1991. Model protocol for disinterment and analysis of skeletal remains. *Manual on the Effective Prevention and Investigation of Extra-*

Legal, Arbitrary, and Summary Executions. United Nations Publication #E.91.IV.1.

Burns, K. R. 1986. Forensic anthropology and human rights issues. In *Forensic Osteology: Advances in the Identification of Human Remains*, ed. K. J. Reichs. Springfield, IL: Charles C. Thomas.

Burns, K. R., and W. R. Maples. 1976. Estimation of age from individual adult teeth. *Journal of Forensic Sciences* 21 (2): 343–356.

Caplan, Y. H., ed. 1997. *Medicolegal Death Investigation, Treatises in the Forensic Sciences*. Colorado Springs, CO: Forensic Sciences Foundation Press.

Carver, R. 1990. Called to account: How African governments investigate human rights violations. *African Affairs* 89 (356): 391.

Catts, E. P., and N. H. Haskell. 1990. *Entomology and Death: A Procedural Guide*. Clemson, SC: Joyce's Print Shop, Inc.

Chamberlain, A. 1994. *Human Remains: Interpreting the Past*. Berkeley, CA: University of California Press.

Danner, M. 1993. The truth of El Mozote. *The New Yorker*. December 6.

Department of Public Information. 1995. *Basic Facts about the United Nations*. New York: United Nations.

Di Maio, V. J. M. 1985. *Gunshot Wounds: Practical Aspects of Firearms, Ballistics, and Forensic Techniques*. New York: Elsevier.

El Equipo de Antropología Forense de Guatemala. 1995. *Las Masacres en Rabinal, Estudio Historico-Antropologico de las Masacres de Plan de Sanchez*. Guatemala: Chichupac y Rio Negro.

Fazekas, G., and F. Kosa. 1978. *Forensic Fetal Osteology*. Budapest: Akademiai Kiado.

Fierro, M. F., ed. 1986. *CAP Handbook for Postmortem Examination of Unidentified Remains*. Skokie, IL: College of American Pathologists.

Finnegan, M., and F. P. Schulter. 1975. Forensic discrimination between American negro and white. *American Journal of Physical Anthropology* 42: 300.

Fuller, J. L., and G. E. Denehy. 1977. *Concise Dental Anatomy and Morphology*. Chicago, IL: Year Book Medical Publishers.

Geberth, V. J. 1983. *Practical Homicide Investigation*. New York: Elsevier.

Geberth, V. J. 1997. *Practical Homicide Investigation: Checklist and Field Guide*. Boca Raton, FL: CRC Press.

Genovés, S. 1967. Proportionality of the long bones and their relation to stature among Mesoamericans. *American Journal of Physical Anthropology* 26: 67–77.

Gibbons, A., ed. 1992. Scientists search for "the disappeared" in Guatemala. *Science* 257 (July 24).

Gilbert, B. M., and T. W. McKern. 1973. A method for aging the female os pubis. *American Journal of Physical Anthropology* 38: 31–38.

Gill, G. W., and S. Rhine. 1990. *Skeletal Attribution of Race*. Maxwell Museum of Anthropology, Anthropological Papers No. 4.

Gill, G. W. 1995. Challenge on the frontier: Discerning American Indians from whites osteologically. *Journal of Forensic Sciences* 40: 783–788.

Grauer, A. L., ed. 1995. *Bodies of Evidence: Reconstruction History through Skeletal Analysis*. New York: Wiley-Liss.

Greulich, W. W., and S. I. Pyle. 1959. *Radiographic Atlas of Skeletal Development of the Hand and Wrist*, 2nd ed. Stanford, CA: Stanford University Press.

Gruschow, J., E. Stover, and J. L. Thomsen. 1989. Medicolegal investigation of political killings in El Salvador. *The Lancet* (June 17): 1377–1379.

Gustafson, G. 1950. Age determinations of teeth. *Journal of the American Dental Association* 41: 45–54.

Gustafson, G. 1966. *Forensic Odontology*. New York: American Elsevier.

Haglund, W. D., and M. H. Sorg, eds. 1997. *Forensic Taphonomy: The Postmortem Fate of Human Remains*. Boca Raton, FL: CRC Press.

Hanihara, K., and T. Suzuki. 1979. Estimation of age from the pubic symphysis by means of multiple regression analysis. *American Journal of Physical Anthropology* 48: 233–240.

Hannibal, K. 1992. *Taking Up the Challenge: The Promotion of Human Rights, A Guide for the Scientific Community*. Science and Human Rights Program, American Association for the Advancement of Science, Publication 92-32S.

Hannibal, K. 1990/1991. AAAS sponsors forensic mission to Brazil. *Report on Science and Human Rights*. AAAS Committee on Scientific Freedom and Responsibility (Winter) XII (2).

Hayner, P. B. 1994. Fifteen truth commissions—1974 to 1994: A comparative study. *Human Rights Quarterly* 16: 597–655.

Hoffman, J. M. 1979. Age estimations from diaphyseal lengths: Two months to twelve years. *Journal of Forensic Sciences* 24: 461–469.

Human Rights Internet and The International Centre for Human Rights and Democratic Development. 1995. *Funding Human Rights: An International Directory of Funding Organizations and Human Rights Awards*, 2nd ed. Ottawa, Canada: Human Rights Internet.

Inman, K., and N. Rudin. 1997. *An Introduction to Forensic DNA Analysis*. Boca Raton, FL: CRC Press.

Işçan, M. Y., and K. A. R. Kennedy. 1989. *Reconstruction of Life from the Skeleton*. New York: Alan R. Liss.

Işçan, M. Y., S. R. Loth, and R. K. Wright. 1984a. Age estimation from the ribs by phase analysis: White males. *Journal of Forensic Sciences* 29: 1094–1104.

Işçan, M. Y., S. R. Loth, and R. K. Wright. 1984b. Metamorphosis at the sternal rib end: A new method to estimate age at death in white males. *American Journal of Physical Anthropology* 65: 147–156.

Işçan, M. Y., S. R. Loth, and R. K. Wright. 1985. Age estimation from the rib by phase analysis: White females. *Journal of Forensic Sciences* 30: 853–863.

Joyce, C., and E. Stover. 1991. *Witnesses from the Grave, The Stories Bones Tell*. New York: Ballantine.

Katz, D., and J. M. Suchey. 1986. Age determination of the male os pubis. *American Journal of Physical Anthropology* 69: 426–235.

Kaye, B. H. 1995. *Science and the Detective: Selected Reading in Forensic Science*. New York: VCH Publishers.

Killam, E. W. 1990. *The Detection of Human Remains.* Springfield, IL: Charles C. Thomas.

Kirschner, R. H. 1994. The application of the forensic sciences to human rights investigations. *International Journal of Medicine and Law* 13 (5–6).

Krogman, W. M. 1939. A guide to the identification of human skeletal material. *FBI Law Enforcement Bulletin.*

Krogman, W. M. 1962. *The Human Skeleton in Forensic Medicine.* Springfield, IL: Charles C. Thomas.

Krogman, W. M., and M. Y. Iscan. 1986. *The Human Skeleton in Forensic Medicine*, 2nd ed. Springfield, IL: Charles C. Thomas.

Lollar, C., ed. 1990. Forensic scientists uncovering fate of Brazil's "disappeared" with help of AAAS. *Science* 250 (December 21).

Maples, W. R., and M. Browning. 1994. *Dead Men Do Tell Tales.* New York: Doubleday.

Marieb, E. N., and J. Mallatt. 1992. *Human Anatomy.* Redwood City, CA: Benjamin/Cummings Publishing Co.

Matson, J. V. 1994. *Effective Expert Witnessing*, 2nd ed. Boca Raton, FL: CRC Press.

McKasson, S. C., and C. A. Richards. 1998. *Speaking as an Expert: A Guide for the Identification Sciences from the Laboratory to the Courtroom.* Springfield, IL: Charles C. Thomas.

McKern, T. W., and T. D. Stewart. 1957. *Skeletal Age Changes in Young American Males.* Natick, MA: Quartermaster Research and Development Command, Technical Report EP-45.

Méndez, J. 1991. Review of a miracle: A universe by Lawrence Weschler. *New York Law School Journal of Human Rights* 8 (2): 577.

Molleson, T. 1994. The eloquent bones of Abu Hureyra. *Scientific American* 271 (2).

Moore-Jansen, P. M., S. D. Ousley, and R. L. Jantz. 1994. *Data Collection Procedures for Forensic Skeletal Material.* Report of Investigations no. 48. Knoxville, TN: University of Tennessee.

Neier, A. 1990. What should be done about the guilty? *The New York Review of Books* (February 1): 32.

Ousley, S. D., and R. L. Jantz. 1993, 1996. *Fordisc 2.0.* Knoxville, TN: Forensic Anthropology Center, Department of Anthropology, University of Tennessee.

Padgett, T. 1992. Subtle clues in shallow graves. *Newsweek* (August 31).

PDR Medical Dictionary. 1995. Baltimore, MD: Williams and Wilkins.

Pearson, K. 1917–1919. A study of the long bones of the English skeleton I: The femur. London: University of London, University College, Department of Applied Statistics, Company Research, Memoirs, Biometric Series X, Chapters 1–4.

Pickering, R. B., and D. C. Bachman. 1996. *The Use of Forensic Anthropology*. Boca Raton, FL: CRC Press.

Pickering, R. B. 1994. *Seminar in Forensic Anthropology*. Sponsored by the Forensic Sciences Association of Thailand and the Institute of Forensic Medicine, the Surgeon General's Office, and the Royal Thai Police Department (unpublished manuscript).

Pyle, S. I., and N. L. Hoerr. 1955. *Radiographic Atlas of Skeletal Development of the Knee*. Springfield, IL: Charles C. Thomas.

Rathbun, T. A., and J. E. Buikstra. 1984. *Human Identification: Case Studies in Forensic Anthropology*. Springfield, IL: Charles C. Thomas.

Redsicker, D. R. 1994. *The Practical Methodology of Forensic Photography*. Boca Raton, FL: CRC Press.

Reichs, K. J., ed. 1986. *Forensic Osteology: Advances in the Identification of Human Remains*. Springfield, IL: Charles C. Thomas.

Reichs, K. J., ed. 1997. *Forensic Osteology II: A Decade of Growth*. Springfield, IL: Charles C. Thomas.

Robertson, B., and G. Vignaux. 1995. *Interpreting Evidence: Evaluating Forensic Science in the Courtroom*. New York: John Wiley and Sons.

Salcedo, D. 1993. Forensic anthropology in Guatemala: A project report. *Report on Science and Human Rights*. AAAS Committee on Scientific Freedom and Responsibility XIV (Winter/Spring): 1.

Saferstein, R. 1995. *Criminalistics: An Introduction to Forensic Science*, 5th ed. Englewood Cliffs, NJ: Prentice-Hall.

Saferstein, R., ed. 1982. *Forensic Science Handbook*. Englewood Cliffs, NJ: Prentice-Hall.

Sellier, K. G., and B. P. Kneubuehl. 1994. *Wound Ballistics and the Scientific Background*. New York: Elsevier.

Shipman, P., A. Walker, and D. Bichell. 1985. *The Human Skeleton*. Cambridge, MA: Harvard University Press.

Skinner, M., and R. A. Lazenby. 1983. *Found! Human Remains: A Field Manual for the Recovery of the Recent Human Skeleton*. Burnaby, BC: Archaeology Press, Simon Fraser University.

Skolnick, A. A. 1992. Game's afoot in many lands for forensic scientists investigating most-extreme human rights abuses. *Journal of the American Medical Association* 268 (August 5): 5.

Snow, C. C. 1983. Equations for estimating age at death from the pubic symphysis: A modification of the McKern-Stewart method. *Journal of Forensic Sciences* 28: 864–870.

Snow, C. C., E. Stover, and K. Hannibal. 1989. Scientists as detectives investigating human rights. *Technology Review* 92 (February/March): 2.

Snow, C. C., and M. J. Bihurriet. 1992. An epidemiology of homicide: *Ningún nombre* burials in the province of Buenos Aires from 1970 to 1984. *Human Rights and Statistics: Getting the Record Straight*, ed. T. B. Jabine and R. P. Claude. Philadelphia, PA: University of Pennsylvania Press.

Spirer, H. F., and L. Spirer. 1993. *Data Analysis for Monitoring Human Rights*. Washington, D.C.: American Association for the Advancement of Science.

Spitz, W. U., and R. S. Fisher. 1980. *Medicolegal Investigation of Death: Guidelines for the Application of Pathology to Crime Investigation*, 2nd ed. Springfield, IL: Charles C. Thomas.

Stewart, J. H., and W. F. McCormick. 1984. A sex and age-limited ossification pattern in human costal cartilages. *Journal of Clinical Pathology* 81: 765–769.

Stewart, T. D. 1979. *Essentials of Forensic Anthropology*. Springfield, IL: Charles C. Thomas.

Stewart, T. D., ed. 1970. *Personal Identification in Mass Disasters*. Washington, D.C.: Smithsonian Institution.

Stimson, P. G., and C. A. Mertz. 1997. *Forensic Dentistry*. Boca Raton, FL: CRC Press.

Stover, E. 1985. Scientists search for Argentina's missing. *Clearinghouse Report on Science and Human Rights*. AAAS Committee on Scientific Freedom and Responsibility VII (September): 2.

Stover, E., and T. Eisner. 1982. Human rights abuses and role of scientists. *BioScience* 32 (December): 11.

Stover, E. 1981. Scientists aid search for Argentina's "desaparacidos." *Science* 211 (4486) (March): 6.

Stover, E. 1992. *Unquiet Graves: The Search for the Disappeared in Iraqi Kurdistan*. A report published by Middle East Watch and Physicians for Human Rights.

St. Louis, M. E., and J. N. Wasserheit. 1998. Elimination of syphilis in the United States. *Science* 281 (July 17): 353–354.

Suchey, J. M., D. V. Wiseley, and D. Katz. 1986. Evaluation of the Todd and McKern-Stewart methods for aging the male os pubis. In *Forensic Osteology: Advances in the Identification of Human Remains*, ed. K. J. Reichs. Springfield, IL: Charles C. Thomas.

Timms, R. F. 1993. *Principios de Arqueologia Forense*. San Jose, Costa Rica: Universidad Estatal a Distancia.

Todd, T. W. 1920. Age changes in the pubic bone, I, The male white pubis. *American Journal of Physical Anthropology* 3: 285–339.

Todd, T. W. 1921. Age changes in the pubic bone, II: The pubis of the male Negro-White hybrid. *American Journal of Physical Anthropology* 4: 1–26.

Trotter, M. 1970. Estimation of stature from intact long limb bones. In *Personal Identification in Mass Disasters*, ed. T. D. Stewart. Washington, D.C.: Smithsonian Institution.

Trotter, M., and G. Gleser. 1952. Estimation of stature from long bones of American whites and Negroes. *American Journal of Physical Anthropology* 9: 311–324.

Trotter, M., and G. Gleser. 1958. A re-evaluation of estimation of stature based on measurements of stature taken during life and of long bones after death. *American Journal of Physical Anthropology* 16: 79–123.

Trotter, M., and G. Gleser. 1977. Corrigenda to "Estimation of stature from long limb bones of American whites and Negroes." *American Journal of Physical Anthropology* 47: 355–356.

Weissbrodt, D., and P. W. Fraser. 1992. Report of the Chilean National Commission of Truth and Reconciliation. *Human Rights Quarterly* 14 (4): 601.

White, T. D. 1991. *Human Osteology.* San Diego, CA: Academic Press.

INDEX